The
Lakers

The
Lakers
A BASKETBALL JOURNEY

Roland Lazenby

A Division of Howard W. Sams
A Bell Atlantic Company

This book is dedicated to the memory of Jim Pollard, the original "Kangaroo Kid," a warm, wonderful man and a true Hall of Famer.

Published by Masters Press
(a Division of Howard W. Sams, a Bell Atlantic Company)
2647 Waterfront Pkwy E. Dr, Suite 300, Indianapolis, IN 46214

Published 1993

First Masters Press edition published 1995

10 9 8 7 6 5 4 3 2 1

Printed in the United States of America

Library of Congress Cataloging-in-Publication Data

Lazenby, Roland.
  The Lakers / Roland Lazenby. -- 50th anniversary ed.
    p. cm.
  Includes bibliographical references (p.)
  ISBN 1-57028-062-2
  1. Los Angeles Lakers (Basketball team)-- History. I. Title.
GV885.52. L67L39   1995   95-42148
796.323'64'0979494--dc20   CIP

"But now the ROUND TABLE is dissolved
Which was an image of the mighty world;
And I, the last, go forth companionless,
And the days darken round me, and the years,
Among new men, strange faces, other minds."

And slowly answered Arthur from the barge:
"The old order changeth, yielding place to new,
And God fulfills himself in many ways,
Lest one good custom should corrupt the world.
Comfort thyself: what comfort is in me?"

The Passing of Arthur
Alfred, Lord Tennyson

Contents

Credits:

New typography by Leah Marckel
Cover design by Christy Pierce
Front cover photos © Steve Lipofsky, with the exception of the picture of
George Mikan, contributed by Roland Lazenby

Acknowledgments

I have many people to thank for their generous help on this book:

Mitch Chortkoff, the veteran sportswriter of the LA Copley Newspapers, unselfishly gave me the benefit of his many years' experience reporting on the Lakers. Lon Rosen, Magic Johnson's friend and agent, made a special effort in explaining and interpreting the saga of Showtime. Gary Vitti, the Lakers trainer, took the time to relate his many experiences with the team. For the Minneapolis Lakers, Sid Hartman and John Kundla graciously provided extensive help, as did Jim Pollard before his death. Also pivotal were Bob Steiner of California Sports, Inc., and John Black, the Lakers director of public relations. Both extended professional courtesies to me, as they do for the many writers, broadcasters and reporters covering the team.

Deserving special recognition are George Witte, the editor at St. Martin's Press who advised and guided me through the project, and his assistant, Ann McKay Farrell.

For help in the editorial review of this project, I am indebted to my wife, Karen Lazenby, and Rick Moore, Tim Orwig, and Diddy Deane. I must also thank Billy Packer, always a good friend and always willing to talk hoops. Jenny Byrd contributed key library research on AIDS and other topics.

There are the many people who agreed to be interviewed about the Lakers. Some offered extensive interviews in person. Others agreed to short sessions after basketball games and practices, and numerous others granted telephone interviews. Their stories and recollections make up the heart of this book. They include: Kareem Abdul-Jabbar, Red Auerbach, Jesse Barkin, Elgin Baylor, Bill Bertka, John Black, Alex Blackwell, Marty Blake, Mike Bloom, Frank Brickowski, Jerry Buss, Elden Campbell, Tony Campbell, Butch Carter, Mitch Chortkoff, Doug Christie, Jack Kent Cooke, Bob Cousy, Vlade Divac, Larry Drew, Mike Dunleavy, Charlie Eckman, James

Edwards, Robert "Jake" Embry, Rudy Garciduenas, Sid Goldberg, A.C. Green, Ted Green, Dick Harp, Merv Harris, Les Harrison, Sid Hartman, Chick Hearn, Gerald Henderson, Bailey Howell, Lou Hudson, Rod Hund-ley, Earvin "Magic" Johnson, John Kundla, Bob Kurland, Stu Lantz, Mary Lou Liebich, George Maskin, Hampton Mears, Jon McGlocklin, Vern Mikkelsen, Bones McKinney, John McLendon, Jr., Pete Newell, Billy Packer, Anthony Peeler, Paul Pentecost, Randy Pfund, Jim Pollard, Lorin Pullman, John Radcliffe, Pat Riley, Lon Rosen, Josh Rosenfeld, Bob Ryan, Frank Ryan, Fred Schaus, Dolph Schayes, Byron Scott, George Senesky, Paul Seymour, Bill Sharman, Bob Steiner, Jerry Tarkanian, Jack Tobin, Gary Vitti, Jerry West, Jamaal Wilkes, Herb Williams, and James Worthy. New interviews for this updated edition include Nick Van Exel, Eddie Jones, Del Harris, and Anthony Peeler.

Finally, I would like to thank Tom Bast of Masters Press for his belief in this book, as well as managing editor Holly Kondras for seeing it through the publishing of the paperback edition.

1

Musings from Big Pink

WAIKIKI, HAWAII, OCTOBER 10, 1992

Basketball is a game of lobbies.

Jim Valvano, the late, great hoops humorist/coach, first stumbled upon that notion some years back. He was sitting in a lobby somewhere when he realized just how central they are to the sport. Regardless of the event—the NCAA's Final Four, the NBA Finals, the All-Star Game, or any basic college tournament—the hotel lobby provides sanctuary for that odd collection of people who follow the games. Fans, former players, broadcasters, writers, analysts, young statisticians, old coaches, equipment salesmen—they all find their way to the bar stools and couches, where they kibitz until the wee hours, replaying games, advancing and testing theorems, trading tales and gossip, talking hoops.

They smoke; they drink; they dream; they commune with the great basketball spirits.

And I am one of them, a deep sub on life's all-lobby team.

It is October 10, 1992, and I am alone at 5:00 A.M. in what you might call the ultimate lobby, the Royal Hawaiian at Waikiki, also known as "the Pink Palace of the Pacific," with what is arguably the ultimate basketball team, the Los Angeles Lakers.

Well, the Lakers aren't exactly with me. They're upstairs in their rooms asleep or tossing and turning or whatever. But they are *here,* in this somewhat frayed version of Paradise.

The occasion is their fall training camp, the start of the franchise's forty-sixth season, and the circumstances are plump with significance. Earvin "Magic" Johnson, Jr., is attempting a comeback, to see if he can extend pro basketball's Age of Camelot for another glorious season. To do so, he will have to test his HIV-infected blood against the gauntlet of the National Basketball Association's long, hard schedule.

Which is why I am here, to see how this whole thing is going to unwind.

1

Just a few moments ago I was stumbling through the hotel's closed and darkened seaside restaurant when I encountered the morning manager, who directed me to the veranda and an urn of rich, deep Hawaiian coffee.

"The restuarant opens at six-thirty," she told me sternly.

So now I sit alone on a veranda couch, a prisoner of eastern time zones, charged and ready to go. My inner clock says 11:00 A.M. But this stately old pink hotel is dead, save for a custodian resolutely dustmopping the marble floors and the workers jingling the china as they set up for breakfast down in the restaurant.

A breeze blows oceanward, and a soft rain has begun to fall. Fifty yards away, the blue waters of Waikiki slosh peacefully and recuperate from the daily assault of humans covered in suntan oil.

Upstairs, Johnson (he is Earvin or "Buck" to the folks who know him, Magic to those who don't) is already awake and supercharged by his bountiful energy, ready to attack his morning. The newspaper has been read, and he has begun making phone calls back to the mainland, his preparation for another day in what has to be the most eventful year any athlete has ever experienced.

Yet, despite all his energy, it's a sour, stomach-churning morning for Earvin.

Normally he is overwhelmingly positive, always moving, always focused on the light, always seeking the good and right path to success. Always winning. Games. Friends. Prizes. Women. Fans. Money. Whatever trophy there is to be won at the moment, Earvin Johnson is locked in on it. It may be nothing more than a game of h-o-r-s-e with an eleven-year-old at his summer basketball camp. Too bad, kid. He'll smile; he'll entertain you; he'll even take time with you. But he ain't gonna lose to you.

It's a gift from his mother, Christine, this power of the positive, and it magnifies his special basketball skills, making them even more potent. If he didn't have basketball skills, the saying goes, Earvin Johnson would still be successful at something, simply because of this great positive power. He probably wouldn't be a world-famous millionaire. But this natural homing device would have him locked in on promotions and relationships and advancement, on every good thing that he could find in his path.

But for Earvin Johnson basketball has been an express lane to the top. When he was seventeen, he and his Everett High team in Lansing, Michigan, won a state championship. By nineteen, he was a sophomore and the team leader at Michigan State, and the prize was the NCAA title. At twenty, the stakes rose yet again, and he pushed the Lakers to the NBA's "World Championship."

Now, he's thirty-three and owns five diamond-studded NBA championship rings, a major portion of an East Coast Pepsi distributorship, and a hugely successful sportswear company and has nearly a dozen lucrative endorsement contracts with major corporations, ranging from a Spanish meat company to SkyBox, the trading card publisher.

To cap it all, Lakers owner Jerry Buss has quite unselfishly given Johnson a $14.6 million contract extension, guaranteeing him more than $19.6 million over the next three NBA seasons, whether he plays a single game or not.

But the money is only part of the fun.

Earvin Johnson's the darling of Hollywood, with show biz's biggest names eagerly paying $500 a night for a courtside seat at the Great Western Forum to watch him direct Showtime, the famed Laker fast break, with his no-look, peekaboo, wraparound, gotcha! passes. Never mind that Showtime has become Slowtime in recent seasons, the stars squeal, they freak, they feel like cheerleaders, they love Magic.

"He's got something," said Michael Ovitz, the Hollywood power broker of power brokers. "He's a star among stars."

If you don't believe that, just count the friends.

Let's see, there's Arsenio Hall and Eddie Murphy and Paula Abdul and Janet Jackson and brother Michael and Rob Lowe and Spike Lee and Charlie Sheen and Jack Nicholson and Lou Gossett and Denzel Washington and Don Johnson and Whitney Houston and Lionel Ritchie and Robin Givens and Pee Wee Herman . . .

Pee Wee Herman?

"Pee Wee, he's just down home," Johnson once said of actor Paul Reubens.

The list, of course, could go on. But you get the picture.

Outside of his rival Michael Jordan, Earvin Johnson is the most successful, most charismatic, most celebrated player in the world. If you still don't believe it, the people who have lived and worked with him are filled with endless tales of his appeal. They don't mean to talk about it, but they do, because although they've witnessed it, they still can't quite believe it. They knew, for example, that he was *big* in the United States. But in October 1991 the team went to Paris to play against European teams in the McDonald's Open. Everywhere the Lakers went there were crowds chanting over and over, "Ma-jeek! Ma-jeek!"

Johnson would look across those crowds, would hear them intoning his name, would feel their energy charging the very air, and his motor would hum all the harder, rotating to a hypercharge of Positive. What was Positive at it purest state?

Invincibility?

Deification?

Who knew? Earvin Johnson didn't spend much time with such questions. He just knew that he was moving at the upper realm of human existence, and he knew he could negotiate that realm with the same ease that he executed a no-look pass on the Lakers' fast break.

People were *his*.

The sense of power was incredible. But Earvin Johnson wasn't necessarily into power. He was into Positive.

Back in the good old USA, the worshipers were quieter, almost awe-struck, regardless of who they were. And once they had been in Johnson's presence, they wanted to be in it again and again, to be near *him*. Especially after Laker games. It was almost like that line from *Field of Dreams*.

People will come.

"After every game, we'd have this entourage, this line of cars behind our team bus, that would follow us to the airport in hopes of getting a glimpse of Earvin, maybe an autograph," says Lakers broadcaster Stu Lantz. "It was hilarious. We'd look out the window at the line of cars and laugh. That's the kind of effect he had on people, and they weren't all women. There'd be families. There'd be the dad, the wife, and two kids, following the bus. We'd pull to the airport runway gates—we'd drive straight onto the runway to meet our charter—and the gates would close, and they'd all get out of the cars and run out to the fence, hoping to see *him*."

Gary Vitti, the team's trainer and Johnson's longtime friend, recalled that Earvin once wore a white sweatshirt when he went to speak at a high school about drug abuse. When he returned, the sweatshirt was covered with pink lip prints from teenage girls.

"Covered with pink lip prints," Vitti said again, as if he still couldn't believe it.

Pink lip prints, like rose petals strewn before an emperor.

Magic the God.

It's enough to make Hugh Hefner envious. It was Hef, after all, who created the American *Playboy* ideal. A midwesterner like Johnson, Heff filled his Chicago mansion with luscious naked beauties right from the pages of his magazine.

But it was Earvin Johnson, perhaps more than any other male, who had come to live that American *Playboy* ideal. Heck, even Hef had to pay for his Playmates. But Earvin had 'em for free. Brown ones. Black ones. White ones. Yellow ones. Two at a time. Three at a time. Even six at a time! Or he'd try a foursome, one from each of the major color groups.

It didn't take him long after he arrived in Los Angeles in 1979 to learn that he had taken up residence at the prime end of the world's casting couch. Hollywood offered an abundant supply of beauties, many of whom were eager to get to know a basketball star. Back then the Lakers' dapper guard, Norm Nixon, was the reigning ladies' man, and Johnson was an inexperienced understudy. Butch Carter, now a Milwaukee Bucks assistant coach, came to the Lakers as a rookie in 1980 and found Johnson marveling at Nixon's popularity. One day Johnson walked through a hotel lobby and three women gave him their phone numbers—to take up to Nixon's room.

"At the time, Norm Nixon was the king of LA," Carter recalls with a laugh. "When we'd go out somewhere, the women would ask, 'Where's Norm? Where's Norm?' "

Nixon had such a smooth rap that his teammates took to calling him "Savoir Faire," or "Wa" for short.

It wasn't too long, however, before Johnson was making his own time. Taking the Lakers to championship after championship, he lit the incandescent lamps of his own stardom. Captivated by his smile, by the career shortcut that an association with him might offer, those Hollywood ladies began asking, "Where's Magic?" They, too, simply wanted to be with *him*.

As Johnson later explained, he thought it only proper that he *accommodate* these women, a comment that brought howls from feminists, which in turn brought a quick apology from Johnson for his insensitivity. But the sheer numbers of people seeking him were proof enough. That's exactly what he did. He accommodated them.

It has been said often that Los Angeles became Magic's city. More accurately, it became his harem.

Magic, of course, was his public persona, the fellow who turned in wondrous performances nightly on the floor at the Great Western Forum. Earvin, on the other hand, was his private sanctuary, the person who had been that sweet, chubby adolescent son of deeply religious Christine Johnson back in Michigan.

Earvin was the good guy.

Magic was the satyr.

His excesses became the stuff of legend around the Lakers. He would later estimate that he had sexual relations with 300 to 500 women annually. Even more amazing was the discretion with which he rang up these numbers. Outside of a small inner circle of Laker staffers and players, few people knew exactly what he was doing. "When I first started with the team, it was astounding," said Rudy Garciduenas, the equipment manager and another good friend of Johnson's. "But it was an existence, a way of life, with Earvin. I came to understand Earvin and the way he did things, his love for women, females in general. That's the way it was.

"When you're a person of that stature, it's almost expected. All the movie stars get the same attention. Michael Jordan, you can't get near him. It's part of the business."

But Mike Jordan is married and monogamous, and what's more, he works in Chicago, a virtual dead zone compared with Hollywood. The nightclub life in Los Angeles was an irresistible playground for Johnson. After all, there were thousands of beautiful young women, and there was only one Magic Johnson. "Earvin and I would go out to the clubs, and you'd just have to shake your head," Garciduenas said with a laugh. "Every male wants to be that way, or dreams of being that way for just one night. But with Earvin, it was reality. . . ."

Actually, the tales of his exploits had to struggle to keep up with the reality. There was a series of rumored liaisons in public places with a prominent TV newscaster. There was sex in a movie theater. Sex in an elevator. Sex in a corporate boardroom. Sex in a thousand hotel rooms.

One of his favorite spots for frivolity was the Lakers' locker room sauna. Sometimes he would have sex there with women immediately after games, then slip on a bathrobe or towel and go back to his locker to calmly field questions from the press. "Everyone knew he was doing that," said one Laker staffer.

"It's difficult to imagine," Garciduenas said, "but Earvin was used to doing anything he wanted, really. And people loved Earvin so much that nothing he did was wrong. It was never really hidden from anybody, what Earvin did. He was always pretty up-front with it. That was part of him. You had to learn to accept it."

This phenomenon, of course, wasn't exclusive to Earvin Johnson. The modern professional athlete in all major sports has discovered that physical prowess, fame, and fortune attract large numbers of women. The Atlanta Hawks' Dominique Wilkins, once known as one of the league's most notorious bachelors, has met quite a few ladies over the years. "They want the thrill of being with an athlete," he explained in a *Sports Illustrated* article. "And they don't want safe sex. They want to have your baby, man, because they think that if they have your baby, they're set for life. That's the hard fact of it, because if they had a life, they wouldn't be hanging around the hotel or showing up at the back door of the arena trying to pick up a player."

"We don't even have to try," said Phoenix Suns guard Kevin Johnson. "We come into town, and the women come out in force. They call the hotel, they follow the bus. They hover and wait to get you."

Such reactions are typical of many NBA players, says a former Lakers public relations assistant. "They act like these women are such a problem for them. But the guys perpetuate the behavior."

Besides, many women see the pursuit of NBA players as an expression of liberation. If men can chase skirts, what's wrong with the ladies lying in wait until one of their sexual fantasies happens along?

Robin Power, a stunning Los Angeleno who has identified herself as one of Johnson's lovers, says NBA players are her favorite pastime and she can get just about anyone she wants. The secret, she says, is strategic positioning to greet a player. From there, the goal is eye contact. Then they have to notice her kelly green silk minidress, her long, thick, dark hair, her breathtaking cleavage. . . . The whole package fairly screams her message: *I want your sex.*

She always gets her man, Robin Power boasts.

Once Earvin Johnson surrendered to this crowd, he found he could have just about what he wanted when he wanted it. By the time Norm Nixon left the Lakers in 1983, Johnson was well on his way to assuming the throne, even playing the role of social director, introducing players from visiting teams to some of his favorite ladies.

Competitive as they were, some of his teammates gave Johnson a run for the money in this studhorse sweepstakes. Sex became the game within the game.

"I couldn't believe how they all shared notes in the locker room," Lorin Pullman said. " 'My God,' I thought, 'this is like they're still in high school.' "

Some went so far as to keep stats, although the results were often much disputed, what with the male ego showing a propensity for overestimation. But for Johnson, keeping score was almost moot.

"It didn't do any good to keep count," Rudy Garciduenas said, "because there was always going to be somebody new. It just wasn't any good to count or to try to keep track of any of them."

There was, however, a code for Johnson's sexfest. He never allowed a woman to stay overnight with him. That was reserved for his college sweetheart, Earleatha "Cookie" Kelly, who would become his wife in September 1991 after years of stormy relations over his womanizing. She couldn't bring herself to break off her relationship with him, although she tried for several months. Yet she also couldn't stomach the scene in Los Angeles, so she remained in Michigan during his first decade in the league. Johnson was unrepentant about his indulgences, and his token acknowledgment of her was that he booted his partners out of bed before sunrise.

Besides, he had always told Cookie that his first love was the game. And for the game, he saved himself. No sex before tip-off. None. He wanted nothing to keep him from performing his best. Sex was the game *after* the game.

And the Forum Club, the arena's exclusive restaurant and bar, comprised a large part of the playing field. Basketball had never seen anything quite like it, and probably never will again. Before Laker games, it was the spot for power dinners with LA's elite. After games, it was transformed into a swinging singles bar, throbbing with energy and celebrity and celebration. At the height of Showtime, the Lakers lost only four or five home games a season, meaning that the Forum Club was a place to see and be seen with winners. Players from both teams would hustle to shower and don their Armani suits for a swing through the crowd to scope the lovelies. "Any athlete who walks in there is already spotted," said Laker guard Byron Scott. "He's got three, four, or five girls who already spotted him, and it depends on which one he wants to go with."

The atmosphere was so thick with women that Laker wives and regular girlfriends were often forced to make an appearance to check out who was zoomin' who. "They had to do that to make sure these women knew their guy was accounted for," a former Laker employee explained.

Away from Los Angeles, the hotel lobbies generated another level of excitement. "When our bus would pull up to a hotel you'd see sixty people out there waiting and forty of them would be women," Byron Scott said. "It was like going around with a rock group. It was just amazing."

The "road" left the wives and girlfriends at a distinct disadvantage. Under coach Pat Riley, the Lakers had an "excess baggage" rule barring wives and girlfriends of players from traveling with the team because they created a distraction. Riley would later explain that his "excess baggage" distinction didn't mean the wives. Yet the ban against them was so strongly implied that when wives did travel to away games, they would hide from the coaches.

Which meant that players faced fifty to sixty nights per season alone on the road. "I always felt that contributed to the excess," one former Laker staffer said. "If you wanted your wife or girlfriend along, what was wrong with that? You're not going to walk through the bar or lobby looking for women if your wife is upstairs in your room."

Many times, though, the Lakers didn't have to go to the action in the lobby. It came to them. In 1989, Lorin Pullman, Kareem's publicist, was traveling with the team during Abdul-Jabbar's retirement tour. Somehow the front desk in one hotel got her room number mixed up with Johnson's. She returned that evening to find messages from six different women slid under her door.

Each city has its regular group of women eager to meet and greet NBA teams. They keep an eye on the schedule; they know when the circus is coming to town. Sometimes they request autographs, these requests in many cases a means of arranging liaisons, with a player writing his room number alongside his signature.

For every game, for every play-off series, the hotels come alive with the ubiquitous autograph seekers, who hang in the shadows, waiting until players or coaches or anybody who looks famous happens by, then silently extending a pennant or a trading card or a program or a scrap of paper to be signed, often doing so with averted eyes.

There are shy, pimply adolescents and supercharged grade-schoolers and lonely grandmothers and middle-aged men and attractive women and women not so attractive, even entire families, with little children and a wife trailing a father still obsessed by his adolescent sports fantasies, all of them drawn by a power, a mystery, they don't quite understand. They only know they want to encounter it, to get something notarized to prove to themselves that they encountered it. Later, they will hold these signed scraps of paper, treasuring and fondling them, all the while wondering at the mystery and the power, feeling both fulfilled and empty, and very big and very, very small.

One night in the Charlotte Marriott in March 1990 after a Lakers/ Charlotte Hornets game, the lobby and hotel bar were filled with dozens of attractive, well-dressed young women who had come out with hopes of meeting a player.

One woman had brought a wrapped gift for a Laker player whom she had spent time with on a previous Laker trip to the North Carolina city. He ignored her most of the night while partying with his teammates (Johnson was on the dance stage leading scores of people in the Electric Slide). Later, when the bar closed, this Laker would motion for this woman with a nod of his head, and she would hurry to slip away to his room.

While she waited, I asked her why she had come to the bar. She explained that she was a secretary with limited prospects. The chance to be with a player, although this one was married, offered her a dramatic opportunity to broaden those prospects, she said.

"It's exciting," she said with a smile as she looked at the Lakers dancing and laughing and clapping together onstage.

When ordinary people sensed his power, it only confirmed for Johnson his special status. All of these people couldn't be wrong. He had it all. Fame. Fortune. Sex. Adulation. Success.

In 1990, a contractor was set to install an outdoor basketball goal at Johnson's new Beverly Hills ridgetop home that afforded him grand views of the city. Did Johnson want the goal on the street side or ravine side of the house? the contractor inquired.

Why does it matter? Johnson asked.

If you miss a shot on the ravine side, the ball's likely to wind up down in the canyon, the contractor replied.

"Put it on the ravine side," the star decided with a smile. "Magic Johnson doesn't miss."

He was invincible.

Invincible people don't need protection, and like many men, Johnson disdained condoms, even as the contagion of the Acquired Immune Deficiency Syndrome spread through the population.

There are reports that with his unprotected sexual activity, Johnson began to cause concern among the team's management, and that the Lakers went so far as to contact the NBA league offices in New York for help in persuading Johnson to change his thinking.

The team, however, denies that it ever contacted the league.

In his early years as owner of the team, Jerry Buss prided himself on his playboy reputation and frequented the LA club scene with Johnson. Despite their friendship, Buss said he didn't think of reminding Johnson about protection. "Magic was a mature man," Buss explained. "Plus I didn't realize there was as much activity as there was."

Gary Vitti did, however, and as AIDS fears gained prominence the team's trainer began carrying condoms and distributing them to the Lakers. Vitti made a point of always asking the players if they were protecting themselves.

Yeah, everything's cool, Johnson would say.

Vitti would ask this question frequently, and he wondered if Johnson was fibbing. And it would later haunt Vitti that he didn't do more, didn't confront his friend.

In that regard, Vitti came to consider Johnson's fate his fault. After all, he reasoned, he was the trainer, the person most responsible for the players' well-being.

"I felt I let him down," Vitti said. "I let myself down. I didn't do what I was supposed to do. Somehow I should've made him more aware, made him understand."

Others, of course, thought that Vitti was being unnecessarily hard on himself, that despite their close friendship, Johnson would always be deaf to Vitti's pleas. "Earvin wanted to live his life his way," Garciduenas said. "Once he made up his mind, he wasn't going to change it for anybody."

With Johnson's appetite, Laker players and staff marveled at his durability. And in a sense, they all came to believe in his infallibility. After all, wasn't he the Magic man? Wasn't he the person with the special gifts and the broad smile? Wasn't he the deliverer of miracle plays and championships?

A few years earlier several players and staffers had discussed sex and sexually transmitted diseases at training camp in Hawaii. Inevitably, the discussion turned to Johnson. ("We always talked about Magic and the wild shit that he did," explained one staffer.) And one of the players laughed and said, "Shit. If that motherfucker doesn't have it, you can't get it."

The group laughed hard at that assessment. Magic was indestructible. He was so potent that sexually transmitted diseases couldn't affect him. Like M. C. Hammer's anthem. "U Can't Touch This." Protected by providence, Magic didn't need condoms.

That comment would become something of a comic refrain around the Lakers over the ensuing months whenever the topic of Johnson's sex life arose in conversation: "If he doesn't have it, you can't get it."

THINGS FALL APART

Earvin Johnson was on vacation in August 1991 when he phoned Cookie Kelly. "I'm ready to get married," he told her. "I think it's time."

They had been through this several times before, only to have their plans fall through. So Kelly was understandably cautious. "Are you sure?" she asked.

"This is it," he said. "I want to do it."

Now.

"They had to hurry it up," recalled New York Knicks forward Herb Williams, an old friend. "So she didn't get time to set up a big wedding or anything."

There was time, however, to negotiate and sign a prenuptial agreement in which Kelly gave up claims on Johnson's estimated $100 million in wealth. Such harsh details aside, they assembled a quick wedding in Lansing. It was a small affair. Williams and Isiah Thomas and Mark Aguirre of the Detroit Pistons were among the guests, who also included Darwin Payton and Dale Beard, two old friends.

The joy and relief were obvious in Kelly's eyes, Williams said. "She's a nice girl. She has a nice head on her shoulders. She had a nice job. I mean she could have had a whole lot of other guys, whoever she wanted. But she had always been there for him, no matter what."

Two weeks later, the Lakers opened the season with an abbreviated version of training camp in Palm Desert, California. Johnson arrived there in poor shape, with the idea that he would work himself into condition during the team's twice-daily practices. From there, the Lakers jetted to Boston for two quick exhibition games with the Celtics, then on to Paris to play in the McDonald's Open, the international exhibition tournament, where they played another two games, barely beating a Spanish team, Joventut Badalona, for the championship.

It was in Paris that Cookie Kelly Johnson learned she was pregnant.

By then the grind of playing himself into shape while crossing time zones had begun to show on Johnson, and the fourteen-hour plane trip home offered little relief. He arrived in Los Angeles with a face drawn and tired. But there was little time to rest. Back home, the Lakers faced two more exhibition games in the GTE Everything Pages Shoot-out, where they again beat Boston, then lost to the Milwaukee Bucks.

From there, the schedule called for them to fly to Utah for another game, then to head off to Vancouver, British Columbia, that night after it was over for yet another game the next night against the Seattle Supersonics. From there, they were scheduled to fly back to Los Angeles that night after the game in Canada in order to hold practice the next morning at the Loyola Marymount University gym, their regular practice facility.

It was an idiotic schedule, Johnson thought. Boston. Paris. Los Angeles. Utah. Canada. What a terrible way to start the season. He didn't want to go to Utah and he was vocal about it. But this was what he got paid the big bucks for. He knew it was part of the deal. So he went anyway.

The Lakers had just checked into their hotel in Salt Lake City that afternoon of October 25 when Johnson got a message from Lon Rosen, his agent, stating that he had to return to Los Angeles immediately.

Vitti's response was disbelief when Johnson informed him. His first thought was that Johnson had arranged a doctor's excuse to miss the rest of the trip.

Nah, Vitti thought, Earvin wouldn't do that.

So the trainer called Michael Mellman, one of the team's doctors, and asked what was up.

"I can't tell you about it at this point," the doctor said. "Something has shown up abnormal on Earvin's physical exam. He has to come home."

The league's salary cap had prevented the team from increasing Johnson's $2.5 million annual contract, yet his salary had become dwarfed by younger players coming into the league whose agents were negotiating megadeals of $3, $4, and $5 million per year. To compensate Johnson more fairly, team owner Jerry Buss had arranged to give his superstar a $3.6 million low-interest loan.

But to get the loan, he had to have a life insurance policy.

To get the policy, Johnson had been required to undergo a rigorous physical exam. It seemed that the results were now in.

After speaking with Mellman, Vitti still couldn't figure it out. So he went to Johnson and asked him what was going on.

"Gary, I don't know," he replied.

Female Laker fans are fond of pointing out that Vitti is a smaller, Italian version of Tom Selleck. Since coming to the Lakers in 1984, Vitti had become close friends with Johnson. If there were a human version of the star's guardian angel, Vitti would be it. In fact, he watched over all the Lakers' health like a private eye, noting details, offering advice, serving as a combination drill sergeant/big brother. Outside of his wife and two daughters, the Lakers are Vitti's life.

And his memory is like a family photo album, particularly when it comes to the details of Johnson's career. This sudden call home was virtually unprecedented. A superstar was never called home from the road. Vitti knew something had to be terribly wrong, and as the trainer, he prided himself on knowing everything about each athlete's health. But now he didn't know, and it was driving him crazy.

Mike Dunleavy, who was then the Lakers coach, was also confused by Johnson's sudden departure. To find out what was wrong, he phoned Mitch Kupchak, the team's assistant general manager.

"Mike," Kupchak said, "I don't know anything about it. All I know is I got a call from Lon Rosen and he said he was scared to death."

In Los Angeles, Rosen picked up Johnson at the airport. They proceeded immediately to Mellman's office. In the two hours before Johnson arrived, the agent had sat in Jerry West's office, talking with the general manager. Together they had tried to figure what was up. Rosen, himself a former Laker employee, thought his friend and client had cancer. After all, Johnson's half sister, Mary, had died of cancer just a few years earlier.

Back in Utah, Vitti wondered if it weren't a heart condition. That was the fear with big men like the six-foot-nine Johnson. But over his years in the league Johnson had passed batteries of stress tests with flying colors. It wasn't his heart. For hours, Vitti wracked his brain. *What could be wrong?*

In the middle of the game with Utah that night, the trainer realized the problem.

"It's like somebody hit me in the head with a sledgehammer," Vitti recalled. "Bang. He's HIV positive."

He didn't know for sure. But he *knew*. And that was worse than not knowing.

In the second half of the game, second-year guard Tony Smith suffered a badly sprained ankle. Smith had played well in the preseason, and just when it appeared he was going to earn more playing time, he messed up an ankle. As Vitti examined the ankle in the locker room, Smith lay on the training table sobbing. Suddenly Vitti grabbed Smith by the shirt and pulled him up inches from his face.

"What are you crying about?" he demanded. "Are you crying because of the pain? Are you crying because you're bummed out that you got hurt?"

Smith was too stunned to answer. He looked at Vitti like he was crazy.

"You know," Vitti said, relaxing, "you're gonna get better."

The ankle, Vitti thought to himself, would take at worst six weeks to heal. But Earvin was not going to get better. Somewhere down the road—it might take months; it might take years—he was going to die of some AIDS-related complex. This wasn't Magic Johnson who was going to die. This was Earvin, Vitti's friend. Johnson was a big star, yet he treated Vitti like a brother, coming to dinner at his house, taking time to be nice to Vitti's parents. Most NBA trainers didn't get such respect and attention from stars. But Johnson was loved by all the Laker staffers. Many pro ball players are so focused on their own grand existence, they often fail to notice the people around them doing the little things that make their worlds go round. Not Johnson. He always noticed. Every staffer at the Forum. The ushers. The scorekeepers. The custodians. The public relations people. He knew them by name. What's more, he liked them, and they knew it. After all, they inhabited a special world together at the Forum. He made all of them feel a part of Showtime. If a ball boy needed a car for the prom, Johnson knew it. Here, kid, take the keys and don't scratch the paint. If a public relations assistant was stuck in a low, blue mood, Johnson wasn't above having a bottle of champagne sent over. Just like that, a bottle of Dom. The idea of such a gesture would never occur to most NBA players.

"Earvin is probably one of the most special people there is," explained Rudy Garciduenas, the equipment manager. "Everybody knows what he can do on the floor, as far as playing the game. They've seen him for years now. But off the floor is the Earvin I like to think about, because Earvin always cared enough to ask you, you know, how you were doing. And not every once in a while. It was every day. He would always check with you."

The players, the staffers, the coaches had all come to understand that Johnson was a part of them. It was his energy, his positive power, that picked them up and carried them to levels they could never reach on their own.

"Earvin was the roller coaster," Garciduenas explained, "and we were all just along for the ride."

The Lakers lost in Utah that night, and as the players boarded the team plane for Canada they all wanted to know what was wrong with Magic.

Vitti told them he didn't know. But he *knew.*

At eight the next morning, Vitti's motel phone rang in Vancouver. It was Mellman.

"Mickey, you don't have to tell me a thing," Vitti said quickly. "I already figured it out. Earvin is HIV positive isn't he?"

"I knew you would figure it out," the doctor said. "Earvin wanted you to know. We're only telling a few people. No one else is to know. No one. No coaches. No players. Absolutely no one. Earvin said he wanted you to know, and he said he would meet you early in the morning before practice at Loyola."

The flight home from Canada that night was good for Vitti. It gave the trainer time to sort out what he wanted to say to Johnson the next morning. The locker room at Loyola was empty and quiet when he and Johnson met around eight. But there was little to say at first. They cried together. Vitti knew that everyone dies of AIDS. No one survives. And there was no way Johnson would be different.

"You're gonna beat this thing," he told Johnson. "I'm gonna help you. You're gonna eat right, sleep right, exercise. I'm gonna keep you healthy."

The good news was that Johnson had found out early, which meant he could take medication to slow the spread of the virus. People usually don't learn they have AIDS until symptoms of disease appear. Otherwise, the virus works insidiously. Fortunately, Johnson's life insurance policy had required that he be tested for HIV. He had a head start on fighting the virus. Regardless, Vitti knew that eventually it would take over his friend's body. The right regimen could slow the onset of the disease. Some people had tested positive, then lived as long as a decade without developing symptoms. But Vitti knew these were the exception, not the rule. His and Johnson's immediate concern was how to handle the news. Johnson needed time to talk to counselors, to lawyers, to doctors. He needed to examine his options.

"We came up with this bullshit that he had the flu," Vitti said.

The media were told that Johnson would miss some practice and games. That story would get them about ten days, which would be time enough to figure out what to do.

Except Johnson didn't make it easy on Vitti, who had to answer reporters' questions about the star player's condition. Johnson appeared at a Los Angeles Raiders game and sat on the sidelines. He's sick with the flu, yet goes to a football game and has a good time? It didn't make sense to the media.

Each day, Rosen, Johnson's agent, would phone Vitti to go over the details. "I had to confide in somebody," Rosen explained. They hated lying to reporters, but they had no choice. After a few days, the flu story began to wear thin. So Rosen phoned the trainer. "Veets," he said, "I've decided to announce that Earvin has begun light workouts under supervision."

"What the fuck does that mean?" Vitti asked.

"I don't know, Gary," Rosen replied. "What are we gonna do? We've got to tell them something."

These stories may have held off the media, but they didn't add up for Dunleavy, the team's thirty-seven-year-old head coach. Concerned about the strange situation, he went to Kupchak's office. "Something's not right here," he told the assistant general manager. "This is way off the wall. If Earvin has cancer or AIDS and you know it, you'd better let me know. I've got about a week before the season starts, and if he's not going to be in the lineup I've got to start making some plans."

Dunleavy was told that something very bad had come up, that it would have a major impact on the team. "I knew from that standpoint that I had about a week to prepare," he recalled. "So I began immediately changing our plays around, running different things for different guys. Some players were scratching their heads, wondering what the hell I was doing."

Fortunately, the team had traded for veteran guard Sedale Threatt during the off-season. Threatt was an NBA journeyman known for his smooth shot. But over most of his eight pro seasons he had rarely played more than fifteen minutes a game. Suddenly Dunleavy found himself placing the burden of running the Lakers, with their flock of $500-per-night fans, on the shoulders of a career reserve.

"If nothing else, this'll be interesting," the coach thought.

Amazingly, Johnson's circle of friends, family, and advisers kept their secret for almost two weeks. Johnson's family knew. Cookie Kelly's family knew. Plus the doctors and a few other select counselors. But few in that group understood the implications of the news.

Least of all Johnson.

For most of the time, he and the people around him thought that testing HIV positive meant that he had AIDS. They would soon learn the difference, but at that moment there was much to sort out. For Johnson, the question was what to do with the information. His first inclination was human. It was his body, his infection, his business only. He was not going to tell anybody that he had AIDS. That was a gay disease, and people would think he was gay.

But he didn't have to think long about it to realize that his infection could not remain his own dark secret. "There was no way to know what was correct," recalled Rosen. "But very quickly Earvin knew that keeping it quiet was impossible. We knew it would get out. Let's face it. He's Magic Johnson."

Vitti and others close to Johnson agreed. "He absolutely had to go public with it because of the thousands of women that he'd had sexual relations with," the trainer said. "Even if only one of them was HIV positive because of him, and you had sex with that woman and became HIV positive, indirectly you could hold Earvin responsible because he knew that he had it and didn't notify the woman. He had a moral and ethical responsibility, so he went up there like a man and did what he had to do."

First, he was retested to make sure the original results were correct, and Cookie was tested. Her negative results helped calm his anxiety, although it was explained to the couple that it sometimes took months for the virus to show up.

Once Johnson faced the inevitable, his advisers began making plans for a press conference. That Wednesday night, November 6, Rosen began making phone calls from his home, notifying the key people. In each call, he stressed the necessity of confidentiality. Everyone understood. Later that evening, he met with a small group to plan the conference. Then Rosen went to Dunleavy's house and informed the coach that Johnson was HIV positive.

That next morning, the team was practicing at Loyola Marymount when Vitti got a call from Lakers general manager Jerry West.

"Gary," West said, "get everybody out of the gym. Get them in their cars. Tell them to go home and change and be back at the Forum at two o'clock. I don't care what they have to do. I don't care what their schedule is today. Tell 'em no matter what it is to cancel it.

"Get them out of the gym now. We have a leak, and the press are on their way to Loyola to interview them about it."

This presented a problem, because the players had not been told of Johnson's plight. One or two may have figured it out on their own, but there had been no official word on it. And the grapevine had been surprisingly quiet on the matter.

The players began complaining about this abrupt change of plans and strange directive from team management.

"Hey, look," Vitti told them testily. "No matter what you've got to do, cancel it. We've got a press conference today. Believe me, this is going to change your life."

Before leaving, Byron Scott and James Worthy paused to shoot free throws.

"What do you think this is about?" Worthy asked.

"I don't know," Scott replied. "It's probably about Earvin." He paused, laughed nervously, and said, "He might have AIDS."

Then he and Worthy looked at each other. "Naw," Worthy said. "I hope that's not the case."

"I pray to God that's not it."

"I hadn't heard anything," Scott later recalled. "Something just made me say it. We were there with him as far as on the road and had seen all the girls and what he did."

On the way home, Scott and several others heard noon radio broadcasts announcing that Magic Johnson had tested HIV positive and was retiring. Still, two or three players arrived at the Forum unaware of what was about to unfold. They had been listening to tapes or CDs in their cars or were simply tuning in to another planet.

When the team assembled in the locker room at two, Vitti asked if everyone knew what it was about. Two or three players raised their hands and said they didn't.

"Well, Earvin wanted to tell you himself," Vitti said, "but since the other guys know, it's pretty ridiculous that you don't. Earvin has tested HIV positive. That's why he hasn't been with us. He's having a press conference today to announce his retirement."

Each moment of the entire day would stay with Vitti long afterward. For a time he couldn't stop thinking about it. Over and over again, he would replay the events, until he began wishing he could get them out of his mind. Then he realized he didn't want to turn them loose at all. It was the worst day of his life. Yet he insisted on reliving it over and over.

Garciduenas felt much the same way. "It was one of the worst emotional experiences I've ever been through," the equipment manager said, "because we felt that it was such a loss, because there's such a stigma that follows this disease around, because it's life-threatening. . . .

"But Earvin came down and told us before the press conference. We all got to be with him for a little while."

First, Johnson met privately with Dunleavy. Although the coach was starting only his second season with the team, Johnson had a genuine affection for him. Dunleavy had been a journeyman NBA player, which contributed to his unassuming coaching style. He had all the confidence and competitiveness of great coaches, but Dunleavy lacked the bluster. Together, he and Johnson had retooled the Lakers into a team that had just lost the NBA championship to the Chicago Bulls. They had held great hopes for the 1991–92 season.

His voice breaking, Johnson told the coach that his career was over, that things would be alright, that he would get through the circumstances as best he could.

From there, Johnson turned to his next great task—telling his teammates.

"He came in," Vitti said. "He had on a blue suit and a white shirt, and he looked really good and distinguished. I can just see him so vividly. He told the team that he had this virus, you know. 'I got this virus.' You know the way he talks. 'I can't play basketball anymore.' "

Weeping as he spoke, Johnson paused to talk about the "wars" he had been through with his longtime teammates Worthy, Scott, and A. C. Green and how special those wars had been. Then he went around to each of the twelve players and the coaches and Vitti and Garciduenas and hugged them and spoke privately with each one.

"To have him confirm it was like somebody had just reached in and grabbed my heart and pulled it out," Byron Scott said.

"The guys broke down crying, the whole room," Dunleavy said. "Everybody felt for Earvin. We felt like we had lost somebody, and yet he was still there."

Assistant coach Bill Bertka, who had been with the Lakers in one capacity or another for parts of three decades, took the news hard. In his sixties, Bertka, affectionately known as Bert, was a father figure to Laker players and coaches alike.

"I really tried to be strong for Earvin, because he's so strong," Vitti said. "Bert was next to me. I was the last guy. Bert's a stoic, Scandinavian kind of rock, icy type of guy. He's a pillar of strength. Earvin put his arm around Bert, and Bert's knees just buckled.

"To see that man, who's like the toughest guy I know . . . I just came unglued. Earvin came over to me. I was trying to gather myself up."

Vitti told Johnson, "We've already been through this, you know."

"Yeah," Johnson said as he hugged Vitti. "But it doesn't make it any easier."

Behind the emotion were the questions. There remained quite a bit of confusion among the staff and players. What was "HIV positive?" Did Earvin have AIDS? "It's really something we didn't know that much about," Garciduenas said. "Once you mention the word, or that somebody you know has it, basically people write them off and don't understand that people still have a life to live and they can prolong their life and it's not gonna happen for years down the road. But once you mention it, everybody just associates it with death.

"That's why it hit everybody on the team so hard. Everybody who had been involved with Earvin for any period of time just couldn't handle it. It was devastating."

Upstairs, a throng of media waited for Johnson, with CNN and ESPN planning live feeds of the press conference to their audiences.

"Earvin went in the bathroom and washed his face," Vitti said, "and went upstairs and got in front of those cameras like it was nothing. He went from this huge emotional scene to going up there and standing in front of the world, like the strongest man that ever lived. He did what he had to do."

Just before the press conference, the players were provided brief counseling, with a question-and-answer session about the virus. Right before he went on camera, Johnson was reminded that he didn't have AIDS but had merely tested positive for the Human Immunodeficiency Virus, HIV.

"Good afternoon," he told a worldwide audience moments later. "Because of the HIV virus that I have attained, I will have to retire from the Lakers today. I just want to make clear, first of all, that I do not have the AIDS disease. I know a lot of you want to know that. I have the HIV virus. My wife is fine. She's negative, so no problem with her.

"I plan to go on living for a long time, bugging you guys like I always have. So you'll see me around. I plan on being with the Lakers and the league, and going on with my life. I guess now I get to enjoy some of the other sides of living that I've missed because of the season and the long practices and so on. I'm going to miss playing.

"I will now become a spokesman for the HIV virus. I want people, young people, to realize they can practice safe sex. Sometimes you're a little naive about it, and you think it could never happen to you. You only thought it could happen to other people. It has happened. But I'm going to deal with it. Life is going to go on for me, and I'm going to be a happy man. . . .

"Sometimes we think only gay people can get it, or 'it's not going to happen to me.' Here I am, saying it can happen to anybody.

"Even me, Magic Johnson."

The Laker players and staffers watched these strange events unfold, heard the follow-up questions from the overflow crowd of reporters, and sat around numbly as the session wound to a close.

"Then," Vitti said, "we all just went home and turned off our phones."

MONEY

Lon Rosen was a child of affluence in the 1970s. His dad was a successful advertising executive, which meant that Rosen existed in that untouchable teen world that only well-to-do California kids can know. Beaches. Music.

Opportunity. Fun. Great Expectations. All wrapped in an elite package of LA Cool.

There was only one problem with Rosen. He wasn't a native. He had spent his childhood in Jersey and New York, coming to Los Angeles just in time for high school. While other kids worked on their tans, he wanted to hustle. Back in Jersey, it had been a matter of getting snow-shoveling jobs, then paying his pals to do the work while he took his cut off the top for closing the deals. He had a nose for action, and like a lot of folks from Jersey, he had a thing for hoops.

Before long he was developing his own little tricks for sneaking into Laker games at the Forum. He was so good at it that Laker staffers got tired of seeing him there. They figured they might as well put him to work. Before Rosen knew it, he was part of the game crew, charged with doing small-time promotional chores and gophering.

He didn't realize it at the time, but he had just gotten the first big break of his professional career.

That work, in turn, led to a series of internships and part-time jobs with the team while he was studying cinema/television at the University of Southern California. All of which put him in position in the fall of 1979 to meet Magic Johnson, the Lakers' new rookie from Michigan State.

Johnson had just turned twenty in August, and Rosen was one of the few people in the organization the same age. Often, when Johnson had to make public appearances, team officials would send Rosen along to help the rookie find his way around. Thrown together, the two, as Rosen tells it, "had nothing in common and everything in common, a black kid from Michigan and a Jewish kid from LA."

They became friends, something Johnson needed badly at the time. "Earvin really didn't know what to do with himself," Rosen recalled.

Johnson had spent most of his life in Lansing, in the protective environment of his family, helping his father haul garbage on weekends and shoveling the snow off playground courts in the wintertime. An instant millionaire who had always been perfectly happy without any money, Johnson was lost in the expanse of Los Angeles. It seemed his wardrobe included only sweatsuits and T-shirts and jeans. He had a two-bedroom apartment in one of Jerry Buss's buildings in Culver City, just ten minutes from the Forum, and that became his outpost. Unsure of the surroundings, he spent long hours there battling homesickness. One of his few contacts was longtime Laker administrative assistant Mary Lou Liebich, who had served as an unofficial mother figure to many rookies over the years.

Liebich said she couldn't recall a rookie who spent more time at her desk than Johnson. "Earvin would come in grinning, talking a mile a minute," she recalled with a laugh. "He always said, 'How ya doin', sweets?'" Johnson would visit there, then head over to Public Relations for more small talk. It was obvious he didn't have anything to do.

It became Rosen's task to rescue the rookie from this social nether-world. The intern was the perfect pal to help Johnson learn the area. Rosen knew the hot spots, the ways to find fun, the tricks to coping with the city's oppressive traffic. They went to Southern Cal football games and Dodger baseball games and movies and night spots together. It was easy and fun.

As was Rosen's job with the team. It helped that he was a natural at the promotions business, which was something the team's new owner, Jerry Buss, wanted to emphasize.

In his early twenties, Rosen soon moved into a full-time job with the Lakers as director of promotions, which paid all of twelve thousand dollars a year. It was a hustle job, meeting and greeting the many people who wanted to attach themselves to the team's image. Rosen set up dozens of small-time deals—printing jobs, media spots, all the usual things that keep a team's name in public view. But Rosen's friendship with Johnson made him more than just another flack. He was close to the team's star and over the next few years found a role as part of then-coach Pat Riley's trusted inner circle.

As if all this wasn't exciting enough for a Jersey kid, Rosen found himself in charge of Jerry Buss's new idea, the Laker Girls, the owner's plan for charging the atmosphere at the Forum. They weren't cheerleaders, per se. They were dancers, among Southern California's best. Buss wanted them visible. Rosen was merely in charge of quality control. He had to select the dance group each year from auditions. Tough as it was, he struggled to stay away from the casting couch mentality. "I could have," he said with a laugh. "But I didn't."

Still, a jiggle is a jiggle, and hey, somebody had to do it. So Rosen sat and watched the bump and grind, the step and slide, and called on his expertise to make the selections. Sometimes people offered advice, but Rosen mostly did the dirty work himself. That was how he tabbed an eighteen-year-old choreographer named Paula Abdul in 1983. Later, the team would turn the chores over to a dance professional, but in those early days of Showtime, the pleasure was all Rosen's. Yet when the time came to give it up, he wouldn't complain. "I was getting married," he explained. "And the Laker Girls can put undue stress on a relationship."

As could his hours. He worked 270 nights per year promoting events at the Forum: LA Kings hockey games, circuses, the Lakers, you name it. It was the kind of job that introduced him to everybody on the LA scene. Agents. Promoters. Entertainers. The Hollywood stars sitting at courtside, many of whom were often desperate for a ticket. Rosen chuckles at the time Ron Reagan, Jr., phoned desperately looking for two seats to a big game and promised, "I'll introduce you to my father!" Reagan got the seats, but Rosen never met the prez. It didn't matter. Rosen knew virtually everybody else, or at least someone who did.

His real promotional trial by fire was the 1983 NBA All-Star Game at the Forum, for which Rosen signed Lionel Ritchie to sing the national anthem. Those plans, however, were ditched the week of the event when a league official asked, "Who's Lionel Ritchie?"

Rosen got Marvin Gaye as a replacement, then watched in horror the day before the game as Gaye ran through a five-minute version of the national anthem with the rhythm track to "Sexual Healing" as the backbeat. There was no way that CBS would put up with a five-minute national anthem.

Rosen had to walk up to Gaye and ask if he could trim the number a bit, and would he show up an hour early tomorrow to do a run-through?

Gaye frowned and mumbled something about being at the Forum at 11:30.

The next day 11:30 passed, then noon. With the 12:37 game time looming, it was panic city for Rosen. He scrambled to find a Forum usherette who said she could do the anthem. Rosen was set to take her to center court at 12:25 when Gaye appeared with his entourage of five. He strolled to the mike and turned out a two-minute, twenty-four-second version of pure soul sweetness.

"People started to clap; players were dancing to it," Rosen recalls.

But upstairs at the Forum offices and in New York at the CBS switchboard, the phones were ringing. The national anthem and "Sexual Healing"? People were outraged.

Fortunately, Rosen saved the soundtrack, and when Gaye was killed months later, the Lakers played it as a tribute to him.

The real bottom line, though, was that Rosen quickly learned to maneuver in a world of high-priced athletes and entertainers. His friendship with Johnson was just another angle that helped ensure his success. On the side, Rosen began aiding Johnson with small agenting chores. The team frowned on some of the activities, because Rosen was still employed there. But there was little doubt that the help was needed.

Trust had become a big factor to Johnson. He had watched as poor business management left Kareem Abdul-Jabbar nearly bankrupt in the mid-1980s. Besides, Johnson was unhappy with his own representation. He sensed his popularity and figured that a special shoe and clothing line with his name on it would be tremendously successful. But the conventional marketing wisdom was that white buyers would never support a product named for a black athlete. This irritated Johnson no end, because he knew it wasn't true. Then he watched as Michael Jordan's shoe and clothing line, Air Jordan, encountered phenomenal success.

Which, in turn, started Johnson's competitive juices to flowing. He didn't like losing at anything. Like basketball and sex, business was just another game, and money was how you kept score.

Johnson's then-agent, George Andrews, lived in Chicago and enjoyed a broad client base. Too broad, Johnson thought. He was being over-looked. Los Angeles was too far away for Andrews to be effective. In the meantime, Johnson was losing millions in endorsement opportunities. And that meant he was falling short of his ultimate goal. Johnson dreamed of becoming a major player in the business world after his Laker days were over. He wanted badly to own an NBA team, and that required immense wealth, far more than the savings from a mere player's salary. To attain his goals, he had to reach into that vast grab bag of corporate endorsement money.

Johnson's spunky young friend, Rosen, was an unusal choice as a new agent for a superstar. It was a big gamble, to turn over his multimillion-dollar interests to a twenty-something kid with no real experience striking big-time deals. Besides, Rosen could be snotty, and some people questioned if Johnson was making a good decision.

"Lon was a good guy, but he could be very abrasive sometimes. He could be arrogant and condescending," said a Laker staffer. "But he was young. Jerry West had some talks with him about it. Lon learned not to show that side of himself unless he really needed to."

Rosen readily conceded that West helped him a lot. "Like anybody, I had to be put in my place a time or two," he said.

On September 1, 1987, Rosen gave up his job as the Lakers director of promotions and became Johnson's agent. His first job was to renegotiate his client's contract. "Overnight," he said, "I moved across the table. It caught Jerry Buss by surprise."

Rosen then turned his attention to finding companies eager to associate themselves with Magic Johnson's image. And Rosen had even greater ideas. He had read a magazine article about superagent Michael Ovitz, the head of the powerful Creative Artists Agency, who represented the very best of Hollywood and arranged for them the deals that nobody else could strike. Rosen wanted Ovitz to take Johnson to the upper realm of power and wealth.

Johnson, after all, was Magic.

It was well known that Ovitz had never represented an athlete. But, as promotions director for the Lakers, Rosen had gotten to know Joe Smith, the president of Capitol Music–EMI and an associate of Ovitz's. Smith, a longtime fan and friend of Johnson's, agreed to set up a meeting between Ovitz, Johnson, Rosen, and himself.

At that meeting, Ovitz explained, "I don't do athletes." But the talk went well, and Ovitz was a Laker fan. He liked Johnson, so he agreed to a second meeting, this time at Le Dome, that classy, cool eatery for huge Hollywood types. Rosen gave Johnson background material on Ovitz to read to prepare for the meeting, which the player dutifully did. Things got off to a good start when Johnson walked into Le Dome and the patrons, normally dripping with Hollywood hauteur, gave him a standing ovation.

Ovitz was amazed. The superagent had brought his biggest clients there, and nothing like this had ever happened. After that and a series of follow-up meetings, it became only a matter of the Magic charm, which was no contest.

Ovitz, the superagent who didn't do athletes, suddenly was doing one. He took over Johnson's corporate strategy and restructured it, limiting his endorsements to create value for megacontracts with equity positions. Rosen and Johnson, the two buddies who had started their relationship munching Dodger Dogs at the ballpark, had reached that platinum level.

In 1987, when Johnson switched agents, he was making less than $1 million annually in endorsements. By late 1991, the corporate deals for Earvin Johnson had stacked up to quite an impressive portfolio, about $10 million annually. They didn't quite match Michael Jordan's (estimated at $15 to $20 million), but they were getting close.

This competition with Jordan had forced Johnson to work all the harder. He had to win. In the 1980s, the two superstars didn't care much for each other. Jordan had mistakenly believed that James Worthy, his old friend and teammate at the University of North Carolina, had been snubbed by Johnson at a benefit game. But after a while Johnson and Jordan came to understand that their differences were more imagined than real. Soon their rivalry became friendly, in basketball and business.

Jordan would tease Johnson. Look at those junky Converse shoes of yours, he'd say. You need something nice like my Air Jordans.

"That talk made Earvin work harder," Rosen said.

By 1990, Johnson and Jordan felt so comfortable with one another that they considered playing one-on-one in a giant pay-per-view television deal. Isiah Thomas, as president of the NBA Players' Association, protested that the game violated the agreement between the league and its players, which it did. For a time, Johnson and Jordan considered briefly retiring to play one-on-one, then resuming their careers. But they dropped the idea.

Which didn't really matter. Their business one-on-one match was even hotter than the basketball version. Jordan had Nike. Johnson was Converse. Jordan had Wilson equipment. Johnson endorsed Spalding. Jordan sipped Coke. Johnson gulped Pepsi. Even though he was younger, Jordan had the head start. Johnson was down on the scoreboard. But he enjoyed being the underdog and was coming on strong.

Then the HIV nightmare struck.

At first, Rosen barely had time to consider the financial implications. He had planned to contact the key people at each of Johnson's corporate affiliations. Converse. Campofrio (the Spanish meat company). Nestlé. Pepsi. Spalding. Tiger Electronics. Virgin Electronics. But when the news leak blew the announcement schedule, Rosen had time to reach only four of the companies on the list—Pepsi, Converse, Spalding, and Nestlé.

His announcement brought immediate speculation that corporate America would quickly dump the Magic act. Whether contacted or not, all of Johnson's corporate affiliations phoned or faxed back messages of support, to Rosen's relief. But within days, Nestlé quietly dropped plans to air a commercial with Johnson that had already been produced.

The spot featured Johnson shooting a ball and delivered the standard Nestlé's candy message: "It's scrumptious."

"Their feeling was that it wasn't the right thing to do," Rosen said of the spot. "We disagreed, but it was certainly within their rights to change plans."

Converse also announced that it was supportive of Johnson, but the message had a rather hollow ring to it. Since 1990, the shoe company had ceased to include him in its marketing plans, although it continued to pay him a seven-figure sum each year. Johnson had asked to make commercials for Converse, and although the company wouldn't have to pay him any more money, it declined. So he asked to be released from his contract. The company declined that request, too. Part of the problem had been Converse's financial problems. Converse's parent company, Interco, had filed for bankruptcy protection in 1991, and Johnson was left standing in line with the other creditors. He couldn't get out of his contract because the bankruptcy court counted his relationship among Converse's most valuable assets. Although the shoe company regained its feet and resumed sending checks to Johnson, it still owed him several missed payments. He was left stranded in shoe limbo, so to speak.

Adding to the misery was the fact that the shoe contract, originally negotiated by George Andrews, had been reworked into a long-term deal. Johnson was caught in Converse's clutches through 1995. That, of course, was just fine with Nike and Reebok, the major powers in the shoe industry. If they couldn't have him, both Nike and Reebok told Rosen they'd rather Johnson be with Converse, where his name wouldn't be used to take some of their market share.

Within days after the announcement, condom companies and a pharmaceutical firm made offers for Johnson's endorsement. Rosen and Johnson declined, deciding that striking a deal there would make them seem eager to exploit the health issue. But Johnson did soon sign a $5 million three-book agreement with publishing giant Random House, which put him in a unique class. Of the estimated 11 million people in the world who had tested HIV positive, he was perhaps the only one to turn his status into a tidy financial gain.

FRIENDS

Friendship is a strange concept in the exclusive little world occupied by celebrities. Most, of course, are mere acquaintances arranged for career strategies. In 1989, Johnson threw a thirtieth birthday party for himself and invited five hundred of his "closest friends." But when his big trouble struck two years later, he had no trouble paring that group down to a short list of people who needed to be notified before the news broke. The list included Jordan, Pat Riley, Arsenio Hall, Larry Bird, Michael Cooper, Abdul-Jabbar, Isiah Thomas, and Kurt Rambis. Johnson asked Rosen to make the calls.

Each was understandably shaken by the news.

Hall was so disconcerted that he wanted to cancel the taping of his late-night talk show, but Rosen talked him out of it.

Riley, who had been hired as coach of the New York Knicks, wanted to miss his game against the Orlando Magic that night and hop a plane to LA. Rosen said there wouldn't be time, so instead Riley and the Knicks held a moment of prayer before tip-off in Madison Square Garden.

Rambis, however, abruptly left practice with the Phoenix Suns, where he was then playing, to fly to Los Angeles for the press conference. Abdul-Jabbar was in town and wanted to know immediately what he could do to help. Why don't you come over to the Forum and support Earvin? Rosen suggested. So the giant center, always a ponderous presence in the Laker locker room, came to the Forum that day.

Abdul-Jabbar had watched Johnson's transformation during their years playing together. "Back in October 1979, Earvin was innocent, just a wide-eyed kid with very special talent," Abdul-Jabbar said later. "No hidden agenda. He just wanted to have some fun. He was where he wanted to be. Having it go from that to where it ended up was tragic. I'm angry at myself, because I guess somehow I feel I should have warned him. I didn't do anything, or couldn't do anything. He was very much a man who was gonna live his life the way he wanted to live it."

Rosen liked to think of himself as one of the most competent promoters in the business, but there was nothing to prepare him for the deluge that followed Johnson's announcement. The two fax machines in the agent's office began spewing out messages from around the world, and this would go on nonstop for days.

It didn't take long for Rosen to realize he was overwhelmed.

In the hours just before the announcement, Rosen had been in frequent contact with NBA commissioner David Stern. Johnson's announcement had to be done correctly, and that required Stern's full consultation. It was Stern, after all, who had been credited with resurrecting the NBA after he became commissioner in 1984. In the 1970s, the league had been plagued by an image of drug abuse and boring games. A lawyer, Stern immediately attacked those problems. He instituted a tight drug policy, one that was fair and tough; then he set out to market the game and its exciting young superstars—Magic Johnson and Larry Bird—as a "Fantastic" form of entertainment. Everything he did worked famously for pro basketball, and in 1991 team owners rewarded Stern with a new multimillion-dollar contract.

Now, he was earning his money in crisis management. In the hours leading up to the announcement, he gave his full attention to the matter.

After Johnson made his disclosure, Rosen phoned the commissioner again to ask for more help. The agent was faced with a massive public relations crisis. Could the league send someone to help out?

It was an unprecedented move, the league office of a pro sport dispatching one of its employees to assist a "retired" player's agent. But Stern didn't hesitate.

"He's very sharp," Rosen said of the commissioner. "Magic having AIDS was a crisis that could have ripped the league apart if it wasn't handled correctly, and he knew it."

Stern went after this problem just as he had attacked the drug problem when he took over in 1984. "The big problem was no longer the NBA and drugs," Rosen said. "It was excessive sex."

The obvious choice to help was Josh Rosenfeld, the NBA's newly named director of international public relations. A former Laker public relations director, Rosenfeld was a close friend of both Rosen's and Johnson's. They trusted him completely.

Rosenfeld flew immediately to Los Angeles. "I walked into Lon's office and found two fax machines going full speed with the paper stacked to the ceiling," Rosenfeld recalled. He would spend two weeks helping Rosen sort out the communications and control the damage.

In the few days after the announcement, an estimated one hundred thousand letters flooded the Lakers' and Rosen's offices for Johnson. From there, the figure would go higher. There were people with AIDS, people who knew people with AIDS, people who wanted to send donations to the Magic Johnson Foundation, hastily formed to raise money to battle the disease.

The most urgent messages Rosen got the night of the announcement were from other players on other teams. "Ten prominent NBA players phoned that night," the agent said, "most of them asking, 'What can I do? How can I get tested?' They were scared to death."

In the United States, AIDS is thought to be largely a disease for gays and serious dope shooters. Of the 45,506 new AIDS cases reported to the Centers for Disease Control in 1991, approximately 52 percent involved homosexual males.

The news flash that Thursday in November gave hoops junkies around the world reason to pause. Was Magic bisexual? On playgrounds in every city, in every small town, the balls stopped bouncing as the debates began. *Magic Johnson, one of the two or three greatest players in the history of the game, is a sweet man? No way, Jack.*

The night of the announcement, *USA Today* basketball columnist Peter Vecsey was asked during a television network interview if Johnson was a homosexual. Vecsey, a former Green Beret who had been known for years as the league's juiciest gossip columnist, replied that he didn't know for sure because he wasn't always with Johnson.

Lon Rosen heard the exchange and was outraged. The agent phoned Vecsey at home that Saturday and demanded to know why he hadn't taken up for Earvin. Over the years, Johnson had come to think of Vecsey as a friend. He often took the time to talk to him, to offer his perspective on the many stories the columnist dredged up, the kinds of stories that infuriated general managers and coaches all over the league.

How could you not defend Earvin? Rosen demanded. "You know he's not gay."

Vecsey said he couldn't be sure of that. He said he'd heard rumors for years that Johnson had been seen frequenting gay bars.

"Peter," Rosen retorted, "Earvin is six-nine and black. He can't put on a hat and sunglasses and sneak in and out of gay bars."

Vecsey would later use the comment in his column, which further infuriated Rosen. He had assumed the conversation was private. The remark would leave the agent open to criticism for his insensitivity.

Johnson loathed the idea that people would think he was gay. He and Rosen decided they should move quickly to counter the negative publicity of the announcement. Johnson wanted to appear that Friday night on Arsenio Hall's nationally syndicated late-night talk show. Plus he decided to do an interview with LA sportscaster Jim Hill, an old friend, and to write an article for *Sports Illustrated* with writer Roy S. Johnson, coauthor of Johnson's book, *Magic's Touch*.

"We knew," Rosen explained, "that by going to the people Earvin felt comfortable with, people who would protect him, the message would get out."

Hall and Johnson had become close friends over the previous four years. Hall had first moved into the late-night talk show circuit as a replacement in 1988 when the Fox network fired Joan Rivers. It was a short-term assignment, and Hall's staying in the business required that he sell the idea of underwriting his own show to the top guns at Paramount.

Hall learned that the studio bosses were going to attend his show one night, so he phoned Johnson and asked him to come on as a last-minute guest. Johnson's appearance, Hall reasoned, would demonstrate for Paramount that he could deliver big-name personalities. Johnson was all smiles and hugs and handshakes that night (Little Richard and Mike Tyson also appeared), and the Paramount people were duly impressed, paving the way for Hall to get his own show.

Now, Johnson needed to defend himself, and he was calling in the favor. He wanted to go on Hall's show and explain his situation.

Hall didn't think it was such a grand idea and was worried that the appearance would be a disaster. The host didn't think that he could hold up under the emotional duress. He made several phone calls trying to get Johnson and his advisers to change their minds. But Johnson was determined.

Reluctantly, Hall agreed.

Contrary to fears, Johnson's appearance was a slick success, for Johnson and for the show's ratings. Among several pointed questions, Hall asked if Johnson was gay.

Johnson replied that he wasn't, and the studio audience applauded enthusiastically. He also called for people everywhere to practice safe sex, a plea that later brought broad criticism because Johnson hadn't pointed out that the best protection against sexually transmitted disease was abstinence. Johnson quickly tailored his future messages to include that option.

In the dressing room at Hall's show, Johnson also did his interview with Hill, then sat down and talked with Roy Johnson for the *Sports Illustrated* piece. "By now I'm sure that most of America has heard rumors that I am gay," he wrote. "Well, you can forget that. Some people started the talk during the NBA Finals in 1988 and '89 when I kissed Isiah Thomas on the cheek as a pregame salute to our friendship and our respect for the game. But actually I've been hearing that kind of talk for a long time. . . .

"I sympathize with anyone who has to battle AIDS, regardless of his or her sexual preference, but I have never had a homosexual encounter. Never."

In the days after the announcement, Johnson rented a beach house in Maui and retreated there with his wife and four of his best friends and their wives. Included in the group were former Laker guard Larry Drew and his wife. Given his release by the Lakers, Drew had been in Italy trying to catch on with an Italian team when news of Johnson's plight broke. Drew dropped his plans and returned immediately to Los Angeles. Already Johnson was feeling the first withdrawal pangs for the game. It helped having Drew, a former teammate, in Hawaii.

Also, the doubt grew in Johnson's mind. Had he made the right decision? He certainly didn't feel sick. It was good to have the group around him, and it was also good to get away for walks on the beach. His life, always a storybook, had changed abruptly, sending his destiny spinning off in strange directions. Maui was nice. He loved the place. The islands offered a healing atmosphere. In the past, he had loved going there after a long, brutal season. He could let the sun heal his tired, aching body. In fact, he liked Maui so much that he wanted to purchase a home there and spent part of his week looking at real estate. But he really wasn't ready to retire. Johnson's nature demanded that he be busy with something. When he wasn't, he tended to get cranky. Plus, there was another distraction. The tabloid bloodhounds, having gotten a scent of a story, had tracked him to Maui. He spent some time around the pool at the Westin Hotel, until the tabloids sniffed him out there. These intrusions hastened his return to the mainland. It was easier to find privacy in Los Angeles. Besides, he wanted to find out what his new life would be like, to find some positive direction. And, mostly, to find out if he could play again.

Back in Los Angeles, he returned to some of his old routines. He arrived early at the Forum before Laker games, dressed in playing gear, and went through his shooting warm-ups, with the ushers and early bird fans there to cheer him on. He would then shower and dress, and for a time he even sat on the bench with the team. But that was too close to the action. He could taste it, like a junkie licking a rock of cocaine. He wanted the game. On the bench, it was in his nostrils. So he backed off and moved up into the stands.

His doctors, however, had said from the very start that they wanted him to continue exercising. He had begun taking AZT, the medicine thought to help slow the spread of the virus, and his physicians were eager to see how he adjusted.

He missed his daily playing fix so much that he settled for pickup games at Sports Club LA. His doctors cleared it. Spreading the virus by playing basketball was virtually impossible, they said. At the sports club the stallion of professional basketball tried to find satisfaction by mixing with the usual pickup crowd. Overweight salesmen. Awkward schoolboys. And a smattering of former college players.

Instead of James Worthy on the wing, there'd be a thirty-one-year-old stockbroker, with a million-dollar pass smacking him in the face. Let that happen to a rookie in training camp and Johnson would be raggin' all over him. It didn't matter where, he didn't like to miss an assist. But at the club, he forced himself to smile. After all, these people accepted him. They boxed out on rebounds and played hard defense. There was no AIDS fear here. Johnson appreciated that. It was Positive. Once he found it, he locked in on it and was like a kid on a playground again.

Yet ultimately, all it did was stoke his habit. He wanted the game. His departure had been too abrupt. The lights. The media. The crowds. The autographs. The locker room. The fellas. The team. The travel. The purpose. It had all been there one moment, then gone the next. He hadn't been able to squeeze it one last time.

He was healthy. He wanted to play again, maybe full-time. And if not full-time, he at least wanted some type of good-bye.

Over the 1988–89 season, Kareem Abdul-Jabbar had retired with a farewell tour. In each city the Lakers visited, the opponents would have a pregame ceremony honoring the forty-two-year-old center, the game's most prolific scorer. There would be gifts and speeches and applause. It drove the rest of the team nuts. As James Worthy explained, it was like playing two games. They'd warm up and get ready to play; then the farewell salute to Kareem would drag on interminably. Meanwhile, the players would get stiff, then they'd have to play again.

Johnson, too, would get irritated at times. But he also took a lot of pleasure in watching the crowds, taking in the pageantry, and hearing the testimonials. It made him think ahead to his own departure. On some nights, as Johnson stood in line for the national anthem behind Gary Vitti, he would lean forward as the music started and whisper in the trainer's ear, "Can you imagine what it'll be like when they do this for me?"

Kareem was a great player, Vitti said, but he was aloof and understood by few. If the opposing teams did this much for Kareem, Johnson wondered, what would they do for him? He loved everybody, and everybody loved him. What kind of retirement bash would they throw for him?

Just trying to imagine it set his flywheel spinning. Sparks flew. Positive.

After a couple of weeks of playing pickup at the club, he decided to put together a group of skilled players, mostly former pros and college players, who could offer more of a challenge. This group included Mike Dunleavy, Larry Drew, and former Syracuse star Stevie Thompson. They became Johnson's unofficial support group, and most of them managed to meet him whenever he could get a free gym. Seven A.M., 10:00 P.M., it didn't matter. They just wanted to help.

This higher level of competition served to drive his desire up a notch. By late December, Johnson was phoning Rosen nearly every day to discuss a comeback. The agent stalled him. Johnson also repeatedly discussed the issue by phone with his father, Earvin Sr., back in Lansing. Like Kareem, Worthy, and other Laker stalwarts of the 1980s, Johnson had a strong, successful father. Earvin Sr. was six-foot-four and industrious. In addition to his job at an auto plant in Lansing, he ran his own garbage-hauling business on weekends. As a youth, Johnson had helped his father haul that garbage. As an adult, he constantly sought his father's guidance.

Earvin, if you feel good and you want to do it, go on back to playing, his father told him.

In early January, Johnson phoned Rosen. "Just tell them I'm coming back next week," he ordered.

But Rosen again found a way of stalling. In the days after the announcement, the agent had flown to New York for a parley with the NBA's top executives—Stern and assistants Gary Bettman and Russ Granik. Earvin will want to play in the All-Star Game in Orlando, Rosen told them. After all, his name is on the All-Star ballot, and this will be an excellent farewell.

Stern and his associates immediately agreed. That would be a very good idea, they said. After all, Johnson had been the linchpin of the league's success. There wasn't one good reason not to let him play.

It was quite a collision, Earvin Johnson's churning nature of Positive against centuries of dark Negative, the great public fear of contagion. Leprosy. The black death. Cholera. Typhoid fever. Polio. AIDS. Regardless of the disease, the victims were outcasts. Fear was the only currency. And even the undertakers didn't want the dead.

To the general public, AIDS was a disease of gay boys and whores and drug addicts and hapless blood transfusion victims. Earvin Johnson fell in at the head of their parade rather uneasily in late 1991.

With his revelation, he had announced his intention to become "a spokesman for the HIV virus." He would quickly discover that this role was far more complicated than he imagined.

To his credit, he studied hard, learned about the disease, and played his part. Where other celebrities with AIDS had chosen to slink off and die quietly, as was their right, he attacked the circumstances with all of his Positive might.

Asked if the virus had brought him "bad days," Johnson replied, "I'm not a bad day person. Every day I wake up, I'm happy. I'm ready to go do something. The virus can only make you have a bad day if your frame of mind is like that. So I'm not down about it. I'm not trying to say, 'Why me?' I'm going on. It's happened, and I'm dealing with it. But it hasn't stopped me from living and enjoying life."

In the days after his announcement, AIDS hot lines across the country had been jammed with callers seeking information and counseling. The cards and letters to his foundation filled a large storeroom at the Forum, where the bags of mail were packed to the ceiling. It would take platoons of volunteers weeks to open each piece, discarding the small amount of hate mail to focus on the frantic pleas for help from some writers and the support offered by others. In the first two weeks after the announcement, his Magic Johnson Foundation took in more than five hundred thousand dollars in unsolicited donations. (NBA player Rex Chapman alone sent a fifty-thousand-dollar check, even though he hardly knew Johnson.)

The outpouring of public love encouraged him and, to some degree, all AIDS victims. It was said time and again that surely God must have selected Johnson to fight this disease. Who else could rally the public against fear, against centuries of prejudice toward the victims of contagion?

He had been raised in a religious household. His mother, Christine, was a devout Seventh-Day Adventist, and his father, Earvin Sr., was a good Baptist. From an early age, young Earvin was taught about the presence of God in life. Now that he was confronted by death, Johnson reconnected with his spiritual background. Somehow, with pro basketball's Sunday games and practices, he had never found much time for churchgoing. But with his abrupt departure from the game, he had time for church again. He and Cookie quietly began attending worship services in Los Angeles.

And Johnson soon began repeating what others were saying about him: he must have been selected by God to fight this disease.

Thus inspired, Johnson moved quickly to make good on his promises to join the AIDS fight. In addition to setting up the Magic Johnson Foundation to raise money for AIDS research, he lent his name to a book, *What You Can Do to Avoid AIDS*. And he and Arsenio Hall produced an AIDS awareness video, *Time Out*. Beyond that, Johnson joined broadcaster Linda Ellerbee for a well-received AIDS special for children on the Nickelodeon network (which Nestlé supported, thus atoning for canceling his commercial shortly after the announcement).

Johnson said he especially wanted to reach "the young people, because I'm trying to make sure that what happened to me doesn't happen to them."

He also continued the heavy load of charitable work he had done before his "retirement," including benefits for the United Negro College Fund, the American Heart Association, and the Muscular Dystrophy Association.

In February, Johnson again held the annual dinner he sponsors for the MDA. "It was overwhelming," said Bob Gile of the MDA. "We had more people than ever before."

Yet Johnson soon discovered that unlike his other charities, his AIDS involvement went beyond the realm of feel-good. Shortly after the announcement, he had agreed to serve on President George Bush's commission on AIDS, and in mid-January Johnson went to Washington to attend his first commission meeting. There he encountered New York AIDS activist Derek Hodel, himself sick with the disease. Hodel talked of the immense power that Johnson had brought to the AIDS fight, how the basketball player overnight had attracted publicity to the issue that activists hadn't been able to garner in a decade of work. "Mr. Johnson, already you have given people with HIV great hope," Hodel said. "By your will to live, by your will to beat this thing. Your taking control of your illness and your positive attitude show great courage. Sadly, they will not be enough to keep you alive."

Hodel's speech and his lambasting of the Bush administration for weak support of AIDS research deeply affected Johnson. He had been nervous about going to Washington, about commenting on this very complicated issue.

He didn't want to mess up, especially not in front of the bank of media covering the commission.

That night, when he got back to his hotel room, Johnson phoned Rosen in Los Angeles. He told his agent that Hodel had opened his eyes for the first time to the frustration, to the reality, that people with AIDS face. He had learned more from that simple speech than from all the other literature he'd read.

"That struck a nerve in Earvin," Rosen said. "It was a reality check."

"They had all these charts," Johnson explained. "They showed the African-American numbers from ten years ago up to now, and in every category they just kept going up and up and up. We lead in every chart. Children. Adults. Women. I just had to sit back and take a deep breath."

But if AIDS shocked him, it also broadened his public. Everywhere he went, he electrified crowds like never before. "I never had to be escorted into places," he said of the attention. "Now you gotta come in with six guys on you, trying to get through the crowds. It's been different."

Soon Johnson began limiting his public appearances. Without realizing it, he had quickly become a poster child, the patron saint of the disease. Over time, he would become increasingly uncomfortable with that role. Just why was difficult to explain. But this much was true: He wanted his old life back. God had made him to be a basketball player. That's what he did best. It was the motor that drove his success, his Positive. It was his life force, and Earvin Johnson wanted to live.

The announcement that Magic Johnson would play in the NBA's forty-second All-Star Game in Orlando in mid-February 1992 was hailed as another great step forward for the enlightenment. Suddenly, it wasn't just another boring All-Star Game. It was Magic Johnson's Grand Finale, the Farewell event, the greatest public relations opportunity that AIDS awareness campaigners could imagine.

The game would be broadcast worldwide in 90 countries, and more than 960 journalists would be there, to see an HIV-infected athlete compete against the world's best basketball players. If only for a brief time, AIDS victims worldwide could emerge from the shadows to feel a bit normal. One of their own was playing in the big game.

Unfortunately, many NBA players didn't quite see it that way. They were worried that playing against an infected opponent could have disastrous results. After all, it was a brutal sport. Players fought for rebounds and loose balls. Scratches, cuts, fat lips were a part of every game.

In January, Cleveland guard Mark Price and Portland forward Jerome Kersey expressed publicly their concern about the situation. Their questions bothered Johnson only a little. They weren't his friends and weren't particularly powerful. They didn't matter.

But then A. C. Green and Byron Scott told reporters they didn't think Johnson should play in the game. He was crushed at the news. They were like family. Both players later explained to him that their comments were taken out of context. Scott said he was concerned about Johnson's health.

Green, on the other hand, said he didn't see how Johnson could be honored as an All-Star if he was retired. Johnson didn't take it well.

"It made it clear to me that 'Okay, you're not a part of this team anymore,' " he said. "I had felt like I was a part of it up to that point, but that just put the *t* on the end of *retirement.*"

With the comments, Johnson for the first time began to feel the ostracism that other AIDS victims lived with daily. He felt different and alone. Others were frightened of playing with him, and that was depressing. During a low point in early January, he was shooting around before a Forum game with the Miami Heat when Miami center Rony Seikaly asked if they could play one-on-one. Johnson happily agreed. Usually pro players dabble at one-on-one during warm-ups, and the games are nothing more than silly little shooting contests. But Seikaly seemed intent on making this competitive. He played defense and went after rebounds. Johnson didn't know Seikaly very well. But he knew the young center was sending him a message. The gesture was a simple kindness, one Johnson wouldn't forget.

"He took me right out there and played," Johnson said of Seikaly. "People were putting fear in other people's minds. He had no fear at all. We just played."

While his close friends were expressing doubt, here was someone Johnson hardly knew, telling him everything would be alright.

The NBA, too, went to great lengths to make things alright. Part of the strategy was a massive information campaign, for both athletes and the media. In the coming months, the league would establish a policy for bleeding players. If someone sustained a cut or scratch in a game, time would be called and the player removed until the bleeding was stopped and the wound bandaged. Team trainers would treat all such cases while wearing latex gloves.

Afterward, only one question remained for the players: "If it's so safe for us to compete against an infected player, then why is the trainer wearing the gloves?"

The All-Star Game in Orlando was the NBA at its marketing best. The league teamed with Walt Disney World to throw a rousing party. On Friday night of All-Star Weekend, the Magic Kingdom was opened to the media and the NBA's special guests. There were marching bands and Disney characters and free shows and an endless flow of booze and seafood and hors d'oeuvres. Among the throng of journalists was Bogdan Stanculescu, a broadcaster from recently liberated Romania. "I ask myself what more can men do here?" he said while surveying the surreal atmosphere of Disney's World Village.

It was an orgy of sport and capitalism.

The lobbies of the Disney hotels were a basketball junkie's dream. The media hospitality room on the second floor of the Contemporary Resort served as the late-night hot spot for the couches-and-bar-stool crowd. Among the throng on Saturday night was Les Harrison, the former owner/coach of the Rochester Royals (today the Sacramento Kings). Now in his eighties, he remained as brash as the old days, when he used to bark and yell and bait the officials from the Royals' bench.

A small crowd gathered around while Harrison talked of his chief rivals of yesteryear, the Minneapolis Lakers, and launched into an animated critique of his great guards, Bobby Wanzer and Bob Davies. In the midst of this harangue, Harrison was introduced to Christine Johnson, Earvin's mother, and her sweet smile brought an abrupt calm over the old man. One of the first owners to integrate pro basketball, Harrison turned all charm, telling Mrs. Johnson he was honored to meet her.

She returned the compliment, saying it was nice meeting a pioneer of the game.

Harrison said it must be something to be the mother of such a special person.

Indeed it was, she replied. For example, she had run into her son's fourth-grade teacher in a grocery store a few months back. The woman recalled a story about Magic. It was the first day of school in her first year of teaching, and the class was giving her fits. Spitballs were flying. Children were yelling. Suddenly young Earvin stood up and told his classmates to get in their seats, behave, and listen to the teacher. In a blink, he restored order to the room.

"She told me, 'I will never forget him,' " Mrs. Johnson said proudly.

Told later about his mother's anecdote, Johnson laughed and said, "She shouldn't be telling you my childhood stories. The teacher just came in that first year, and the class could sense she couldn't handle us. So I just stood up and told everybody to shut up and behave. I've always tried to do the right thing and be a leader. That was just one of those situations."

And now the All-Star Game was another of those leadership situations, and Johnson wanted to make the most of it. During the preliminary press conference he had talked about how wonderful Sunday was going to be, how it would be a triumph for AIDS victims everywhere. "No matter what negative comes, I've always been a positive person, always been upbeat," he said. "As long as you have your family and friends supporting you, that's all you need. I have to be out there for myself and I have to be out there for a lot of people, whether they have disease or handicaps or whatever, and let them know that they can still carry on."

On Friday night of All-Star Weekend, Herb Williams had dropped by Johnson's room to find Isiah Thomas there sharing a laugh and a quiet conversation with Magic. Williams figured Johnson had come to Orlando to put in a cameo appearance, take a bow, and enjoy the weekend.

"I'm winning the MVP," Johnson announced.

"What you mean?" Williams said, laughing.

"I've had the guys at the club running five-on-five," Johnson said. "My game is right. I feel good. And when I leave here I'm taking that trophy home with me."

First you noticed the brunette. She was really quite nice. Then you noticed that she had a millionaire in tow. Lakers owner Jerry Buss stood with his date at courtside. A hand jammed in one pocket, he nervously chewed a fingernail on the other. A few feet away, Johnson was warming up for the All-Star Game, and Buss was trying to get his attention through the throng milling about.

Finally Johnson spied him and came over, smiling. He shook the owner's hand, draped a long arm over his shoulder, and gave a squeeze. Buss was another old friend. Almost like a father.

In fact, Kareem Abdul-Jabbar thought Johnson and the owner were too close. "It kind of got to be like a family thing," Kareem said, "where Earvin got to be the favorite child. I think they did things to placate me. Up until the year I retired, I was the highest-paid player in the league. So I don't have any complaints. They paid me well; they appreciated what I did. But I never got to be a part of the family thing, because my own personal integrity made Dr. Buss uncomfortable."

Some observers believed that the stone-faced, seven-foot-two, 260-pound Abdul-Jabbar intimidated the owner. Others just thought their personal styles were simply different. Buss loved the high profile his association with the team brought. Each game night he packed his skybox at the Forum with an array of impressive people. Actors. Lawyers. Executives. Intellectuals. Celebrities of all kinds. Afterward, he enjoyed taking them to the locker room to meet his stars. Abdul-Jabbar hated schmoozing and crowds and glad-handing. He wanted no part of Buss's celebrity games. Johnson, on the other hand, loved the associates that the owner brought to the locker room. He set them at ease and made them feel welcome, while Kareem grabbed a shower and made a quick exit.

Buss and Johnson were kindred spirits in other ways. The owner exuded informality with his blue jeans and open-collared shirts. He fancied himself a playboy and took great delight in dating beautiful young women. Although he usually dated them only once or twice each, he liked to keep their pictures in photo albums, which he proudly showed to visitors and friends.

And he was a great dancer. In the fifties, when he was in school, he loved the cha-cha, the polka, the mambo. "But the rage was the jitterbug," he said. "I loved it and did it all the time." When the late seventies came along, he got caught up in the *Saturday Night Fever* craze. "I took disco lessons and tried to imitate John Travolta," he said with a laugh.

When Johnson joined the team as a rookie in the fall of '79, the owner began going to the clubs with his star rookie. "He would dance; I would dance," Buss explained. He had other favorites among the Lakers, but Buss soon learned a lesson about becoming friends with lesser players. It hurt too badly when they had to be traded or released. Johnson wasn't only a great friend; he was a safe one. No owner in his right mind would ever trade a player like Magic.

For the past dozen years, they had celebrated championships and weathered hard times together. Buss, a poor boy who had used his quick mind to earn a doctorate in chemistry and later to find wealth in Southern California real estate, had seen his holdings drop appreciably in the mid-1980s, as the recession slowed the cash flow from his properties. Creditors complained, and the LA business media had a field day reporting it. But Buss never missed a payday to his players, and eventually he consolidated his holdings and got everything headed in the right direction again.

Those times had been easy compared with the news about Johnson. Buss had gotten word the very day Johnson learned he was HIV positive. In some regards, the owner took it worse than anyone else. Each day over the next two weeks he phoned Rosen to check on Johnson, always breaking down sobbing during the conversation. "Just tell me what I can do for Earvin," he told the agent.

Why don't you call him? Rosen suggested.

Buss couldn't bring himself to do that. We have to meet in person, he said. When they did, Buss was again torn with grief. He assured Johnson that although the agreement was unsigned, his new megacontract was good. Many people offered Johnson support in this low period. But none was bigger than Buss.

And no one was happier to see Johnson playing at the All-Star Game. Buss didn't have to say much standing there at courtside. They both knew what it meant to each of them.

Before all big games, Johnson was nervous, sleepless, anxiety-driven. The All-Star Game was no different. He had not played against pro competition in almost four months. He was a proud man and did not want to make a fool of himself in front of the world. James Worthy told him to relax. "Just kick it, man," he said. Don't worry about messing up. If you shoot an air ball, people are going to boo. Just laugh with 'em and have fun.

Johnson did just that, and the Orlando Arena that afternoon answered with an outpouring of love, 23,000 people showering him with their appreciation. It began as he took the floor and lasted all afternoon.

As Michael Bolton finished the national anthem, Johnson bit his lip and blinked. His eyes turned to liquid pools but stopped just short of spilling into tears. The East players, led by Isiah Thomas, came over, breaking that barrier between opposing teams, and took turns hugging him. Enough of this, he said. Let's play.

Rubbing his hands slowly, nervously, Johnson led the West starters to midcourt for the opening tip. Soon after it began, the game was over, at least from a competitive standpoint. The West quickly outclassed the East, leaving much garbage time, but easily the sweetest garbage time in the century-old history of basketball.

For the record, the West won, 153–113, but the Magic moment had nothing to do with the outcome. With just under three minutes to go in the game, Johnson first played Isiah Thomas one-on-one as the other players cleared out of the way. He stopped Thomas on defense, then hit a three-pointer at the other end as the crowd whooped.

On the next possession, he found Dan Majerle of the Phoenix Suns with a patent no-look assist, again to the crowd's great delight. Finally, he matched up one-on-one with Michael Jordan, stopped the superstar on defense, then lofted in another trey at the other end, setting off yet another tumultuous celebration.

With fourteen seconds left, Isiah Thomas grinned broadly and picked up the ball. The game had to end on Johnson's big shot. For his style and charisma and twenty-five points and nine assists, he was named the game's MVP, just as he had predicted on Friday night.

"I will cherish this the rest of my life, no matter what happens," he said. "I'm in a dream right now, and I don't ever want to wake up."

Johnson said he hoped to capture the weekend in a bottle, cap it, and never let it go. Instead just the opposite happened. His life escaped with a rush after that. The eyes were hardly dry from the All-Star Game when a week later the Lakers retired his number 32 in another emotional ceremony at the Forum. In the aftermath of the two events, he again felt an overwhelming urge to return to playing. But again his advisers and friends urged him not to, and he listened. Instead, he turned to serving as a broadcast analyst for NBC. He had always been good at talking the game, despite his fractured diction. In his early years in the league, he rivaled Yogi Berra's legendary ability to author malapropisms. ("I only know how to play two ways," Johnson once said. "That's reckless and abandon.")

Although he received diction and voice coaching to improve his opportunities in broadcasting, it was impossible to eliminate the goof-ups. He talked so much, they popped up everywhere. (Even in his HIV announcement, he talked about the virus that he had "attained.") The network audiences, though, showed little concern about this. Sports fans had once loved Dizzy Dean's wacky sayings in baseball. They were nothing if not original. The same was true of Magic and hoops. The ratings were good. The network big guns liked him, and that's all that mattered.

The Lakers, meanwhile, labored on without Johnson as Worthy, forward Sam Perkins, and center Vlade Divac all missed great chunks of the season with injuries. Regardless, Sedale Threatt, the journeyman backup, delivered solid, steady play at point guard, a pleasant surprise for the team's management, although his effort went largely unnoticed by many in the Forum crowd who were paying high prices to see a superstar. Simply, the fans were used to seeing Magic Johnson, and no matter how good Threatt was—and he was pretty good—it wasn't the same.

As for his playing urges, Johnson focused his attention on the upcoming Olympic Summer Games in Barcelona, where he would play on the "Dream Team," the first American men's basketball team to be comprised largely of professional players. Johnson had won a championship at every level, but his trophy case lacked an Olympic gold medal. He wanted one badly.

Again there were some rumblings about an HIV-infected athlete competing, but those were minor. Still, there were plenty of other major distractions. In April, Los Angeles erupted with urban riots, creating a holocaust that was broadcast live by the networks, particularly CNN. The fires and violence and looting left more than fifty people dead and resulted in billions of dollars in damage. The violence spread within blocks of the Forum, with some Laker players and staffers watching television inside the arena's offices as the bizarre events unfolded outside. In that regard, the concrete shell of the Forum became a bunker. But even it wasn't considered safe enough. With Threatt's leadership, the team had managed a late win that miraculously put the Lakers in the play-offs for the sixteenth consecutive time. And the riots forced the team to move one of its home games to Las Vegas in the first-round series against Portland. The Lakers lost three games to one, which immediately turned the focus to next season. Would Johnson attempt a comeback?

The answer was a resounding maybe.

In early June, his NBC broadcasting schedule for the play-offs conflicted with the due date of Cookie's pregnancy, so they agreed to induce labor, which allowed Johnson to perform as Lamaze coach during the delivery. The result was Earvin Johnson III, a fat, wide-eyed son, complete with all his fingers and toes and an HIV-negative blood test.

Much elated and relieved, Johnson returned to his busy schedule. His autobiography, *My Life,* with cowriter William Novak, was on a rush schedule. Charged with advance promotion, Johnson attended the American Booksellers' Association convention in Anaheim, where he hobnobbed with the publishing industry's power buyers. He was greeting a line of well-wishers at a reception when a forty-three-year-old woman gave him a pair of her daughter's ballet slippers to sign. When he complied, the woman was obviously thrilled. She thanked him, turned, walked a few feet, and collapsed, instantly dead of a heart aneurysm.

Johnson was shaken. Did she die because of the excitement of meeting me? he asked. Rosen assured him that wasn't the case. Johnson wrote her family anyway, offering his condolences.

What strange thing in his life could happen next? he asked.

Of the thousands of athletes at the Olympics, it was Earvin Johnson who loomed over the games. Crowds everywhere in Barcelona greeted him with the familiar chant, "Ma-jeek. Ma-jeek." His answer was to avoid them and the media throng's endless questions about AIDS. The first day in Barcelona he told them he would answer health questions just that once and from then on it would be only basketball.

Still, it was difficult. He was a world-class player at the world's competition. And he was infected with the world's disease. The populations of Africa, Asia, Europe, and North America were threatened by the spread of AIDS, according to the World Health Organization. And Johnson was easily the most visible of all the victims. Wherever he took a step, they took a step. Whenever he played, they played. The only real question seemed to be: did he empower AIDS victims or trivialize them? The answer seemed to be that he did both. But the major result of his participation was again positive. The world watched in early August as he stood on the awards platform with Jordan, Larry Bird, and his other teammates to receive the gold medal in men's basketball.

As his turn came to receive the medal, the crowd roared. He acknowledged them with a bow, smiling, not too broadly, a tight smile, packed with happiness. The noise grew when he bent to have the medal draped about his neck. Then he rose with the applause, punched the air in exhilaration, and unleashed the full smile, a bright beam to the world. A soon-to-be AIDS victim had just claimed the gold. He, who wanted to win everything, now possessed the only trophy he hadn't owned.

This one felt the best of all, he said. It was "the greatest feeling I've ever felt winning anything."

With the Olympics over, Johnson finally faced the question. Would he play again in the NBA? He originally planned to make his decision two weeks after the Summer Games. Instead, he dragged on for eight weeks, unable to make up his mind, which left general manager Jerry West twisted in knots. If Johnson wasn't coming back, West needed to sign a first-rate guard to strengthen the backcourt. Sedale Threatt had worked out well, but the team needed a point guard, a ball handler to run the offense. If Johnson didn't play, that opened a position on the team under the NBA's salary cap rules for another big-money player. Free agent Rod Strickland was available, and he was just the kind of guard West was looking for. Strickland seemed eager to come to the Lakers, but he couldn't wait for Johnson's decision.

Each day West would phone to grouse at Rosen about Johnson not making up his mind.

"Jerry," Rosen would say, "you're only happy when you're miserable."

The general manager fussed, but he didn't put any real pressure on Rosen, even as he watched Strickland give up on the Lakers and sign with Portland. "I believed all along that Magic would come back," West explained later.

If Johnson came back, West knew the Lakers could again be a great team, capable of claiming another NBA title. The general manager craved that greatness. "If you win a championship, the summers are fun," he said. "If you don't, they're terrible."

Johnson was in the final stages of renegotiating his contract with team owner Jerry Buss. Normally, West was the tough guy negotiating all Laker contracts. But Buss and Lon Rosen had been discussing a new agreement for several years. They had first begun talking at training camp in Hawaii in 1990, although under league rules the deal couldn't actually be signed until after the 1992 play-offs.

During the 1991 off-season, Johnson and Rosen had gone to Spain for a promotional appearance for Campofrio, the Spanish meat company. While there, Johnson was offered $20 million to play a season for a Spanish pro team. In September 1991, Rosen met again with Buss at the owner's house to discuss the new contract. "I used the Spanish offer as leverage," Rosen said. But he asked Buss for much more than $20 million. "It was a huge figure," Rosen said with a chuckle. "Jerry said, 'That's very high. A lot of money. More than I'm willing to pay him. But we'll keep talking.'" Buss did not want his superstar playing for another team, even if he was at the end of his career.

The nature of Buss's dealings with Johnson had always been love/business. In 1981, Buss the owner had given Magic what seemed like an incredible deal, $25 million for twenty-five years. But spiraling player salaries soon dwarfed those numbers. In 1987, Joe Smith of Capitol Music-EMI had helped Johnson renegotiate the deal into a $2.5 million annual package. Seemingly miffed at Smith's involvement, Buss pointed out that he could easily take away Smith's floor seats at the Forum. "Of the 128 seats out there, 96 belong to lawyers," Smith told him. "So if you want to deal with them instead . . ." Buss said he was only kidding. But the lesson in his toughness didn't escape Johnson's advisers. The owner may have loved Magic, but he meant business.

Rosen and Buss had planned to resume contract discussions in November 1991. But then Johnson's test results came back positive, which left the owner in a deep emotional funk, forcing him into virtual seclusion. Just before Johnson announced to the world that he was HIV positive, Buss pulled Rosen aside. "Look," he said. "I'm still giving him his contract."

By then, the matter was no longer a business deal. Buss was operating on pure emotion. In fact, the new contract made absolutely no business sense, because it jammed the Lakers against the salary cap for another three seasons, making it more difficult for West to arrange trades and other player deals. "Jerry Buss had no obligation whatsoever to do that for Earvin Johnson, but that's the way he is," Rosen said of the deal they eventually struck.

Buss had a history of generosity toward other people involved in the Lakers' run of championships. James Worthy, former coach Pat Riley, Michael Cooper, even West, all had gotten fat contracts and bonuses from Buss. But the league's salary cap had prevented him from doing the same for Johnson. Some people would later question his wisdom in giving Johnson the new deal, Buss said. "But I don't think people looked at the way Magic handled himself. At no time in his career did you see that he was unhappy with his contract."

For a while, the contract Joe Smith negotiated allowed Johnson to make the money he deserved, Buss said. "But then basketball contracts went into the stratosphere and Magic was left behind."

Buss had always told Johnson that he would be the highest-paid player on the team. But making that happen within the salary cap had been impossible. Johnson never complained, although Buss sensed that he expected something to be done. Sometimes Magic and Buss went to prizefights at the Forum. "He enjoyed the fights," Buss said, "and we'd have dinner together. A lot of the talking Magic and I do is at the fights. I told him in one of those talks that I would take care of it. He could have complained about his pay. He could have caused a lot of problems. But Magic Johnson is too professional to do that.

"Because he treated me so honorably, I returned the favor."

The "favor" was a whopping one-year, $14.6 million contract extension, bringing Johnson's guaranteed income to $19.6 million. It was the largest single-year contract in the history of pro basketball. To reach that figure, Buss and Rosen had examined past Laker payrolls to determine just how much Johnson had been underpaid. "This was Buss's way of paying Earvin back for all those years," Rosen said.

The owner and the agent reached an agreement shortly after the Olympics and notified the league office, as NBA rules required. There was only one problem. Johnson still didn't know if he wanted to come back. Rosen decided to delay the announcement of the new deal until after he made up his mind.

Either way, Johnson couldn't lose. If he decided not to play, Buss still guaranteed his money.

The man doing the bench presses can do one more. He *needs* to do just one more. How does he know this? Because Magic Johnson is telling him so.

This man doesn't know Magic Johnson, but here the big guy is in World's Gym, shouting at him, cheering him on. *One more rep. That's right. Push it. Push it. Big effort. C'mon now. Bi-i-iggg effort!*

It would go on each day like that, six days a week, after the Olympics, through August and September. As he had promised, Laker trainer Gary Vitti took charge of getting Johnson ready for the 1992–93 NBA season. First thing each morning, Vitti, Johnson, Byron Scott, and Duane Cooper, the Laker's second-round draft pick, would troop over to the UCLA gym for some quality hoops competition. That's where all the pros and big-name college players meet in the summer for pickup games. Johnson was the king of the court, organizing a little, establishing what needed to be established, mostly figuring the sides so he could win. "He ran the show," Vitti said. "Just like the old days."

Johnson didn't say he was coming back, but everybody around sensed he was. New Lakers coach Randy Pfund sensed it. Jerry West sensed it. Vitti did, too. But he didn't worry about it like the others. Like many of Johnson's friends, Vitti wasn't so concerned whether Johnson played in the NBA again. But if he was going to play, the trainer wanted to make sure his friend was in the best shape possible. So they pushed it every day, even when they went to Hawaii for Johnson's basketball camp.

Each day in LA after their sessions at UCLA, they'd head to World's Gym to lift weights. "He filled the gym," Vitti said. "He'd walk up to people he didn't know, people who were lifting, and pump 'em up. Motivate 'em. Push it. Push it. He was so full of life. He was so happy."

The only thing that dragged him down was trying to make the decision. His wife, Cookie, and most of his advisers weren't hot on the idea of his playing. You have nothing to prove, Arsenio Hall told him.

Johnson's doctors did not advise for or against playing, although they suggested that if he did play, not to attempt to cover the full eighty-two-game schedule. He planned to avoid back-to-back games and long, grueling road trips, anything that might weaken his immune system and hasten the onset of AIDS. Johnson hoped to play about sixty games on the schedule, which wasn't without precedent. Over the 1961–62 season Laker forward Elgin Baylor was called to military duty and appeared in only forty-eight games, mostly on weekend passes from service. Yet Baylor was still able to help the team to the league's championship finals. Johnson would settle for similar results this time around.

But in Boston, the Celtics' Larry Bird had briefly contemplated being a part-time player and rejected it. He wouldn't want to approach the game without a complete effort, he said. So he announced his retirement. The same problem remained for Johnson. Like Bird, his trademark had been all-out effort and commitment to the game. Basketball was his first love. How could it now become a mistress? "Every time Earvin looked at the schedule, he changed his mind about something else," Gary Vitti said. At first he was going to play no back-to-back games. Then it was some back-to-backs. Should he travel to Boston? What about New York? His doctors reminded him that a set plan would be difficult. Much of what he did would depend on his health. After all, this was new territory.

One morning during a pickup game with his pro friends, the tension boiled over. Journeyman Jim Farmer argued with him over a foul call, and Johnson exploded with rage. "That's the maddest I've ever seen Earvin," said longtime pro James Edwards. "It took ten to fifteen minutes to calm him down."

He kept charging toward Farmer, and other pros had to step between them. Don't leave early, Johnson finally told Doc Rivers, one of the peacemakers. I just might jump him when you're gone.

By the next morning, however, Johnson had regained his sunshine. Just to prove it, he picked Farmer first on his team.

Although he hadn't announced it, his comeback intentions were clear. "Earvin doesn't say much to anyone," Jerry West explained. "He does things by the way he feels. But if you've been around him long enough, you get to know what he's thinking."

New Jersey Nets coach Chuck Daly, Johnson's Olympic coach, came to Los Angeles on business and heard that a group of pro players was moving from court to court around the city to avoid crowds of spectators. Daly was told that if he appeared at a certain public court early one morning he might actually catch the action. Daly was there at nine, just in time to see Johnson going at it. Daly saw the fire in his eyes and didn't need to see any more. Johnson would be back.

"A lot of people didn't know what to expect," equipment manager Rudy Garciduenas said of Johnson's decision. "But a lot of people knew that Earvin couldn't be without the game."

Cookie knew, too, and finally she consented as well.

"I'm back," he announced, with his wife and Dr. Michael Mellman at his side at a news conference at the Forum on September 29.

God had put him here to play basketball, he said, admitting that at first his doctors had been opposed. "But they've never dealt with anyone as big and strong as I am. I continued to work out and do what I was supposed to do, and now I'm in a position to come back and play, so here I am. I'm back, baby."

HAWAII

If it is to be a long, hard road back, what better place to begin than Paradise? Breezes. Blue water. Groomed beaches. Leis. Soft morning rains. Beautiful Polynesian people. Pineapple music. Flowers. Grace. Just the thought of camp in Hawaii had always set Johnson to thinking about the possibilities. The same is true for his teammates. They've been waiting all summer. Lifting weights. Getting therapy to heal old injuries. Planning for a new start. But this camp has Johnson spinning like never before. For much of the past two weeks he has transcended the mere Positive to reach the absolutely beatific realm of joy that he has known on few previous occasions. Baby, he's back!

One of his first big moments was the "box" that the Laker ball boys delivered to his home from the equipment manager. As usual, it was filled with his practice gear. Socks. Jocks. Jerseys. Sweats. Shorts. All of it new and fresh and crisp and clean, just as the season is new and fresh and crisp and clean and alive. Johnson practically salivated at the freshness of it, the bland smell of the cotton, the tightness of the elastic, the brightness of the purple and gold outfits, the crème of the socks and jocks.

The box was the sign, like a robin in spring. It was time to begin again. And Earvin Johnson, point guard, team leader, Magic man, knew just how he wanted everything to be. To ensure that, he went to Hawaii a few days early with team management, to survey the familiar gym at the University of Hawaii, to bounce the balls, to take those early shots, to put everything in his universe in order.

It is a new season and Earvin Johnson is alive with it.

This was never more evident than at the team banquet two nights ago here in the hotel, a private, intramural affair from which the media are barred. "It's a ritual that everybody anticipates and looks forward to," Rudy Garciduenas says of the banquet. "It marks the beginning of the season. It's a chance for the players to get together, to be introduced to one another. With Earvin especially, it was a big deal. He would always be ready. It was time to kick ass. Time to go to work."

After the meal, Jerry West spoke to the group, reminding the players of league policies on gambling and fighting, of how they should conduct themselves as Lakers. Always remember that you're a representative of the team, he told the new players. The talk was surprisingly devoid of the "Laker tradition." The job, as West sees it, is to live up to tradition, not talk about it.

Then both Garciduenas and Gary Vitti addressed the group about routines and procedure for equipment and training. As they spoke, the energy built in Johnson. The furrows of his face deepened into a frown. Finally Garciduenas and Vitti finished, and it was time for Johnson to play drill sergeant/mother hen to the rookies.

"The young kids are called up in front of the room," Garciduenas explains, "and they're asked to introduce themselves, to say their school, what their major was. And they sing either their alma mater's fight song or a song of their choice. While they're up there, Earvin addresses the group. He basically challenges the young guys and tells the veterans, 'Let's go to work. We want to win. Let's get another championship.' Earvin likes to have fun. He really looks forward to the rookies. He orchestrates that whole thing. He gets up there with 'em and shows 'em exactly how he wants them to stand at attention and salute. Earvin really gets into that. He makes 'em march and step to.

"When they go through their little routine, they step forward and say their name. He shows 'em exactly how he wants it done. He goes through the whole thing with them and helps them with the words of the songs."

There are three rookies this season: Anthony Peeler, the first-round draft pick out of the University of Missouri; Duane Cooper, the second-round pick out of Southern Cal; and Alex Blackwell, a free agent from Monmouth College in New Jersey. All three thought Johnson was kidding when the session began. But the frown deepened in his face. And it didn't quite register with them. Magic Johnson playing Mickey Mouse hazing games? And serious about it? On another team, with another person, it wouldn't have floated. But this was the Lakers and Magic Johnson. "Rookies, come to the front!" he boomed, his eyes glaring. "I want you just like in the army. Stand at attention. Say your name and your school and your hometown. . . ."

The rookies stepped to and tried to be serious.

There was, after all, some reason behind it. During a recent season, one of the team's top draft picks couldn't manage in eleven takes to announce his name, school, hometown, and major. The players and coaches howled with each successive screwup. But underneath the hilarity developed a hard edge of worry. Something had to be wrong. And it was. The player would later reveal an inability to remember even the simplest plays. And despite impressive physical talents, he had to be cut.

Blackwell, Peeler, and Cooper sputtered through the silliness of the thing, but they got through it. Only one of the three knew his alma mater's fight song. So Peeler sang a rap, which he had put together for a video in college. "He rapped about himself," Cooper recalls with a laugh. "It was kinda short."

Blackwell, a large, friendly guy from a small college who eventually made the team despite being a long shot, giggled his way through "My Country 'Tis of Thee." Then Cooper launched into rapper Ice Cube's "A Gangsta's Fairytale" but only managed a few lines before forward A. C. Green, who is seriously religious, protested the excessive profanity. So Cooper shifted gears, singing "Always and Forever."

"See, they didn't think I had that kind of talent, where I could do that," Cooper said. "So I broke it down for 'em."

His voice was so strong, so nice, that the team rose for a standing ovation.

Looking back on it, each of the rookies would later prize the camp experience with Johnson. "That's why Earvin was always excited about camp, because he loved playing with the younger guys," Garciduenas said.

"That's where it all begins," Johnson explained later. "That's where you set the tone."

"He started out really strong on us and got us serious from the git-go," Peeler said.

"He took it serious," Cooper agreed, "because he wanted to see us build the Laker tradition. He had to do the same thing, and he wanted us to follow in that tradition."

Johnson, of course, has not been completely honest here. He went through no such routine as a rookie in 1979. And in 1980 rookie Butch Carter sang no songs. Nor did he play any army games. But when it became clear that Carter was going to make the team, the veterans invited him down to the hotel bar for a drink. Carter, who didn't drink, ordered a soda, and the rest of the guys ordered rounds of mixed drinks. After a time, they excused themselves and said they'd be back in a minute.

Carter waited alone for a while, then realized they weren't coming back. He, too, got up to leave, only to have the bartender catch him going out the door. Somebody needed to pay the bill.

Welcome to the club, rook.

For Johnson, the rookie initiation was far too important to confine it to a mere ceremonial stiffing for the drinks.

He had brought incredible energy to camp as a rookie in 1979. The Lakers then were a tired group of veterans, and he zapped them with a high charge, so high that they took to calling him "Young Buck" and later "Buck" for short. The name stuck over the years.

As did his enthusiasm. Johnson knew that youth is energy and life and freshness, and that each year the rookies brought the team abundant supply of those qualities. So he focused on the rookies and made them the ritual. He made his own tradition. He drew from their youth and energy and enthusiasm and passed it along to his tired veteran teammates. It became, "Stand in line!" Sing your song. State your credentials. We'll see if you fit. And if you do, we'll make a trade. Our leadership and tradition and wisdom, even our fatigue, for your youth and all that it brings.

Earvin Johnson knew all of this. That, as much as the game itself, was why he was in camp again. To draw on the life force. To get that super-charge from the rookies. To break away from everything that was bad and negative, to restart his Positive, to focus on the trophy at the end of the season, comfortable in the supremacy of its purpose.

Camp was where it all began, and camp was where he could find whatever it was that he had lost.

TROUBLE

But on this soft rainy morning in Hawaii, Earvin Johnson is not so positive as he was two nights ago. The first stone in his path back to NBA stardom came just yesterday when columnist Dave Kindred of *The Sporting News* urged Johnson "to tell the whole truth about how he acquired the AIDS virus. . . . He [Johnson] said unprotected heterosexual sex did it; numbers say that's highly unlikely."

If Johnson was hiding the fact that he acquired the virus through homosexual activity and his lie caused research money to be diverted into the wrong areas, then that lie would be "reprehensible," Kindred wrote.

Rosen said he probably never would have even noticed the article, but Thursday, October 8, radio station KMPC in Los Angeles picked it up as a story. Johnson Accused of Dishonesty About Aids. "KMPC started it," Rosen said. "They called me. If the radio station hadn't brought it up, we wouldn't have made an issue of it."

Soon other reporters were calling, and Rosen was infuriated. He got a copy of the column and faxed Johnson a copy in Hawaii.

Kindred, a veteran, well-respected sportswriter, had based his column not on any specific information that Johnson was bisexual, but on statistics of the disease in America. The odds are roughly one in five hundred that a man can get the virus through unprotected heterosexual activity, Kindred quoted one study as showing.

However, AIDS worldwide is largely a heterosexual disease. (Seventy-five percent of the millions worldwide have contracted it through heterosexual activity.) In Africa and Asia, an estimated 98 percent of all victims catch the virus heterosexually. Rosen believed that Kindred had misunderstood the statistics and had failed to take into account the worldwide picture, which suggested that heterosexuals could catch the virus quite easily. That, health officials had told both Johnson and Rosen, was an important message in the United States, where AIDS was wrongly considered just a gay problem.

It so happened that John Rawlings, editor of *The Sporting News,* phoned Rosen about another story that day. And Rosen demanded an immediate retraction of Kindred's column. We can't do that, Rawlings told Rosen, but we'll give you equal space to tell your side of the story.

Why should Earvin Johnson help you sell more newspapers? Rosen replied. He told the editor that if the column wasn't retracted, Johnson would never again speak to a representative of *The Sporting News.*

"Kindred never called me; he never called Earvin," Rosen said. "He just wrote his opinion."

In Hawaii, Johnson read the faxed column and was infuriated. "The thing about it is, if he knows something, why didn't he say it?" he told a small group of sportswriters that afternoon. "Why didn't he come out like a man and say it? . . . I was hoping he would say something so I can sue him real good, really good. That's why he didn't say anything. He doesn't have any information.

"You know that if something was happening, first of all the *[National]*

Enquirer, all the magazines would have it by now. So how is he going to know something that nobody else knows? . . . Be up-front. I've been up-front, so why couldn't he be up-front?

"I don't care if they have an opinion on whether I come back, because that's their job," Johnson said. "That's what they're supposed to do. Everybody's going to say something about this situation. I knew that when I came back.

"But don't point no finger about something that's happened, if you're not going to come out and be up-front."

The Sporting News story would be followed by others on the issue, and within days Jan Hubbard, *Newsday*'s NBA writer, would produce a story saying that a prominent NBA player was spreading rumors about Johnson's sexual preference.

Within hours, the issue had been ignited and tossed onto the media's agenda. John Black, the Lakers' director of public relations, had a sour look screwed on his face the next day at practice. He knew the firestorm was about to begin. "Everywhere we go," he said, "there are going to be the same questions. Over and over."

Added to the uncertainty were the questions over Johnson's status. Which games would he play? On what days would he take off? If he took off, did that mean he was sick? Suddenly every little thing required an explanation. In camp, he had taken a Sunday morning off and watched drills from the sidelines. Later, the writers asked him about it.

"Age factor," he said.

"Did you say AIDS factor?" a writer asked.

"*Age* factor," he reiterated.

With everything open to interpretation, John Black began looking for a slogan to characterize the upcoming season, something funny to break the tension. He didn't have to search too hard. The slogan soon enough emerged on its own. It seemed that every time the PR director provided the press with an update on the team, he was forced to conclude it by saying, "Everything is subject to change."

There it was every day, that same phrase. Very quickly the writers would come to expect it. And Black would find a laugh in reminding them. Remember, he would say, "subject to change."

2

The Lakers

The fifty-four-year-old man studies the goal briefly, then delivers a perfect sixteen-footer. Plop. The ball settles through the net and hits the floor with just enough spin that it heads back to the shooter. He hardly has to move to retrieve it. Then he starts the process over. He studies the goal, and this is the most unsettling thing. Jerry West has sighted the goal probably no fewer than two million times since his grade school days, when he first began lofting a ball at a hoop suspended above the dirt outside his Cheylan, West Virginia, home. And now, forty-some years later, he pauses, studying again, as if he is seeing something for the first time, discovering something that the rest of us can't see. He launches another; the arc is perfectly elliptical. Plop. When he first came into the NBA in 1960, the shot was flat, and people noticed it, because they notice everything about rookies (or they think they do). It wouldn't do to have a flat shot. So Jerry West set out to fashion the perfect ellipsis. Plop.

People also noticed that as a rookie he seemed to have trouble going to his left. That wouldn't do either. So West worked at that, too, and spent more time going left than, say, Angela Davis. He went left so much that people guarding him forgot there was a right.

It is all wasted motion now. Jerry West is on his way to becoming an old man. An administrator. A general manager. And he professes not to remember anything about his great playing days. "Roland," he later tells me with more than a trace of testiness, "I don't know if I'm going to be much help for you on this book. I don't live my life in the past."

We both know this isn't true. Within minutes, he'll tell me a half-dozen stunning little stories from murky yesteryear, and later he'll be quietly irritated that he has dredged up his misery for yet another journalist. It is obvious that West loathes many of his memories. But to understand the Lakers, you have to attempt to understand Jerry West. He is the mystic who leads this team, working, as he explains it, "in my own weird way." He is

51

the franchise's past, present, and future, its moral compass in the land of Babylon. It may sound corny, but West is the Lakers' connection with whatever spirituality basketball holds. He may, in fact, be the only mystic to head up an NBA team, to head up any American professional sports franchise.

"Jerry West is a visionary kind of guy," explains Kareem Abdul-Jabbar.

"The bottom line is, my number-one priority in life is to see this franchise prosper," West once said. "That's my life. It goes beyond being paid. It goes to something that's been a great source of pride. I would like people to know that I do care. It's not a self-interest thing. I do care about the winning and the perpetuation of the franchise. That's the one thing I care most about. I don't care about the pelts and the tributes. I like to work in my own weird way, working toward one goal, that's a winning team here."

He offered that admission three years ago, and in the interim he considered an attractive offer to join the Sacramento Kings. The money was good enough to secure his and his children's future. But he just couldn't bring himself to leave. West joined the Lakers as a rookie when the team moved to Los Angeles in 1960, and he has remained in one capacity or another ever since, except for two seasons of bitter feuding with then-owner Jack Kent Cooke in the 1970s. Many observers like to point out that those two seasons were the only times that a Los Angeles Lakers team didn't make the play-offs.

He takes another studied shot here at Klum Gym. Plop. The small crowd gathered before this Sunday morning session of training camp takes notice. West doesn't shoot much. Maybe once or twice a year. Which means he misses a shot about as often. But it is no longer about hits and misses. For West, shooting is like being reminded of an old, irretrievably lost love. "I wonder, 'What the hell am I doing this for?' " he says of shooting. "It's a part of my life that was there at one time, and it's not there now."

I first interviewed Jerry West a few years back in Dallas, where he had gone on a scouting trip. I remember thinking that you don't have to spend too much time with him, perhaps a matter of minutes, before you sense his anguish. It's not a flaming pain, but a deep, slow-burning one, a complicated anxiety, the kind that can kill people, especially former great athletes. But so far, it hasn't killed Jerry West. Instead he wears his anguish like an after-shave: every day.

He is one of the most successful general managers in the history of American professional sports. Before that, he was one of the greatest basketball players ever. He averaged 27.1 points over his fourteen-year career and 29.1 points in the play-offs; only Michael Jordan has a higher play-off scoring average. That should be enough for anybody, you think. But it obviously isn't enough for Jerry West. Which makes you wonder why.

How can one person demand so much of life?

"Jerry always seems like he's having a terrible time, or something bad is impending," says Kareem with a laugh. "He's always worried."

West, Abdul-Jabbar says with another chuckle, reminds him of the pilots in the film *Catch-22* who are about to fly off into combat. This sense of foreboding seems to keep his angst spinning.

"Jerry is the most impatient man I've ever met in my life," says John Black, the team's public relations director. "I love the guy. He's hilarious. He and I had lunch with Mitch Kupchak [the Lakers' assistant general manager] the other day. We're only a quarter of the way through our meal, and Jerry's already done and drumming his fingers on the table. Everything he does is done at a hyper speed. You should see him play golf. It's hilarious. He walks up to the ball and whacks it. Never takes a practice swing or anything. He used to play a lot of golf, but now he only plays a few times a year. And he always shoots 70 or under. If he shoots a 71, he's pissed."

As an executive, he still travels like a player. A single road bag. His crisp white dress shirt neatly tucked inside with his other items. No hangers. No suit bag. He's still a Spartan, still moves unencumbered as he did when he ran the backcourt for the Lakers for fourteen seasons. He still glides through his tasks with a proficiency that startles the opposition.

Yet his every move is haunted by the same old questions: What does it take to close? What does it take to finish? What does it take to win? Most people are happy for a partial answer. But life has taught West a different lesson. Six times in the 1960s, he and the Lakers faced the Boston Celtics in the NBA Finals. Six times they lost. On their seventh try for a championship, the Lakers met the New York Knicks. They lost again. They finally won in 1972, then lost an eighth time in the Finals the next year.

"I don't think people understand there's a real trauma associated with losing," West says. "I don't think they realize how miserable you can be. Particularly me. I was terrible. It got to the point with me that I wanted to quit basketball. I really did. I didn't think it was fair that you could give so much and play until there was nothing left in your body to give and you couldn't win."

Yet the more elusive it proved to be, the more the championship came to have an almost mesmerizing hold on him. "The closer you get to the magic circle, the more enticing it becomes," he said. "I imagine in some ways it's like a drug. It's seductive because it's always there, and the desire is always there to win one more game. I don't like to think I'm different, but I was obsessed with winning. And losing made it so much more difficult in the off-season."

He played college basketball at West Virginia University, and as a six-foot-two junior forward he led the Mountaineers to the 1959 NCAA championship game where they lost by a point. "I had my hands on the ball about midcourt with no time left on the clock," he recalled, "and I said, 'If I could have just gotten one more shot . . .' But it wasn't to be. Those are the things, frankly, that stay with you more than the wins. Those are the things that really are wearing.

"My basketball career has sort of been on the tragic side of everything. It hasn't been on the positive side. It was so close, yet so far away."

The worst loss by far was the 1969 NBA Finals, where the Lakers, highly favored to win the title, lost the seventh game to the Celtics at the Forum. It was their sixth and final loss to Boston. West was named the MVP, the first and only time in NBA Finals history that the award went to a member of a losing team. The gesture was nice, but it didn't address his agony.

"It was like a slap in the face," he said. "Like, 'We're not gonna let you win. We don't care how well you play.' I always thought it was personal. It got to the point where I didn't think I was doing enough. I was searching everything that I had ever done in my life for a reason, looking for an answer why. Why couldn't we win it? That's why it became so personal. It almost controlled my life."

The championship failures only embedded his superstitions deeper. Before each home game, he would take the same circuitous route to the Forum, using the same back streets. Once in the locker room, he would tear a stick of gum in half, placing the pieces on each side of his locker in exactly the same places. He would try anything to alleviate the curse of the Celtics. "Jerry couldn't even wear a green sportcoat or a green shirt for a lot of years," Bill Sharman, onetime Lakers Coach, said. "Green really rubbed him the wrong way."

But to West, the enemy wasn't the Celtics. In his mind, there was no enemy. There was only the obstacle, and that was the game itself. His unfortunate compulsion was perfection in a sport that never allows it. Yet he came as close as anyone. One great night as a player, he made all twelve of his free throws and sixteen of seventeen field goal attempts. He also had ten rebounds, twelve assists, and ten steals.

"I had nights where you just couldn't guard me," he said.

At times, though, West tended to brood over the flaws in his game, said Fred Schaus, who coached him in both college and the pros. "When he was not playing well, he'd kind of go into a shell. He wouldn't talk to anybody, not the coaches or his own teammates. If he wasn't playing well, he was tough to live with."

"I was nervous all the time," West said. "But then again, I was a nervous player. That's where I got my energy from."

In 1971, the Lakers held a Jerry West Appreciation Night at the Forum, and Boston center Bill Russell paid his own plane fare to Los Angeles to address the crowd. "The greatest honor a man can have is the respect and friendship of his peers," Russell told West that night. "You have that more than any man I know. If I could have one wish granted, it would be that you would always be happy."

Strange, this coming from Russell, the dominant Celtic center, who had more to do with West's unhappiness than any other single human being.

Finally, in 1972, the Lakers powered their way to a championship. But for West, the finish was rife with irony. After years of losing, his emotions were nearly empty, and when the Lakers got it, the title seemed anticlimatic. "I played terrible basketball in the Finals," he said. "And we won. And that didn't seem to be justice for me personally, because I had contributed so much in other years when we lost. And now, when we won, I was just another piece of the machinery. It was particularly frustrating because I was playing so poorly that the team overcame me.

"Maybe," he said after a moment's thought, "that's what the team is all about."

It seems logical that at least part of his current anguish stems from those long-ago frustrations. But only West knows for sure. Or maybe nobody knows. But West does know this—no matter how great he was way back when, he has accomplished things now as general manager of the Lakers that he never accomplished as a player. In the 1980s, his team won five NBA World Championships, two of them over the Celtics. He has vanquished the curse of the green. But that's a paradoxical triumph for West. It both increases and lessens his anguish at the same time.

Pain, it seems, is a central ingredient to his mysticism. "I hope these things stay with me," he says of his anxieties. "If I weren't like this, I probably wouldn't work."

Listening to Jerry West, you think that there really should be a Field of Dreams. Somebody should be hearing the voice.

Ease his pain.

There are times, of course, that West remembers his playing days fondly. He was adored by the fans at the Forum, and he remembers their appreciation. But losing the championships has obscured so much.

And then there is the matter of his retirement.

West loathed Jack Kent Cooke, the smug, pompous, self-made millionaire who owned the Lakers from 1965 to 1979. Cooke knew a little about basketball, but he knew lots more about business and making money. In West's eyes, Cooke devalued the game, making it and the people employed by the team simply a part of the business process. For West, basketball was the end, not just the means.

It was just after training camp in 1974 that he finally got fed up and quit. The official excuse was a torn stomach muscle. That was a public relations smoke screen. His disagreement with Cooke "started over money, but then it became personal," West said.

The owner had told West that he and center Wilt Chamberlain were making the same salary. "I thought they were both getting $250,000 a year," said Pete Newell, then the Lakers' general manager.

But in September of 1973 when Chamberlain abruptly "retired" to become a player/coach in the rival American Basketball Association, West learned that Cooke had been paying Chamberlain $400,000. The owner justified this by arranging a side deal with the center for other services. "Jerry wasn't upset that Wilt was getting the money," Newell said. "He was upset because Cooke had told him he was getting the same deal. It wasn't the money. It was the fact that he was told one thing, and another happened. Jerry is not petty, but he believed that he had not been given what was rightfully his. After all, Jerry had been with the team long before Wilt got there. Jerry was a superstar in his own right and a big draw. A lot of people had come to the Forum over the years to see him play."

"I always have viewed trust as an important factor," West said, "trust in a coach, trust in the people you've got around you. And I lost that trust with Jack Cooke. I just felt I wasn't compensated correctly."

Angered, West told his agent to attempt to have his contract renegotiated. "He basically told my agent to go to hell," West said, "and that was as ugly, as bitter . . . I felt I was deceived. When you feel that you're deceived you don't want any part of the organization that deceived you."

He knew he could have played two more years and wanted to play. But not for Cooke. "I could've played another very good year," West said. "Every athlete says that. But I could've, and I knew I could've. But I could never have played for the Lakers again, and I wasn't going to play for anybody else."

Newell begged him to change his mind. "It just crushed me when Jerry phoned and said, 'Pete, I'm going to retire.' "

"There's no question about it; Jerry West should have played another two years," said Laker broadcaster Chick Hearn, who was the team's assistant general manager at the time.

West, though, was as steadfast as the West Virginia hills. He retired at thirty-six, walked away the day after a dazzling performance against Portland in a preseason game. Newell recalled that Portland's Geoff Petrie was then touted as the league's next young superstar guard, and the Lakers were eager to see how West played against him.

"Jerry had something like thirty-four points that night," Newell said. "It was just like Jerry to make a statement like that."

"I played one preseason game," West said. "I went to training camp. I was in real good shape, but I felt no excitement sitting in the locker room.

I didn't think that was fair to the people who enjoyed watching me play, just as I don't think it's fair today for an athlete to go out and play when they shouldn't play, when they play only for the money, for their own emotional well-being. I think athletes should be realistic about when their careers are over. Mine was over, maybe not physically, but mentally."

For this reason, training camp for Jerry West is always mixed, full of promise, but full of reminders, too. And when Magic Johnson's career fell apart during the 1991 preseason, it led West to think again of his own departure. "At least I retired when I wanted to," he said. "Magic didn't have the chance to do that."

DETROIT, MINNEAPOLIS, THEN HOLLYWOOD

The Lakers began life in 1946 as the Detroit Gems in the old National Basketball League (NBL). No one recalls exactly where the first training camp was held, but it seems likely they had one, probably at Detroit's Holy Redeemer High School gym. The Gems had been started on a whim by a Michigan jewelry store owner named Maury Winston, a rabid fan who figured a basketball team would be a good promotion for his business.

Big mistake.

Even the good pro teams had few fans and got no press in 1946.

The Gems were terrible. They finished 4–40, the worst record in modern pro basketball, and Winston lost thousands of dollars. One night a mere six paying customers showed up to see the Gems play, and Winston later resolutely issued each of them a refund. "Maury Winston seemed like a real nice guy, but he didn't know too much about about basketball," recalled Sid Goldberg, a sports promoter of that era. "He was in over his head."

Thoroughly whipped by season's end, Winston quickly sold the franchise for $15,000 to an enterprising group of investors from Minneapolis. They, in turn, renamed the club the Lakers (Minnesota being the land of cold, clear lakes), thus setting in motion a curious and wonderful karma. From its meager beginnings, the team has gone on to win thirteen league championships, or nearly a third of the pro titles since World War II. On another thirteen occasions, they have lost in the NBA Finals, a league record.

When they didn't win, the Lakers still remained competitive. Just four times in their forty-six seasons of existence have they failed to make the play-offs.

But the story is about more than winning. With their verve and style, the Lakers rescued pro basketball from its plodding pace and laborious nature. They've always been at the vanguard of the sport's western movement, at the cusp of its innovation, at the hot spot of whatever star quality the NBA could muster. In its early years, pro basketball was an eastern game, played in underheated gyms in cold cities. The Lakers were the force that tugged the game west and into the new age. To pro basketballers in 1947, Minnesota seemed like the far reaches of the universe, until the Lakers once again expanded the horizon and relocated in Los Angeles in 1960.

To Hollywood.

To basketball as entertainment. To Showtime.

It was the perfect place for a team that had always understood the preciousness of star quality. Long before they arrived in Tinseltown, the Lakers were the league's main gate attraction. They brought pro basketball its first dominant giant, George Mikan, and its first jumping jack, Jim Pollard. The Minneapolis Lakers teams they anchored won six pro championships and rated marquee billings at Madison Square Garden, where they were the regular centerpiece in the doubleheaders that the NBA sponsored in its early seasons.

Despite the success in Minneapolis, the team's tenure there ended badly, in near financial collapse, and the move to Los Angeles in 1960 was a desperate gamble for survival. "Call me for anything, but don't call me for money," Lakers owner Bob Short told Lou Mohs, the team's general manager, when he sent the club packing west.

Once there, the team boasted the game's exciting young players, Jerry West and Elgin Baylor, who led the Lakers to one play-off battle after another. Their performances attracted the early Hollywood crowd, Doris Day, Danny Thomas, and Pat Boone, who sat courtside in the LA Sports Arena and brought pro basketball its first real taste of glamour.

Then in the mid sixties came new owner Jack Kent Cooke, who built his own arena, the Fabulous Forum, a building with a studied ambience to attract the city's wheelers and dealers. The game's first self-declared sex symbol, Wilt Chamberlain, arrived in 1968, and after losing in seven league championship series, the Los Angeles Lakers finally won the 1972 title, with West and Chamberlain as aging superstars.

Chamberlain departed in '73 and West in '74, and Kareem Abdul-Jabbar arrived a year later, only to endure four frustrating seasons until the team drafted Magic Johnson. On the brink of the Showtime era, Jack Kent Cooke grew weary of ownership. He was buffeted by a stormy divorce and agreed to sell out to real estate whiz Jerry Buss in 1979. With Johnson in the backcourt and Abdul-Jabbar looming inside, the Lakers evolved into the greatest team in the history of the game. They won five NBA titles in the 1980s and could have won another four if not for injuries and miscues.

With their success came money. Lots of it. The Lakers became the glitter in the NBA's pot of gold. The financial growth has been astounding to witness, said Sid Hartman, a Minnesota newspaper columnist who ran the Lakers in their early years. "We paid Maury Winston $15,000 for the franchise in 1947," he recalled. "Bob Short bought the Lakers in 1957 for $150,000. He in turn sold them to Jack Kent Cooke in 1965 for $5.2 million. Cooke sold it to Jerry Buss in 1979 for $67.5 million. Now it's probably worth $200 million."

Financial World magazine figured in 1991 that the number was more like $150 million. But Buss vehemently disagrees. The $200 million is correct, he says. The annual operating profit alone is about $32 million for the team and the Forum.

Which is why Buss can afford to bring his team to Hawaii for training camp. The Washington Bullets go to West Virginia. The Atlanta Hawks train in Chattanooga, Tennessee.

But for the Lakers, it's the allure of the islands.

Which only embellishes and deepens the team's image. The Lakers are modern American society's very definition of cool. To be the Lakers is to be hip. That's why the Hollywood types pay $500 each night to sit courtside in the Forum, the great Mecca of cool. To rub shoulders with that wonderful elusive feeling. Cool. The Lakers personify it.

Cool is ineluctable celebrity. Jack Nicholson, the archetypical American somebody, sits courtside every night. Untouchable. And when he can't be there, when he's on location for another of his films, he has fresh videotape of the team delivered daily. Nicholson is so cool he doesn't even have to do interviews. Why should he? He possesses the perfect image. He's the emperor of cool.

Cool is distant, unapproachable knowledge, typified by Kareem, the great Oz of basketball, who behind his big frame and scowl is just another frightened you or me. "He was cool," Nicholson once said of Abdul-Jabbar, a cool endorsement if there ever was one. Cool is jazz, too, and Kareem owned a monstrous collection.

Cool is money, lots of it, and Jerry Buss knows how to make it and how to make it work for him.

Cool is good, as in very good, as in the best. Earvin Johnson brought that element to the equation, along with enthusiasm and energy, which is a dangerous mix. Enthusiasm and energy can be very uncool, unless they're controlled. Johnson controlled them, just like he did the Showtime fast break. Which maybe made Earvin the coolest of all.

Cool is youth and biting humor. Laker broadcaster Chick Hearn (how cool is the name?) possesses both of those. He first broadcast a Laker game in the spring of 1961, and has only missed two games since. That's more than twenty-five hundred straight broadcasts, not to mention road trips, bumpy flights, bad food, noisy hotels. He's pushing eighty these days, but you'd never know it, and it has nothing to do with the hair color. Chick is eternal. The Lakers don't keep him around for nostalgia trips. His mind is like a steel trap, lying in wait for the weaker brains on the team bus, hoping somebody—a coach, a player, the driver—will take the bait on one of his practical jokes. Chick is cool because he wears the broadcast headset. He's tuned in to knowledge that others don't have. Cool is knowing. Chick knows.

Which raises another question:

Where does Jerry West fit in in this land of cool?

To understand West, says longtime friend Pete Newell, you have to understand that he's from West Virginia. In other words, he was country when country wasn't cool. He came to Los Angeles in 1960 with a flattop haircut, skinny legs, and a high-pitched mountain twang, like he had just fallen off the turnip truck. Bumpkin personified. It was the age of the Beverly Hillbillies, and the shy, serious country boy found a Hollywood eager to lampoon him. Elgin Baylor first called him "Tweetie Bird" because of the high-pitched voice and the skinny legs. West hated that.

Then Baylor came up with another name. Zeke from Cabin Creek. West wasn't even from Cabin Creek. He was from nearby Cheylan. He hated that name, too. Zeke from Cabin Creek. "I've never seen Jerry walk by an autograph yet," Newell says of West. He signed because he believed he owed it to the fans. But when they asked him to sign "Zeke from Cabin Creek," West refused.

Catchy as the name was and eager as the team was to build a following in Los Angeles in the early years, Chick Hearn constantly referred to West as Zeke on game broadcasts, until West's first wife, Jane, quietly asked him to quit using it.

"Jerry was never a very secure kind of person," Newell says. "Believe it or not, he has never had a great self-esteem. Everybody thinks more of Jerry than he does of himself. That's the West Virginia in him."

West Virginia. Almost heaven? Bullshit. Almost Appalachia. Coal mines. Poverty. Ignorance. Black lung. Strikes. Violence. Family feuds. The Martins and McCoys. West was the son of a mine electrician, so he had it better than most. But it was a long way from Los Angeles.

Or was it?

"As a player, he would get down on himself," Newell says.

It doesn't make sense. He led East Bank High School to a state championship as a senior, then listened as more than seventy colleges across the country begged him to play for them. Jerry West without confidence? All great players have confidence. How could he succeed without it? West got by, Newell says, because "he was driven for it. The drive was greater than the fear of not succeeding."

Which still leaves that one big question.

Where does Jerry West fit into this cool equation?

Cool is a lifelong commitment? Cool is obsession? Cool is puritanical? Cool is humorless?

Hardly.

Could it be that for many years now Jerry West has had the lonely job of protecting cool from itself?

THE GENERAL MANAGER

"Maybe I'm spoiled," West says. "Maybe the success of this team has spoiled me a little bit. I try to be objective. It makes no sense that I'm not happy. I should be happy. The reason I tend not to be happy is goal setting. You want to stretch yourself. You want to stretch your players and make them try to take that last step, and that's to end their season with a win. If you do that, you're gonna have a fun summer."

In other words, West always wants the thing he couldn't have. Another championship.

It is a relentless goal. He has suffered from ulcers and sleepless nights in recent seasons, particularly after games, when he twists and turns, running back every play in his mind. At the end of the 1989 season, a spot mysteriously appeared on his lung, frightening West and his family. It later went away, but doctors weren't sure what it was. The fear made him appreciate his family more, but it didn't dull his drive.

"I do think this job is wearing," he says. "There's a lot of pressure on you."

The translation, of course, is that he puts a lot of pressure on himself.

West, it seems, is constantly mindful of his burden, of *being* the Lakers. "Since I came here in 1960," he said, "the Lakers have always had one or two players that have been at the top of the league in talent. In perpetuating this franchise, our next move is, where do we find another one of those guys?"

Most people are lucky, he says, to have one Magic Johnson in a lifetime. But West is obsessed with finding the next great one, "that one unique player who can get through the tough losses and come back and compete the next night. Those players are rare in this league. They'll play hard every night. They'll play in every building. They'll play in every circumstance. That kind of person is the most difficult to find."

Seeing the athletic talent is easy, he says. The hard part is identifying what can't be seen. He knows this will be nearly impossible, particularly when he didn't see it in Magic the first time around.

But then no one really did.

"I felt he would be a very good player," West said of Johnson. "I had no idea he would get to this level. No idea. But see, you don't know what's inside of people. You can see what they can do physically on the court. The things you could see about Magic you loved. But you wondered where he was gonna play in the NBA. But he has just through hard work willed himself to take his game to another level. I don't think anyone knew he had that kind of greatness in him."

Identifying that player, seeing the unseeable, is just the first part of West's impossible task. Then he must manipulate the NBA's Byzantine personnel structure so that the Lakers get the rights to that special player. That has become nearly impossible with the league's salary cap and expansion.

"The problem is, it's like a poker game," he says. "Any team that has a player play ten years is probably going to be out of chips pretty soon. So you have to try like crazy within the scope of this league to keep your team young and productive. In the past, we've been able to bring in younger players and phase out older players at the end of their careers. That's where we are again. Are we willing to take a chance on keeping guys who maybe have four or five years left in their careers?"

The important thing for players, he also says, is to believe that the team offers a family atmosphere.

Business and family. We've all been told that they don't mix. But for years, the Boston Celtics' Red Auerbach made it happen. He kept the family circle yet still managed the tricky business deals that brought his franchise sixteen championships.

Fred Schaus says West has become the premier general manager of his time. What Red Auerbach did with the Celtics in the 1960s and '70s West has done with the Lakers in the '80s and '90s. "I admired Auerbach in the past, and I admire West now," Schaus said. "Their teams are finishing high in the standings and they're drafting low. That's why it's so hard to remain competitive."

Others have echoed Schaus's assessment. West is every bit as cagey as Auerbach was, Abdul-Jabbar says.

This comparison wears on West. I don't want to be Red Auerbach, he says. I want to be myself. He maintains that his success as a general manager—"If I've had any," he says—has nothing to do with the competitiveness he showed as a player.

"I have to disagree with him," Schaus says. "Play golf with him, or any game of skill. Cards or anything. He's such a competitor. He wants to be the very best at doing anything."

Told of Schaus's comment, West acknowledged that competitiveness does drive him as a GM. "But it's so different," he said. "Being a player, it's a wonderful feeling to win an important ball game, to compete against the best players. Being a general manager is so much more subtle, so much more frustrating. It's a completely different feeling. Every once in a while, when you get something done as a general manager, you really feel good about it. You really do. Finding and drafting players and watching them develop, that's where you get your satisfaction."

But by and large, West gets far more agony than satisfaction from his job. During games he's a bundle of nervous energy and sometimes winds up out in the Forum parking lot while the outcome is being settled. Or he can be seen standing near section 27, peeking past the ushers at the action, his body twisted with tension.

When he does sit, he sometimes watches the game with Chick Hearn's wife, Marge. Usually West can determine in the first three or four minutes how the Lakers are going to do. If the prognosis is bad, he's up quickly, stepping on poor Marge's toes as he makes an early exit. He retreats from there to his office, where he watches the rest of the game on television. There he can express his disgust in solitude. West gets easily offended if the game isn't played right.

Perhaps West's greatest agony has come over the past year, since the revelation of Johnson's infection. West has been torn between two issues in recent months, his concern and love for Johnson and his dedication to the team. The issues have been so difficult for him that he will not discuss them.

But now Johnson is back in uniform, and West has assembled a deep, talented roster to play with him. James Worthy, Sam Perkins, and Vlade Divac are back with the team, apparently recovered from the injuries that sidelined them last season. The Lakers are filled with hope and eager to meet the challenge of the upcoming season.

West, too, allows himself to hope.

They all do.

Jerry Buss. Chick Hearn. Magic Johnson. Jerry West.

They're all here in Hawaii, eyeing the future.

This team has been good to all of them. And they've been good to each other. Now they want it to end right, to sustain itself.

They want Magic to live. They want AIDS to be cured. They want to win basketball games.

They want the great and wonderful life they lived in the 1980s to go right on being great and wonderful in the 1990s. After all, they have to, because they're charging people $500 a night to sit close by and take it all in.

Which leads you to think that success isn't so much a corrupter as it is a spoiler.

Byron Scott says that when you get down to it, the only element in the equation of cool that really matters is winning. Everything else, the style and Hollywood glitz, become pointless without it.

"The expectations around here are very high," as West says.

They all just hope that once again Earvin Johnson is up to meeting them.

3

In the Beginning

The man waited quietly in the Detroit airport, a mix of defeat and relief on his face. Maury Winston, owner of the Detroit Gems, was making his exit from pro basketball. It was the summer of 1947, and he had had enough. Enough bad deals. Enough coaching problems. Enough losing.

Winston, the proprietor of a Detroit jewelry store, had founded the team just a year earlier, in 1946, when everything was booming in the aftermath of World War II. The old National Basketball League, in operation since 1937, had shrunk to just three clubs during the war. But with peacetime, a lot of people suddenly wanted to own a pro team. Which, in retrospect, seems a little crazy. The sport had been around for fifty years, and in that time nobody had figured out how to make any money from it.

The NBL had expanded to eleven teams in 1946. And another pro league, the Basketball Association of America (BAA), formed that same year with another dozen teams. Three painful seasons later they would merge to form the NBA, but in 1946 it was a basketball free-for-all.

And Maury Winston was the big loser.

He had paid about $1,500 to join the league and another $5,000 for a performance bond. He had bought uniforms and about a dozen balls and shelled out another $40,000 or so for salaries. (The average pro contract ran about three grand back then.) To coach, he got Joel Mason from nearby Wayne State. At the time, Mason was known mostly for his football background. He had played end for the Green Bay Packers. At Wayne State, he was the backfield assistant, but he also coached a little basketball. So Winston signed him up.

Wisely, Mason didn't give up his day job. He kept coaching and teaching phys ed while running the Gems.

"He worked about thirty-six hours a day," explained Paul Pentecost, Mason's longtime friend.

But it wasn't enough to rescue the hapless club. "They were a ragamuffin team," said Sid Goldberg, a retired sports promoter.

64

Mason and Winston had signed mostly local college players. The best-known of the group was Wayne State's Howie McCarty, a guard with a one-handed shot. As something of an innovation, the Gems also signed Willie King, a former Harlem Globetrotter who played fourteen games for the club. It was one of the isolated early attempts to integrate pro basketball. It didn't matter. The Gems were depressingly bad, the only consolation being that their pain was practically anonymous. "I don't think we gave them any attention," recalled George Maskin, the night sports editor for the old *Detroit Times*. "We might have run a paragraph or two in the paper and that's about it."

Games often drew fewer than one hundred paying fans. One night late in the season, only six people showed up, and Winston issued each a refund. Part of the problem was the venues. The Gems played some of their games at Holy Redeemer High School, but often it was wherever they could find an open court. Once or twice, they even managed an appearance at the Olympia, a Detroit arena, but only as a warm-up game for a better-known pro team.

"They should have been called the Nomads," Paul Pentecost recalled with a laugh. "They didn't know where they were gonna play from one night to the next."

Mason watched his team run out to a 3–13 record and decided he'd had enough. He turned the coaching duties over to guard Fred Campbell, and the Gems coasted from there, winning once in their last twenty-eight games to finish 4–40. Pro basketball had never seen such a terrible team and wouldn't again for many, many seasons. Usually, when clubs were this bad, they died with barely a whisper. Sometimes teams didn't even have to be bad to disappear. Their names were colorful, but that wouldn't prevent them from littering pro basketball's graveyard. The Anderson Duffy Packers. The Toledo Jeeps. The Cleveland Chase Brass. The St. Louis Bombers. The Chicago Stags. The Indianapolis Olympians. The Youngstown Bears. The list of franchise cadavers could go on.

But the Detroit Gems were different. It was from their seed of misery that the Lakers' great championship tradition would grow. The miracle of survival would come in a phone call that summer of 1947, as Maury Winston was wondering what to do about his disaster. The caller was Sid Hartman, a young newspaper reporter who represented some Minneapolis businessmen. They wanted to buy Winston's terrible team. Better yet, they wanted to pay $15,000 for it.

"We were looking for a franchise," Hartman recalled. "A lot of them were available. For $15,000 you could buy about anything in those days."

The Minneapolis investors could have started a new franchise much more cheaply. Or, as Hartman suspected, they could have waited a week or two and gotten Winston's team for almost nothing. But they had plenty of money and didn't want to wait. The Gems had their bad record, and that was worth a lot. Hartman had done his research and learned that the Chicago American Gears were headed for trouble. Owner Maurice White was drinking heavily and planning to break away from the NBL to form his own league. The Gears had a sensational young center named George Mikan, and if Chicago folded, the Gems with their terrible record would have first shot at signing him. And even if Mikan wasn't available, the Gems' record would mean the top pick in the 1947 draft.

That was incentive enough for the people in Minneapolis. They paid Maurice Winston $15,000 for the Gems. The transaction took place in the Detroit airport. Sid Hartman flew in, signed the papers, and gave Winston a check. The deal took all of fifteen minutes.

The Minneapolis people didn't want anything from the Gems. Not the players. Not the name. Not the equipment. "Even the uniforms weren't worth a damn," Hartman said.

Only the franchise and its rotten record.

From that Sid Hartman figured he could make a pretty good beginning.

When he began running the Lakers in 1947, Sid Hartman was all of twenty-four and still had a paper route on the side plus his job as a sportswriter for the *Minneapolis Star Tribune*. Strange as this combination seemed, Hartman was only a product of the times. First the Great Depression, then World War II had rocked his generation. Hartman had started in the news business at age nine during the depression with his first delivery route and was soon hanging around the newsroom at the old *Minneapolis Times*. There he found an escape from the bad family life that haunted many households in that era. His father drank heavily, which meant that the streets were a good place to be if the old man was in a bad mood. Besides, Hartman loved sports, and in the 1930s the newspaper was where you found out all about them.

"I got to know the sports editors," he said. "They kind of adopted me."

By the time he was in high school, he had added the chores of a part-time sportswriter to his news route, bringing his paycheck to a grand total of $23 every two weeks. But writing and delivering the news made for a grinding schedule that left little time for academic work. At seventeen, he dropped out of school, a few months shy of graduation. He would later earn a diploma with night courses at North High School in Minneapolis. But that didn't really matter, for Hartman was already on his way to becoming an established sportswriter.

His obsession in those days was University of Minnesota athletics. He attended virtually every practice of every sport, waiting, watching, listening for bits of information to fill his columns and stories. He developed a gossipy style, and people read his work because he didn't just talk about the games; he talked about the people. Soon he owned a little black book, which he filled with the phone numbers of coaches and sports editors all over the country. When visiting college teams played against the Golden Gophers, Hartman made a point of having a friendly chat with the coaches. Then afterward he would send a short note thanking them for taking the time to talk with him. In time, he would own the phone numbers of many great coaches of that era, including Adolph Rupp, Ray Meyer, Hank Iba, John Wooden, and Pete Newell. Hartman would later boast that he had more unpublished numbers than any other reporter in the country. The coaches, in turn, would invite Hartman to attend their clinics, many of them held at summer resorts in Minnesota.

Over the ensuing seasons, Hartman would expand these cordial relationships into a nationwide network. "At one time," he said, "I was sending out 1,600 Christmas cards a year."

Among his many acquaintances, Hartman would become particularly good friends with Maurice Chalfen, who promoted ice shows and other entertainment around Minneapolis. Chalfen, in turn, introduced Hartman to Ben Berger, a little Polish immigrant who loved to smoke cigars and roll them in his fingers like George Burns. Both Chalfen and Berger, who owned a chain of movie theaters in North Dakota and Minnesota, were quite wealthy. Before long, the young sportswriter had convinced these middle-aged millionaires that they shared his dream of bringing a professional sports team to Minneapolis. Berger wanted one because it would increase his standing in the community. Hartman simply longed to manage a pro club. It was an escape fantasy for him. If he brought a team to Minneapolis, then maybe he could give up the drudgery of his circulation job and instead spend his time wheeling and dealing for athletes. Football and baseball franchises seemed impossible to obtain in 1946. But Hartman saw that basketball was easily within reach. Besides, he loved the game.

Having built his fortune in North Dakota, Berger knew next to nothing about hoops. But the immigrant loved this country (he would later title his self-financed biography *Thank You, America*); he loved a sense of community. He owned a cluster of theaters in Minneapolis and served on a local prison advisory board. But he wanted to do something more for the city. Hartman convinced him that a hoops team would be a perfect gift. Berger wasn't so sure, but he agreed to test the idea. To see how pro basketball would go in the area, Berger and Chalfen promoted a game in Minneapolis at the end of the 1946 season between the Oshkosh All-Stars and the Sheboygan Redskins, two National teams. The event drew about five thousand, a smashing success in that era of cold gyms and lopsided balls. Seeing the crowd, Berger and Chalfen gave Hartman the nod. He had an open checkbook to begin assembling a team.

After buying the Gems franchise, Hartman moved quickly to sign players. His coaching contacts paid off handsomely. "Nobody scouted in those days. Nobody had the money to do that," said Marty Blake, the former general manager of the Milwaukee/St. Louis/Atlanta Hawks, who today serves as the MBA's director of scouting. "Hartman knew basketball, and he had a lot of coaching contacts from his newspaper business. They told him who the good players were."

Tops on the list was a Coast Guard veteran from California, Jim Pollard, the crown prince of Amateur Athletic Union basketball (AAU). At six-foot-six (he would always list his official height at six-three), Pollard was a rare bird in 1940s basketball. He could run and jump and dunk and dribble and pass. He could even execute a reverse jam, though not with so much twist and style as modern dunkers. No one envisioned a midair slam dance in 1947. But he could play above the rim. Many of the players in that whites-only era were mechanical, one- and two-dimensional athletes. Not Pollard. He was a prototype for the future. Hartman would later compare him to Michael Jordan, but Pollard actually was more like Scottie Pippen. He was a terror from the wing.

The fans called him "the Kangaroo Kid." Later, Billy Cunningham would earn the nickname, but Pollard was the original.

"We used to know when Pollard had been in the building," Horace "Bones" McKinney, who played for the Washington Capitols, recalled, "because the tops of the backboards would be clean where he raked them." Pollard was fast, too, McKinney said. "You couldn't press him either. He was too good moving with the ball. He'd get by you in a cat lick." Because of that, he often would serve as the Lakers' primary ball handler. If he played today, Pollard would be a big point guard, said John Kundla, his coach.

Pollard had played center during high school in Oakland, California, then graduated in December 1940 and spent the spring playing with Golden State Creamery, a local AAU team, where the veterans showed him the game. It was his lucky break. "Those old-timers took me and taught me how to play forward, how to shoot outside and play facing the basket," Pollard recalled. "By the time I got to college, I was a pretty well made forward." Indeed. That fall, he enrolled at Stanford and as a freshman helped lead the Cardinal to the 1942 NCAA championship.

But it was wartime and Pollard left Stanford after one year to enter the Coast Guard, where he dominated the California military leagues. After the war, he settled back into AAU ball. On the East Coast, pro basketball was the big game. But on the West Coast, there were only the AAU leagues, and they were every bit as good as the eastern pros. Most teams were sponsored by top corporations (Twentieth Century-Fox in Hollywood had a club) who put the players on their company payrolls. "They paid you under the table a little bit," Pollard said. "They called it 'expenses.' Some of the guys made pretty good money."

For 1946, Pollard and the Oakland Bittners (sponsored by a grocery chain) tore up the field in the national AAU tournament in Denver, which created something of a frenzied interest among the eastern pro teams. Just about all of them wanted Pollard. Robert "Jake" Embry, owner of the Baltimore Bullets, flew to Denver to try to sign him. Les Harrison of the Rochester Royals made an offer, too. But Pollard declined both. He liked playing with the Bittners just fine, he said.

Hartman, though, called him up and turned on the charm. "I liked Sid," Pollard recalled. "I had another team [Rochester] that actually offered me more money." But Hartman convinced him the Minneapolis team (the name Lakers wouldn't be chosen until right before the season) could be very good. Besides, the deal was pretty sweet, $12,000 a year, plus a $3,000 signing bonus, big money in those days. But Pollard struck a tougher bargain. He signed only after Hartman agreed to bring along three of his Bittner teammates. "The guy we wanted was Pollard, but he insisted we bring in his buddies," Hartman said.

In their second season of competition, the Basketball Association of America and the National League were in the throes of a bidding war over talent. As a truce, the two leagues agreed to meet in Chicago to discuss the situation. Hartman attended the meeting, where BAA commissioner Maurice Podoloff started off the proceedings by discussing how tough it would be for any team to sign Jim Pollard. That's when young Sid Hartman raised his hand and stood up. "Mr. Commissioner," he said smugly, "I want to let you know that we've already signed him."

If other pro teams didn't take notice that these Minneapolis people were serious about winning, Hartman quickly gave them more to think about. Next he paid the Chicago Stags $25,000—very big money in those days—for the rights to two pro veterans, Tony Jaros and Don "Swede" Carlson. Carlson was a six-foot forward and Jaros was a journeyman guard, but they were Minnesota natives, good for building interest in the team, Hartman figured. "Berger and Chalfen had plenty of money," he explained. "They could afford it."

Finding a coach was Hartman's other big chore. He first offered the job to Joe Hutton, Sr., at Hamline University, but Hutton decided he liked his security at the college rather than risking that a pro team would survive. So Hartman turned to John Kundla, the twenty-something coach at St. Thomas College, a small four-year Catholic school in St. Paul. Hartman made several trips to Kundla's apartment in northeastern Minneapolis to talk the young coach into joining up. Kundla played a lot of softball in those days, and Hartman would hang around the backstop, trying to work his sales pitch between innings. Kundla finally agreed but demanded a three-year contract. "Kundla was young and had nothing to lose, so he took the job," said Laker forward Vern Mikkelsen.

In those days, however, even young coaches considered the pro game an invitation to ruin.

Despite Hartman's quick success in building a team, he couldn't run the club alone because that conflicted with his newspaper job. To serve as general manager Berger hired Max Winter, a Minneapolis bar owner with a background in sports promotions and marketing. Hartman then moved into the background, working the club's deals behind the scenes for a seventy-five-dollar weekly salary, which meant that he could give up delivering newspapers.

"Sid was what you call an ambassador without portfolio," said Marty Blake, the former Hawks general manager who today serves as the NBA's director of scouting. "Sid was a consultant. Consultants are people who never have to take the blame when things go wrong."

Hartman was so discreet in his workings that years later some of the team's followers would be astounded to learn of his involvement. "Sid kept his name out of everything. He had to," said John Kundla. "As soon as Max Winter came in, Sid went behind the scenes."

Yet Hartman continued to arrange promotional deals for the Lakers and was always in the team's offices, just as he had once shadowed athletics at the University of Minnesota. Only now, instead of a cub reporter hanging around practice, Hartman was one of the major players. To avoid a conflict of interest, Hartman seldom wrote about the Lakers. When he began putting together the deal to bring the club to Minneapolis, Hartman had approached his editors and asked for permission to be involved. The editors were eager to have a pro team in Minneapolis, Hartman said, and they readily gave permission. "The newspaper knew what I was doing," he said. "All newspaper reporters had PR jobs on the side in those days. The idea of conflict of interest was much different then."

Yet Kundla wondered how much the editors knew of Hartman's involvement. It wasn't until decades after the events that Hartman revealed the full extent of his effort, Kundla said, which left some of the team's followers wondering if the newsman wasn't trying to take more credit than he deserved. Yet there is no question that Hartman was the deal maker who built the team. "Sid ran that club the first year, as much as Max Winter did," Pollard said. "It was Sid Hartman who negotiated with me and signed the Bittners. When I got to Minneapolis, I'd never heard of Max Winter."

Even with Hartman's wheeling and dealing, the team needed a sharp business mind to manage its day-to-day affairs. Winter was perfect. "Max had an excellent promotional mind," Pollard said, "and Sid Hartman made the basketball decisions. Max was a good combination with Sid because Sid was very, very impetuous. If you played a bad game, Sid would say, 'We ought to get rid of him; make a trade.' Max was the one who always said, 'Now you gotta sit down and think about this.' Max was a good leveler for Sid. Sid had a lot of good ideas and worked like heck."

Winter, however, was older, wiser, and a natural promoter. Shortly after his hiring, he announced a newspaper contest to name the team. Once that was settled, Winter turned to other chores. He made the Lakers the first team in pro basketball to have its own cheerleaders, the Lakerettes, a group of modestly dressed high school girls from the suburbs. And each year, Winter called in a producer from New York to make a promotional film on the team, which provided steady grist for the newsreels of the era as the Minneapolis Lakers won championship after championship.

At first, even winning wasn't enough to bring out fans in Minneapolis. Most games were played in the Minneapolis Auditorium, which seated about nine thousand. Often, in the early years, the Lakers would draw as few as twenty-five hundred people, which left Winter looking for ways to make the atmosphere more cordial. He employed an orchestra to play before the games and went so far as to have crews available to jump-start fans' cars in the parking lot on cold Minnesota nights. As the Lakers kept winning, these efforts paid off. Minneapolis became a model of success for pro basketball. "There were two or three years in a row when we took in more money than Madison Square Garden," Hartman said.

If nothing else, the team would show that success could be manufactured in a hurry. It's true that Winter and Hartman brought the front office an air of intrigue, Kundla said. "But they saw the possibility of everything."

And that was essential. To make it in pro basketball in the 1940s, you needed vision. It wasn't a sport for people who couldn't smell trouble or see opportunity.

NUTS

Jim Pollard recalled that the first Laker training camp in 1947 was held at a community center in northwest Minneapolis called the "Nuthouse." Pollard wasn't exactly sure how the building got its name, but it was certainly emblematic of the state of professional basketball in the 1940s. You had to be a bit loony to play.

From the game's early days in 1896, pro hoopsters had always played with fearlessness. They were competitive, hard-driving men. After Dr. James Naismith invented basketball at a YMCA training school in late 1891, the sport spread rapidly through the YMCA's network of clubs. Many early pros had first played the game on YMCA teams and become quite good at it. The better they played, the more they wanted to play. This, in turn, led to conflicts with YMCA officials over the use of the gym.

Basketballers wanted to play *all* the time. And when the YMCA said no, the players went elsewhere, to local armories or Masonic temples or hotel ballrooms. Any place would do, just so long as it had a high ceiling and decent lighting.

To pay for the building, the players had to charge admission, which meant they were no longer amateurs, a scandalous development to Victorian sensibilities. Pro basketballers were quickly labeled as outcasts. A YMCA official wrote in 1898 that "when men commence to make money out of sport it degenerates with tremendous speed. It has inevitably resulted in men of lower character going into the game."

Addicted as they were, the early players paid this condescension little mind. While money was a motivation, it wasn't the force that drove the first pros. Basketball was too risky a venture for that. Most who played and promoted it needed day jobs to get by. Still, the pro game grew steadily, and within a few decades the very biggest stars could pull down $2,400 a year, about three times the earnings of the average laborer. Still, the vast majority of early players made little or nothing. And their game remained a stepchild as leagues and franchises sprang to life across the Northeast, flowered briefly, then died. The surviving teams were mostly barnstormers who traveled about the country playing the locals. These early pros saw basketball as it was played in every region, and they incorporated the best ideas into their styles. They developed quick, short passing offenses and ran them off the post, an innovation that quickly found its way to the college game. Joe Lapchick, an early pro who later coached St. John's and the New York Knickerbockers, described this snappy passing style as "making the ball sing."

The first pro club, The Trenton (New Jersey) Basketball Team, formed in 1896. They wore velvet shorts with tights and played their home games at the local Masonic temple. After a few games, the team manager, a carpenter named Fred Padderatz, strung chicken wire around the Masonic temple court to keep the ball in play. Supposedly, Padderatz built it in response to an editorial comment in the Trenton *Daily True American* that "the fellows play like monkeys and should be put in a cage."

Within a few seasons the "cage" was the standard for pro games, although college coaches sneered at it. From Padderatz's chicken wire there developed a system of rope and wire cages draped about the court, some strung fifteen to twenty feet high for keeping the ball in play. Thus basketball came to be known as the "cage game" and its players the "cagers."

The cage frequently resulted in wicked injuries and burns as players hurled themselves against it going after loose balls. Fans were said to be fond of poking knitting needles, lighted cigarettes, and other prods through the netting. In some Pennsylvania mining towns, spectators took to heating nails and tossing them onto opponents shooting free throws.

Soon other YMCA teams sought to match Trenton's success, which brought the rapid spread of "cager" teams throughout New England, New York, Pennsylvania, and New Jersey. Unlike the college game, which disdained the continuous dribble, early pro rules allowed players to take a series of two-handed, single-bounce dribbles. As a result, the game had a rough nature, what you might call "the original ugly," with broad, hulking men dominating the ball up and down the floor, forcing their way near the goal to score. Head-on collisions were numerous, particularly in the small gyms of the era, many of which presented other obstacles, such as hot stoves, steam pipes, and even posts in the middle of the floor supporting the roof. (Legend has it that the posts in the middle of the Trenton YMCA floor led the original idea of "post" play.)

The "cage" game died in the 1920s, but pro basketball steamed on, as a series of leagues rose and fell. Any stability came from the great teams: Harlem's Renaissance Big Five, an all-black team better known as the Rens; the Original Celtics, a New York club that garnered wide attention; and the Philadelphia SPHAs, the South Philadelphia Hebrew Association team run by Eddie Gottlieb. Despite the inconsistency of the leagues, these teams survived because they barnstormed, playing as many as two hundred games per season.

By the early 1930s, some basketball promoters found they could attract a decent crowd if they combined the games with a dance afterward, the only problem being that sometimes the "fans" were more interested in the dance. It wasn't unusual to have women in heels interrupt play with an inadvertent stroll across the floor. Back then, the game was played in three periods. The pros would play a period; then the fans would dance awhile. Then the pros would play another period. A popular venue was the old Broadwood Hotel in Philadelphia, a nightspot for Jewish singles, where the SPHAs played. "The floor was slick, a lot of dance wax on it," recalled Robert "Jake" Embry, owner of the old Baltimore Bullets. "The players were used to sliding and shooting. They'd dribble, slide about five feet, and shoot."

Very ugly.

During the late 1930s and '40s, pro basketball organized itself around the *Chicago Herald American* tournament. Each year, all the country's good pro teams, regardless of what league they played in, would meet in Chicago to settle who was best. Known simply as the "world tournament," the competition helped build public interest in the game. It was the place where the great early black teams, the Rens, the Washington Bears, the Harlem Globetrotters, were free to take on the all-white clubs, with the best men winning.

But, as fascinating as it was, the tournament couldn't do much to make pro basketball a stable business or change the lot of the average player. Like the pros in Trenton a half-century earlier, the teams of the 1940s still sported fancy uniforms (the rave was satin). Yet the day-to-day life of the players was a bit ragged. Training methods were minimal. At home, the teams usually employed a trainer of sorts, "but on the road, each guy took a roll of tape with him," said George Senesky, who played in the forties. "You knew how to tape your own ankles."

And as nice as the jerseys looked, there was no such thing as a clean road uniform. "You couldn't wash them; they had to be dry-cleaned," Senesky said. "On the jerseys, you could see the salt marks on them after a while. You had to hang it up in your room after the games so it would dry out. There was no equipment manager. You were responsible. But nobody complained about it. We were so glad to have the opportunity, so glad to be there."

Which makes you wonder why.

But as Les Harrison, owner/coach of the Rochester Royals, used to say, "This is still better than carrying a lunch bucket every day."

Out of an average $3,000 salary, a player would take home about $2,000. "A lot of us always thought it was going to get better the next year," Senesky said. "The best ticket was $2.50, and 50 cents of that was tax. The owners weren't making money either."

The shaky finances contributed to pro basketball's goofy image. In short, the whole game was a "nuthouse." You had to love it to play it. And then, as George Senesky pointed out, you often wondered why you did.

MINNEAPOLIS

Renamed the Lakers, basketball's worst franchise immediately set out to change that status in 1947, the only problem being that the key people weren't exactly sure what they were doing. The coach had gotten most of his experience running high school teams, the front office was steered by a twenty-four-year-old sportswriter, and the core of the roster was a group of AAU players.

"We didn't know what it was all about," Jim Pollard admitted. "I'd only seen about two pro games. And Kundla didn't know any more about the league than I did."

Still, hope was high. The owners chartered a DC-3 to fly the Lakers to their first game against the Oshkosh All-Stars and legendary six-foot-four center Leroy "Cowboy" Edwards, an aging star who could hook with either hand.

"I'll always remember him," Pollard said. "That's when I knew I wasn't a center. Edwards started out guarding me. He was muscular and slow. So the first time down the floor I gave him a good fake and drove around him for an easy basket. I said, 'Geez, this is easy. This guy is supposed to be good.' The second time down the floor, I faked and went around him and he just put his arm out. Boy, he clotheslined me good and put me about three rows up in the bleachers. 'Hey skinny,' he said, 'that's no way to do in this league.' "

Cowboy made his point, but the Lakers won that first game and arrived home to find their wives, the owners, Hartman, and Winter at the airport waiting to celebrate. They loaded up in cars and went down to the Rainbow Cafe for a big meal. "I don't remember Sid and Max ever being more excited than that first game," Pollard said. "It really was a thrill because we didn't know what to expect."

After three games, they acquired Herm Schaeffer, a six-foot-one guard, from the Indianapolis Kautskys. A wise, experienced ball handler, Schaeffer could run the floor show. "He was a master at the pick and roll," Kundla said.

One game later, the last piece of the dynasty, the biggest piece, fell into place as Sid Hartman had hoped it would. Maurice White, owner of the Chicago American Gears, had broken away from the NBL to form his own league, the Professional Basketball League of America, with George Mikan as the drawing card. It was an ambitious plan with twenty four franchises across the country, including such new hoops territories as Houston, New Orleans, and Atlanta. But White was drinking heavily and insisted on controlling the payroll for all of the teams out of his Chicago office. Part of his plan was to begin the season earlier, in September.

That plan only hastened his demise. The PBLA folded two weeks into the season, and White lost $600,000.

As Hartman had hoped, the six-foot-ten Mikan was suddenly free to negotiate his own deal with another team, and the Gems/Lakers had first crack at him. Several other BAA clubs were hot on the big center's trail, but he agreed to come to Minneapolis first to talk business.

Winter and Hartman spent a long day negotiating with Mikan, but his lawyer, Stacy Osgood, advised him to pass on their offer. Besides, Osgood pointed out, they had to catch the last plane to Chicago.

As Hartman prepared to drive them to the airport, Max Winter called him aside. If they leave town, we'll never sign Mikan, Winter said. He suggested that Hartman take a long route to the airport so that Mikan would miss his flight.

"I drove around and made sure he missed the plane," Hartman said, chuckling.

Mikan had to stay overnight, and the next day he agreed to a one-year, $15,000 contract.

Hartman could hardly contain his glee. Within a matter of months he had assembled the makings of a dynasty, a team that would win six championships over the next seven seasons. "That," Hartman would say forty-five years later, "was the most fun I ever had in my life."

BIG GEORGE

The lenses in George Mikan's glasses were a quarter-inch thick. He once said trying to see without them was like driving a car without wipers during a rainstorm. His eyesight had been reason enough to get him cut from the basketball team at Catholic High in Joliet, Illinois. But Mikan was so tall (he had grown six inches while convalescing from a broken leg as an adolescent), people kept telling him he should play the game. Plus, a scholarship could pay for his education. He wanted to go to Notre Dame, but that was a costly proposition in 1942.

Instead, he enrolled in classes at DePaul, with the idea that he would catch the train down to Notre Dame over Christmas break and try out for the team. The war was on, and just about every college coach was looking for athletes. Mikan was too tall and too blind to go into the service. So he figured that Notre Dame coach George Keogan might be interested.

"He's too awkward, and he wears glasses," Keogan supposedly said after watching Big George work out.

"Keogan told me to return to DePaul, that I'd make a better scholar than a basketball player," Mikan recalled.

He took that advice, and went back to DePaul and resumed classes. But that spring he caught the eye of Ray Meyer, the school's new basketball coach.

"There's my future," Meyer said to himself.

Mikan underwent a miraculous development at DePaul. The clumsy, unpolished prospect seemingly blossomed overnight into the premier player in college basketball, the big-time gate attraction during World War II. Remarkably, he developed agility while growing from six-foot-eight to six-ten. By the 1944–45 season, Mikan's junior year, he and Oklahoma A&M's Bob Kurland had become prototypes for what future generations would come to know as a "force." But when Mikan entered college in 1942, most coaches had little regard for tall players. Basketball was still the domain of the little man. Considered too awkward for the game, the big guys were called "goons."

Both Mikan and Kurland soon proved that they weren't goons. "George and I opened the door to the idea that the big man could play the game," Kurland said. "Which in our day was, by eastern standards, played by guys five-ten, five-eleven, who were quick, took the set shot, and so forth. We opened the door for what the game is today."

Mikan and DePaul won the 1945 National Invitational Tournament, in those days the college game's prized trophy. In one NIT game, Mikan scored fifty-three points, an incredible sum for the slow pace of 1940s basketball, and he twice won the NCAA scoring crown. All of this from a guy who hadn't been able to make the Notre Dame varsity three years earlier.

"He was an awkward kid at first," Ray Meyer once explained, "but he just kept improving. I guided him, but he had talent, and he just kept getting better and better. The superstars are like that. They have something inside."

Mikan had something outside, too: wide shoulders and a pair of bruising elbows. But he wasn't just a brute. Meyer, then a young, ambitious coach, sensed that he could develop Mikan. He hired a co-ed to give the center dancing lessons to improve his agility, and he set up drills with Mikan guarding a five-foot-five teammate one-on-one, to teach Mikan to move his feet defensively. Jumping rope and shadowboxing were also part of the regimen, as was alternately playing catch with a tennis ball and a medicine ball. Then Meyer made him work on his shooting and faking. First 250 right-handed hooks each day. Then 250 left-handed. That grueling repetition would become a staple of basketball how-to manuals as "the Mikan drill." Soon Meyer's awkward protégé had developed a simple but punishing style around the basket, based on a solid drop step.

"George didn't have a lot of moves," Jim Pollard explained. "He never fooled you very often. Some of those old centers gave great fakes. Not George."

Mikan would get position down low, drop his inside foot back, and pivot toward the hoop. As he did, he'd lead his motion with his inside elbow. "He didn't get called for the offensive foul because he had both hands on the ball," Pollard said. "He'd take it up in the air with both hands. If he took a hand off the ball and threw the elbow, he was going to get called for the foul. But George seldom did that. He was smart."

The foul lane was only six feet wide in those days, which allowed him to set up and score. "If you let Mikan get position, it was over," said Mike Bloom, a defensive specialist in the 1940s. "He would back in to the basket and go to work with those elbows."

"When he got you in that pivot, you couldn't do anything about it," agrees Horace "Bones" McKinney, who played against Mikan.

"Mikan was great with those elbows," said Paul Seymour, who played for the Syracuse Nationals. "He used to kill our centers. Used to knock 'em down, draw the foul, then help 'em up and pat 'em on the fanny."

The Chicago American Gears signed Mikan to an unprecedented five-year, $62,000 contract in the spring of 1946, after he had completed his college eligibility, and he went right to work for them, even playing in the *Chicago Herald American* tournament that spring, where he was named the MVP. But that fall Mikan claimed that the cash-thin Gears were cutting his paychecks short and held out for nineteen of the forty-four regular-season games. He and the team worked out their differences still in time for him to lead the Gears to the NBL championship that spring of 1947.

His size and dominance made Mikan an overnight sensation, and that gave Gears owner Maurice White ideas. Why not start his own league just to showcase the big guy?

Needless to say, if White didn't have enough cash to run one club, he certainly didn't have enough to float a twenty-four-team league. The Lakers, of course, were waiting with a net to catch Big George in the NBL dispersal draft.

Mikan joined the Lakers for their fifth game of the 1947–48 season, at Sheboygan. "I had never seen George," Pollard recalled. "I didn't know what he was like at all. He walked into that locker room at Sheboygan, and I thought that was the biggest-looking dumb character that I'd ever seen for a guy that was barely twenty-three years old. He had these great big, thick glasses, and he had this homburg hat on. I said to myself, 'What the hell's a guy twenty-three years old doing wearing a homburg and a great big storm overcoat?'

"He walked in and said, 'Hi, fellas; I'm your new center.' I jumped up and said, 'Hi, George; my name's Jim.'

"When we got out on the floor, we threw him the ball and said, 'Show us what you can do.' I played with that big horse for every game for seven years, and that's the only time I ever heard him say, 'Please don't throw me the ball; they're killing me.' The rest of us just threw him the ball and stood there. They ganged up on him and kicked the hell out of George that first night."

The Lakers lost their first five games with Mikan, making it immediately obvious that before they could rush off to harvest championships, they had to learn to play together. It wasn't easy, because Mikan's and Pollard's individual styles were so different. Pollard was a slashing driver, but Mikan clogged the middle, leaving his teammate little room to drive. "Pollard could really leap. He got hurt playing with Mikan," said Paul Seymour of the Syracuse Nationals.

"George was great if he stayed on his side of the lane," Pollard said. "But a lot of times, as soon as I got the ball on the wing, he would come over to my side of the lane. I would tell him, 'Stay over there a minute.' But that wasn't his style of play. When we first started playing together, I couldn't very well go to the middle because he was there.

"When I started to drive, he'd go to the basket. So he'd bring his man, six-eight, six-ten, down to the basket where they'd kick the hell out of me. At that time, George didn't know what I could do. He'd go to the basket, and I'd flip the ball to him and he'd miss it. I kept telling him, 'You better get your hands up because nine out of ten passes are going to hit you right in the face.' After a while, he learned to give me that one count, to give me that step and give me room to drive, and then he could come in. If his man switched off on me, I'd flip him the ball. It made it easier for George, too. But we had to learn that. It took us awhile."

From that awkward chemistry, Mikan and Pollard built a deadly pick-and-roll routine, which Kundla called the J&G (Jim and George) play. Needless to say, it was the coach's favorite because most opponents couldn't stop it.

"It was a simple little play," Kundla said proudly. "But it was very successful."

The Lakers ran it again and again that season on their way to a league-best 43–17 record. In the play-offs, they moved aside Oshkosh, Tri-Cities, and Rochester to claim their first championship.

"After we won, we had to hustle to catch a train out of Rochester," Pollard recalled. "On the way out, we picked up a couple of six-packs. We put 'em in the stainless-steel sink in the men's room on the train. Then we sat there and celebrated our first championship with the train rattling all around and the wheels rolling underneath."

In those days, the Lakers did just about all their traveling by train except when management chartered an occasional DC-3. With Minneapolis so far west of the other franchises, the scheduling was brutal. They rode all night to Chicago, then got off the train and grabbed a cab across the city to yet another station, where they caught the 8:00 A.M. train to Minneapolis. The league champions arrived home the next afternoon at 2:30, almost too tired to celebrate with the small group of family and friends waiting at the station.

Still, it was hard not to be elated. In one season, the franchise had changed names, management, rosters, and status, having gone from worst to best.

Just before the 1948 play-offs, the Lakers entered the last of the *Chicago Herald American*'s "world" tournaments and played their way to the finals, where they beat the aging Rens, the all-black barnstorming team from New York. The Lakers were all white, but their most widely publicized contests were against all-black teams, particularly their five-year, seven-game series with the Harlem Globetrotters.

In 1948, the Globetrotters were the most popular pro team in the country. "Most people back then weren't aware of pro basketball beyond the Harlem Globetrotters," explained George Puscas, a basketball publicist of that era. "That game between the Lakers and the Globetrotters gave the pros some identity. It helped the NBA tremendously as it was emerging."

The games were played in Chicago Stadium (Chicago was the 'Trotters' hometown) and in Minneapolis. "We had people waiting in line here at 3:00 o'clock in the morning to get tickets," Sid Hartman said. "You couldn't get in Chicago Stadium. There were mobs. Everybody thought the Globetrotters were a super team."

The fan interest wasn't particular to basketball. American society remained deeply segregated after World War II, but white spectators were curious and eager to see black athletes in action. Black baseball teams in Philadelphia regularly drew larger crowds than the white clubs.

The Globetrotters had gotten their start in Chicago in the 1920s with a portly twenty-three-year-old promoter, Abe Saperstein, from Chicago's north side. He began booking the team as the Savoy Big Five. (They played their home games in Chicago's Savoy Ballroom.) By the 1930s, the name would evolve to the Harlem Globetrotters. Saperstein settled on that because Harlem identified the players as black and Globetrotters suggested world travel.

In later years, they would become known for their humor and slick ball-handling routines, often performed to the accompaniment of "Sweet Georgia Brown." But in the early days, the Globetrotters played their basketball straight. They did, however, thrill fans with a warm-up "circle," which over the years evolved into the world's classiest ball-handling routine. The entertainment and humor were said to be a means of deflecting the ugly racial moods the team sometimes encountered on the road. Plus, if the local teams had fun and the crowd laughed, people didn't mind losing, and the Globetrotters were often invited back.

Their breakthrough to the big time didn't come until the 1939 season, when they stacked up a 148–13 record, good enough for an invitation to the Chicago "world tournament." The Globetrotters lost a close game to the Rens, but the outcome established just how good they were. For 1940, the 'Trotters (with Bernie Price, Babe Pressley, Sonny Boswell, Hillery Brown, and Inman Jackson) won the world tournament, beating the NBL's Chicago Bruins (owned by George Halas) 31–29 in overtime. The victory was soon followed by new red-white-and-blue uniforms and a team bus, and the Globetrotters were on their way.

In the 1940s, Saperstein signed two major stars. Reece "Goose" Tatum, a baseball player from Arkansas, had huge hands, long arms, and a wonderful wit. And when Oklahoma's Langston University team beat the 'Trotters one night, Saperstein promptly lured away the star player, Marcus Haynes. Building on Tatum's creativity, the Globetrotters left the straight game to offer fans their hugely entertaining brand of hoops, filled with gimmicks, gags, and top-notch ball handling. The transition to a comedy club increased the fame and popularity of the 'Trotters. But they paused in this conversion long enough to take on the Lakers in a serious showdown.

"They had some great players on that team," Hartman said. "Marcus

Haynes, Goose Tatum, Sonny Boswell, Sweetwater Clifton, and Babe Press-ley were all great players. And they dropped their comedy against us. They wanted to win."

The 'Trotters beat Minneapolis in 1948 and again in '49, which left the Lakers grumbling that Abe Saperstein had used his own refs. The victory, though, boosted morale in the black communities across the country. To many African-Americans, the Globetrotters' win was another knock against segregation. The Lakers, though, thought little, if any, about the social implications. They were eager for revenge. They didn't like playing the Globetrotter games in the first place, because they received no extra pay for them. Plus they didn't like the idea of playing a comedy team. And losing made it much worse.

"The first two games, Saperstein hired the refs," Kundla said. "After that, we said, 'You get one ref, and we'll get a referee.' "

The second game in 1949, played before a crowd of 10,122 at the Minneapolis Auditorium, resulted in a 68–53 Laker win. In 1950, the teams met twice, with the Lakers winning both, by sixteen and fifteen points. The first game was played at Chicago Stadium before 21,666 fans, an astounding turnout for that era.

"The third year we played 'em we kicked the hell out of 'em in Minneapolis," Pollard recalled. "It was no contest. They only had eight or nine guys on their squad in Minneapolis. Then we played 'em a few days later in Chicago. They must have had fifteen or sixteen players. Every time we threw the ball to Mikan, they grabbed him. In the first half alone, he hit ten or twelve free throws."

The Chicago game also marked the Lakers' first televised broadcast. Rollie Johnson, manager of WCCO in Minneapolis, did the play-by-play. Late in the second half with the Lakers leading by 10, he walked over to the bench and asked Kundla to call a time-out so that the station could get in a final advertisement. Moments later, as Pollard pulled down a rebound and raced upcourt, apparently headed for an easy basket, Kundla called time-out.

"Jim came over to the bench with this look on his face and asked me what was the matter," Kundla recalled. "I told him Rollie needed a time-out. He got so mad at me he wouldn't go back in the game."

The Lakers still coasted to the win and again swept games in 1951 and '52, which brought an end to the series (except for one final Lakers win in 1958). "Saperstein didn't want to lose, and we kept on beating them," Hartman said. "So he finally cut out the series."

The final blow was an 84–60 Laker win at Chicago Stadium in January 1952. "We beat 'em so bad in Chicago, he wouldn't play us again," Kundla said. "After the game, Abe took a walk, he was so upset. They couldn't find him for hours."

*   *   *

Just before the 1948–49 season, Minneapolis and three of the NBL's best teams—Fort Wayne, Rochester, and Indianapolis—crossed over and joined the new league, the BBA, a move that would lead to the formation of the NBA. But it also brought howls of protest from the remaining National owners, who claimed the Lakers and other teams had sold out to the competing league. The National League gets no modern recognition, but it was far better than the BAA, said Syracuse Nationals owner Danny Biasone, who was often fond of pointing out that after the leagues merged, National teams won the first seven championships.

The BAA, though, had the big money and the big markets.

Begun in 1946 by a group of hockey teams and arena owners, the BAA had franchises based in Boston, New York, Washington, Chicago, Baltimore, Philadelphia, and St. Louis. The BAA's best arenas, Boston Garden, Madison Square Garden, and Chicago Stadium, were the sports palaces of that era. The National League, on the other hand, was a decade older and had many of the name players. But its teams were located in smaller markets—Fort Wayne, Syracuse, Rochester, Dayton, and Oshkosh—with small, often dingy buildings. That situation changed overnight with the move of the four NBL teams, which took up residence in the BAA's Western Division with Chicago and St. Louis. The result was a nicely balanced twelve-team league.

Pollard recalled how excited the Lakers were at finally getting to play in the big cities and arenas, particularly New York and Madison Square Garden. The new league had a big-time feel to it, and the Lakers quickly showed they belonged. The Royals won the Western Division regular-season crown with a 45–15 record, while Mikan and the Lakers finished just one game back at 44–16. The best Eastern Division team, the Washington Capitols (coached by twenty-nine-year-old Red Auerbach), finished 38–22.

Minneapolis closed the schedule with Mikan, the league's leading scorer, ringing up forty-eight and fifty-one points against New York, fifty-three against Baltimore, and forty-six against Rochester, incredible totals in that era of forty-minute games. When it came to winning, the big, affable Mikan could be incredibly tough and just a little mean, Pollard recalled. "Toward the end of a ball game, if we were ahead by 20, George would come over to the bench and say, 'Let's beat 'em good. Let's kick the hell out of 'em so they don't want to play us ever again.' "

Powered by Mikan, the Lakers steamed into the 1949 play-offs and overwhelmed whoever happened into their path. They swept both Chicago and Rochester 2–0 on their way to dumping Auerbach's Capitols, 4–2, for the championship. Mikan scored 303 points in ten play-off games. "George gloried in that 'I am number one' feeling," Pollard said. "That's why he was so successful. He wanted that spot, wanted to be number one, wanted you to be a little bit fearful of him on the court."

Mikan would get his wish time and again over the coming seasons. He would stay on top, and opponents would be quite fearful of him and his powerful drop step and leading elbow. His intensity would burn bright for five more seasons, all of them immensely fun for the Lakers. But then, almost as quickly as it had been put together, the team would fall apart. And in the aftermath the participants would have plenty of time to wonder why.

Sweet as it was, success bred its own sort of contempt for the Minneapolis Lakers. From time to time, problems arose between Pollard and Mikan, then-forward Vern Mikkelsen said. Both were great athletes, yet Mikan did most of the scoring and got most of the recognition. The little problems could have been big ones, "but Kundla handled that situation just beautifully," Mikkelsen recalled. "Our offense was built around George, and it would have been stupid not to use him."

One night the marquee outside Madison Square Garden read: "Tonite: Geo. Mikan vs. the Knicks." More than anything, that incident summed up his stature in those early years of the game. He was the league's draw, just as he had been for college basketball. "Accolades were something that I had no control over," Mikan said.

The real rub, of course, was Pollard. He was a masterful player, a former leading scorer in the AAU leagues, and he admitted that the attention given to Mikan bothered him. "The thing about Mikan, everything revolved around him, and he got too much publicity and he tried to do too much himself because of it," Pollard said. "But he was a hell of a competitor. We'd get through a game and his question was, 'Did we win?' That was the idea of the whole game. That made us all on George's side, because he was a winner.

"I used to get on George's case all the time. George and I always argued. But when we stepped on the floor, George and I always played to win, the hell with who got the points."

The biggest irritation was Mikan's refusal to pass the ball when he was double-teamed, Pollard said. "It wasn't that he was selfish. It was more a matter of pride." During one season, Mikan suddenly began passing out of the double teams, and the Lakers went on an eight-game winning streak, with everybody scoring in double figures. "Then we went to New York, and George always wanted to put the big show on in New York," Pollard said. "George had thirty-eight or thirty-nine points that night, and no one else was in double figures. We lost, and afterward we went drinking with friends. Mikan was at one end of the bar drinking. I told the guy I was drinking with to go up there and ask Mikan how we could have an eight-game winning streak with everybody happy and then come here and lose. My friend went over and asked him that, and then George roared, 'I'm gonna kill that goddamn Pollard!' 'You'll never catch me, George!' I yelled back at him. That was our way of picking on George. He was the bellwether of our club, and we all picked on him."

Pollard admitted the friction between the stars was "something that could have torn the team apart. But Kundla kept a very even keel, and he didn't pick on anybody. He seldom made a big deal out of offensive mistakes. But boy, would he get upset about defense."

"Kundla gets no recognition, and he should be in the Hall of Fame," Mikan agreed. "He did a great job of molding the team, taking care of the players' idiosyncrasies."

Keeping the Lakers' abundant talent controlled and focused took its toll on Kundla, a shy, quiet man who by every January was gulping milk to combat the ulcers left over from his duty on a navy landing craft in the Pacific during the war. It wasn't that he couldn't get angry. He just didn't very often. "He had a very, very slow fuse, but when it finally erupted, then look out," Mikkelsen said.

Kundla was successful both because of and despite of his youth. His age allowed him to joke with his players, to engage in the silly fun experienced by adults who are paid to play games. Four decades later, the Lakers still couldn't agree on who rubbed the Limburger cheese in whose hat. Mikkelsen swore that reserves Tony Jaros and Bud Grant (he was a Laker reserve for a couple of seasons before going on to coach the NFL's Minnesota Vikings) ruined several of Kundla's hats. Kundla, though, was sure that he was the one who pulled the cheese trick on somebody else.

Kundla also recalled the time his players stuffed pornography in his luggage, which his wife found later.

Then there was the infamous train ride early one very cold morning to a game against the Fort Wayne Pistons. Because of the extreme cold, the Lakers' train experienced several delays, and it soon became apparent they weren't going to make the game on time. At Milwaukee, a messenger boarded the train with a telegram from Pistons owner Fred Zollner, telling the Lakers that he would send the Pistons' team plane for them.

"They were the envy of the league because they flew to all the games," Vern Mikkelsen said of the Pistons.

The Lakers got off the train, but no one realized that Kundla had gone to the dining car to drink milk for his ulcer. As the train pulled out of the station, the players standing on the platform saw the coach looking plaintively out a window two cars back. Kundla didn't see his players and didn't know of the developments until a conductor later informed him.

As planned, the team caught the plane and made the game at North Side High School in Fort Wayne, where the Pistons played their home games. The Lakers, in fact, had a lead at intermission and had returned to the floor just before the start of the second half when they heard a murmur from the crowd.

Kundla had walked in the gym door wearing his storm coat and toting his suitcase. "He walked in pretty sheepishly," Mikkelsen recalled. "At the time we were winning, but we wound up losing the game. We gave John plenty of trouble on that."

The Lakers were the kind of team that could laugh about losses, because there weren't that many. When tight situations arose, they always seemed to have an answer. "George Mikan had a tremendous, total confidence that he could get the job done," Mikkelsen said. "He would make believers out of us. Late in close games he always wanted the ball. The tremendous competitor that he was, he would say, 'Let me have the ball. I'll get it done.' More often than not, he did."

4

Time on Your Side

There was no shot clock in pro basketball in the late 1940s, which meant the game was interminably slow, particularly if the Minneapolis Lakers were involved. George Mikan or Jim Pollard would control a defensive rebound: then the league champions would begin their methodical assault on the opponent's goal. At the offensive end, the Lakers would hold the ball and wait for Mikan to lumber upcourt and take position down near the basket. Only then would they go to work. Even at this pace Mikan's spectacles would often fog up, and play would be stopped while he toweled off and wiped the lens dry. After he had dominated the league for a couple of years, opponents grew impatient with these pauses to refresh. They complained that if Big George wanted to wipe his glasses, the Lakers should call a time-out.

That was only fair, the league decided.

So John Kundla shifted his time-out strategies to make sure his center had a clean windshield. Kundla also kept a spare set of Mikan's specs in his coat pocket. No one would accuse the young Laker coach of not knowing who punched his meal ticket. The entire offense was built around Mikan, and in two years of competition no one had been able to stop him when the game really mattered.

But as strong as the Lakers seemed after winning two straight championships, they were a machine with a definite need for replacement parts in the spring of 1949. Herm Schaeffer was a smart ball handler and a good passer, but his age was beginning to show. In the frontcourt, Don "Swede" Carlson was the last of pro basketball's six-foot forwards. He had been crafty and tough enough to average about eight points a game over two seasons in Minneapolis. Of playing with Mikan, Carlson once said, "I used to like to pass him the ball, cut around him, and then listen to the sound the guy guarding me made when he ran into George." But the game was changing rapidly in 1950. The players were getting larger.

"If he stood up straight, he was six-one," Pollard said of Carlson. "As the game got bigger, they moved him out."

Knowing that the team needed to upgrade, Max Winter and Sid Hartman found three good picks in the 1949 draft. The top prizes were thought to be six-foot-seven forward Vern Mikkelsen, a power player out of Minnesota's little Hamline College, and Bob "Tiger" Harrison, a guard from the University of Michigan.

Almost as an afterthought, the Lakers drafted five-foot-nine guard Slater "Dugie" Martin out of the University of Texas. Martin had been an All-American in the high-speed offense run by Texas, but few thought he was big enough to survive in the pro game. His best offer had come from the Phillips 66ers, one of the top AAU teams of the era, but the 66ers wanted Martin to hold down an office job in addition to his playing duties. Martin would later explain that he just couldn't stomach the idea of sitting behind a desk.

So he accepted a low-grade, $3,500 offer from the Lakers, where his value was held suspect by Kundla, who had little say in the team's personnel moves. Martin had scored easily in the up-tempo offense he played in college, but how would this slightly built Texan fit into the Lakers' plodding floor game? At first the answer was: not very well at all. Kundla gave Martin scant playing time, and when he did play, the little guard seemed overwhelmed. Muscular Frankie Brian of the Anderson Duffy Packers scored forty points against him in an early game, a severe blow, because Martin's long suit was supposed to be his defense. On offense, he was caught in a tug-of-war between the coach and the star. Kundla inserted him into a game at St. Louis with the idea that he would pass the ball to Mikan, then cut to the hoop. But the center angrily told the rookie guard not to cut because he was clogging the middle. Martin was intimidated by Mikan and kept quiet when Kundla called him to the bench for not following instructions.

"Kundla didn't use me much until our next trip to St. Louis when Herm Schaeffer was hurt," Martin recalled. "Schaeffer, a nice fellow, came up to me in the locker room before the game. 'Don't be afraid to take your shots,' he said. 'You're letting the big guy cramp your style.' I had one of those lucky nights where everything I threw up went in. I hit eight straight shots from the floor. They came just in time to save my job."

Before long, the veteran Schaeffer had stepped aside and was teaching the rookie how to run the team. Martin soon showed that his quickness gave the Lakers another weapon. And his coach came to love the little guard's style. Both Martin and Kundla had served in the navy in the Pacific during the war. Both thought like coaches, and their mutual understanding grew from there. Martin, the high-scoring college player, became a low-scoring, ball-distributing pro guard, running the Lakers' lumbering offense.

Later, after helping the Lakers to four championships, Martin would move on to the St. Louis Hawks and direct them to yet another title, accomplishments that landed him in the Hall of Fame.

"He wanted to win," Kundla said of Martin. "He didn't care who made the points."

With Martin in the lineup, Kundla kept the offense moving at a pace that matched Mikan's abilities, but this retooled group could also get up and move, with Martin running the break and Pollard on the wing. "If the fast break was there, they'd go on you," said Paul Seymour, who played for the Syracuse Nationals. "But most of the time they waited for Mikan to come down the floor and then set things up."

"We didn't fast-break that much," Pollard said, "because Mikan and Mikkelsen were not that quick, and you didn't want either one of them to dribble. But Martin always wanted to go. He was always looking for the fast break."

The rookie adjustment for Mikkelsen, the son of a Lutheran minister, was just as difficult as Martin's, and just as important to the team's development. At six-foot-seven, 235 pounds, he had played center in high school and college, but he was forced to shift to forward in the pros, which meant that he played facing the basket for the first time in his career. The new position suited his skills. He could leap and knew how to get rebounding position. In adjusting, he developed a bit of an outside shot, although he made his living on the offensive glass.

"I didn't see the ball much," Mikkelsen said of his first few years in the league. "I didn't have to. Mikan and Pollard did most of the scoring. When they had an off night, I cleaned up on the boards."

Before the 1950 season was over these rookies would help make the Lakers into a blueprint for modern teams. Building around the 245-pound Mikan, the dominant center, and Pollard, the quick, acrobatic small forward, the Lakers transformed Mikkelsen into the original "power" forward. And Slater Martin filled the role of ball handler, or what would come to be known as a "point guard." The six-foot-four Harrison, meanwhile, found a place in the lineup as the off guard.

"We were the first team to have those types of players filling the roles," Pollard said, "and we became the model for all the modern teams that came after us."

There is a lingering perception today that the old Lakers couldn't play the modern game. Wrong, says Marty Blake, the former Hawks general manager who today serves as the NBA's director of scouting. "The Lakers were a great team. Mikan and Mikkelsen and Pollard and Martin—they could have played today. Mikkelsen would be making $2 million a year, for God sakes. These people today don't realize how good they were."

The Lakers were also the first fully athletic team capable of dunking at will, but the ethic of that era didn't allow for such overtly macho statements. "All of us could dunk except Slater Martin," Mikkelsen said. "But we weren't allowed to much, because Kundla wouldn't let us. It was frowned on as hotdogging."

Pollard recalled getting a steal once and taking the ball in for a jam only to have it hit the back of the rim and sail out to half court, leaving him to endure an unusually vociferous ragging from Kundla during the time-out.

"They could all dunk," Kundla agreed. "But usually they just shot the ball. In practice they did a lot of dunking. But otherwise we kept away from that. You didn't want to embarrass another team or player. Wilt Chamberlain was the one who really started the dunking in games in the late fifties."

As if their talent wasn't enough, the Lakers also got a boost on their home floor, the Minneapolis Auditorium, where the court was narrower by a few feet. "That made them much more effective," said Dolph Schayes, who played for the Syracuse Nationals. "We always had a difficult time with them. If you double-teamed George, then Mikkelsen would clean up. And Pollard was able to drive, and he was a great passer."

"They used to say that when Mikan, Mikkelsen and Pollard stretched their arms across that narrow court, nobody could get through," Syracuse coach Al Cervi said.

Paul Seymour, who played for the Syracuse Nationals, laughed at the memory of trying to play against the Lakers' frontcourt. "Those three big bastards made every court look narrow," he said. "Mikkelsen was a brute."

Minneapolis would need all advantages for the 1950 season, as the six surviving teams of the NBL—Syracuse, the Anderson Duffy Packers, Tri-Cities Blackhawks, Denver Nuggets, Sheboygan Redskins, and Waterloo Hawks—merged with the BAA to form the National Basketball Association, a seventeen-team league aligned in three cumbersome divisions. The old Western Division became the Central, where Minneapolis and the Rochester Royals battled to a tie with 51–17 records. Both had 33–1 home records, and the division title came down to a single tiebreaker game. With Mikan scoring thirty-five, the Lakers won at Rochester, 78–76, to claim the division. From there, the Lakers swept both Fort Wayne and Anderson 2–0 to meet Syracuse for the championship.

The Nationals held the home-court advantage, and the series opened at State Fair Coliseum, just outside Syracuse, where the Nats had a 34–1 record. But Mikan scored thirty-seven points, and rookie "Tiger" Harrison hit a forty-footer at the buzzer to give Minneapolis the first game. In the giddiness of the victory, the Lakers made a major mistake in the locker room. Mikan told reporters that he was allergic to all the smoke in the arena, which made the Syracuse papers the next morning. "That next night all the fans came out smoking cigars," Mikan said.

"You could hardly see across the floor," Kundla agreed. "It was filled with smoke."

Mikan alleged that Kundla had slipped up and told reporters about his allergy, but Pollard said he distinctly recalled Big George making the comment. Either way, the smoke screen allowed the Nats to grab the second game despite thirty-two points from Mikan. In retrospect, however, it was only good for a laugh. The Lakers snuffed Syracuse in six games. If you counted Mikan's two NBL titles, with Chicago and Minneapolis, he had been the center of four straight championship teams, and the competition realized that even making him take a time-out to wipe his glasses wasn't going to slow the juggernaut.

THE NEW GAME

The Lakers ran off the league's best regular-season record in 1951. And, as he had the two previous seasons, Mikan won the scoring crown. But as the schedule came to a close, their luck turned bad. Mikan suffered a hairline fracture of his ankle. Even that didn't sideline him. Doctors placed his foot in a cast and used ethyl chloride to numb his pain.

"He played, but he was at half-speed," Kundla said.

Half-speed of slow must have meant that the Lakers were almost motionless. They still moved into the Western Conference finals again to meet their old rivals, the Rochester Royals. "It seemed we were always neck and neck, with every game going down to the wire," Kundla said.

Between 1949 and 1954, the Lakers won 267 games. The Royals won 266. Twice they finished ahead of Minneapolis in the regular-season standings. But in the head-to-head meetings, the Lakers usually won. (Over the four years, the Lakers won thirty-eight and lost twenty-eight against the Royals.)

"To me, our games with Rochester, that was the greatest basketball ever played," Hartman said. "There was some science to it, some finesse to it."

The Royals presented a slick look, with fancy ball handling, smooth passing, and a lot of quickness. Hall of Famer Bob Davies ran the offense. A former MVP of the NBL, he had once played ninety games for Rochester while coaching his former college team, Seton Hall, to a 24–3 record. (Imagine a modern college coach pulling that off.) Teamed with Davies in the Royals' backcourt was one of his former Seton Hall players, All-American Bobby Wanzer. Red Holzman, who later coached the Knicks, was the backup.

The players for both teams enjoyed a high regard for one another. But the front offices of the two clubs seemed to be engaged in a running blood feud. Rochester owner/coach Les Harrison had hired the first trainer in the league and had helped to break the NBL color line in 1946 when he added

Dolly King to the club's roster. When reporters questioned the move, Harrison told them, "If he can play, he can play."

Such accomplishments aside, Harrison was viewed as a villain in Minneapolis. Sid Hartman alleged that Harrison once had tried to convince the Lakers' Herm Schaeffer that he was underpaid, an act for which the Lakers were always trying to retaliate.

In one regular season game at Rochester, the Lakers managed to tie the score on a buzzer-beating basket, then won in overtime. Afterward, they sat exhausted in the locker room and listened through the thin walls as Harrison screamed at Chickie Shapiro, his scorekeeper, for not sounding the horn soon enough.

"Les Harrison was a strange duck," Hartman recalled.

Another time, the Royals were playing in Fort Wayne when Davies hit a long shot. As Davies fired it up, referee Pat Kennedy blew his whistle but somehow inhaled and sucked the ball of the whistle into his windpipe. He passed out and collapsed. Harrison then supposedly ran onto the floor and screamed at Kennedy, "Pat, Pat, quick before you die, did the bucket count?"

Harrison hated that he couldn't beat the Lakers for a championship. In 1947, he had gone so far as to pay $25,000 to acquire six-foot-nine Arnie Risen from Indianapolis in an effort to battle Mikan. When that didn't do the trick, he added bulky forward Arnie Johnson to the mix.

"Mikan and Risen had great battles at center," Pollard said. "Risen couldn't stop George, but George had a heck of a time stopping Risen, too. And Arnie Johnson was a big bull, and he had great battles with Mikkelsen. Our game was all 'underneath the boards and battle like heck.' Their game was all outside set shooting with Wanzer and Davies and Red Holzman."

With Mikan injured in the 1951 play-offs, the Royals finally had their chance. The Lakers quickly won the first game at home. But then Harrison moved Red Holzman into the starting lineup, and the Royals took command. With Mikan slowed, the Lakers collapsed, losing the next three games. From there, Harrison's team went on to beat the Knicks for the title. That left Mikan burning. He couldn't stand the idea that Rochester had taken one of his championships.

Mikan returned from his ankle injury in the fall of 1951 and encountered a new game. A year earlier, in November 1950, the Pistons had run a stall against the Lakers. Only thirty-six shots were taken the whole game, and Fort Wayne won, 19–18, on a last-second bucket by Larry Foust. But the fans had booed loudly throughout; the NBA couldn't afford to lose what little entertainment value it had mustered. Something had to be done to counteract Mikan's nearly unstoppable offense. The league rules committee decided to widen the lane from six feet to twelve.

As a result, Big George's scoring average fell from 28.4 to 23.8 points per game, and he finished second in the scoring race behind Philadelphia's young jump shot specialist, Paul Arizin. "Actually, the rule change opened up the lane and made it more difficult for them to defense me," Mikan said. "Opposing teams couldn't deter our cutters going through the lane. It moved me out and gave me more shot selection instead of just short pivots and hooks. I was able to dribble across the lane and use a lot more freedom setting the shot up."

Beyond that, it meant a few more shots for Pollard and Mikkelsen, both of whom averaged more than fifteen points for the first time in their pro careers. Heading into his third season, Mikkelsen was starting to find himself. "Widening the lane opened the middle and allowed these marvelous one-on-one deals," he explained.

Each season when training camp opened, Slater Martin stood up and addressed the team in his Texas drawl. Had they all signed their contracts? he would ask. Then he would explain that the only way they could earn more money would be to win the championship, and the only way to win the championship was to feed the ball to number 99, Big George.

But with the lane widened, the Lakers wouldn't be able to depend on Mikan as much. Sid Hartman knew the team needed better outside shooting, and he knew where to find it. Sitting on Rochester's bench was six-foot-two Pep Saul, a two-handed set-shooting artist. "We had been rotating Pollard outside, but we needed better shooting," Hartman said.

The newspaperman knew that Les Harrison would never agree to trade or sell Saul to the Lakers. "He wouldn't give us anything," Hartman said. "We had a bitter, bitter rivalry." Instead, Hartman called coach Clair Bee of the struggling Baltimore Bullets and told him that he would give him $5,000 for Saul.

"Do you think I can get him from Harrison?" Bee asked.

"You can get him for about $1,500 and keep the change," Hartman told him.

Which Bee promptly did, sending Saul to the Lakers just a few days after acquiring him from Rochester. "Harrison was furious when he realized what had happened," Hartman said. "He went to the league and protested, but he couldn't do anything. It was a legitimate deal. Saul's outside shooting was just enough to open up our inside game. He helped us win three straight championships."

Minus their top young guard but $1,500 richer, the Royals resumed their annual battle with the Lakers. Once again, Rochester nosed Minneapolis aside in the regular season, this time by a single game. But the Royals again numbered among the Lakers' play-off victims, as Minneapolis met the New York Knicks for the championship.

In a surprise, the young Knicks forced the Lakers to a seventh game. Each year, the Lakers had to stage their play-off games in nearby St. Paul instead of the Minneapolis Auditorium because of a scheduling conflict. But for Game 7 on April 25 the auditorium was open, which spelled doom for the Knicks, who hadn't won in eleven tries there spanning four seasons. The Lakers won in a swirl, 82–65, giving quiet John Kundla his fourth championship.

FOUL, FOUL, FOUL

Fortunately for pro basketball, the Knicks and Lakers met again for the championship in 1953. Minneapolis won the Western Division regular season title with a 48–22 record. New York claimed the Eastern Division with a 47–23 finish, one game worse than the Lakers.

The '52–53 season had been a rough, foul-infested year for pro basketball, where strategy had moved toward fouling, as coaches attempted to play the percentages. Officials called an average of 58 fouls per game. Instead of shooting 1,500 or 1,600 free throws in a season, teams were shooting 2,300 or 2,400. It was ugly. And the play-offs were even worse. Boston and Syracuse engaged in a four-overtime battle featuring 107 fouls and 130 free throws. In that game, Bob Cousy scored fifty, but thirty of them came from the line. Through the maze of flailing arms and the steady shrill of whistles, New York somehow finished off Boston in the Eastern Division, and the Lakers escaped Fort Wayne in the Western.

Mikan's scoring average was down to 20.6 per game, second in the league behind Philadelphia center Neil Johnston. But Slater Martin had crept into double figures at 10.6 points, mostly by taking advantage of the defenses that always packed in around the Lakers' frontcourt. Martin would never take a shot unless it was an absolute necessity. Nevertheless, he hit .410 from the floor that season, eighth best in the league, an indication of just how many long set shots those old-timers took.

In the championship series, the Knicks quickly established that they had a new confidence and were out to accomplish something. They stayed with the Lakers through three-quarters of Game 1 in Minneapolis (played in a local armory, not the auditorium, because of another scheduling conflict). At that point, according to the old script, the Knicks were supposed to wither sometime in the fourth. Instead, they produced a thirty-point period that brought a surprise ending: 96–88, New York.

"We had had a tough time with Fort Wayne in the previous series and were a little weary," Kundla said of the defeat.

Just like that, the Lakers had lost their home-court advantage. The next night they evened the series with a 73–71 win. But with a change in the championship format, the next three games were to be played in New York, which left the Knicks and their fans thinking championship. "I can still see the clippings," Mikkelsen said. "The New York newspapers were all saying that the series wouldn't go back to Minneapolis. They were right. It didn't."

Mikan was an old hand at playing in the Big Apple, dating back to his college days and the doubleheaders in Madison Square Garden. "They sort of liked me in New York," he recalled. "And I liked New York. Even today when I travel, people will come up to me and say, 'I saw you play in the Garden.' "

In what the Lakers viewed as their sweetest championship, they blasted the Knicks three straight in New York's old Sixty-ninth Regiment Armory. The first half of Game 3 was tight, partly because Mikan was experimenting with a turnaround jump shot. For help in handling their center, the Lakers had employed DePaul coach Ray Meyer, an old friend of Hartman's, as a consultant. "Ray had tremendous control over Mikan," Hartman explained. "Ray didn't say much during the first half while George was working his jump shot. He just sat there. But in the locker room at halftime, he said, 'George, take that jump shot and stick it up your ass.' "

Properly admonished, Mikan ditched the jump shot and went back to the old drop-step. With that, the Lakers turned on a fourth-quarter blowout that ended 90–75. The Knicks fought back in Game 4, which turned into another foul fest. With twenty-eight seconds left and Minneapolis leading 69–67 the Lakers' Jim Holstein went to the line and missed. But Minneapolis rookie guard Myron "Whitey" Skoog controlled the rebound and scored for a 71–67 lead. Connie Simmons hit two free throws for the Knicks to bring it to 71–69, and New York even got a final shot to tie it. But Harry Gallatin missed with a hook, and suddenly the Knicks were down 3–1.

Kundla gave the team the next day off, so they toured Broadway's clubs after the game. Billy Eckstine was the music rage in those days, and Pollard, Mikkelsen, and Holstein liked to croon his sweet bass tunes to each other in the shower. That night, they caught him at a Broadway club. The singer finished his act and came over to their table, even bringing Count Basie along to chat. The Lakers dragged back to their hotel rooms about 4:30 A.M., and Kundla waited until game day before he made them sweat it out in a one-hour practice.

Game 5 was set for Friday, April 10. The Lakers opened a solid lead in the second, then stretched it to twenty points in the third, only to see it slip away when Mikan developed foul trouble early in the fourth. Perhaps that's where party time caught up with the Lakers. The Knicks pushed back, paring the lead from twelve to five, then down to 84–82 with under two minutes left. But all they could do was foul, and the Lakers made enough of their free throws to stay ahead. Plus, with a jump ball after every late foul (as was the rule then), Mikan controlled the outcome. That was enough for a 91–84 win and the Lakers' fifth title.

Which meant another trek to Broadway.

"That was an evening to remember," Mikkelsen said wistfully. "It was high-test stuff, even in those days."

Pollard recalled that only one local writer followed the team to New York, so at 4:00 A.M. they returned to their hotel to make a collect call to another reporter who had decided not to make the trip. "We just wanted to let him know what he had missed," Pollard said.

The Lakers' sweet memories didn't end with 1953, although they went into the 1954 season with Mikan sporting an array of battle scars. Over his amateur and professional career, he had suffered two broken legs, and broken bones in both feet, as well as fractures of his wrist, nose, thumb, and three fingers. He once figured that he had received a total of 166 stitches.

Quite simply, opposing teams found the only way they could stop him was to get rough.

"Nobody gave George anything," Pollard said. "He earned his baskets."

The beating had begun to take its toll on Mikan's game, as his scoring average dipped to 18.1 points (third in the league behind Neil Johnston and Bob Cousy). One constant that remained was the bickering among the stars. The Milwaukee Hawks had a preseason series with the Lakers in 1953. "We played 'em seven straight games in the preseason and lost all seven," former Hawks GM Marty Blake recalled. "In the seventh game we were leading by twenty points, and John Kundla put on a press. We lost, and our owner, Benny Kerner, had me go out and buy a ten-dollar trophy and give it to 'em."

The season opener that year was also against the Hawks, in Milwaukee, but the Lakers lost after Pollard and Mikan got into a shouting match in front of press row. Pollard recalled that Mikan failed to warn him about a pick, Pollard got whacked, and his man scored easily, leaving the two Laker stars screaming at each other as they ran back down the court. The next night they played in New York and the newspapers were filled with speculation that the Laker dynasty was coming to an end because of the feud.

Mikan and Pollard shared a laugh about the incident over breakfast, then went out and beat the Knicks soundly. "George and I were always very critical of each other, very frank," Pollard said. "But that helped our relationship, because nothing festered. We always got it off our chests."

This fussing duo first carried the Lakers to the league's best record, a 46-26 finish, and from there to the team's sixth championship in seven seasons, a spirited seven-game conquest of the Syracuse Nationals. It had been a great ride, but Mikan abruptly ended it after the season by announcing his retirement. Each season he had signed a one-year contract with the team. "We always sweated signing him at the end of every year," Hartman said. "His last year in the league he made $35,000."

But the center and the Lakers couldn't come to terms for the 1954–55 season, so at age twenty-nine he retired. Some observers said it was none too soon. The league adopted a twenty-four-second shot clock for the upcoming season, which didn't suit his style. Without him, Minneapolis finished 42–30, third best in the eight-team league, and still made it to the 1955 Western Finals, where they lost to Fort Wayne. Afterward, Pollard decided that he, too, should retire.

The team started badly in 1955–56, and Mikan decided to attempt a comeback in December. Frank Ryan, his law partner and agent, was negotiating a new contract with Max Winter and asked for $35,000. "I'd rather sell you my interest in the team for that kind of money," the general manager supposedly replied. Winter then left for his annual trip to Hawaii without wrapping up the deal. When owner Ben Berger heard about Winter's comment, he offered to lend Mikan the money to buy the GM out. Berger had long thought that Winter had gotten too much credit for the team's success. Mikan, who was strapped for cash at the time, took Berger up on the deal. He borrowed the money, bought out Winter, and resumed his playing career. With the sale of his stock, Winter left the team to play a major role in the development of the Minnesota Vikings as an NFL expansion franchise.

Mikan, however, later decided to sign the stock over to Berger and focused instead on playing himself into shape. He averaged about ten points over thirty-seven games, and it was obvious his best days were past. "It was stupid for him to come back," Hartman said. "He had taken a lot of punishment during his career. His knees were shot."

With its faster format, the pro game was racing off to a new level, leaving Mikan and his Lakers to exist in their own special amber. Yes, he had been a four-eyed, wavy-haired goon, but before age thirty he had mastered the pro game of his time, leading his teams to seven championships in eight seasons (including two National titles).

"Mikan ran the whole show," former Laker Larry Foust once observed. "He was an athlete despite what some people say about his bulk, and nobody ever had better offensive moves under the basket. When George played, he owned that lane."

THE TRADE NOT MADE

It was in the heart of Minnesota's bitter winter of 1956, with the Lakers struggling along, that Sid Hartman hatched his best and last idea for building the next great team. For the first time in its decade-old history, the team faced a losing season.

That, in turn, started Hartman to thinking. Why not lose in a big way and get the first pick in the draft that spring? The newspaper reporter knew that having once ruled the league with a strong center, the Lakers again needed a powerful player in the post. Only now, with a shot clock pacing the game, that center must have quickness and agility to go with his size. Hartman didn't have to ask his college coaching friends too many questions before he identified their candidate as the next great pro center: Bill Russell of the University of San Francisco.

Russell was six-foot-nine and ran the 440-yard dash in forty-nine seconds. Better yet, he was a shot-blocking terror who had led San Francisco to the 1955 NCAA championship (and was about to take the Dons to the '56 title as well). Pete Newell, then the University of California coach, and Hartman's other West Coast sources had told him that while Russell wasn't much of an offensive player, he was virtually changing the game with his defense.

To draft him, the Lakers would have to finish last. To finish last, they would have to get rid of Vern Mikkelsen, who in his seventh season had become a rebounding and scoring force. Hartman says that in January of 1956 he struck a deal with the Boston Celtics. The Lakers would trade Vern Mikkelsen for Boston's rights to three Kentucky players—Frank Ramsey, Lou Tsiropoulas, and Cliff Hagan—who were in the service but would be available for the 1956–67 season. Without Mikkelsen, the Lakers would surely finish last, Hartman figured.

But, according to Hartman, just before the transaction was made, then–Celtics owner Walter Brown asked Ben Berger if he could back out of it. The Celtics and Lakers had always enjoyed good relations, and Berger agreed, which left Hartman furious.

History clearly records that the Celtics badly wanted a rebounder at the time, but Celtics president Red Auerbach said he never would have made such a deal. Hartman, however, said that the two teams had even signed the papers to make it official.

John Kundla said that he clearly recalled the plans to trade Mikkelsen and that he lobbied Berger against it. Mikkelsen didn't want to leave Minneapolis, Kundla said. "And I would never have been in favor of losing games. I wanted to win games."

Hartman said he went so far as to contact Pete Newell to see if the Cal coach could ask Russell if he would play in Minneapolis. Hartman said that Russell, through Newell, indicated that he would like to be a Laker.

In a 1992 interview, Newell faintly remembered Hartman contacting him about the situation but didn't remember speaking with Russell. As things turned out, the Celtics made a deal during the 1956 draft that brought Russell to Boston, where he led the Celtics to eleven championships over thirteen seasons.

"We wanted to finish last. If we had traded Mikkelsen, we'd have finished last," Hartman said. "And we'd have had Russell. There'd be no Los Angeles Lakers today, no Boston Celtics mystique, if we had made that deal."

Hartman said that he left the team then, telling Berger, "You go get somebody else to run it."

"Berger decided to sell the team after that," Hartman said.

Bob Short, a local businessman, and a group of investors bought the Lakers for $150,000 the next season, and three years later they moved it to Los Angeles, leaving a distinguished but uncertain past in Minneapolis.

OLD TROPHIES

In the mid-1980s, a Los Angeles Lakers staffer was digging around in a storage room in the bowels of the Forum when he discovered several tarnished and broken trophies. They were literally in pieces, but the employee brought them out into the light and was startled to find that he was holding several league championship trophies from the days of the old Minneapolis Lakers.

What happened next is difficult to understand. Somehow, an undetermined party simply threw them away. Fortunately, someone at the Forum retrieved them from the garbage bin. Today the trophies have been restored and are in a private memorabilia collection in Los Angeles.

"Can you imagine that? That's unbelievable," said an obviously disturbed John Kundla when told about the trophies. "That hurts."

The incident is typical of the Minneapolis Lakers' plight. Today they are pro basketball's forgotten team, a dynasty without a city. As Lakers owner Jerry Buss once explained, the Lakers now mark their beginning from the time they moved to Southern California. What happened in Minneapolis belongs to Minnesota.

Or perhaps it belongs to no one.

The Minneapolis Lakers, if they're alive, are all old men now, inhabiting a world where they work their golf games in between doctor's appointments. Once every few years or so they steer their recreational vehicles down the highway to reunions, where they try to remember the old games and take turns fussing about the NBA's chintzy retirement benefits.

Sometimes, in a fit of guilt, they'll try to make amends for offenses committed forty years ago. Jim Pollard was getting ready for a Laker reunion in Minnesota in 1992 when he got a call from Blackie Towery of the old Fort Wayne Pistons.

"You still mad at me?" Towery asked cautiously, his voice on the phone suddenly spanning four decades with an olive branch.

Towery, the Pistons' enforcer, had once punched Pollard in front of the Fort Wayne bench and knocked him into the bleachers, setting off a brouhaha. Pollard had been furious at the time but laughed on the phone and later had fun telling the story to his teammates at the reunion.

Over the years Max Winter had often recalled the fracas. The little general manager, it seems, had gone to Pollard's aid. "I threw my best Sunday punch at him," Winter used to say. "He brushed me off and threw me into the second row, too."

These, of course, are mostly forgotten stories now. Like the old Lakers, they belong to no one in particular. Time and circumstances have slipped by, leaving the basketball they played in another age, one that few remember. And even fewer understand.

5

Chapel Hill

THE DEAN SMITH CENTER, UNIVERSITY OF NORTH CAROLINA, OCTOBER 29, 1992

Paul Ensslin awaited Magic Johnson in heaven. Blue heaven. That's just what it seems like, the University of North Carolina's Dean Smith Center, with its vast expanse of sky blue seats stretching way up there to the rafters. The Lakers' flight to North Carolina was late, and that worried Ensslin, the thirty-two-year-old sports editor of The *Chapel Hill News*. He had planned on interviewing Johnson ever since he learned the Lakers would play a Halloween night exhibition game against the Cleveland Cavaliers here in the Smith Center, better known as the "Dean Dome," ground zero of Carolina's "blue heaven" hoops cult. It was noonish on this Thursday, and the big building was empty, except for Ensslin and a small group of local writers awaiting the arrival of the Lakers for practice.

The game's publicist had just informed them that the team was coming to practice directly from the airport and that they would be an hour late. Ensslin was worried he wouldn't have enough time to interview Johnson. But the young editor did what sportswriters often do. He waited.

One of the *News*'s staff writers, Lee Weisbecker, was working on a story about Ricky Lumsden, a local middle school student with a brain tumor who idolized Magic and hoped to meet him and maybe even get a pair of his sneakers after the game. The paper's editors, Weisbecker later explained, saw this as a story with tremendous emotional appeal. A kid, with a terminal illness, getting a pair of shoes from Johnson, who himself might be dying before too long.

Ensslin, however, had another mission. He wanted to do a straight interview with Johnson about how a superstar coping with HIV infection makes a comeback in the NBA. Ensslin figured this might be the only chance he would ever get to talk with the Lakers guard. After all, you just didn't know how long a superstar like that would be around. Most of the other writers there were waiting to interview Sam Perkins and James Worthy, both of whom had played at Carolina. That, in fact, was the reason this preseason pro game was being staged in Chapel Hill, to draw on local interest.

At last the Lakers arrived, with Perkins and Worthy among the first players on the floor. Most of the writers immediately encircled them and began asking questions. Ensslin, though, waited for Johnson to appear. Then the young editor approached him and asked for an interview.

"Hang on a second," Johnson said, his shoes still untied. "Take care of this, John," he said to team public relations director John Black, who explained that Johnson would be happy to talk in a few minutes.

So Ensslin again waited.

Johnson, meanwhile, stretched and limbered up, then picked up a ball and dribbled around. This done, he sat down to tie his shoes. Finally he got up, walked over to Ensslin, and announced, "I'm ready."

The editor asked him how it felt to be back with the Lakers. "Basketball is my life," Johnson said, bouncing the ball between his legs. "It's what I love. It's my way to escape. There's no substitute for being on the court."

Ensslin went on to ask a number of questions, many of which Johnson had answered again and again over the three weeks since training camp in Hawaii. The main topic, of course, was AIDS, which was something he preferred not to discuss, Johnson explained. "Because of my celebrity status and my position as a role model, I can understand how people would want to talk about it. It wouldn't be right to totally ignore it, but I've tried not to let it affect me too much."

With the 1992 presidential election just five days away, the next logical issue was Johnson's protest resignation from President Bush's commission on AIDS. If Bush wins the election, what advice would you offer him? Ensslin asked.

"I'm not a political person, and I'm not one to give advice to the president," Johnson replied. "He's got his own agenda right now, and we'll just see what happens after Tuesday's election."

Johnson told Ensslin that he had tried to be a good spokesman for AIDS awareness, and the editor asked about the video Johnson had made with Arsenio Hall. Directed by Malcolm-Jamal Warner, the video had been roundly criticized. The Los Angeles Unified School District rejected it for use in schools because of distasteful content and a jumbled, overly long format. "It was not initially intended to go to the schools," Johnson said. "It was made for kids to watch at home with their parents. If some people find it shocking, well, AIDS is shocking."

The interview ran for fifteen minutes or so, during which Johnson said he was healthy, said he hoped to be a Laker for a few years to come, said he had responded to press reports of rumors of his bisexuality and didn't care to address the matter again.

Ensslin ran through all the topical issues and, as reporters often do when they sense an interview is winding to a close, he scrambled among his thoughts for another question. Then it just popped into his head. "There are questions you gotta ask," Ensslin explained later. "I think he was worried about it, so I asked it. He looked real belligerent when I did. He looked at me like he couldn't believe that I asked such a question. But why shouldn't I have asked it? I'll never get another shot at it."

Ensslin asked Johnson if he feared dying.

The player's face, so often amiable, turned suddenly hard. "Why should I?" he replied before turning away and abruptly ending the interview. "I just live, baby."

As Lakers public relations director John Black had feared, the media interest in Earvin Johnson had swollen with each passing day of the 1992–93 exhibtion season. At every turn, there were new questions to be answered. It soon became apparent that the only practical solution was to hold a press conference before each preseason game, which Johnson quickly came to detest. He longed for the way things were, the good old days, when he could have quiet time in the locker room before each game. Time to read fan mail. Time to think about the game. Time with his teammates. Time, even, for an occasional chat with a writer or two.

But that was all gone now, disappeared in a swirl of controversy.

In its place was the press conference. In every city, there was a new group of reporters with the same questions. Johnson, the smoothest of media creatures, who had always been comfortable with the limelight, was no longer comfortable. So far, the situation hadn't affected his on-court performance. But it hadn't helped either.

His first big step back had come October 16 in Honolulu's sold-out Neal Blaisdell Arena with the opening exhibition game of the 1992–93 season. Johnson played twenty-seven minutes and finished with fourteen assists, five points and four rebounds as the Lakers defeated the Portland Trail Blazers 124–112. A night later, the teams met again, but Johnson sat out and the Lakers lost by twenty-nine points. That, unfortunately, would emerge as something of a pattern in the preseason. When Johnson played, the Lakers won. When he didn't, they lost. Still, the exhibitions confirmed that Jerry West had assembled a deep roster. Johnson and Byron Scott had proven themselves one of the best backcourts in league history. Behind them were Sedale Threatt and Tony Smith and the rookies, Anthony Peeler and Duane Cooper. A. C. Green, Elden Campbell and newly signed veteran James Edwards were the backups in the frontcourt, where the starters— Worthy, Perkins, and Divac—were all healthy again after missing much of the '92 season with injuries.

Yet there was little doubt that everything depended on Johnson. His presence made the game so much easier for all the rest. Watching them in camp, the beat writers realized that this season could be very special for the Lakers. "With Magic back, they can be very good," said Mitch Chortkoff, who has covered the Lakers for years.

The Lakers returned home to play Philadelphia on October 20 in the first round of their annual preseason tournament, the GTE Everything Pages Shoot-out. Before the game, Johnson told a small group of writers that a well-known NBA player was smearing him around the league as a bisexual. Johnson said he had confronted the player twice and each time the player denied it. "If you're gonna be a man, be a man," Johnson told the writers. "If you're gonna say something behind my back, then when I come to you, be a man. Say you said it."

On the court that night, he again held form: fourteen assists, twelve points, and five rebounds. They won by twenty-seven, the only disappointment being that merely 12,600 showed up at the Forum to see Johnson's official homecoming after a year off. Although Johnson said little about the five thousand empty seats, the team's staffers sensed it hurt him. Over the past dozen years, the Forum regulars had come to consider his greatness routine. But if the fans needed a reminder, they received it the next night when he sat out and the Lakers lost to the Knicks.

Two nights later, the Lakers moved south to San Diego to play the Sacramento Kings. Again he played, this time passing out thirteen assists, and again they won, by sixteen. If nothing else, the exhibition games showed Johnson that his "game senses" had become dulled. All the pickup ball he had played, and even the Olympic competition, couldn't begin to prepare him. The players were so large and quick. To go against them, he needed his reflexes at their sharpest, but that would take time. In years past, he could often find a seam in the defense, then hit it quickly, squeeze his big body through, and make it to the basket. Now, those seams closed up before he got there. He had lost a step. Plus he had forgotten other little things, such as the touch it required to loft a shot over big defenders. In the past, he usually found a way to fool them. Now they blocked his shots.

By the time the Lakers reached San Diego on October 23 for an exhibition against the Sacramento Kings, news reports had identified Isiah Thomas as the prime suspect in slandering Johnson. Lon Rosen would later be accused of tipping off the press, which the agent strongly denied. Actually, the rumors themselves were an old item in NBA gossip circles. About three weeks after Johnson first announced his infection, Laker trainer Gary Vitti had gotten a call from another NBA player, a former Laker, who told Vitti that Isiah Thomas had phoned the player's teammate and told him that Johnson was bisexual. The former Laker had called Vitti to confirm it.

"I got a little nasty," Vitti said. "I told him, 'You know, if I had heard something like that, I would never, ever repeat it. If it's true—it's not—but if it is, so what?'

"This guy said, 'But I just thought you should know.' "

Vitti struggled with whether he should tell Johnson about the phone call and decided not to. First of all, he hadn't actually heard Thomas tell anyone anything. Second, he didn't want to unload more troubles on his friend. Johnson would find out soon enough, he figured. Later in the 1991–92 season, Vitti had dinner with then-coach Mike Dunleavy and learned that coaches from other teams had passed along details about the gossip to Dunleavy, who relayed them to Johnson. In Hawaii, after the issue spilled over into the news, the trainer told Johnson that he had heard about the rumors months earlier but had chosen not to pass them along. He said he knew the rumor wasn't true, and even if it was—Vitti reiterated that he knew it wasn't—it wouldn't matter anyway.

As if the Thomas news wasn't enough that morning in San Diego, the media swirl thickened yet again when Phoenix Suns president Jerry Colangelo told broadcaster Jim Lampley that Johnson should not play because other players feared his infection. Colangelo's opinion made big news. He was one of the league's most powerful figures, and he seemed dead set against Johnson's return.

That afternoon Lakers public relations director John Black and Johnson took a forty-five-minute limo ride to a *Sports Illustrated* photo shoot at the Sheraton Torrey Pines in La Jolla. On the way, they discussed Colangelo's opinion, and Black surmised that the Suns executive feared that Johnson's return meant the Lakers would again rule the Western Conference. Colangelo had traded for forward Charles Barkley in the off-season with the hope that Phoenix might finally win an NBA title. Johnson now threatened Colangelo's plans, so he was attacking, Black said.

"You're exactly right," Johnson said, putting up his hand for a high five.

Then the conversation turned to Thomas, and Johnson told Black how disappointed he was. Johnson said that he and Thomas were no longer really close, that their friendship had begun unraveling a few seasons back when the Lakers and Pistons met twice in the NBA Finals. In fact, he said, their closeness was more of a media creation than reality. (Yet the players themselves had fostered that notion by professing their friendship in numerous interviews. Beginning with Pat Riley in 1984, the Laker staff had always held a dim view of the Magic-Isiah friendship.)

"I think Earvin met Isiah at an All-Star Game, and over a weekend they took a crash course in friendship," Gary Vitti would later explain. The trainer quickly added that he didn't mean that Johnson and Thomas weren't friends, but that pro athletes were so different from everyday people. "They're different," Vitti said, "and you have to judge them differently. They come from a different frame of reference than we have. We created these people since they were kids. If you could play, we took care of you and gave you whatever you wanted."

Scholarships. Travel. Hotels. Meals. Acquaintances. Shoes. Clothing. Gifted athletes inhabit an insular world where they never hesitate to ask for things because they've been given everything. Although this "world" makes the athletes rich, it leaves them very insecure as to who their real friends are, Vitti said. "A lot of them have never experienced really, really true friendships. They're not really sure who their friends are because of who they are or what they are."

Herb Williams, however, considered both Johnson and Thomas close friends and had known them since their days playing Big 10 Conference basketball in college. He was a high-scoring freshman at Ohio State while Johnson was the freshman star at Michigan State. When their teams first met in Lansing, Johnson had come up to Williams after the game and offered to show him the town. That night, they toured all the local hot spots. "We just hung out," Williams said. "I had read a lot about Magic and was watching to see if he was ego-tripping. But he was just a regular, down-to-earth guy."

They discovered they had very similar backgrounds. Both were midwesterners from large families where the parents worked hard to keep ahead. Both of their fathers were auto workers, and their mothers had jobs in food service. "Family meant a lot to both of us," Williams said.

Their friendship grew and came to include first Mark Aguirre, another star from the Midwest, and later Thomas, who was two years younger than the others. Soon the four of them made a tight group that spent their off-seasons together looking for fun.

But it was Thomas who shared special circumstances with Johnson. They both had magnetic personalities; both were point guards, controlling the destinies of their teams. More important, both were emotional, and both were absolutely obsessed with winning. Other talented people talked about success, but a select few were completely dedicated to it. Magic and Isiah were.

As young pros, Johnson, Thomas, Aguirre, and Williams shared the same Chicago agent, George Andrews. They mixed business and pleasure, taking vacations together with wives and girlfriends, appearing at each other's camps and benefit games. Particularly Magic and Isiah. "I've seen how close they were and the different things they did together," Williams said. "When Isiah was dating his fiancée [his wife, Lynn], when he wanted to go see her, Earvin would go with him. He would stay in the hotel while Isiah was out there visiting with his fiancée. They was always together in the summertime."

The world was their playground. Carriage rides in Central Park. Beaches in Hawaii. Theme parks in Ohio. They were young and rich and could be wherever they wanted to be at the drop of a plastic card on an airline counter. But the best times were often simple. They would blast basket after basket in all-night pickup games on the court at Johnson's house. Or they'd gather in Lansing, where again the main course would be hoops, followed by a visit to the house of Dr. Charles Tucker, Johnson's longtime friend and adviser. There they'd relax in the basement with a cold beverage and attempt to be regular guys, as much as young millionaires could be. At night, they'd go to the local clubs, where crowds would gather around Isiah and Magic, while Williams and Aguirre would hang back, just out of the limelight, amazed at the swirl of humanity their friends could generate.

Isiah considered the older, more successful Johnson a mentor. Thomas wanted badly to lead the Pistons to a championship, and he would make late-night phone calls to Johnson on the West Coast, seeking advice on how to build a championship mentality among his teammates.

"I hate that I taught him," Johnson would say later, only half-jokingly. "That's the only thing. I should go back and kick myself."

For, if winning bonded Isiah and Magic, it also came between them. "What hurt that relationship more than anything else," Williams said, "were the championships. Once you win them, and as many as Earvin did, you become so big-time, you have so many people around you that do certain things for you."

Quite often these people aren't the best to deal with your friends because things get miscommunicated, Williams said.

Yet even after Johnson's Lakers beat Isiah's Pistons in 1988, the friendship seemed strong, Williams said. It was only after the Pistons beat the Lakers in 1989 that things began to sour. Obviously, Johnson didn't like losing, even to a friend. And the always emotional Thomas got caught up in his team's accomplishment. "It seemed like, 'You were the man. Now I'm the man. I don't need you,' " Williams said.

Lon Rosen thought the problems had actually begun during the 1988 Finals. Johnson and Thomas had kissed each other on the cheek as the series began (which led some misunderstanding souls to wonder if they weren't involved romantically). But the intense seven-game series soon led to hostility. In Game 4, which the Pistons won in a runaway, Johnson knocked Thomas to the floor, and Thomas leaped back up in his face.

Was their friendship over? reporters asked afterward.

"It was nothing personal," Thomas replied. "Just business."

"That's all it is," Johnson agreed when told of the comment. "It's business."

The next night, before Game 5, Thomas's son, Joshua Isiah, was born, and Johnson never phoned to acknowledge it, which hurt Thomas. That, Rosen said, was a big factor in the fraying of their friendship.

If that was the case, it didn't show in the off-season. "We love each other," Johnson declared later that summer.

But the frequency of their late-night conversations declined after that.

There was no way, Johnson would admit later, that their competition could not get in the way of their friendship. The next year when the Pistons came to Los Angeles to meet the Lakers for another championship, Thomas found that Johnson had changed his phone number. So he drove by Johnson's house and ran inside to speak with him. They talked about ten minutes. Johnson had an injured hamstring, and the Pistons were marching to the title, awkward circumstances for winners who would be friends.

One of their last truly friendly visits was at the All-Star Game in Orlando, when Herb Williams found them laughing and joking in Johnson's room. Johnson invited both of them to a party one of his friends was having, and they both showed up. But the crowd was large. Johnson sat in a private section, and Isiah sat there with him, seemingly wanting to visit, Williams said. "But Isiah had his wife and his mother with him, and I really don't know if he wanted to be in that situation. People kept crowding around and they really didn't have a chance to talk."

After a short time, Isiah left.

Six months later tales of their feud surfaced in the newspapers, and what was cool became frigid. Johnson told a small group of writers that the reason he was upset was that the player he suspected of talking—he wouldn't identify him as Thomas—was one who had spent a lot of time with him socially and knew that he wasn't bisexual. "Those guys know me," he said. "I'd been hanging out with them. That's what ticked me off. I don't know what I'm going to do about it."

Thomas, for his part, denied that he was the culprit. Privately, he told the Detroit sportswriters he trusted that there was no way he would spread rumors about Johnson, because those same rumors concerned him and were related to their pregame bussing before the 1988 Finals tip-off. Those reporters liked to think they knew Thomas and could tell if he was lying. Those reporters told others that they thought Isiah was telling the truth, that he hadn't spread the rumors.

"I didn't hear Isiah say anything," Herb Williams said. "I just heard people say that when they heard Earvin had the virus, the first thing that popped into their minds was, *Is he gay? Well, him and Isiah was real tight, so what about Isiah?* So then Isiah said, 'We're not that tight.' "

It seems that Isiah's denial somehow got twisted into the rumor, Williams said. "That made things pull apart. Even if he didn't say it, once things hit the papers, somebody should have called. Either Earvin should have called him or Isiah should have called. They should have talked it over, because the first thing Earvin thought, 'Man, this is my friend. Me and Isiah were tighter than anybody.' For him to say something, that's got to really hurt, especially at a time when you need somebody.

"If this had happened a few years ago, if people had said what they said, either Isiah or Magic would have gotten on a plane and flown to the other one," Williams said. "They would have sat down and talked it out. And when they left everything would have been straight. . . . But when you win championships, the people around you, you don't know whether they're for real or not. I think that's what happened more than anything else. The people around them kind of tore them apart, because they didn't sit down and talk when the frustration first started. And that's a shame. Because it's hard to find a good friend, and when you do, you shouldn't let anything come between you, especially nothing petty like he said, or she said, or whatever."

After whipping the Kings in San Diego, the Lakers headed east for their final three exhibition games, the first being another meeting with the Kings in St. Louis. Johnson, however, passed on this game and instead flew to Chicago with his wife and Rosen for a taping of the "Oprah Winfrey Show." The appearance marked the opening of his promotional efforts for his new book, *My Life*. His unofficial agenda was to defend his sexuality, and the book provided a good basis for that with a brief account of his many encounters. This would soon prove to be a disaster, because in several key interviews Johnson told far more than the book revealed. "He was surrounded by so much controversy it destroyed the hero," Gary Vitti said later. "I mean the hero is still there, but for a lot of people it has been destroyed. When he started talking about six women at a time on the Oprah Winfrey show and stuff like that, he lost a lot of people.

"He felt he had to say these things about six women," Vitti said. "He felt he needed to defend himself. He didn't want people to think he was gay."

Lon Rosen remembered sitting horrified as Johnson launched into similar detail during an interview with ABC's "PrimeTime Live." The agent saw an unusual face on his friend and client that night. "He looked so sad," Rosen said. "I felt really bad for him."

They had discussed the need for Johnson to limit what he said about his affairs, but he was his own man. The spontaneity with the media that had served Johnson so well over the years suddenly became a terrible problem as he went into explanations and descriptions of his behavior. "He said it," Rosen said, "and I knew it was gonna cause a lot of shit."

Shortly thereafter, Rosen informed Random House, the publisher, that Johnson would have to discontinue his promotional efforts. Other things were planned, but the publicity wasn't in Johnson's best interest.

In Chicago, while they were waiting to tape the Winfrey show, Rosen and Johnson again read of Colangelo's criticism of his return. Johnson was puzzled because he had always considered the Suns' president a friend. Yet now Colangelo was attacking him, campaigning against him. He handed the newspaper to Rosen, who was furious about the comments. He phoned

Russ Granik, the league's deputy commissioner, and asked him to step in.

Granik, in turn, contacted Colangelo but had no luck in quieting him. Granik phoned Rosen back and said that Colangelo had a right to speak his mind.

"They couldn't stop him," Rosen said.

At first, Johnson planned to skip the Lakers' games in St. Louis and Memphis, making only the final exhibition stop in Chapel Hill. However, he changed his mind and announced that he would play in Memphis against the Bullets, which prompted a sellout in St. Louis based on speculation that he might play there, too. He didn't, but the Lakers won for the first time without him. Then they won with him in Memphis, and good feelings about their prospects abounded.

But the baggage Johnson carried to North Carolina had left him weary. That Thursday night after his encounter with Ensslin he phoned Rosen and said he didn't want to practice the next morning.

Early Friday, Rosen got a call from Jerry West. "Something's up," West said. "Earvin didn't go to practice."

Vitti and new coach Randy Pfund also called. The trainer was particularly concerned. Since Johnson's return, Vitti had taken extra caution, making sure that the star stayed away from any teammate with a cold. He didn't want anything to tax Johnson's immune system.

Rosen assured all of them nothing was wrong. "He just wanted a break," he explained. "He didn't want to deal with the press today."

Before the game that night, Johnson had to attend a reception hosted by SkyBox, the trading card company. He arrived on time and happily schmoozed with the corporate guests. But afterward came yet another pregame press conference. Much as he disliked it, Johnson pushed ahead. About two dozen reporters awaited him in the Smith Center's pressroom.

What had amazed him about his return? asked the first questioner. "The most amazing thing is that everything you say now will be printed," Johnson said, laughing hard at his answer.

Is dealing with the virus a problem? "I just live with it, and just go on," he replied. "People make a bigger thing of it than I do. I don't think about it. I just go."

"Did you anticipate the media attention being this big with your return?" he was asked.

"You really didn't know," he said, his reply interrupted by a gargantuan sneeze. "Excuse me. I've been dealing with the media for a long time. Whatever happens really doesn't surprise me. They have a job to do. Everybody wants a story. So be it. I'll deal with it. It's fine. Because once you hit the floor, it's all about basketball. I can do this now, but another 45 minutes from now I'll be doing something I love to do."

Another writer asked, "Do you have anything left to accomplish in basketball, now that you've won an Olympic medal, NBA titles, and an NCAA championship? What you're doing now, is it just to be playing, or are you making a statement about the HIV virus?"

"I'm making a statement, but I'm also playing to win the NBA championship," he said. "I just don't play basketball to play it. I play to win, and I've always played to win. I only know how to do that."

After that, John Black ended the session, saying that Johnson would be available after the game.

"He was composed," one writer said afterward, sounding surprised. "Very composed."

The game began just like hundreds of other Laker road games. Ready to broadcast, Chick Hearn sat courtside, his left hand on his stopwatch as he read over stats. As usual, Magic Johnson examined the game ball, bouncing it near the Laker bench, rolling it in his fingers, then pausing to eye its roundness. Satisfied, he passed it to official Dick Bavetta at midcourt. Then came the player introductions, and as usual, the applause for Johnson was the loudest. But it was far from deafening on this Halloween night. The 21,500-seat arena had 9,000 unsold seats. Exhibition pro games, even with Michael Jordan on the bill, seldom do well in Chapel Hill.

Those who did attend quickly realized it was not one of Magic Johnson's best nights. First, he tried his "Junior skyhook" over Cleveland's Craig Ehlo; it rolled off the rim. Moments later, Worthy broke open on the wing and called for the ball, "Whew! Whew!" Johnson shoveled an underhand three-quarter court pass that just missed Worthy's outstretched fingers and sailed into the end zone. Johnson grimaced and snapped his fingers.

About midway through the first period, he attempted to back Ehlo down near the goal. Working from the right side, Johnson reversed left and right while Ehlo leaned in and snatched at the dribble. Going to his left, Johnson suddenly whirled about-face, and Ehlo hit his right forearm. Foul. As he walked to the free throw line, Johnson examined first one arm, then the other.

Watching from the bench, free agent Sean Higgins told Gary Vitti that Johnson had gotten scratched. So the trainer caught the attention of official Ed Rush in front of the Laker bench. "Ed, you oughta check Magic," Vitti told him. "Somebody on our team thinks he has an open wound."

Rush then halted the free throw proceedings to examine Johnson's arms. Obviously annoyed at this intrusion, Johnson told Rush he didn't have any injury. After looking at his arms, the official agreed and walked back over and told Vitti, "Gary, he doesn't have anything."

"Fine," Vitti said. "I'm just telling you what I was told."

Moments later, during a time-out, Vitti decided to examine Johnson's right arm himself. "He sits down," the trainer recalled. "I get kinda nosy. I turn his arm over. I see this small scratch. No bigger than a fingernail. I could easily have looked the other way. But you're supposed to cover open wounds. I pull a 4-by-4 gauze pad out of my jacket pocket. I hand it to Magic. I said, 'Put this on your arm and wipe away the perspiration.' I got a cotton-tip applicator and sprayed some benzoin on it, which is a sticky, adhesive substance. I painted his arm with it. Never put my fingers on the wound. Yeah, I held his arm, but I never put my fingers on the side of the wound. I made it sticky so we could put a bandage over it. Then he went back out and played."

With about three minutes left in the half, Vitti decided to put a sweatband over Johnson's small, clear bandage as additional protection. Later, the Occupational Safety and Health Administration would cite Vitti for a safety violation for failing to wear latex gloves during the bandaging. "I didn't forget to put the gloves on," Vitti explained later. "I chose not to. It was a nonbloody wound in a controlled situation, one that was so small the official couldn't see it.

"There was a lot of controversy about players playing with Magic. I felt this was the perfect opportunity to make a statement. If I put the gloves on, that would have sent a mixed message to all of these players. 'Gary, you're telling us to play with Magic Johnson because we can't get HIV. But now he has this fingernail scratch. It's a nonbloody wound and you're putting gloves on? Now if I can't get it, why are you putting those gloves on? What are you trying to say? It's okay if he bleeds on me, but not on you?' "

This whole scenario played itself out with most people in the arena failing to notice. Neither public relations director John Black nor the Laker broadcasters noticed it. Nor did most of the reporters in attendance. Photographer Brad Isbell on the baseline took pictures of Johnson receiving treatment, but outside of that, little attention was paid to it. (According to Lon Rosen, Johnson had gotten cut during the Olympics, another small cut on his finger, covered by a Band-Aid, and no one even noticed.)

Properly bandaged, Johnson continued play, but the results were mixed at best. Early in the third period, he zipped a pass the length of the court, right into a seam in the defense, to find Worthy breaking for an easy slam. But moments later he rifled a no-looker to Worthy in the post and caught him unaware. "Shit," Johnson muttered as he hustled to get back on defense.

A little later, he spied Perkins flashing open in the lane and attempted to push a pass over the top of the defense. Another miss. Johnson paused there, shaking his head and gazing in dismay into the upper empty seats of Blue Heaven.

Having missed all but one of his shots, he again attempted to back down inside for an easy score in the fourth period. He faked one way and pivoted the other, but the shot fell off. "God!" Johnson yelled in disgust. Rookie Alex Blackwell, hustling to make the team, rose up and slammed home the miss.

With Johnson playing 28 minutes and making just one of 10 shots, the Lakers lost. Afterward, a crowd jammed the hallway outside the dressing rooms, and about two dozen media people waited inside for Johnson to finish dressing. "I'm ready," he said after about five minutes, still barefoot.

"Were you a little frustrated out there tonight?" asked Leonard Laye of the *Charlotte Observer.*

"Just short. Too short," Johnson said. "It seems to happen sometimes when you've been on the road for a week. You shoot everything short. A lot of 'em I should have made."

"How's your conditioning?" someone else asked.

"I'm in shape," he said. "Everything's ready to go. Kind of tired of exhibition, ready to get the real deal going."

It was an easy group to talk to. The reporters, just about all of them from basketball-crazy Carolina, wanted to quiz him about hoops. He was asked about his eagerness for the start of the regular season a week away, was asked about the 15 pounds he had added with weight lifting, about plans for him to play forward, about the team's experimenting with the lineup.

Finally, someone mentioned his arm. "You kinda got nicked a little on the arm?" a writer said. "Is that a problem at all?"

"No. No-o-o-o," Johnson said. "Everybody, anybody who gets cut, not just me, anybody, you just go, get it fixed. Boom. Come right back."

"Nothing special to worry about?" the writer asked.

"No," he said. "That's everybody. Not just me. Everybody in the league."

Impatient with this silliness, someone else asked Johnson to evaluate the preseason. Then another writer wanted him to compare his Michigan State team with Duke's national champions. After that, someone wanted his analysis of the upcoming NBA season. Then came more questions about the development of the team, followed by a request that he talk about the great 1979 game Michigan State had played against North Carolina in Chapel Hill. He rolled sweetly and expansively over these subjects.

Finally, another question brought him back to the unpleasantries at hand. "Does the controversy take some of the luster off your comeback?" he was asked.

"Naw," he said. "No. You gotta remember something. People are gonna have their own opinions, and so be it. But once Friday [the regular season] starts, it doesn't matter. I'm out here tonight. Boom. I'll be out there Friday night, and once you play all that will die down. Everybody needs something to write about right now. It's exhibition time."

"In fact, it's probably good it happened at exhibition time," a writer suggested.

"Yeah, it's good," Johnson said, not sounding convinced. "But it's gonna happen. I knew it when I decided to come back, because even mentioning about coming back, people had their own opinions even then. It's fine. You know, I've handled everything in my life. The majority of it's been good. Ninety percent of it good, 10 percent of it bad."

"You've said God chose you to be the person to do this," another writer said. "Do you still feel that way about coming back? That a lesser person, a lesser talent, couldn't have pulled it off like you have?"

"It's been tough," he admitted. "First of all, I'm a strong person. Second of all, I was already financially secure. So you had both of those things working. Anybody else, it was gonna be a problem, see. The best about all of this, I own both of my houses. No mortgage. Everything that comes in to me is mine. When it happened, it wasn't like, 'Oh, man, what am I gonna do now?' It was none of that. I just ran my businesses. Just like when I retire, I'll step into the suits. I'll have to wear a suit every day. That's the only difference."

Then he was asked what kind of impact he'd have as the first NBA player with HIV. "The impact will be just that. Just that. I'm just happy it was me," he said, bubbling into a clear, perfect laughter, almost like a baby chuckling in a crib.

"I'm like a guinea pig," he added, his voice turning suddenly serious. "I like challenges. It's fun. It's no fun when you don't have challenges. This is one of them."

Then he was asked about the rising percentages of heterosexual HIV infection. The gay community had gotten the message out to its members about protection, he said. "Now it's just us being blinded by whatever it is."

It was his role to fight that blindness, he said, and playing basketball helped him do it. "Look at this. I'm in North Carolina right now. Boom. The message is out. I'm here. I'm playing. I'm talking to you. Boom. It'll be in the papers tomorrow. Next time I'll be in Philly. I'm gonna be in Cleveland. In Chicago. See? So the message gets out even bigger."

Playing in the Olympics helped broadcast the message? someone asked.

"Oh, man," Johnson said. "That's the whole forum. That's what I wanted. So I got the whole forum."

"We educated them," he said, his eyes gleaming.

Team officials ended the session moments later and ushered the media out of the locker room. Most of his teammates had dressed quietly and gone to the bus. There waiting in the background in his wheelchair was Ricky Lumsden, the boy with the brain tumor. His sad face brightened a little when a team assistant handed him a pair of shoes. A family friend would later declare that Lumsden got "Magic Johnson's last shoes," which would create something of a controversy because a Smith Center employee would claim that he got the shoes, snatched 'em away right in the locker room.

Who could tell? Even Earvin Johnson didn't know which were which. He simply finished dressing, gathered his things together, and hurried out into the night, leaving his playing career behind.

Later, after it happened and they were all stunned again, the Laker staffers and players would look back, searching for a clue. PR director John Black thought of the airport in Dallas. Because the team's charter plane was in for repairs, the Lakers had spent the preseason traveling on commercial airlines. So they had gotten up early that Saturday morning to catch a flight home and had changed planes in Dallas. When Johnson traveled, he usually avoided the crowds and autograph hounds. In the old days, when they always flew commercially, he would sit by the window in first class with stone-faced James Worthy on the aisle in hopes that this would put off people from bothering him. He would avert his gaze out the window so that no one could catch his eye. On the preseason commercial flights, he had again used Worthy as a screen. In the airports, the players always found an out-of-the-way place to play cards while they waited.

But in Dallas on this first Saturday of November, Johnson left the protected area and stepped out to accommodate the fans. Soon there were dozens of people waiting for autographs.

His teammates quickly grew impatient. C'mon Earvin. Let's play.

Go on without me, he said, signing every scrap of paper in sight. In the past when he signed, he tried not to pay attention, because the conversations could drag on and he could become overwhelmed. But on this day, he looked at all of them, taking in each and every sweet, wide eye. Smiling. Chatting. Squeezing the Positive right out of his fans.

"That's really weird," Black remembered thinking.

That night, after he got home, Earvin Johnson phoned Lon Rosen and told him he was retiring. Again. For good.

The agent was stunned. "If you're retiring because you got cut, you're a chickenshit," he told Johnson.

"No, it's not that," Johnson said. "It's no fun."

The controversies, the hassles. It wasn't right for him. Plus he could see that his presence was changing the game. Because players from other teams feared him, they might not play as hard as they could. And that would hurt the game, he told Rosen. Above all, he didn't want to hurt the game.

Johnson said he didn't want to let down all the children with HIV. He knew how many had written him and told him they were counting on him to keep playing. As long as he played, he knew they could play, because other kids wouldn't have an excuse for keeping them out.

"But I can't play," he told Rosen. "It's no fun."

They agreed to meet at a quiet restaurant that Sunday morning for breakfast. They had just gotten seated at one of their favorite little eateries when a man sitting nearby said, "Magic, I just got my season tickets. I'm so glad you're back."

This isn't going to be easy, Rosen thought.

The agent waited around that day, thinking that maybe Johnson would change his mind. By 4:00 P.M. it was clear that wasn't going to happen. So he phoned Jerry Buss and told him.

"Is he sure?" Buss asked immediately. "Has he talked about it? Maybe he's just reacting to the cut."

The agent and owner talked at length, and at last Buss realized the decision was firm. "Look," he said, "if this is what Earvin wants . . ."

Next Rosen phoned Russ Granik, the NBA's number-two man.

Talk him out of it, Granik said.

So Rosen again phoned Johnson to see if he was absolutely sure.

"I'm sure," Johnson replied.

That Sunday morning, forward Karl Malone of the Utah Jazz was quoted in the *New York Times* as saying he was concerned about playing against someone infected with HIV. The news of Johnson's decision and Malone's quotes would swirl in the media, causing some people to mistakenly think that Malone's comments helped force Johnson from the league.

Malone's opinions only reinforced his decision, Johnson would explain later.

Through Rosen, he released a statement: "It has become obvious that the various controversies surrounding my return are taking away from both basketball as a sport and the larger issue of living with HIV for me and the many people affected. After much thought and talking it over with Cookie and my family, I decided I will retire—for good—from the Lakers."

A big part of the problem, he would say, was the fear he saw in the eyes of the Cleveland players after he was cut.

There was no fear in my eyes, the Cavaliers' Ehlo said.

However, Cleveland's Gerald Wilkins readily admitted he didn't like playing against an HIV-positive opponent.

Vitti, though, said the controversy was just a part of the equation. Johnson had forgotten how difficult life is in the NBA, the trainer said. "Then all of a sudden training camp starts and training camp's a bitch. We're all over the place, and he's not playing quite as well as he thought he would. . . . It was like, 'This isn't that great anyway. And on top of it, these guys don't wanna be with me. So what am I doing this for?' And then boom. He just quit."

Without Magic Johnson, the Lakers opened the season against their crosstown rivals, the Clippers, that Friday, November 6, and Byron Scott hit a

15-foot jumper in overtime to give Randy Pfund his first win as a head coach.

Johnson, meanwhile, had other battles to fight. That morning he had been greeted by news reports that a Michigan woman, a lover from his past, had filed a $2 million lawsuit against him, claiming that he had infected her with HIV in 1990. The woman also claimed that she had first notified Johnson that she was infected during the summer of 1991. This, of course, raised serious questions about just when Johnson had learned of his infection.

Johnson, through his lawyer, admitted that he had had sex with the woman. But he said he didn't know whether she gave the infection to him or he to her. Ultimately, the courts would rule in Johnson's favor on many of the major issues in the case. But on this first Friday in November, his public image had taken another serious blow.

That night, he held yet another press conference at the Sports Arena before the Lakers game. "I definitely want to come back," he said, "but I won't. . . .

"It's a different hurt this year. After going through training camp and knowing what we had on paper as a team, it's more difficult than last season. Am I at peace? I probably won't be until a month or two into the season when I know I'm out."

He spoke in a crowded side room just as the game was set to begin. The national anthem blared in the background. "I'll never disappear," he promised as the session closed. "I don't know how to. I love to live. When you disappear, you stop living."

6

Elgin: The Soul of a New Machine

MINNEAPOLIS, 1957

Bob Short and Frank Ryan scrambled to buy the Minneapolis Lakers in 1957, only to realize after the deal was done that they had hitched themselves to a wild ride, the kind that could make or break them. Years later, after they had salted away their millions, they could scoff at their folly. But at the time it was no laughing matter. Rather, it was a gut-twisting spin through a financial house of horrors, complete with lawsuits, judgments, indecent exposure allegations against a star player, a plane crash landing, and countless other tingling moments of drama.

When he first got started in pro basketball, Bob Short only wanted the fame, fortune, and fun associated with owning a team. Little did he know all the extra thrills that came with the territory. But Short was built for rough terrain. "He'd give you the shirt off his back and fight you for a nickle," Frank Ryan said of his partner. Some associates thought you were more likely to get the fight than the shirt, but nobody doubted Short's acumen. "Bob was a very aggressive, outspoken individual," recalled Jim Pollard. "If you knew what you were talking about, you could challenge him. But if you didn't, he'd shove you in a corner."

The son of a Minneapolis fireman, Short burned with all sorts of ambitions and was willing to work 14 hours a day to reach them. He had served as an assistant U.S. attorney in Minnesota after earning his law degree from Georgetown University in the 1940s. From there he moved into the murky world of the trucking business. His drive and the money he made there helped him become a force in the Minnesota Democratic party. He would launch an unsuccessful bid to become lieutenant governor in 1966 and would serve as the national treasurer for Lyndon Johnson's presidential campaign. Yet even politics couldn't compare to the strange intrigue Short found in the nascent NBA in 1957.

He had wanted a pro sports team in the worst way and had looked at the possibilities of football and baseball, which were nil. Then he and Ryan, an old classmate and friend from the University of Minnesota, learned that Ben Berger was hoping to sell the Lakers to out-of-town interests. Berger was quoted in a newspaper article as saying that he would give local buyers a week to put together an offer. Otherwise, the Lakers would go.

Within days, Short and Ryan had pulled together a group of 30 investors and offered Berger $150,000. That was good enough, and in a blur Bob Short found himself at the controls of a strange machine. The investors quickly named Short team president and formed a 12-member executive board to oversee operations. Their first move was to boot John Kundla upstairs as general manager and hire George Mikan as coach.

The big jolt came shortly thereafter. Forward Clyde Lovellette, the team's leading scorer and rebounder, was accused of exposing himself to a woman at a popular St. Paul nightclub. A future Hall of Famer, Lovellette would go into law enforcement after his playing days and become known as a born-again Christian. But at the time, Kundla and the new owners feared a public relations disaster. Without questioning Lovellette about the incident, Kundla quickly shipped him to the Cincinnati Royals in exchange for the first pick in the 1958 draft and veteran Ed Fleming.

The new owners then used the pick to draft Rodney Clark Hundley, better known as "Hot Rod," out of West Virginia University, where he had been a showboat, flipping behind-the-back passes and infuriating opponents with his dribble-king routine. Once, late in a game, he had even shot hook shots for free throws. "They thought Hundley would have fan appeal," Kundla said of Short and the new owners. "They were desperate to make it entertaining."

Few disagreed that the Lakers needed something. The team's attendance had plunged since the twilight of the Mikan glory years. "There's such a thing as winning too much," Sid Hartman observed. "People in Minneapolis seemed to lose interest when the Lakers dominated the league every year."

Upon acquiring the Lakers, the new owners threw $50,000 into the team coffers for operating capital. It disappeared in two weeks, creating an immediate need to trim overhead. So Kundla sent 7-foot center Walter Dukes to Detroit. With the frontcourt stripped of Lovellette and Dukes, the Lakers soon headed into a downward spiral, losing games and money.

In his first pro game, rookie forward McCoy Ingram, a 6-foot jumping jack, got the ball after a jump ball and promptly shot it into the opponent's goal. That proved to be typical of what would become a season of confusion for the Lakers. On many nights, attendance in the 10,000-seat Auditorium totaled no more than 900. As the gate receipts went down, the unpaid bills stacked up. Soon the club faced judgments and court actions totaling $40,000, forcing Short to call an investors' meeting at the club's offices. He walked in with a cashier's check for $40,000 and offered to purchase a block of the team's stock that had been authorized but unissued. The other

Left: John Kundla, the Minneapolis Lakers' first coach, led the team to five league championships. *(Naismith Memorial Basketball Hall of Fame)*

Below: At 6'10", center George Mikan was such a dominant force that the foul lane was widened to help negate his strength. He was basketball's first true "big man." *(Naismith Memorial Basketball Hall of Fame)*

Right: Minneapolis forward Jim Pollard teamed with Mikan in a potent Lakers offense. *(Naismith Memorial Basketball Hall of Fame)*

Below: Vern Mikkelsen was a bruising rebounder and scorer at forward for Minneapolis. *(Naismith Memorial Basketball Hall of Fame)*

Fred Schaus coached the great Los Angeles teams of the early 60s, but fell short four times to the Celtics in the championship series. *(Naismith Memorial Basketball Hall of Fame)*

"Hot Rod" Hundley was a flashy ballhandler and entertainer, and later a Lakers broadcaster. *(Naismith Memorial Basketball Hall of Fame)*

Right: Elgin Baylor. *(Naismith Memorial Basketball Hall of Fame)*

Below: Jerry West defends against Hal Greer. *(Naismith Memorial Basketball Hall of Fame)*

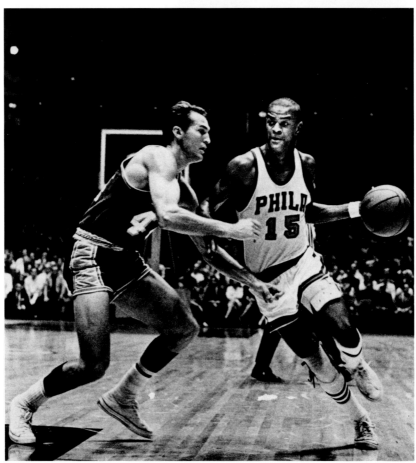

Rudy La Russo. *(Naismith Memorial Basketball Hall of Fame)*

Forward Harold "Happy" Hairston. *(Los Angeles Lakers)*

Wilt Chamberlain dunks. *(Naismith Memorial Basketball Hall of Fame)*

Owner Jerry Buss. *(Los Angeles Lakers)*

Broadcaster Chick Hearn.
(Los Angeles Lakers)

Three key Lakers of the early 1980s: Michael Cooper (left), Jamaal Wilkes (below, left), and Norm Nixon (below, right). *(Los Angeles Lakers)*

investors were asked if they wanted to buy the stock to cover the debts. None did, so Short paid up, pushing his interest in the club to near majority status while diluting the other investors' holdings. Three years later, a group of investors would sue Short and Ryan over the move. Short would pay nearly $500,000 to settle the case, which left him and Ryan as the team's sole owners.

But in 1957, Short's $40,000 was badly needed, and even that wasn't nearly enough.

As the losses mounted, one investor complained that with Mikan's low-key coaching style, the bench seemed mighty quiet. How about getting the subs to do a little cheering? the investor asked.

The question was good for a laugh. The roster was stocked with notorious partiers, led by veteran guard Bob "Slick" Leonard, Dick Garmaker, Corky Devlin, and Hundley. Hundley and Leonard had teamed up in training camp as a pair who liked to drink, smoke, and run around all night. Mikan, who missed his playing days, wanted to run around with them, but Leonard and Hundley declined, pointing out that having the coach along just wouldn't be fun. The Lakers' road trips were dominated by marathon late-night poker games. "There was a lot of gambling," Kundla said. Mikan lost so much money to Leonard that it was he who named the player "Slick," Hundley said.

And when the Lakers weren't gambling, they were barhopping. Hundley seemingly knew every hot spot in every city. One Friday night in St. Louis, Bob Short saw Hundley standing in front of the team's hotel waiting for a cab to take him off to another good time. Knowing that the Lakers had a game the next afternoon and that Hundley needed his rest, Short tried to get the player to stay in his room. "Hey, you guys go on up to your room," Short said. "I'll send a woman up. You can take care of your business and then go on to bed and get some rest for tomorrow."

"Bob, you know I don't work that way," Hundley said, draping his arm around Short's shoulder. "The thrill is in the chase, baby."

Finally, after a night of partying, Hundley and Leonard missed a flight from New York to Syracuse. Furious, Short called them both in. Hundley met with the owner first. Short explained that he was fining them $1,000 each in an effort to get them to tone down.

Waiting outside Short's office on pins and needles, Leonard asked Hundley, "What did they hit us with?"

"The big one," Hundley replied.

Damn, Leonard said. A hundred bucks.

Hundley laughed.

Leonard made only $9,000 and Hundley $10,000 yearly. Short promised that if they behaved they'd get their money back at season's end. Hundley had to think about it. Was giving up his good times worth it?

By midseason, the Lakers' record stood at 9–30, and the executive committee decided it was time to fire Mikan. To bear the bad news, the committee dispatched Kundla to St. Louis, where the team was playing a road game. The move left Big George fuming, but the owners softened the blow by promoting him to general manager as Kundla closed out the season on the bench. "They just traded jobs," Hundley said. The Lakers went 10–23 down the stretch to finish at 19–53, worst in the league.

Two seasons after Sid Hartman had wanted the Lakers to finish last in order to get the first pick in the draft, they finally reached his objective, discovering in the process that being at the bottom didn't necessarily mean the view was up.

BAYLOR TIME

The draft prize claimed by the Lakers for their descent into purgatory was one Elgin Baylor, who supposedly had gotten his surname at birth when his father glanced at his wristwatch and liked the sound of the name on the face. "Elgin has more moves than a clock," his college coach, John Castellani, once said of Baylor. Time, it seems, was the reigning motif of his style of play. Michael Jordan and Julius Erving would later gain notoriety for their "hang time," that mysterious ability to jump and remain in the air, to "hang," while gliding to the hoop. But it was Baylor who possessed the original commodity. Driving to the basket, he would leave the floor, often not quite sure what he wanted to do, simply relying on his hang time to open his options. Because he was an excellent passer, he could usually find someplace to put the ball for a teammate. Failing that, he could resort to a lay-up (he seldom chose to dunk). The implication here is that Baylor was a gliding featherweight. Not so. He was 6-foot-5 and 225 pounds, a powerful rebounder with another special gift for following his own shots and correcting the misses. Hot Rod Hundley, today a broadcaster for the Utah Jazz, likes to tell people that Baylor was a shorter version of Karl Malone.

In Baylor resided the grace and creativity of Jordan with the bull power of Malone. "He just might be the best player I ever saw," said Laker broadcaster Chick Hearn. "He was doing things that Dr. J. made famous 20 years later, the hang time and so forth. But Elgin didn't have the TV exposure. Nobody did in those days."

"Baylor was really the first to have body control in the air," Hundley said. "He'd hang there and shoot these little flip shots."

Added to Baylor's dynamic mix was the curiosity of his nervous tick, a twitching of his face, which Hearn liked to describe as a "built-in head fake," leaving defenders confused as Baylor headed around them to the basket. Kundla said that soon after Baylor's arrival in Minnesota, schoolboys across the state were attempting to emulate the twitch. Visiting at Laker practice one day, one of Baylor's college teammates greeted him, "Hey, Elgin, you still shaking the leaves off your head?"

Baylor saw a doctor about the condition and was told that it was simply a nervous reaction, nothing to worry about. Kundla first noticed it one day when Baylor was late for practice. The coach asked why, and the nervous rookie began twitching. The condition also negated Baylor's poker face. Every time he got a great hand he twitched, and his teammates folded. But mostly the condition was a factor on the court, where the player with "more moves than a clock" shook defenders with a tick. "If they stopped to think about it, he was gone," said John Radcliffe, the Lakers' longtime statistician.

You didn't have to see Baylor but once to know he was headed for greatness, said NBA scout Marty Blake. For John Kundla, that opportunity came with the 1958 Final Four in Louisville, where Baylor had led little-known University of Seattle to a meeting with the University of Kentucky. With the help of a little Kentucky-fried home cooking, Baylor accumulated three quick fouls that day and his team lost to Adolph Rupp's Wildcats, but Kundla had gotten the picture. Elgin became Bob Short's great hope.

The Lakers made him the first pick of the '58 draft, and Baylor, a Washington, D.C., native, sent his uncle to negotiate the contract, a $22,000 deal. "If Elgin had turned me down, I'd have gone out of business," Short said later.

He almost did anyway. But Baylor was nothing short of sensational in his rookie debut. One look at him in training camp and the whole team knew he was going to be great, Hundley said. The rookie averaged 24.7 points and 15 rebounds for 1958–59. He was second in the league in the most minutes played and led the Lakers in assists, scoring, and rebounding. The team clunked along to a 33–39 record, while the veterans learned to play with the rookie. By the play-offs, they had gotten the hang of it, dumping first Detroit, then defending NBA champion St. Louis to meet Boston for the 1959 league title. The Celtics, of course, had just set out on their great championship run and buzzed the Lakers in four straight games, the first sweep in league finals history.

Short, though, had reason for elation. His team had shown signs of emerging from its coma, and Baylor was clearly the most exciting player in the league. So the owner hustled to sign Baylor to a long-term contract at $50,000 per year. The light of hope quickly dimmed, however. Kundla had grown weary of the NBA travel schedule and decided to accept the head coaching job at the University of Minnesota. Needing a coach, Short picked John Castellani, who had coached Baylor at Seattle. "They figured he could handle Baylor," Kundla said.

Baylor, of course, didn't need "handling," and if he had, Castellani wasn't the man for the job. His style was pure laissez-faire. Practices amounted to little more than unorganized pickup games. Rookie Rudy LaRusso from Dartmouth recalled Castellani approaching him early in the

season and asking if he had any plays the team could use. Right then
LaRusso realized the Lakers were in trouble.

To make matters worse, Baylor was inducted into the army before the
start of his second season. So the Lakers joined him for basic training at
Fort Sam Houston, moving their training camp near San Antonio. Private
Baylor played soldier all day and wearily joined them for games at night,
where several thousand soldiers would cram the gym to watch.

The team was housed in nearby barracks, which the players soon
trashed. Their partying and poker playing quickly drew the ire of army
brass who demanded they clean up their mess. After that, the high-life
Lakers began slipping across the border to sip Mexican beer and party with
the señoritas.

Despite the disaster of training camp, Baylor opened the season by
scoring 52 against Detroit. A few nights later, on November 8, 1959, he rang
up 64 points against the Celtics, breaking the single-game record set a
decade earlier by Jumpin' Joe Fulks. Seeing that Baylor was on course to
break the record, Boston's Red Auerbach told his players not to let him
score. But the Celtics kept fouling, and Baylor kept dropping in points from
the line.

Soon fans were lining up to see this phenomenal scoring machine
wherever the Lakers played. Baylor's individual heroics, however, couldn't
save the team. They lost their twenty-fifth game (against 11 wins) by
midseason, and afterward Short carried a stack of ballots into the locker
room and asked the players to vote for a coach. Castellani was on the ticket
but was voted out, 8–1. In his place, Short hired the old "Kangaroo Kid,"
Jim Pollard, whose confident, low-key style earned the immediate respect
of the players. One of Pollard's first moves was to outlaw poker playing.
He saw that Leonard and guard Dick Garmaker were winning a lot of
money from Baylor. It wasn't good to have the team's star losing money,
Pollard figured. It wasn't that Baylor was a bad player, but "Slick" Leonard
was that good. "We were pretty much divvying up Elgin's money," Hundley admitted. "But Pollard couldn't stop us completely. We'd still play."

The next thing Pollard faced was convincing Baylor not to play every
minute of every game. The coach wanted the player to rest a minute just
before the end of each quarter so that he would be fresh in the clutch. Baylor
hesitantly agreed.

But for the team's real problem there was no cure. The Lakers needed
a center. The starter was 6-foot-8 Jimmy "Boomer" Krebs out of SMU,
who had a decent outside shot but disliked mixing it up underneath. Still,
Pollard figured that Krebs's outside scoring could open the lane for Baylor
to work inside. One night in Boston, the scheme clicked. Krebs's shot
started falling, which pulled Celtics center Bill Russell away from the
basket. Baylor then worked inside to give the Lakers a lead. But Krebs tired

easily and soon began signaling for Pollard to take him out. The coach ignored his center, but Krebs kept signaling. Finally he committed a foul to stop play. Then, during the free throw, the center came over and simply sat down on the bench. Pollard jumped up and ran over to a nearby official and began arguing. Why are you fussing about the foul? the official asked.

"I'm not," Pollard said. "I'm just trying to buy a little time for my center."

The official laughed but told Pollard to take a seat.

Back on the bench, Krebs refused to go back in, despite Pollard's pleas.

"Forget it, Coach," Baylor said finally. "He doesn't want to play."

The trip to St. Louis on January 18, 1960, was supposed to be quick and uneventful. There were a few extra seats on the Lakers' team plane, a DC-3, so Frank Ryan decided to take his wife and two of his 10 kids along. After all, the team was set to return right after the Sunday afternoon game, which the Lakers lost, 135–119. As if that wasn't enough, a winter snowstorm, laced with sleet, settled across the Midwest that evening. The team arrived at Lambert Field in St. Louis about 5:30 P.M. only to be confronted with a weather delay for their flight home. Then the plane's generator failed, requiring an extra delay for repairs. Finally, they flew out about 8:30 that night, with the pilot keeping the craft low to avoid the planes stacked over St. Louis waiting to land in bad weather.

The DC-3 was off the ground about 10 minutes, just enough time for the Lakers to set up their portable card table, deal a pinochle hand, and light a cigarette, when the generator again blew, taking the lights, heat, navigation devices, and radio with it. The pilot could have turned around, but he had no radio to guide him through the maze of planes already waiting to land in St. Louis. So he pushed on, heading the prop plane up through the storm with the idea that at 15,000 feet he might be able to steer his way to Minneapolis by the stars.

The bumpy, cold flight leveled out at the higher altitude, leading Pollard and Ryan to check on the situation in the cockpit, which was lighted only by a flashlight. "How are things going?" Pollard asked, trying not to sound alarmed.

"Well, we're flying home by the stars," pilot Vernon Ullman, a marine veteran, told them. "I'm not sure what the wind conditions are, but we don't have much to worry about until we start coming down."

Pollard and Ryan put on their best nonchalance when they headed back into the cabin, but it didn't take long for concern to spread among the passengers. Under the best circumstances the Lakers dreaded the vagaries of winter travel. Normally, the prop plane flew through winter storms, not over them, which meant a lot of bumpy rides. The Lakers, though, were a loose bunch, greeting the circumstances with gallows humor, even taking turns steering the plane's controls on clear nights. "There was always somebody up front screwin' around with the pilots," Pollard explained. "They'd flip off the lights or sit in the copilot's seat and fly the plane a little bit. As soon as the plane started dipping, you knew they were screwin' around."

But not on this night. A few days earlier Jimmy Krebs's new Ouija board had warned that the plane would crash, which was something they now remembered. As the engines droned on, the cabin got colder and quieter. The passengers wrapped themselves in blankets and measured their breathing in the unpressurized plane.

The flight to Minneapolis, normally two hours, stretched to three, then three and a half. Ice formed, first on the wings and windows, then in the cabin itself. Worry became fear. Knowing they were about out of fuel and nowhere near Minneapolis, Ullman decided to take the plane down to look for a place to land. As they descended, his copilot opened the cockpit window, reached out, and scraped the ice from the windshield.

Fortunately, the terrain was flat. Shining the flashlight out the cockpit window, the pilots spied a hamlet and a water tower, which read: "Carroll, Iowa." They would later discover that they had strayed about 150 miles off course, but at the moment that wasn't the issue. Ullman began buzzing the town, hoping to awaken someone who might turn on the lights at a local airstrip. It soon became obvious there was none.

Flashlight in hand, copilot Howard Gifford came back to the cabin and explained the situation. We're about out of fuel. We can try someplace else or we might be able to land in a cornfield, he said.

Put this SOB down, the players demanded.

"Okay," Gifford said. "Buckle your seat belts, put your knees up, and say a little prayer. We're going in."

Gifford returned to the cockpit but failed to latch the door, which flapped open and closed as the wind from the open window rushed through the plane, giving the passengers intermittent views of the pilots struggling to land the plane. While Ullman flew, one copilot stretched his arm out the open window to scrape ice from the windshield while another read the altimeter by flashlight.

"The wind was blowing back through there, and the cockpit door was going back and forth, and the pilots were yelling above the roar of the engines," Hundley said. "That wind blowing back through the cabin was cold. It must have been about 20 below zero, but we were sweating."

About 300 feet up, the plane began following a car on a road, its lights barely visible through the storm. But then the car headed up a hill, and Ullman abruptly pulled the plane up, sending jitters through the passengers. Baylor decided to take his blanket and lie down in the aisle at the back of the plane. If I'm going to die, I might as well die comfortably, he thought as he braced himself against the seat supports on either side. Boomer Krebs began making public vows. If the plane landed safely, he'd quit cheating at cards. He'd play hard on the court. And throw away his Ouija board.

"We were all making promises," Hundley said. "Dick Garmaker sold life insurance in the off-season. We later kidded him that he was writing policies and throwing them out the window."

The plane made several more passes, each one goosing the passengers' anxiety higher. At one point, Ullman pulled up to avoid high-tension wires. On the final try, the pilot cut the engines and the plane floated into a cornfield. The crop had been left uncut, and three feet of snow rested on top of the corn. Touchdown was pillow soft.

"That landing was so smooth you could have held a cup of coffee and not spilled a drop," Pollard said, still amazed 30 years later. "That pilot went right down a row of corn, just as straight as a string."

First there was silence after the plane came to a rest, then a knock on the door. "The first guy across the field had a fireman's hat on and a big ax," Pollard said. "He looked at me and said, 'Hi. How're you doing?' "

The passengers cheered and upon emptying from the plane engaged in a joyful snowball fight. Soon they calmed down to realize they had a mile hike across the cornfield in crotch-deep snow to the road. Nobody seemed to mind.

When they got to the road, they found a hearse waiting with the rescue vehicles and cars. "When I saw that hearse I got the shakes," Pollard recalled. "The guy driving it was the village undertaker."

One of the locals standing nearby joked that there'd be no new business at the funeral parlor.

Safe and sound, the Lakers retreated to an old hotel in town, which housed mostly seniors. They brewed some coffee and eventually somebody got the idea to raid the liquor cabinet. Then they broke out the cards. On this very lucky night, Pollard didn't even mind that they played a little poker.

The dangers seemed well defined for the Lakers in 1960. The opportunities, on the other hand, were far more difficult to gauge. Were they real or an illusion?

That winter, Bob Short began talking about moving his team west. Former minority owner Maurice Chalfen had first wanted to relocate the Lakers to Los Angeles after the Dodgers began plans to move there in 1957. But then-owner Ben Berger had wanted to keep the team in Minneapolis, so the Lakers stayed put. For Short, the choice was easier. The team was doing poorly, and the bills were mounting. Part of the problem was their home court, the narrow, outdated auditorium. For years, the team had pestered the University of Minnesota about playing in Williams Arena, only to be turned down repeatedly. Short made one last request and even offered to purchase an iron lung for the university hospital. But the school again refused. Finally, Short announced that if he sold 3,000 season tickets for 1960–61, the Lakers would stay in Minneapolis. But privately he began making plans for a move. It was either that or fold.

Within days after their emergency landing, the Lakers were told they'd have to board the plane again, this time for a flight cross-country to play a series of games on the West Coast. When several players balked at the idea, Short told them they either boarded the plane or found a new job. Reluctantly, they headed west. Their big debut came February 1 against Wilt Chamberlain and the Philadelphia Warriors at the new 14,000-seat Los Angeles Sports Arena near the Southern Cal campus. The event drew 10,202 and featured a preliminary game between the Vagabonds, promoted as "an all-Negro basketball team," and Los Alamitos Navy. In the main event, the Warriors prevailed, 103–96. But that didn't matter. Short and Ryan figured the crowd size was a winner. "We don't want to leave Minneapolis," Short told reporters afterward. "It's more than just a dollar-and-cents thing. It's a civic venture. However, if we can't see a way to operate without constantly subsidizing our investment, we'd ask permission to move our franchise."

In fact, they'd already made their decision, having gotten a similar response two nights earlier in another game at the Cow Palace in San Francisco.

"California seemed the place to go," Ryan said.

Despite their poor regular-season record, 25–50, the Lakers found their rhythm again in the play-offs and took a 3–2 lead against the St. Louis Hawks in the Western finals. But they lost the sixth game at home, their last in Minneapolis, and fell in the seventh in St. Louis on March 26.

A month later, on April 27, Short and Ryan went to a league owners' meeting at the Roosevelt Hotel in New York to ask for permission to move to California. For momentum, Short had announced the previous afternoon that he had reached a tentative agreement for the Lakers to play their games the next season in the LA Sports Arena. That story made the morning papers, but it did little to sway the vote. In a morning session, the other owners voted down Short's request 7–1. They were worried about the increased travel costs to play in California. Plus, the Knicks' Ned Irish hoped to get Baylor when the Lakers folded. Figuring they were doomed, Short and Ryan pulled aside St. Louis Hawks owner Ben Kerner to plead their case as the meeting recessed for lunch.

If we stay in Minneapolis, we'll die, they told him.

Then you'll have to die in Minneapolis, Kerner replied.

The Lakers were finished, they realized.

But as Short and Ryan returned to the meeting after lunch they saw a newspaper headline at the hotel's cigar stand announcing that Abe Saperstein, the founder of the Harlem Globetrotters, had formed the American Basketball League. For years, Saperstein had wanted an NBA team, and the league had held him off with promises that he could add a franchise in California. Finally he had run out of patience and started his own league. None of the owners wanted the competition getting a head start in the vast western market. So they voted again that afternoon. The Lakers won the second time, 8–0, and were on their way to the City of the Angels. Only before they consented, the other owners forced Short to agree to pay each team's extra travel costs for going to the West Coast.

Short turned to Ryan. "That'll break us," he said.

"We're already broke," his partner replied.

After finishing 25–50, the Lakers held the second pick in the draft that spring of 1960. Sixteen games into the 1959–60 season, they had acquired 6-foot-11 Ray Felix to help Krebs in the post, but the combination was barely adequate. They still needed a center. Yet their informal scouting reports all came back the same that spring: *Jerry West is the best white player available.* Forget white, Jim Pollard said after scouting West. Outside of Oscar Robertson, who would be taken first by the Cincinnati Royals in a territorial draft, West was the best player, period.

So West, a skinny, 6-foot-2 forward out of West Virginia, became their choice. The national collegiate player of the year in 1960, he had averaged 29 points and 17 rebounds per game as a senior. Because he possessed lightning quickness and could score, the Lakers figured he would make the adjustment to pro guard. West himself wasn't so sure. In the first session of tryouts for the U.S. Olympic team that spring, he performed miserably. Afterward, he went to see coach Pete Newell. I just don't think I'm playing well enough to help the team at the summer games in Rome, he told Newell. Maybe I don't belong here.

Listen, Jerry, Newell said. If you don't go to Rome, I don't go.

The next day West had a great practice, and he went on to join Robertson and Walt Bellamy on the team that overwhelmed the competition for the gold medal. It was in Italy during the Olympics that West learned from an issue of *Stars and Stripes* of the Lakers' move to Los Angeles. He also learned from the same issue that the Lakers had hired Fred Schaus, his college coach at West Virginia.

This is going to be interesting, West thought.

The earliest settlers in Southern California discovered that the countryside was thick with grizzly bears, those powerful creatures with nasty tempers. By the 1840s the sport of grizzly roping had taken ahold in the region, and it thrived there until 1912, when the last griz' was killed in Los Angeles County. As the indigenous population of noble foes declined, the locals turned to an array of other sports to fill their leisure. Boxing, horse racing, college football, track and field, and minor-league baseball—all came to capture the fancy of the California sporting crowd over the first four decades of the twentieth century.

But big-time pro team competition didn't reach Los Angeles until the Cleveland Rams grew tired of cold weather and sparse crowds and moved there in 1945. Then came the Dodgers from Brooklyn in 1958. When they won the World Series a year later, Los Angelenos suddenly realized that their town, with its sparkling afternoons and balmy nights, made a perfect stop for the big leagues. Both the Rams and Dodgers regularly drew large, enthusiastic crowds to the Los Angeles Coliseum.

But when the Lakers arrived in 1960 basketball was very much an unknown factor in the city's sports psyche. For years the game had existed merely as a sideshow. John Wooden was putting together decent teams at UCLA, but the Bruins played some of their games at Venice High School and others at a little gym on campus. And the hoops program at Southern Cal fared as well as it could at a football factory. Beyond that, the attraction was a mishmash of AAU and junior college teams, none of which could manage more than an occasional back-page paragraph in the local newspapers.

Basketball, it seemed, was an indoor game, and Los Angeles was a very outdoor city.

Yet the groundwork for dramatic change had already been laid with the completion of the 14,000-seat Los Angeles Sports Arena near the Coliseum in 1959. Funded by public bonds, the facility transported basketball into the modern age, as if a giant flying saucer had landed in the neighborhood near the University of Southern California on a mission to show Los Angeles the future. Other arenas in the country couldn't compare to this strange oval. With its space-age decor, the Sports Arena featured elevators to lift spectators to the seating levels and fans to keep the flag waving gracefully during the national anthem. Even the turnstiles were electronic, keeping a running tally of the crowd size on a scoreboard as each spectator entered. Both UCLA and Southern Cal scrambled to play their games there, leaving the Lakers to settle for an unusual number of Sunday and Monday dates.

Short and Ryan, though, were just happy to be there, after struggling to survive in the antiquated auditorium in Minneapolis. They negotiated a three-year lease with a series of 17 one-year options to follow, providing security through the 1980 season, what seemed like a distant signpost at the time.

In a matter of months, the Lakers had moved from the past to the future, with the Sports Arena as their fancy new home. If their presence wasn't enough to consecrate the building, John Kennedy assured the arena's place in history that July of 1960 when he secured the nomination to run for the presidency at the Democratic National Convention there. If observers doubted that basketball was on the rise in Southern California in 1960, they needed to look no further than the new building. It was very big-time.

The players needed no persuasion to abandon Minnesota's snows for Southern California's sunshine. Hot Rod Hundley and Rudy LaRusso jumped in their cars that summer and raced cross-country to Los Angeles, pausing for a night of gambling and partying in Las Vegas, where by sunrise they were down to their last $100 each. Give me your money, Hundley told LaRusso. The young forward, thinking he was making a loan, jumped when he realized Hundley was pooling all their money for a single $200 blackjack hand. LaRusso protested, but Hot Rod brushed him off, then winked when the dealer flipped up an ace and a jack.

"We blackjacked the hand and walked away," Hundley said.

LaRusso popped off his shoes and, still wearing his dress suit, jumped into a nearby swimming pool just as the sun was coming up. Then he lay seven silver dollars on the side of the pool and bet Hundley that he wouldn't take the same plunge. Hot Rod wasn't about to lose, so he straightened his tie and leaped.

Later they were amazed at how quickly those wash-and-wear suits dried out. From there, it was another mad dash to Los Angeles, where they lost each other in traffic immediately after hitting town. It didn't take long, however, to get acclimated. LA was the Lakers' kind of town. Once Hundley found Sunset Strip, he knew he was right at home.

Bob Short and Frank Ryan planned to stay in Minneapolis while owning a team in Los Angeles, which meant they needed a Moses to lead the Lakers to the promised land. At first, Short had given an associate $15,000 to go west and set up the team in 1960. But a few weeks later the owners realized that the money had been spent and nothing accomplished, a dreadful setback. So they selected one of Short's longtime buddies, Lou Mohs, to be their new Moses.

He fit the part. Mohs was tall and broad-shouldered, with a mane of striking white hair. Already in his sixties, he had been toughened by years as a newspaper circulation director, a business that demanded long hours. He would give the Lakers that and more.

A Minnesota native, Mohs had starred in athletics at St. Thomas College. While in the newspaper business, he persisted in his love of sports, going to games whenever possible, even scouting talent for his coaching friends. Mohs was Sid Hartman's circulation boss when the young reporter began running the Lakers in 1947. Mohs was so interested in the team that Hartman feared his boss was trying to move him out of the way to take over the Lakers himself. Thirteen years later, after his career had taken him across the country working for major newspapers, Mohs was finally getting the opportunity to run a team.

He was so happy he didn't care that the franchise was broke. Not long after he arrived in California, Mohs called Short for cash to pay bills.

"Call me for anything, but don't call me for money," the owner told his pal.

Somehow Mohs took that directive and made it work.

"That son of a gun came in with literally nothing to work with," said Chick Hearn. "He worked out of a desk and did it all. Tickets. Money. Everything else. He saved the franchise, no question about it. Literally threw his heart and soul into it."

It was Mohs who lured Fred Schaus from West Virginia to coach the Lakers. For several years the team had tried to attract Schaus to Minneapolis. But Schaus said he turned the job down because he knew the franchise was weak financially. However, the move to Los Angeles meant a great climate, and now the Lakers had West. Plus Mohs offered $18,500 in salary, so Schaus agreed. But if he had known the team's cash flow was so thin he would never have taken the job. Shortly after he arrived, Schaus saw the first signs of trouble: All the equipment suppliers sent their packages COD.

Mohs's answer to the cash crisis was a tightness that infuriated his players. He kept track of every paper clip. "We called him the Black Cat," Hundley said. "He did an excellent job of watching Bob Short's money. But every time he'd come around the locker room we'd get beat."

Only 4,008 paying customers turned out on October 24 to see the Lakers lose their first home game to the Knicks 111–100. The next night the teams played again and the Lakers won, with 3,375 watching.

At least those were the numbers Mohs reported.

Each afternoon at five, he would phone Short in Minneapolis to report the ticket sales from the night before. After one of the early games, Mohs told Short that 4,000 seats had been sold.

"Can't you double that when you give it to the press?" the owner asked.

"Again?" Mohs replied.

"We shared a building with the minor-league hockey team, the Blades, who were next door," recalled Mitch Chortkoff, the veteran Los Angeles sportswriter who worked as a public relations assistant to the Lakers at the time. "There was a crack in the ceiling where you could hear everything that was said in the next room. Jack Geyer, a former sportswriter, was the general manager of the Blades. As a lark, he would listen to Mohs's conversations with Short. Then he would call Jim Healy, a gossip radio guy in Los

Angeles. The reports of Lakers ticket sales would be on Healy's show all the time.

"Mohs could never figure out the leak."

Fred Schaus seemed like an odd coaching choice for the Lakers, but he had credentials. He had been a solid pro player for five seasons with the Fort Wayne Pistons, then had coached West Virginia to the 1959 NCAA championship game, only to lose by a point to Pete Newell's University of California Bears.

Schaus had also coached Hundley. If Jerry West was the obvious link between Schaus and the Lakers, Hot Rod was the spiritual connection. To Schaus and Hundley, basketball was an opportunity to put on a show. With his dribble-king wizardry, Hundley had played the prime attraction for Schaus in the mid-1950s. West Virginia basketball in those days was a forerunner to the Showtime basketball Schaus would eventually bring to the Lakers. With the pep bands blaring, his Moutaineer teams would dash onto the floor before each game and whip through a crisp warm-up with a blue-and-gold ball. Schaus's basketball-as-entertainment approach struck a twangy chord with fans in the dreary, undeveloped mountain state and carried the Mountaineers to a run of Southern Conference titles.

Mohs hoped that Schaus could work the same kind of promotional magic in Southern California. But that wouldn't happen right away. And when it did, it was the players who sparked it.

If Los Angelenos didn't yet realize what had landed in their midst, Baylor gave them the first big clue that November 15 when he scored 71 points, a new single-game record, against the Knicks in Madison Square Garden. Baylor's performances seemed to entrance his teammates. "All of those guys worked so hard for Elgin," recalled John Radcliffe, the Lakers' longtime statistician. Forward Tommy Hawkins was a leaper, but he was undersized, had small hands, and couldn't shoot well. But he and LaRusso set picks, battled for rebounds, and generally did anything to get Baylor the ball.

Which left little doubt that the Lakers were Baylor's team, on and off the court. "It was fascinating to see the domination of his personality over that team," said Merv Harris, who covered pro basketball for the old *LA Herald Examiner*. "Elgin was the boss. He was the most physically dominating player, and his status began with that.

"Whenever Elgin wanted to play poker, they played poker. Wherever Elgin wanted to eat, they went to eat. Whatever Elgin wanted to talk about, they talked about."

"Our nickname for Elgin was Motormouth," Hundley recalled. "He never stopped talking. He knew everything, or he thought he did. We had a lot of fun."

With Baylor and Hundley setting the tone, the Lakers stuffed their off-court hours with laughs and card games and good times. On the court, this energy translated into a basketball sideshow. Baylor was the contortionist, and Hundley was the hotdog, covered in mustard. All of which made for an awkward first-year adjustment for West, the introverted country boy.

"There was not one inch, not one drop, of showmanship in Jerry," Hundley once said of West.

He had grown up on the fringe of the coalfields in little Cheylan, West Virginia (near another little community, Cabin Creek, which would lead to Baylor dubbing West "Zeke from Cabin Creek"). He had traveled in his amateur basketball career, but those experiences did little to prepare him for LA. "It was culture shock when I first started playing," West said, "coming from such a small place to such a big city."

Baylor called this skinnier, hawk-nosed version of a Beverly Hillbilly "Tweetie Bird." West, though, didn't like the names Baylor gave him and didn't like being kidded about his background. All he wanted to do was play basketball. His goal was to play the game as well as he could, and that meant perfect, if possible. And winning was the first test of perfection. If people wanted to watch, that was fine. He just didn't have much to say to them that first year. "I'm not very social," he explained.

Early in the schedule, Schaus gave most of the playing time to the veterans, a situation that frustrated West. Schaus was concerned that bringing the rookie along quickly would place too much pressure on him and ruin his confidence if he failed.

For West, the time as a spectator was unbearable. He let Schaus know that he didn't like it. "I could not learn sitting on the bench," he said. "The only thing I could learn were bad habits. I had to get out there and get over those first-year jitters." He knew he could compete on a higher level than the average player. But no matter how hard he tried or how well he played in practice, his playing time seemed set. As badly as the team needed West's scoring, Schaus wouldn't budge.

"I almost felt that I had to be so much better than the people I was playing with that it was frustrating," West recalled.

Starting in front of West at ball-handling guard was Hundley. "He had fun and did a lot of funny things," Schaus said of Hundley. "But he was a fine player, too. He was a great dribbler and passer, and he played pretty fair defense. He was a scorer, but he was not the great shooter that Jerry West was."

When West, Baylor, and Hundley were named to the All-Star team in January, West had achieved the honor without starting a game. The Lakers soon grew tired of the distraction. "We all knew he was ready to start," Hundley said.

Finally, with the team's record sinking, Schaus gave West the nod. "All of a sudden things weren't very good," West said, "and I had a chance to step in and start, and I never gave it up."

The Lakers began a turnaround with West in the lineup, although it was nothing that the rookie guard engineered by himself. Baylor was in his prime, playing the forward spot in spectacular fashion. He led the team offensively and finished second in the league in scoring (behind Wilt Chamberlain) at a 34.8 points per game pace. "They were only drawing about 3,000 that first year," Mitch Chortkoff said. "But Baylor and West made it into something. Baylor was so spectacular he could sell tickets with the way he played."

The Lakers finished second in the Western Division with a 36–43 record, just enough to make the play-offs. But the Sports Arena wasn't available, so they moved one of their first-round games with Detroit to the local Shrine Auditorium, where they played on a stage. They survived that series, then took on St. Louis in the Western finals. They beat the Hawks the first game in St. Louis and later claimed another at home. Suddenly the series was knotted at two-all. Bob Short and Lou Mohs were ecstatic. This was the turnaround they'd been looking for. They knew it was time to do some serious promoting. And maybe even spend a little money.

Chick Hearn's phone rang just after midnight. With the hours he was putting in, he probably shouldn't have answered it. Since coming to Los Angeles from Peoria, Illinois, in 1957, Hearn had found all the broadcasting work he wanted. Through KNX in Los Angeles, he did Southern Cal football and other local sports for CBS radio. Then NBC-TV hired him for a variety of on-camera duties, so he worked for both networks, radio for CBS, TV for NBC.

The phone rang again.

On the line was Bob Short. His Lakers had tied the Hawks in the Western Finals and were set to play the fifth game in St. Louis that Saturday, March 27. Could Hearn arrange a TV broadcast of the game?

Of course not, Hearn said. We can't set up a TV broadcast on this short notice. But why not KNX radio? It has 50,000 watts.

Short jumped at it. He was ready to take anything he could get.

"The Lakers didn't have any broadcasts that first year despite West and Baylor," Hearn recalled. "They couldn't get anyone to carry their games. No radio station would take them."

Short, however, was willing to buy some air time, and Hearn arranged a KNX broadcast of that fifth game in St. Louis, which the Lakers won 121–112. "We came home to 15,000 in the Sports Arena," Hearn said, "and that was the turning point."

Indeed. The packed house saw the Lakers fall in overtime that Monday; then the Hawks took the seventh game and the series at home, 105–

103. But Los Angeles had discovered the Lakers, and they would never again go begging for a broadcast or a broadcaster. Hearn was hooked for good. And his swift, smart delivery was perfect for selling Southern California fans on Baylor, West, and the Lakers.

"That started it," Hearn said, "and I've been doing it ever since."

With their success in the '61 play-offs, the Lakers gathered a quick following in Los Angeles, and they soon became popular with the Hollywood crowd. Lakers games became a place to be seen. Soon Lou Mohs was fielding regular requests from stars for complimentary tickets.

"Back then, if a celebrity wanted a ticket, he had to come see Lou personally," Mitch Chortkoff recalled. "I remember he got a call from Peter Falk, and Lou had never heard of him. This was before the 'Columbo' TV series. The secretary explained that he was an actor, and Lou said, 'Well, he must be a bad actor if he can't buy his own tickets.' Then we convinced him that this was someone you should give tickets to."

Once Lakers management understood the value of the Hollywood connection, games at the Sports Arena became a parade of stars. Doris Day, Danny Thomas, Pat Boone, and other celebrities moved into regular courtside seats. "The celebrities had tremendous impact," Chick Hearn said. "Put a guy like Jack Nicholson in the front row, and people will come to see the game and the star. Doris Day was a real heartthrob and a real star on the screen. Others would come occasionally. But she was a regular in those early days."

For the Lakers, 1961–62 was one of those golden, fun-loving seasons in which almost everything seemed to go right. Even their only real setback during the regular season had its advantages. After opening the season on another scoring tare, Baylor was called into reserve duty with the army near Fort Lewis, Washington. As a result, he was able to appear in only 48 regular-season games. He made the lineup mostly on weekends or with an occasional pass, and when he did, he was fresh, ready, and virtually unstoppable. His 38.2 scoring average was second only to that of the prodigious Chamberlain.

When Baylor wasn't there, West had to carry the load, which pushed him to do more with his game. Early in his career, West was less secure in his abilities and often deferred to Baylor on offense. Like many great athletes, West was high-strung, sensitive, and somewhat temperamental, Schaus said.

"I didn't feel I was competent enough to be consistent," West said. "I would have outlandish scoring games, but maybe the rest of my performance would not be what it should."

But as his confidence grew, West began demanding the ball in the closing seconds with the game on the line. "I always thought that if we needed a basket, I could score," West said. "I didn't care who was guarding me or what the defense was."

Noticing this late-game trend, Chick Hearn came up with a new nickname for the second-year guard: "Mr. Clutch." West didn't complain.

He scored better than 30 points over the first four games of the season and went on to average 31. Hidden behind those numbers was West's defense. "We didn't keep steals in those days," said Laker statistician John Radcliffe. "But if we had, Jerry probably would have led the league. He used to take the ball away from everybody. He knew how to time it just perfectly, taking it down low off the floor."

Against the Knicks on January 17, 1962, West hit for 63, his career single-game high, by making 22 of 36 shots from the field. The game, though, revealed that the Lakers still weren't an everyday item in Los Angeles. Only 2,766 fans saw the game at the Sports Arena. Still, the team's second star had come into his own. In that regard, the Lakers' looseness made them the perfect team for West, particularly in 1962. "It was an enjoyable year," Baylor recalled. "Our camaraderie was great. On and off the court, we did things together. We enjoyed one another. As a team we gave the effort every night."

Even if you were a bit uptight, it was hard not to enjoy time with the likes of the wisecracking Hundley, Tommy Hawkins, veteran guard Dick "Skull" Barnett, and Rudy LaRusso. Known in Boston as "Roughhouse Rudy" (the nickname courtesy of Celtics radioman Johnny Most), the six-foot-eight, 220-pound LaRusso had developed into a tough-minded forward, able to rebound in traffic and hit his jumper from the key. He was a Dartmouth graduate, yet nothing about him suggested Ivy League. His many antics had once included a down-on-the-floor, rolling-around wrestling bout with a huge stuffed tiger at a Detroit airport gift shop, which left his teammates crying with laughter.

"Rudy was a crazy man," Hundley said.

"They were all just a bunch of real characters," West said of his teammates. "The players then were closer than they are today. There was no reason to be jealous of anyone. No one was making any kind of money at all. We traveled differently back then." Schaus kept this chemistry going by rotating the road rooming schedule without regard to race.

Even with Baylor's intermittent schedule, they won the Western Division with a 54–26 record, 11 games better than Cincinnati, and whipped Detroit 4–2 in the division finals series.

For the league championship they faced the Celtics and fire-breathing center Bill Russell, winners of four titles in five years. To match him, the Lakers had their usual solution, 6-foot-8 Jimmy Krebs and 6-11 Ray Felix. Krebs could score but didn't like to work in the post. A former rookie of the year, Felix could muscle around, do a little rebounding, and play defense. But Russell completely stifled whatever offense Felix could muster. In one game, he took four shots and Russell blocked all four. On a fifth try, Felix backed in and tried to surprise the Celtic center by flipping a shot over his shoulder. The ball sailed over the backboard. Felix then pointed at Russell and exclaimed, "You didn't get that one, baby!"

"Bill looked at him like, 'You're crazy, Ray,' " Hundley recalled.

Fact is, Felix was a little nutty. "He had strange habits," Hundley said. "Like he'd eat his dessert first. We called him Baby Ray, because he called everybody Baby."

Felix always seemed a little confused, too. In hi-lo poker, he'd get the signs mixed up and call a low hand when he had high winners.

Krebs, on the other hand, remained the same player who had taken himself out of the game against Boston in 1960. "Krebs was effective against the Celtics," Schaus said, "because he was a perimeter pivot man. When we sent him outside to shoot, he brought Russell away from the basket." With Russell unable to hang in the lane, the Lakers worked their offense and sometimes got decent shots.

The Celtics won big to open the series in the Garden, 122–108. But the Lakers broke back the next night with a 129–122 upset. A record crowd of 15,180 packed the Sports Arena for Game 3 on April 10. In the closing seconds, the Lakers were down 115–111 when West scored four points to tie it. Then Boston's Sam Jones tried to inbound the ball to Bob Cousy with four seconds remaining. West stole it and drove 30 feet for the winning lay-up, 117–115. Boston coach Red Auerbach complained to the refs that it was impossible for West to dribble the distance to score with only four seconds left. The Lakers bench had feared as much. Everyone there shouted for West to pull up and shoot. But he kept digging for the goal and laid the ball in as the buzzer sounded.

"I had deflected the ball on the run," West explained. "I knew I would have enough time."

The crowd erupted into celebration with the play, but the Celtics promptly killed any thoughts of prolonged jubilation in LA by taking Game 4, 115–103. They headed back to Boston with the series tied at two. There, it was all Baylor. Despite fouling out, he scored 61 points (the record for an NBA Finals game) and had 22 rebounds, while the Celtics' defensive specialist, Satch Sanders, contemplated another line of work.

"Elgin was just a machine," Sanders said later.

Boston attempted to double-team him, but Baylor passed the ball too well for that to work. He carried the Lakers in that crucial fifth game, 126–121. It was one of those nights where Baylor's every effort seemed to guide him to just the right spot on the floor, West said. "He had that wonderful, magical instinct for making plays and doing things that you had to just stop and watch. He is without a doubt one of the truly great people who played this game. I hear people talking about forwards today. I don't see many that can compare to him."

From the high of that Game 5 win in Boston, the Lakers headed home with a 3–2 lead and a real opportunity to win the title. The Celtics, though, again doused the jubilation in Los Angeles by tying the series with a 119–105 win in the Sports Arena.

On Wednesday night, April 16, they faced each other in Game 7 in Boston. The Celtics took a 53–47 lead at the half, despite the fact that Sam Jones was only one of 10 from the floor. The Lakers knew that a prodigious night from Baylor had delivered them earlier, and to win, they would have to have another. He took 18 shots in the first half and made eight.

The Celtics maintained their lead through most of the third and were ahead 73–67 heading into the period's final minute. But West then scored seven in a row to help tie the game at 75, setting up a fourth quarter that would haunt the Lakers for decades.

The Celtics first rushed up by six, then fell back into a tie at 88 with six minutes left. Then Boston went back up by three again. Then the Celtics' Tommy Heinsohn fouled out, joining Satch Sanders and Jim Loscutoff, all of whom had gone down trying to stop Baylor, who already had 38.

But Russell scored on a stickback seconds after that, and Boston breathed a bit at 96–91, which was a mistake. West canned a jumper, and Baylor hit one of two free throws. 96–94. Boston then added two Russell free throws, and West answered with another jumper. 98–96. Then Sam Jones blocked Laker guard Frank Selvy's shot and hit two free throws at the other end. 100–96. LaRusso picked up an offensive foul with a minute to go, and the Lakers seemed doomed.

Selvy, though, saved them momentarily by getting a rebound and driving the length of the floor for a lay-up. Seconds later, he repeated the act, driving the length of the floor, missing the shot, then getting the rebound and scoring to tie the game at 100.

The Celtics got the ball back with 18 seconds left. Ramsey tried a driving hook shot in traffic and missed. LaRusso clutched the rebound, and the Lakers had a shot to win it. Schaus called time-out with five seconds to go.

Schaus set up Baylor as the first option, West as the second, and whoever else was open as the third. Hundley, who was in the game to handle the ball, had fantasized in practice the day before that he made the winning bucket, a set shot. Sure enough, Hundley quickly moved into the opening just where he had fantasized his game winner to be. Mr. Clutch and Baylor were covered.

But Selvy was open on the left baseline. Cousy, who was guarding him, had gambled for a quick double-team on West. Hundley sent the pass to

Selvy, and Cousy rushed back to cover him. It was an eight-footer, one that Selvy always made.

It hit the rim and fell away, to be known forever as the shot that could have ended Boston's dynasty and the Lakers' agony before it ever began.

"I would trade all my points for that last basket," Selvy told reporters afterward. "It was a fairly tough shot. I was almost on the baseline."

The ball came off the rim, and Russell, who would finish with 30 points and 40 rebounds, wrapped it in his arms for overtime. The Celtics escaped with their fourth straight title in the extra period as they built a five-point lead and won, 110–107. The Lakers could only think of what could have been.

"Selvy thought Bob Cousy fouled him," Baylor said. "I thought Cousy fouled him. He took the shot from a spot where he was very proficient. Cousy said he never fouled him. I was in a position to get the offensive rebound. But somebody behind me shoved me out-of-bounds right into the referee. There was no foul call there, either. I looked around and saw Russell and Sam Jones were behind me."

Baylor said that some years later he got a copy of the game's film and confirmed what he had suspected. Sam Jones had shoved him out-of-bounds, away from the rebound, a move that had Jones smiling every time he saw Baylor over the years.

In the locker room, Selvy and Hundley were anguished. Hundley lamented that he should have taken the shot, just as he dreamed.

Selvy sat with his head hanging.

"Don't worry," Hundley told him with a laugh. "You only cost us about $30,000, you bastard."

That's all right, baby, Ray Felix told them. We'll get 'em tomorrow.

Tomorrow, of course, never quite came for those sixties Lakers. Or for Ray Felix. They released him after the season and employed two 6-foot-10 rookies, Leroy Ellis and Gene Wiley, to share time in the post.

By the 1963 season, Hot Rod Hundley's partying caught up with his basketball. His skills declined to the point that he became an end-of-game show. If the Lakers were way ahead or far behind, Schaus inserted Hot Rod to entertain the fans with his clowning and showboat dribbling. He'd pull up beside Doris Day sitting at courtside, give her a wink, and announce, "This one's for you, baby." Then he'd shoot a 30-foot hook shot.

"She was gorgeous," Hundley said.

And the fans loved it.

Opposing teams, however, weren't so amused, particularly if Hundley worked his act on their home floor.

St. Louis Hawks coach Harry "the Horse" Gallatin hated the clown game.

"Don't get too far behind tonight, Horse," Hundley once warned him, "or it'll be showtime."

Over the course of the 1962–63 season, the Lakers would take in $1 million at the gate, then the largest gross in league history. But on the court they had to prove themselves again by beating St. Louis in a seven-game Western Division final. Then they got their second shot at Boston for the league championship. West had missed seven weeks at the close of the season with an injury, and although he was back in the lineup for the play-offs, the team still hadn't worked out all the kinks.

Schaus, though, offered no excuses. After all, they had a score to settle from last year. "If my guys aren't up for Boston, then, by heaven, they'll never be up for anyone," he told reporters. Red Auerbach allowed that his team was tired and ripe for plucking.

Boston still eased by the first two games in the Garden for a 2–0 series lead. Back at the Sports Arena, the Lakers retaliated with a blowout, 119–99, only to see the Celtics take firm command by sneaking away with Game 4, 108–105. Up 3–1, Auerbach was as confident as ever. "We've never lost three games in a row," he told reporters.

The Lakers headed back to Boston and found the stuff to survive. Baylor had 43, West 32, as LA pulled to 3–2, 126–119. The loss fueled speculation that the Celtics had run out of gas, that the younger Lakers were about to surge ahead. "No," Russell said, "Los Angeles is not going to do any such thing."

In Los Angeles, a throng estimated at more than 5,000 converged on the Sports Arena hoping to buy play-off tickets. When they found there weren't any left, the scene turned angry. Management quickly calmed things by offering closed-circuit TV seats in a nearby theater at $2.50 a head. By Game 6, about 6,000 such seats had been taken, to go along with the 15,000 arena sellout. "We were aware we were testing the future of pay television," Lou Mohs told reporters.

The crowd at the Sports Arena on April 24 rode on a tide of hope that the Lakers could turn it around. All the stars were out. Doris Day showed up in a green suit. Danny Thomas puffed on a cigar, while Pat Boone, in a snazzy red jacket, blew bubbles.

But Bill Russell made rebounds a scarce commodity, and Boston held off a fourth-quarter Laker comeback to win yet another championship, 112–109.

"Please," Auerbach crowed to the press, "tell me some of these stories about Los Angeles being the basketball capital of the world."

The Celtics, it seemed, were destined to lord over the NBA with Auerbach stomping and fuming on the sidelines, then toasting each victory with a cigar. It wasn't a pleasant sight for the rest of the league. "At first

I didn't like Red Auerbach," a rival NBA coach once said. "But in time I grew to hate him."

"Red was hated around the league," St. Louis coach Paul Seymour said. "He wasn't a very well liked guy. He always had the talent. He was always shooting his mouth off. If you walked up to him in the old days, he was more than likely to tell you to get lost."

"Red was a very astute judge of talent," Schaus said. "When you have a lot of stars, you have to keep them happy and playing as a team. Red did that. I didn't like some of the things he did and said when I competed against him. Some of the things he said would bother me. But the guy who wore Number 6 out there bothered us more. You had to change your complete game because of Russell."

The idea of finding a center to counter Russell drove Lou Mohs to the brink of excess. "I never saw anybody work so hard all day," Mitch Chortkoff said. "Then he would fly to Texas or somewhere to scout a game and be back in the morning in Los Angeles to work."

"He looked like he always slept in his clothes," Marty Blake said of Mohs. "He was crazy. He used to work until late at night, then get on a plane and go scouting. It eventually killed him."

After searching high and low, Mohs finally found his center, Willis Reed of Grambling, in the spring of 1964. Blake, then the Hawks' general manager, knew that the Lakers were about to take Reed with their first draft pick. "I faked Louie Mohs out," Blake said. "Louie was gonna take Willis Reed, so to keep the Lakers from taking him I came out with a story that the Hawks were going to take Walt Hazzard of UCLA. That forced Louie to use his territorial rights to take Hazzard with the first pick."

But the Hawks didn't take Reed because at the last minute St. Louis coach Harry Galatin didn't think he was good enough, Blake said.

Ironically, the Knicks took Reed with the first pick of the second round, and Gallatin wound up coaching him in New York. Even more ironic was the fact that once Russell retired it was Reed who led the Knicks over the Lakers for the 1970 NBA championship.

Even worse, Bob Short sold the Lakers and never gave Mohs a bonus for working so hard to build the team, Blake said. Blake himself got a $100,000 bonus when Ben Kerner sold the Hawks to Atlanta investors in 1967. Mohs died just months after retiring from the Lakers that same year.

"All Bob Short did was cash the money," Blake said. "Louie never got a dime of it."

The Lakers fell to 42–38 for 1964 and were eliminated by St. Louis in the first round of the playoffs. With Wiley and Ellis maturing, they came back strong for 1964–65 and reclaimed the Western Division title with a 49–31 record. But Baylor suffered a severe knee injury on April 3 in the first game of the Western Division finals against the Baltimore Bullets.

"I went up for a shot, and my knee exploded," he recalled. "I could hear a crack and a pop and everything else."

West and LaRusso were left alone to lead Los Angeles. They got help from their teammates, but it was impossible to replace Baylor. Gone were Selvy and Hundley and Krebs (who was killed in May 1965 in a freakish tree-cutting accident). Wiley and Ellis moved into the starting frontcourt together, and the Lakers also got 14 points per game out of guard Dick Barnett. Jim King, a second-year guard out of Tulsa, rounded out the backcourt. Also filling out the roster were Don Nelson, Darrell Imhoff and Walt Hazzard.

With Baylor out, the load fell on West, who responded by averaging 40.6 points over 10 play-off games, good enough to take them back to the Finals for yet another meeting with the Celtics. But Boston waltzed through Game 1 in Boston 142–110, as K. C. Jones held West to 26 points. "K. C. Jones used to tackle West rather than let him get off a jump shot," Schaus said.

West scored 45 in Game 2, but Boston still controlled the outcome, 129–123. Wounded as they were, the Lakers managed a home win in Game 3, 126–105, as West hit for 43 and Ellis 29. The Los Angeles crowd celebrated by pelting Auerbach with cigars. Game 4, though, was another Celtics win, 112–99, as Sam Jones scored 37. They went back to Boston to end it, 129–96, as the Celtics outscored the Lakers 72–48 in the second half. At the outset of the fourth period, Boston ran off 20 unanswered points, while the Lakers went scoreless for five minutes. At one stretch, West, now thoroughly exhausted, missed 14 out of 15 shots.

"Jerry just carried that team out of sheer will," said Merv Harris, who covered the Lakers for the *LA Herald Examiner*. "By the fifth game of the Finals, he was just a bundle of raw nerves, a wreck."

For Frank Ryan and Bob Short, the championship loss hardly mattered. Now the sole owners, they had hit the jackpot. The team had turned a whopping $500,000 profit for the '64–65 season. Suddenly they had leverage to strike new deals, the biggest being a proposed merger between the Dodgers and Lakers, with Short and Ryan owning 20 percent of the new sports conglomerate. But that deal was delayed while Dodgers president Walter O'Malley negotiated a broadcast deal for his club, and in the interim Jack Kent Cooke, a Canadian millionaire living in Pebble Beach, inquired about buying the Lakers.

Although he owned a minor league baseball team in Canada and one-fourth of the Washington Redskins, Cooke had never heard of the Lakers or even seen a pro basketball game when one of his investment advisers suggested he purchase the team. The more Cooke looked into them, the more he liked them.

At first Short declared the team wasn't for sale, until his financial advisers suggested that he at least hear Cooke's offer. The Boston Celtics had recently sold for $3 million, so Short reached for something excessive. He told Cooke he wanted $5 million for the Lakers. Cooke then asked to see a profit and loss statement and said he'd think about it. The P&L statement Short gave him was a hastily thrown together document, and he couldn't make any sense of it. But Cooke, a self-made man who had begun his career selling encyclopedias and soap, was bored with his life. And he wanted to own a sports team.

So he agreed to the price, which left Short realizing that he had asked too little. Suddenly he remembered that the team had already sold $350,000 in advance tickets for the next season. Short decided he wanted half of that money, too.

Cooke grumbled that he was being held up, but he wanted the team. So he agreed to that, too.

Then Frank Ryan came up with one final request. They wanted cash.

Walter O'Malley had given his blessing to the deal, but he warned Ryan that Cooke was a tough, smart businessman. Make him pay cash.

"We made him put the cash on the cart," Ryan recalled with a chuckle.

Cooke's lawyer said it was outrageous. But Ryan insisted.

Bank guards rolled the $5.175 million on a cart through a tunnel under New York's streets from one bank to another. It took 12 bank vice presidents to count the change. When they finished, Ryan and Short took a certified check from the second bank and headed on their merry way. Moments later they spied yet another newspaper headline. NFL Challenges Cooke's Right to Buy Lakers.

The NFL had a rule forbidding owners from holding other sports franchises. With O'Malley's warning, Ryan and Short suspected that Cooke might use the NFL's rule to force a last-minute cut rate on the deal. "I figured it would have cost us a million bucks to fight the thing in court," Ryan said.

But now the issue was moot for Short and Ryan. They had taken the money and run.

7

Shaq Rules

ORLANDO, FLORIDA, DECEMBER 29, 1992

Wrapped in overcoats and scarves, the Lakers hustled from their bus to the lobby of the Sheraton Orlando North. They had expected to encounter chilly winds on this six-game eastern road trip, but not in Florida. A cold front out of Canada had shoved itself into the Deep South, leaving Orlando feeling a lot like Michigan. The Lakers planned to celebrate New Year's during a four-day stayover here, and already they were lowering their expectations. Last night, they had blown an 18-point lead and lost to the Miami Heat when rookie guard Harold Miner, a Southern Cal player Jerry West had wanted badly in last spring's draft, put on a fourth-quarter show. Laker coach Randy Pfund couldn't find anyone to stop him, not exactly the best beginning for an East Coast trip. To make matters worse, their luggage was lost this morning. It was last seen in the lobby of their Miami hotel, which had been crammed with a mountain of baggage from a Japanese tour group. Sportswriter Mitch Chortkoff wondered if the team's bags hadn't gotten mixed up with those Japanese suitcases.

Nobody seemed to know.

Now in Orlando, the Lakers had a noonish practice scheduled at a nearby Jewish community center, but no equipment, no training supplies, no balls. Fortunately, Pat Riley was no longer the coach. When he ran the Lakers, he focused on every little detail and often exploded when his high expectations weren't met. This was just the kind of mishap to set him off. For Riley, it was the little things that led to winning. He wanted every detail of the team's operation to run perfectly. He might arrive in a city one night and decide that the practice gym Gary Vitti had arranged was too far away. A long bus ride might subtract from the Lakers' competitiveness, so Riley would order Vitti to find a gym closer. But, Pat, Vitti would say. It's ten o'clock at night. How am I going to find a new gym for tomorrow morning?

I don't care how you get it done, Riley would shoot back. Just do it.

143

"We were used to trying to anticipate everything Pat wanted," Rudy Garciduenas explained. "In game situations everything had to be just right. It was like walking on eggshells."

Vitti and Garciduenas might not have put up with such demands from somebody else. But they knew Riley meant nothing personally by these snits. Absolute commitment was the only way he knew to approach the game. Besides, who could argue with the results? He had coached the Lakers to four NBA titles.

When Mike Dunleavy took over as coach in 1990, it took him a while to figure out why the staffers were constantly checking with him about the slightest details. "Those things are fine with me," Dunleavy would tell Garciduenas and Vitti. "Why are you guys going to all this trouble?"

Randy Pfund had served as an assistant to both men, and the Laker staffers liked to point out that now that he was head coach Pfund had merged the best of their styles: Dunleavy's laid-back, low-key approach with Riley's focus on building a team's mind-set through tightly orchestrated practices and drills. That was certainly true, but Pfund's coaching had one profound distinction from his predecessors': Both Riley and Dunleavy had Magic Johnson to run their squads. Pfund had been left high and dry by Johnson's abrupt retirement. With Magic, the Lakers were a powerhouse primed for a championship. Without him, they were an odd collection of players, not really fit for any one particular system. Johnson's leadership had meant that much.

When Dunleavy abruptly left the Lakers after the 1992 season, Jerry West had first approached University of Kansas coach Roy Williams. But Williams wasn't interested, so West considered his options and decided Pfund, who had been a Laker assistant for seven seasons, was the best person to get along with the veterans.

The Sacramento Kings had strongly implied that Pfund could be their head coach if he wanted. And a year earlier Pat Riley had made Pfund a giant offer to become his top assistant at the New York Knicks and even pressured him to take the job. Pfund, though, wiped his brow and shook off Riley's pressure. Now, the wait had been worth it. He readily accepted the Laker job. He knew the roster was aging, that the challenge would be great. But, hey, this was the Lakers. With Johnson back, they had a chance at a championship, and that was too much of an opportunity for Pfund to turn down. Besides, he knew and liked the veterans. They, in turn, liked and trusted him. After all, Pfund was as much a remnant of Showtime as they were. And when he talked, Pfund sounded an awful lot like Michael Keaton. How could you not like somebody as unpretentious as that?

He was a people person, but Pfund's main focus was the X's and O's; he was what sportswriters around the league called a "technocrat," a coach who had never played in the NBA but had assumed his position because of his understanding of the technical breakdown of the game. For years technocrats such as Hubie Brown, Mike Fratello and Dick Motta had held most of the coaching jobs in the league. But that trend had reversed over the past few seasons, with more and more teams opting to hire former players as coaches. For 1992–93, the "technocrats" held only a half-dozen of the 27 head coaching jobs in the NBA. In that regard, Randy Pfund was swimming against the tide, a fact emphasized in mid-December when the San Antonio Spurs fired new coach Jerry Tarkanian and replaced him with John Lucas, a former player.

As an assistant Pfund had often sketched out plays as suggestions for Riley and Dunleavy in crisis situations. Sometimes they had used Pfund's plays; sometimes they hadn't. But through that experience, Pfund had acquired a supreme confidence that he could devise just the right play for the right situation. He knew that if he ever got to be head coach, his plays would always work, that the players would always be captivated by his technical solutions. Only now, two months into his first season as head coach, Pfund was just beginning to understand that he had misjudged the job a bit. He was swimming in a small pool of doubt and uncertainty, not so much about himself, but about the circumstances. The team he had been given to coach was a difficult mix. One part was a group of veterans with vast experience and no legs, while the other was a group of rookies and young players with good legs and no experience. Did Pfund play the veterans and try to win? Or did he play the youngsters and plan for the future? The signals from management were mixed. He was supposed to do both.

"I think Jerry West and I felt we needed to see what the rookies and young players could do," owner Jerry Buss would explain later. "We urged Randy to give them more playing time than he had been giving them. I think Jerry and I were more concerned with development than Randy was. I think we were all unsure. Jerry was torn. I was torn. I think we all felt we could win, but we needed to develop our talent."

It helped that Pfund had a good relationship with West. He felt he could go into the general manager's office any time he wanted to talk things over. Still, Pfund pointed out with a laugh, some days he entered West's office with more caution than others.

A false success had masked many of the personnel questions over the first six weeks of the season. The Lakers had survived the jolt of Johnson's retirement and rushed out to a 13–6 record, capped by a December 15 road win over the San Antonio Spurs. Right then, things had seemed peachy for Pfund. The next night they would play the miserable Dallas Mavericks, and a win there would give the Lakers the second-best record in pro basketball, just in time for a Friday night game in the Forum against the Phoenix Suns, the winningest team in the NBA.

The media had begun talking about the Suns showdown even before the Mavericks game. Pfund warned his players not to take Dallas for granted and even held an extra shooting practice. But the Lakers fell apart in the fourth quarter against Dallas, scoring only 11 points and losing to the worst team in the league, which left Jerry West furious. Then, on December 19, Charles Barkley and the Suns humiliated them in the Forum. After watching the first few minutes, West left his Forum seat with a disgusted look on his face and retreated to his office to watch the finish on television. Afterward the general manager made a rare speech in the Laker locker room. "I don't like our fans cheated for lack of effort," West told the players. "I don't care what player it is, we're not going to stand for it."

He reminded them of their obligations as Lakers: "To take care of yourself off the court and be someone the community can be proud of, to play as hard as possible every night.

"We don't talk about wins and losses here," he said. "If you do those things, the wins will come."

Then West retreated to the Phoenix locker room, where he introduced his young son to Barkley and joked with the Phoenix star about his golf game. Behind the smile, however, West was hurting. The Lakers needed a superstar like Barkley, and there wasn't one in sight.

The general manager figured the speech had done some good the next night when they won in Denver. But sandwiched around Christmas were another pair of losses, meaning that Randy Pfund's team came to Orlando having won just one of its last five games. Which in turn meant that he would spend today, his fortieth birthday, devising a game plan to defeat the Orlando Magic and their new $40 million, 7-foot-1, 300-pound rookie center, Shaquille O'Neal. Pfund and his assistant coaches, Bill Bertka and Chet Kammerer, had already put together one plan. But with their losses mounting, Pfund had decided to tear it up and start over. The Lakers needed a win in the worst way. They would have four more tough games on this trip, including Cleveland and Chicago, and Pfund didn't want the losing to get out of hand.

THE BIG LEAGUES

It's perhaps difficult to convey the love and regard Randy Pfund felt for his father. Lee Pfund had pitched briefly for the Brooklyn Dodgers in the 1940s, and no matter how short his tenure there, the father would always be a big leaguer in his son's eyes. Lee Pfund later coached basketball at Wheaton College in Illinois and had even won a small college championship there in 1957. Randy's father knew all the other big leaguers, and they knew him. To his son, Lee Pfund was somebody successful, important, just the kind of dad that any kid would emulate.

"My father was the guy who always had the keys to the gym," Pfund explained.

Randy Pfund had starred in football and basketball at North High School in Wheaton and could have played for several bigger colleges. But he decided to stay home and play for the old man at Wheaton, where in 1974 he was named honorable-mention All-America. Lest these résumé items sound too lofty, Pfund liked to point out that he only shot 42 percent from the floor as a senior and that he had a teammate who led the nation in rebounding, mostly by gathering in Pfund's misses.

Taking his social science degree from Wheaton in 1974, Pfund hustled up a job teaching and coaching high school in Illinois but was almost immediately restless. After all, the father was a big leaguer, so the son set his sights there, too. He began writing letters to the major college programs around the country to inquire about a job as an assistant. When he got no response, Pfund lowered his notch a bit and went after smaller colleges. A couple of years and a bundle of letters later, he finally got a reply. Chet Kammerer, the coach at Westmont College in Santa Barbara, needed an assistant. There was no pay, but Pfund didn't blink. He quit his job at Glenbard South High School, packed his Fiat X19, and headed west that summer of 1977.

Once there, he found work raising funds for Westmont and talked his way into a job with Bill Bertka's college scouting service. It wasn't the big leagues, but it was close. The scouting service gave Pfund an opportunity to see a lot of hoops, even to rub shoulders occasionally with the Laker staffers and coaches. Eight years later, in 1985, Lakers assistant Dave Wohl left to become the New Jersey Nets head coach, creating a vacancy on the scouting staff. Just about everybody in basketball lunged for the job, leaving Pat Riley to sort his way through 150 applicants, many of them big names. Here it was, a big-league opportunity, only Pfund didn't apply because he didn't think he had a chance. Then Bertka tipped him that the Lakers were interested. Riley likes decisive assistants, Bertka warned Pfund before the interview, so make sure you're demonstrative when you diagram plays.

Pfund promptly broke the chalk drawing up a play for Riley.

Riley, though, hired him because he was single and could handle the long hours. Besides, Riley said, he didn't have "NBA scars."

Pfund liked to joke that his first real scar didn't come until 1990, when he applied for the Lakers head job after Riley left. Dunleavy got it instead but kept Pfund on the staff. Now, however, in this first season as a head coach, the scars were coming fast and furious. "Management" wasn't pleased with Pfund's indecisive substitution patterns and the team's unorganized defensive play. West and Buss began to wonder if Pfund weren't a "career assistant."

The term wasn't necessarily an insult to Pfund. Bill Bertka, one of his heroes, had spent his life as a scout and assistant, and it was hard to find a more loved, respected man in the Laker organization. But Pfund disagreed with his job evaluation. He knew he was head coach material. He pointed out that Johnson's abrupt departure had left him with a crisis to manage. Under Riley, the Lakers had been the greatest running team in the history of the game. Riley liked to establish his team's offense and force opponents to respond. But the roster had aged by the time Dunleavy came to the job in 1990. Because he was a disciple of Golden State coach Don Nelson's post-up, mismatch style of basketball, Dunleavy reduced Showtime to Slowtime, making the Lakers a plodding halfcourt team that searched for an opponent's weakness, then tried to take advantage.

That was good enough to get Los Angeles to the 1991 Finals, but critics pointed out that the Lakers had become too stagnant, too predictable, in their offense by 1992, so Pfund was charged with devising an offense that got them moving. At first, he had toyed with the idea of installing the passing game. Nobody in the organization believed the team could win a championship with a motion offense—players cutting and weaving through screens, looking for an open shot—but at least it would get them moving again.

Then it became clear that Magic was coming back, so Pfund ditched his plans for a motion offense. With Magic, Pfund would put Showtime on the road again, running over, around, and through opponents. But Johnson's abrupt retirement threw these plans into confusion. Training camp had been spent working on the running game. Without him, the Lakers really didn't have a point guard to drive the machine. Instead, they reverted to the post-up game and tried to run when possible. On the side, Pfund began working in practice on the motion offense, which the players found strange and difficult to learn. Pfund knew that whatever he faced this season, building an offense would be a long, tedious process, one that required plenty of patience. He just hoped management would have the same with him.

It soon turned out that the Lakers' luggage hadn't been lost after all. Hotel employees had mistakenly stashed it in a side room, from where it was retrieved, and everything was made right again. They made a quick stop in their rooms, then headed out to the team bus to practice.

As usual, Vlade Divac, the 7-foot-1 Serbian center, was among the first in his seat. "So, Vlade, when you gonna score in double figures again?" asked Rudy Garciduenas. Divac, obviously in a funk, mumbled an unintelligible reply. He had not played well recently. The staffers have a saying: "As Vlade goes, so go the Lakers." The equipment manager's needling was meant to jostle him from this funk. Part of Garciduenas's job description is keeping the players loose, and he's up to the task. (At the team charity

Christmas party for needy children he played a chubby, rosy-faced Hispanic Santa.)

The Lakers have an exact seating plan for all their travel. On the bus, the head coach always has the first seat on the right, Vitti the first on the left. Behind him come the assistant coaches and staff, followed by the media. The back three-fourths of the bus are reserved for the players. It's a domain they guard jealously, making sure reporters don't crowd into their seats. The forward-most seats belong to A. C. Green, who always has a Bible under his arm, and Divac.

The bus filled, and Vitti made one final head count. Someone was missing. He cursed and went back into the hotel, only to emerge moments later with Sam Perkins in tow. His sunglasses pushed to his forehead and a sickly look on his face, Perkins boarded the bus silently. He had recently told Kelly Carter of the *Orange County Register* that he was being treated for depression, then denied it when her story broke. Regardless, Perkins seemed seriously somber about something. Usually pleasant and cooperative, he had stalked off just last night in Miami when the beat writers gathered around him to ask about Carter's story. Perkins loved Los Angeles, and some observers theorized that he was depressed about the prospect of having to leave. With Johnson retired, the Lakers needed to make a roster move, and the talented Perkins was the obvious choice. A lot of other teams wanted him. As the saying goes, you have to give up something to get something. Perkins knew that Jerry West was trying furiously to make a trade, and that he was the bait.

At the Jewish community center four boys immediately encircled Divac with autograph requests. Vlade smiled and stopped to sign. "Make sure he spells it right," Garciduenas advised as he walked by.

Inside the center, people stared in wonder as the giant Lakers took over the gym. The locals were told they had to leave. All did except for an elderly lady in a black leotard who walked up to Alex Blackwell and asked, "Where's Magic?"

Blackwell explained that he had retired.

"Magic Johnson isn't here!?!" she said. "He's my favorite player. Where's Worthington then?"

Blackwell laughed.

Garciduenas again asked her to leave.

"Okay, boys," she said with a wave as she walked off.

The Lakers worked on a variety of things that morning, including a session on the motion offense. For the first 20 games, Pfund had tried rookie Anthony Peeler at point guard. He was a good ball handler, but after 20 games it was apparent his future lay at off guard. Peeler had an excellent outside shot, made all the more dangerous by his explosive ability to drive and dunk. Pfund believed that management had misled him into thinking Peeler could be a full-time point guard. However, West countered that Pfund had come to that conclusion on his own. They did agree, though, that 20 games had been wasted learning this lesson.

Regardless, Peeler was going to play at least 20 minutes per game. And part of the reason for installing a motion offense was to move the Laker big men away from the basket so that he would have room to drive. Byron Scott, who started at off guard in front of Peeler, had also been a slashing driver in his early years, and Pfund was hoping Scott would resume it once the lane opened.

From there, Pfund turned to a discussion of the team's biggest weakness: rebounding. "A lot of times when we took the shot last night there wasn't one goddamn person there," Bill Bertka fussed. Elden Campbell showed the potential to be a good rebounder. But for him to develop, Pfund would have to take more playing time from the veterans. Unfortunately, he badly needed leadership and couldn't afford to anger the veterans. A. C. Green, the team's best rebounder, didn't even have a full-time home in the frontcourt. More and more, Pfund had taken to playing him at off guard. He could help with the rebounding from there, but on offense Green played like a forward, clogging the inside with too many forwards.

The talking done, they scrimmaged. By the end of practice Perkins was again smiling. A somnolent, slow-moving sort off the court, his demeanor often confused fans who thought he was uninterested. But Perkins was prized for his defense, cagey post moves, and long arms. "Oh, yeah," he said and grinned after stealing the ball from James Edwards.

CHICKIE

On the bus ride back to the hotel, broadcaster Stu Lantz wondered aloud how they might make Chick Hearn pay for his rough treatment of drivers. Yesterday, on their bus in Miami, Hearn had asked the driver for football scores. The driver said he didn't know any because he was in St. Petersburg. "Oh," Hearn said, "they don't have radios down there in St. Petersburg, huh?"

For Lantz, the retort brought to mind a 1991 trip to Boston, where their driver couldn't find an airport runway gate in the snow. They had searched for some time when Hearn finally told him, "Hey, driver, you keep this up a little longer, we'll get another per diem."

Lantz had an idea that he and the coaches could arrange for one of their drivers to fake anger with Hearn and invite him off the bus for a fight. That just might teach Chick not to ride 'em, Lantz said. But what Lantz and the coaches really had in mind was revenge for the tricks Hearn always played on them.

"We're gonna get his ass," Lantz said.

"Yeah," Pfund agreed. "We're gonna get him."

"He is the biggest instigator you'll ever see," Lantz says later of Hearn. "He starts more stuff than anybody. The slightest opening and he's there. He gets on the bus. I call it trolling. I'm not a fisherman, but they say trolling is when you throw a line out and move it along hoping to get a bite. Looking for fish to nibble on it. That's what Chick does. He'll get on the bus and throw out a little bit of information that's a lie. He'll say, 'Miami traded Kevin Edwards today.' He says it with such a straight face, and he's just waiting for someone to say, 'Oh, yeah, for who?' Then he's got you. You've hit on his line. It's gotten to the point now that when he says something on the bus nobody says a word, because they don't know if he's trolling."

Hearn, the trickster, first came to Los Angeles in 1956 to broadcast Southern Cal football games. Since Bob Short talked him into broadcasting that first game in 1961, Hearn has only missed two Laker games, both in 1965. On the first, he was on assignment covering a golf tournament for NBC. The second time he was grounded by a snowstorm in Nebraska covering a Southern Cal football game. Otherwise, he has shaken off innumerable colds and illnesses to call the Lakers action.

But his hold on the team is much more than perfect attendance. His crisp delivery and imagination snared Laker fans from the very start. He points out that the Lakers' great games have provided him with ample drama over the years. But he took that drama and blew it up in the minds of his audience. Almost overnight, he made the Lakers seem like the most important event in Southern California.

First it was the trials and tribulations of Elg and Mr. Clutch that Hearn brought to life for radio listeners. Then, in 1965, Jack Kent Cooke added a television package to the format. The owner wanted to move Hearn into that, but he was afraid of losing the radio audience. So he created the "Simulcast," with Hearn broadcasting simultaneously the team's games on radio and television.

"At first, I didn't think it could be done," Hearn said.

But he learned to trim the verbiage for leaner radio and beefier television. His sense of humor and imagination made it work. He gave a special name to everything. When he tabbed Cooke's new building "the Fabulous Forum," the owner promised a little something extra in Hearn's next pay envelope. Sure enough, there on payday was a picture of Cooke himself.

As might be expected, many of Hearn's best adventures over the years have happened off the air. There was that snowstorm in the Midwest one time when the team had to get dressed for a game in a cold railway baggage car—right next to a coffin.

In the 1970s, the Lakers were headed to New York when bad weather and engine trouble forced an emergency landing in Ohio. On the ground, the team was bused to a hotel, where Hearn, broadcast partner Lynn Shackelford, and trainer Frank O'Neill decided to grab a sandwich. They walked into a restaurant down the street and found a man sitting in between three open bar stools. Hearn politely asked the man to move over, he agreed, and Hearn sat on the stool.

Moments later, Hearn felt a gun in his back and heard someone telling him to put his hands over his head.

Thinking it was a joke, Hearn told Shackelford, "You hear that silly sonofabitch?"

"Get your hands up!" the voice boomed.

"If there had been a ceiling 20 feet high I'd have reached it," Hearn recalled.

Behind him were four police officers who had been called to the restaurant because the man sitting in Hearn's seat had threatened to shoot the waitress if she didn't hurry up with his order.

The cops were frisking Hearn when the waitress appeared and quickly identified the culprit, who was led off in handcuffs while Hearn was left quaking.

Today Lantz enjoys a good relationship with Hearn as his broadcast partner. But life in the booth with Chick hasn't always been easy street. During the 1960s, he was determined to work alone. But ARCO, the company broadcasting Laker games, had provided a salary for a color analyst in its 1967–68 contract with the team. Cooke decided if the money was there, they should use it, and Hearn couldn't talk him out of it.

Al Michaels, then in his twenties, was hired because his father was a close friend of Cooke's. "Chick would open the broadcasts by saying, 'This is Chick Hearn with Al Michaels,' " recalled Merv Harris, who covered the Lakers for the *LA Herald Examiner.* "Then you wouldn't hear from Michaels until halftime, when Chick would say, 'And now here's the first half scoring with Al Michaels.' Then Chick would do the second half and at the end say, 'Here's the game scoring with Al Michaels.' After about three games, Hearn went to Cooke and said Michaels was taking too long reading the scores."

The Lakers released Michaels, a future three-time national sportscaster of the year, after he worked six exhibition and four regular-season games.

"Al had a lot of talent," Hearn said. "But I'd never worked with anyone before. I'd always worked alone. I didn't believe two people could do basketball. But I would be proven wrong."

"Chick didn't like Al," Cooke recalled. "Chick didn't think Al had what it took. I thought the boy had a lot of promise. His father was a very dear friend of mine. But I knew it wouldn't work because Chick would dominate the broadcast and Al couldn't get a word in."

"Michaels didn't last long, but that established the concept of Chick Hearn having a broadcast partner," Harris said.

Next came Dick Shad, followed by Hot Rod Hundley. Later would come Shackelford, Pat Riley, Keith Erickson, and Lantz, all former Lakers.

"He was tough," Hundley, now a Utah Jazz broadcaster, recalled. "I said, 'Chick, I'm working with you.' But when they put me in there, he didn't like that."

Hearn would crisply deliver the play-by-play, pausing only occasionally for Hundley to jump in. "You'd say, 'Yeah, great play,' and it would go right back to him," Hundley said. "He'd just cut right in on you. He was rude. But he was a good teacher. I learned everything I know about broadcasting from Chick. After a while, he accepted the fact that I was gonna be there."

"I didn't think it could work," Hearn said of having a partner. "But after we worked at it a while, it ran smoothly, as long as the color and play-by-play men knew when to get in and get out."

The Lakers celebrated Hearn's twenty-five-hundreth consecutive broadcast at a road game in Cleveland in March 1992. Hundley, Erickson, Riley, Shackelford, and Lantz all flew in for the occasion. "It's the most important event of my life," Hearn said. "Oh, yes, I'm proud of this one."

"Chick's the greatest basketball announcer the world has ever known, or will ever know," Cooke said. "There will never be another one like him."

Hearn once had suggested that he would retire with Magic, but that milestone was already in his rearview mirror. "I won't retire until they tell me that I can't do it anymore, that I'm not any good," he finally admitted.

"They will carry him away with his headset on," wrote the LA Times's Larry Stewart.

Randy Pfund spent his birthday in his room, watching videotape of Shaq until his eyes were red. Then he panicked. "The more I watched, the less idea I had how to cover him," Pfund said. What made Orlando so tough was the armada of young three-point shooters they arranged around O'-Neal. If you double-teamed him an instant too long, they broke your back with a trey. Pfund knew his defensive plan wasn't going to work, so he tossed away his pride and began dialing his friends around the league to see what they did with the Magic's young monster in the middle.

After hearing their ideas, Pfund and his assistants sat down to author a new approach. They called it the "Shaq Rules." On defense, the Lakers would swarm O'Neal with the point guard, shooting guard, and power forward all helping Vlade corral him. Once they forced him to pass, the

Lakers would quickly rotate. "I don't want anybody open," Pfund tells them the next morning at practice. They would also have to watch for cutters going to the basket, taking the pass from Shaq, and scoring, he warned.

On offense, they would fast-break, hoping to score before Shaq could get to the other end, the only problem being that he ran the floor well. In the halfcourt, they wanted to "attack the post," the idea being that they could get the rookie in foul trouble. They also wanted Vlade to move to one of the corners, taking Shaq with him. And when Vlade had the ball, he wasn't to back Shaq down as centers often do when they post up. That would only bring him under the goal to rebound and play defense. Instead, the coaches wanted Vlade to fake and drive past Shaq, leaving him on the wing.

They sounded good, but would the Shaq Rules work? Only a rookie, he was averaging 22 points, 15 rebounds, and four blocked shots a game. And he had made instant winners of the Magic, a considerable accomplishment considering they didn't have a power forward to play alongside him.

The Shaq Rules depended heavily on Vlade and backup centers Elden Campbell and James Edwards. With Vlade's inconsistency, you never really knew what you were going to get.

The same was true of Campbell, a 6-foot-11 center forward in his third season. The team badly needed rebounding, and Campbell possessed the physical skills to be a great rebounder, but he, too, was inconsistent and unpolished offensively. He was a local product, having gone to Inglewood's Morningside High. He usually sported a surly countenance. The future of the frontcourt depended on his development, but coaching him required a different approach.

He needed a broader shot selection, so Chet Kammerer (the same who had hired Pfund years earlier) encouraged Campbell to add a jump hook to his repetoire. That would be a good shot around the basket, the coach told him. When Elden resisted, Kammerer shifted strategies, making a $10 bet that his jump hook would get him a bucket in the next game.

Campbell took the bet but only made a limp effort at shooting a jump hook, and the shot didn't fall.

"Where's my $10 at, Chet?" Campbell asked afterward.

"I gotta get change," Kammerer replied.

"I got change," Campbell said. "$50. $100. I ain't shooting no more jump hooks."

Piano notes trilled through the lobby of the Sheraton.

"Where are the boys?" asked the woman sitting at the bar.

"Up in their rooms," replied the bartender.

"What are they doing?"

"They're probably sleeping," he said.

"When are they coming and going?"

"Five-thirty."

"Five-thirty," she said resolutely, as if armed with a golden piece of information.

As soon as the Lakers hit town, their fans had moved into the Sheraton lobby and begun staking out their strategic positions for autographs and other liaisons. As game time neared on Wednesday afternoon, the crowd thickened. Even the man who operated the lobby shoeshine stand wore gold and purple. A longtime Laker fan, he said he'd love to take his little son to this game, but it cost too much. In years past pro basketball tickets had been relatively cheap, but the new age of NBA marketing had arrived in the 1980s, making it a game for the leisure class.

Just as the bartender predicted, the Lakers appeared in the lobby at 5:30 on their way to the bus. Among the expectant fans was a young mother and her two grade school sons. They'd been waiting five hours, long enough for her to find a prime position near the side door the Lakers exited to their bus. When Alex Blackwell appeared in the hallway, she nudged her eight-year-old to get his autograph. He did, but as Blackwell signed, Anthony Peeler and Byron Scott slipped past. The mother, a wholesome, pretty woman, smiled bashfully, averted her gaze, and held the door open for the players. Then she watched, her eyes wide with amazement, as these golden gods, the Lakers, strolled through her life and off into a future mere mortals couldn't imagine.

On the bus, Rudy Garciduenas noted that in Orlando the numbers of autograph seekers seemed heavier than in other cities.

"They're selling them," John Black replied. "The Orlando people said Shaq has had to quit signing. It's the same people over and over again, getting autographs and selling them."

It was minutes before tip-off, and already the Orlando Arena was jumping. In the locker room, Laker assistant Chet Kammerer printed the Shaq Rules neatly on a chalkboard. Vlade Divac sat in front of his locker, sipping water and watching a TV screen in the corner where O'Neal was taking apart the Cleveland Cavaliers' defense.

James Worthy walked in. "Vlade," he said and slapped five with the center, "let's go."

On the video screen, Shaq caught the ball in the paint and scored easily. Kammerer stepped over and punched the rewind button, then re-played the sequence. "Vlade," he ordered, "don't let him catch the ball in there and score. Body him out."

Divac nodded. When he played poorly, the big center felt like he wasn't part of the team. He disliked that loneliness, which made his slumps all the more frustrating. Since coming to the Lakers from the former Yugo-slavia in 1989, he had worked hard to overcome the language barrier, and although he had made great strides and loved Los Angeles, he was still walled in by the cultural difference between himself and his teammates. His best friend on the team was the Bible-toting A. C. Green, whose disciplined, contemplative life-style also set him apart from the rest of the Lakers.

Earlier on the bus, Divac had discussed urban violence with a televi-sion cameraman traveling with the team. They talked about guns and drugs and hate in America. Divac, a Serbian, could relate. He had seen ethnic violence tear his own country apart, taking with it his friendship with Drazen Petrovic of the New Jersey Nets, a Croatian. They had been long-time friends from Yugoslavia's national teams, but Petrovic had refused to speak to Divac the last time they met.

"My country's a war zone," Divac told the cameraman. "LA is cool."

"LA is crazy," the cameraman responded, then added, "It's the world."

"So many crazy people," Divac said, shaking his head.

Pfund knew it wasn't exactly fair that the Lakers expected Divac to be an NBA center. Against the zone defenses in European basketball he had been a special weapon, able to launch shots from the perimeter or drive right past his man. But he lacked the body to muscle inside with NBA centers. The 7-foot-1 Divac was a good rebounder, but his fluidity made him more of a power forward or, even better, a very large small forward.

The Lakers were mixed on whether to trade or keep him and had reportedly tried to work several deals. Divac, though, showed plenty of savvy with this crisis. He simply told writer Mitch Chortkoff that if he was traded he might return to Europe. West was furious after Chortkoff re-ported Divac's threat, because it hurt the Lakers' ability to trigger a trade. Yet some in the Laker organization still saw Divac as an intriguing talent who could be very effective in the right mix of players. After all, they said, hadn't he shown promise playing with Magic, who constantly badgered Divac into playing tough?

Yes, went the answer, but that was true of all the Lakers. A superstar like Magic made everybody shine.

Just before tip-off, Divac shook O'Neal's hand and gestured toward the other side of the center circle, as if saying, "Please, after me." It was not a good sign.

But on his second trip down the floor, Vlade boxed out Shaq, grabbed the defensive rebound, shot an outlet pass to Sedale Threatt, and headed upfloor with confidence in his step. Moments later Shaq got the ball down low and moved to score, but Divac, with a look on his face that said, "Get me help fast," quickly fouled him. The next time, Byron Scott rushed over to double-team, forcing O'Neal to pass. This effort seemed to work, but the other Magic players hit their shots, giving Orlando a 13–8 lead.

Pfund figured he had an advantage in the Lakers' ample size, so he inserted 7-foot-1 James Edwards to play alongside Divac. Moments later, Shaq posted Edwards up, only to find Divac was there to double-team. Caught in this towering trap, O'Neal traveled.

On defense, Shaq sat in the middle of a thinly disguised Orlando zone, and Pfund begged offical Hue Hollins for an illegal-defense call. At the other end, Pfund kept running the Laker big men—Perkins, Edwards, Green, Divac, and Campbell—at Shaq throughout the game, hoping they could contain the giant rookie. Late in the second quarter, O'Neal got the ball for the umpteenth time in the post against Divac. "Go! Go! Go!" Pfund yelled, calling for the double-team. Before the Lakers could get there, the Magic center whirled toward the basket, only to get yet another traveling call.

At the half, the score was tied at 47, and O'Neal had seven points and 11 rebounds. But he found scoring room in the third period and got the fans going with a series of stupendous dunks, which left the Lakers looking dazed. With six minutes left in the game, the Magic were in control, 85–77, and the crowd sensed a celebration. Moments later, Pfund called for the famed Laker trap. It worked, as it had so often in the past. With Anthony Peeler and Sam Perkins doing most of the scoring, they closed the gap. Perkins, in particular, employed the Shaq Rules, taking the ball right in the rookie's face. He scored nine points down the stretch, while the Magic missed free throws. In the closing seconds, Shaq traveled yet again in the middle of a Laker double-team, and the Lakers ended their losing streak at two games, 96–93.

O'Neal finished with 23 points and 23 rebounds, but he also had seven turnovers and for the first time in his pro career he had failed to block a shot.

"You guys look a lot better than you've looked in about two weeks," Pfund told reporters after the game.

"I've almost forgotten how to write a winning story," Mitch Chortkoff quipped. "I'll have to draw on my vast background."

As he talked, the coach admitted he was struggling with his lineup: "The scenario that begins to develop with this team is that with our depth, it's not going to be the same rotation every night. It's not always going to be the same guys. We've obviously got veterans that we go to and count on, but there's also some young players on this team that play with a lot of energy. There are times when they need to be on the floor for us. It's a good mix when we win. But when we lose, it's frustrating. You're back and forth, wondering where you made a mistake in terms of who you had on the floor late in the game."

*   *   *

Vlade Divac sat quietly on the bus back to the hotel. He had scored 12 points with six rebounds in 29 minutes of play, and the coaches were happy with his defensive effort against O'Neal. "I am again part of the team," he said.

At the Sheraton, a crowd waited in the parking lot. "Good game, really good game," said a fat old woman with Coke-bottle glasses as the players got off the bus.

Perkins stared at her.

All around, kids were hurriedly sorting through their trading cards, trying to match printed faces with real ones. The first off, Vlade, Byron Scott, and Blackwell, stopped to sign. Using them as a screen, Worthy quickened his pace and made it to the door without getting stopped. But inside, more were waiting.

Headphones covering his ears, Elden Campbell looked straight ahead and rounded the corner toward the main lobby. From the shadows emerged a kid with a card. "Is Mr. Divac here?" he asked.

"Get out of my face, man," Campbell said and kept walking.

8

Dreams Deferred: Wilt, West, and Cooke

LOS ANGELES, 1965

It didn't take Jack Kent Cooke long to put his personal stamp on the Los Angeles Lakers. A brusque, efficient executive, he immediately set out over the summer of 1965 to transform the team from a small, haphazardly run venture into a sound business. He charged into the task with a flurry of memos and acerbic reminders to employees. Nothing escaped his view, from an occasional Chick Hearn mispronunciation to a receptionist's tardiness in answering the front office phones. If the memos didn't get the job done, Jack Kent Cooke tended to shout. This approach quickly divided his followers into two camps. Those who loathed him and those who liked him. Sort of.

"He was the number-one asshole that ever lived," said Hot Rod Hundley, who worked for Cooke as a broadcaster. "He was totally, absolutely, unbelievably wrapped up in himself and had no respect for anyone but himself."

Cooke's presence immediately changed the atmosphere around the team, said John Radcliffe, who had been a Laker statistician since 1960. "Everybody was on eggshells. We were afraid to make a mistake, because we were gonna get yelled at. It was his style. He didn't hold anything back."

Longtime Laker scout and assistant coach Bill Bertka credited Cooke with giving him a chance to work in the NBA. "Mr. Cooke shouted and screamed at anyone who didn't give him perfection," Bertka said. "He was interested in the bottom line, in success, in winning. That's all he wanted."

Bertka recalled that Cooke once invited him to his home for a breakfast meeting. When Bertka got there, Cooke came to the door in his bathrobe. "Do you want a cup of coffee?" the owner asked as they went inside.

"That would be nice," Bertka said.

"Bill," Cooke said, "I didn't ask you if it would be nice. Do you want a cup of coffee?"

Every conversation with Cooke was a chess match, Bertka said. "It

159

didn't matter what discussion you had with him; he was going to put you on the defensive. That was his tactic on everything."

Pete Newell, who would become Lakers general manager in 1972, knew that Cooke could be irritating, but Newell found the owner's demands for business discipline quite useful. For example, Cooke required Laker employees to record the time and subject of every phone call. Newell soon found that he had a solid record of every conversation, which he used to remind other team's executives of their promises and trade offers.

"Jack was a hands-on owner," Newell said. "He was a workaholic. If you worked for him you were like a doctor. You were on call 24 hours a day, because Jack was on call 24 hours a day. He'd be there at his desk promptly at nine every morning. And he'd require the team staff to be there as well, not a minute late. I'm not saying he got a buggy whip, where he was gonna beat you if you were two minutes late. But the precision he demanded was good for a basketball team."

There were exceptions to his exactness. Cooke could let an employee's honest $50,000 mistake go by without comment, then explode over mere pocket change. "On big issues, he was at his best," Newell said. "He never seemed to panic."

Because he knew business and possessed a flair for marketing and promotions, Cooke concentrated there in his first months with the team. Eventually, however, his voracious appetite for learning turned to the game itself. In time, Cooke would believe that he understood basketball, a misperception that soon rested at the heart of the Lakers' troubles.

"He thought he knew," Jerry West said of Cooke. "He didn't know."

Basically, Cooke was a salesman, and a good one, said Robert "Jake" Embry, former owner of the old Baltimore Bullets. In his youth, Cooke was a saxophonist and bandleader in Ontario. He also peddled soap and encyclopedias and went to work in 1937 for Lord Thomson of Fleet, the British media magnate who owned numerous properties in Canada. Lord Thomson saw Cooke's sales and management skills and sent him to rescue a struggling radio station. Within six months Cooke had turned the business around, prompting Lord Thomson to reward him with one-third ownership of the station. From that, their relationship grew into Thomson Cooke Publishing and Broadcasting Limited, the media business they operated until 1952, when Lord Thomson left Canada for England and Cooke set up shop in California.

By 1965, Cooke was a magnate himself, engaged in a "retirement" life of buying and selling businesses, with a penchant for sports franchises. Just before purchasing the Lakers, he had attempted to gain the rights to an American League expansion team in Southern California but lost out to Gene Autry.

After acquiring the Lakers, he turned his focus on a National Hockey League franchise for Los Angeles. To get that, he had to have a place to play. But the commission for the city-owned Sports Arena turned back his attempts to secure an agreement there. The Blades, a minor league hockey team, already played in the building, and Dan Reeves, their owner, hoped to secure the NHL franchise ahead of Cooke. The commission debate went back and forth until Cooke grew frustrated.

Look, he told Ernest Debs, chairman of the commission, if you keep this up you're going to force me to build my own building.

Debs smirked and said, "HAR, HAR, HAR."

"He didn't laugh," Cooke recalled. "He said the words *HAR, HAR, HAR.*"

Infuriated, Cooke told his lawyers, "Let's depart from this den of iniquity."

They did, and proceeded directly to an architect's office. Never mind that it had been three decades since a privately funded arena had been built in America. Jack Kent Cooke was determined to build his own, a structure worthy of the ancient Romans. He retained Charles Luckman Associates, who had recently designed the new Madison Square Garden. Within weeks, Luckman presented him with a variety of drawings.

"I don't like any of them," Cooke said.

"Well, what do you like?" Luckman asked.

"Something about 2,000 years ago and 6,000 miles east of here," Cooke replied.

Luckman asked what he meant, and Cooke looked over where Richard Niblack, Luckman's designer, was drawing a column. Cooke wasn't even sure what kind of column it was. But he knew he wanted them to ring his new building. He wanted the place built to last. And he never ever wanted it referred to as an arena. He wanted to call it the Forum, and Chick Hearn thought that was a fabulous name.

CELTICS AGAIN

The doctors told Elgin Baylor that his knee injury had ended his playing career, and for a time he believed them. The main ligament in his knee had been severely damaged, and his kneecap had been split, practically in half. Immediately after the injury, he was worried about even walking again.

After a time, the pain subsided, and Baylor found he had some mobility. "The more I thought about it," he said, "the more determined I became to prove the doctors wrong."

"Afterward," West said, "to watch the slow, painful process of him getting better and improving and never really getting back to where he was, that was the thing that was difficult for the rest of us to accept. We wanted him back having all his greatness. He came back and played, and played incredibly well. But he wasn't the Elgin Baylor of old."

By training camp that next fall, Baylor was able to see limited action. Eventually he would return to full speed, but never again would he be the dynamic player he had been. Before, Baylor had dazzled opponents with a fearless approach to driving and rebounding. After the injury, that part of his game diminished.

"It was very, very difficult," he said. "I would try to do a lot of things that I just couldn't do. It was frustrating. But it made me more determined, too. Before I was injured, I loved to penetrate and create, to pass off or take the shot. At times after I returned, I just couldn't do it. My knee wouldn't respond. I couldn't rebound as well. It just wasn't there. I just couldn't run the same. I had to rely more on perimeter shooting and posting up occasionally."

He played in 65 games the following season, 1965–66, and averaged 16.6 points. West scored at a 31.3 clip and became the top option in the Lakers' offense. But Baylor's mere presence made them stronger. They won the Western with a 45–35 record and eliminated the Hawks in a seven-game conference final series.

The 1966 championship quickly turned into another Celtics/Lakers scrap. The Celtics had a 38–20 lead in Game 1 in the Garden, but the Lakers fought back to a 133–129 win in overtime. Baylor had scored 36, West 41. But instead of the glory and the psychological edge falling to the Lakers, the attention abruptly shifted to Boston. Auerbach picked the postgame to announce that Russell would be his replacement as head coach. Working as a player-coach, Boston's center would become the first black head coach in a major American sport.

The announcement made headlines the next morning, while the Lakers' upset was obscured.

With the future of the team settled, the Celtics bore down on the Lakers, winning the second game in the Garden 129–109, then adding two more victories in Los Angeles for a 3–1 lead. The major problem for the Lakers was Boston's John Havlicek, who could swing between guard and forward. Schaus had tried to play LaRusso, a forward, on Havlicek, but it hadn't worked. "No one in the league his size is even close to Havlicek in quickness," Schaus told reporters.

So the Lakers coach used rookie guard Gail Goodrich on Havlicek. West moved to forward, and this three-guard lineup left Los Angeles weak on the boards. But it worked. West, Baylor, and Goodrich lashed back and won games 5 and 6 to tie the series at three apiece.

Once again the championship had come to a seventh game in Boston Garden. The Celtics took a big lead as Baylor and West were a combined 3 for 18 from the floor in the first half. As usual, the Lakers cut it close at the end, paring the Boston lead to six with 20 seconds left. Massachusetts governor John Volpe figured it was time to light Auerbach's victory cigar. The Lakers took fire with that, cutting lead to two, 95–93, with four seconds left.

The fans always rushed the floor to celebrate Boston's championships and chose to do so with time remaining in 1966. Russell was knocked down. Orange juice containers on the Boston bench spilled across the floor, and Satch Sanders lost his shirt to the crowd. Somehow, K.C. Jones got the inbounds pass to Havlicek, who dribbled out the clock for Boston's ninth championship.

No one was more angered by the early cigar than Schaus. He would have loved to shove the victory cigar down Auerbach's throat, Schaus said. "We came awfully close to putting that damn thing out."

Close, of course, but no cigar, as the saying goes. And the following season they weren't even that, finishing 36–45, then capping the season by getting swept by the Warriors, 3–0, in the first round of the play-offs. It was enough to convince Schaus that he needed a break from coaching. He replaced Lou Mohs as general manager and began fielding questions from Cooke about a replacement. The owner admitted he didn't really know coaches and asked Schaus for a list of five suggestions. From *Sports Illustrated* Cooke learned that Butch van Breda Kolff had coached Bill Bradley at Princeton. So van Breda Kolff was listed among the candidates.

"Butch interviewed extremely well," Schaus said. Cooke particularly liked his decisive style. "Butch was a strong personality," Bill Bertka recalled. "They called him the Dutchman. They also called him bullheaded and stubborn."

Van Breda Kolff brought a major change in style to the Lakers. He stressed conditioning and wanted to get the rest of the team involved in the offense along with West and Baylor. (For years, the Lakers had complained that Schaus wanted only West and Baylor taking shots, which meant that no one else had confidence in the clutch.) "When van Breda Kolff came in, he brought an eastern style of play, with all five men moving and everybody sharing the ball," Bertka said.

Schaus, who had been a college coach, had blended his pro experience with the midwestern running game to fashion a pro style for his team. But van Breda Kolff's approach was a profound departure from that, and it took the players half a season to adjust.

Beyond style, he treated his pros like college boys, going so far as to institute a bed check. The only problem was, van Breda Kolff would make the check but wind up visiting with his players, sipping beer in their rooms and talking basketball for hours until they begged him to get some sleep.

"There was a change in the attitude surrounding the team," Jerry West said of van Breda Kolff's tenure. "There was a volatile person who pretty much said what he thought. He felt that was the way to do it. You simply cannot do that at the professional level. He was a purist. But on the pro level it didn't work."

Some observers would argue that van Breda Kolff got the Lakers close to success, the only problem being that they already knew that territory far better than they cared to.

In December of 1968, just 18 months after groundbreaking, Jack Kent Cooke's Forum opened for business. Throughout contruction it had been referred to as "Cooke's Folly," which only steeled the owner's determination to make it a structure that would stick in the Sports Arena Commission's craw for a long, long time. He had looked across Los Angeles and the San Fernando Valley before settling on a 29-acre site in Inglewood, at the intersections of Manchester Boulevard and Prairie Avenue, next to Hollywood Park. Built about the same time, the Spectrum in Philadelphia cost about $5 million, but Cooke plowed $16 million into his Forum. No expense was spared. Each of the 80 columns supporting the roof stood 57 feet high and weighed 55 tons, so large that they had to be formed on the work site.

Construction crews worked double shifts under giant lights to make sure the building was finished on the date Cooke had promised the NHL. The owner painstakingly oversaw every detail of the process. His building would set the standard for ultimate ambience, with unique fully upholstered, extra-wide, theater-style seats, and rows spaced to provide more legroom. It opened on December 30, 1967, with Cooke's face beaming as his Kings defeated the Philadelphia Flyers in a nationally televised hockey game. His old friend Lord Thomson was there, as was Lorne Greene, who served as master of ceremonies.

The next night, New Year's Eve, the Lakers played their first game there, blasting the San Diego Rockets, who had a young sub named Pat Riley, 147–118.

"I was just so proud," Cooke recalled.

A press release boasted that his Forum would "be in essence a modern version of the greater Colosseum of ancient Rome."

The Roman motif set Cooke's creative juices to flowing. A former bandleader, he wrote fight songs and cheers for both his hockey and basketball teams and authored nicknames for his hockey players, then instructed his broadcasters to use them on air. And he designed uniforms for both hockey and basketball. No longer did the Lakers wear their traditional blue and white. Cooke outfitted them in purple and gold, only he hated the word *purple* and insisted that the team call it Forum Blue, which left Chick Hearn advising television viewers not to adjust the color on their sets. In the Forum, the Lakers wore gold, the first time in league history that the home team didn't wear white.

He dressed Forum ushers in togas, with slacks for the men and short pants for the women. "The ladies did not like 'em, to say the least," said Laker statistician John Radcliffe.

Other Forum male staffers were issued purple blazers with gold patches, to be worn with white dress shirts and black ties. One night John Radcliffe wore a gold turtleneck with his and the next day got a terse memo from Cooke reminding him of proper dress. Rod Hundley looked at Radcliffe's blazer one evening and said, "John, you ought to have that thing cleaned and burned."

The new building meant a realignment of celebrity seating. When Doris Day and her husband asked to have their seats moved, Cooke learned that they weren't paying for them. So he informed Day's husband that they would have to start paying, leading Day to decide that she wouldn't be attending any more Laker games. Cooke didn't care. All of Los Angeles seemed to want seats, including Walter Matthau and Jack Nicholson, who gladly paid.

Now all Cooke had to do was make sure he had the kind of team that kept them coming.

Van Breda Kolff's Lakers struggled along until January, when they acquired Irwin Mueller and Fred Crawford, who gave them quickness off the bench. From that point they rolled through a 38–9 run, good enough for a 52–30 finish, second place in the Western behind the Hawks.

"That second half of the season, the team realized van Breda Kolff's vision," Bertka said. "They were really a happy bunch. They shared the ball and moved it around."

Guard Archie Clark, out of Minnesota, proved to be an incredible find, with quickness, strong defensive desire, and an ability to score. He was one of the few players who could carry the team offensively as West had. And Gail Goodrich, now in his third season, had come into his own. They called him "Stumpy," because he was only six feet, but as John Ratcliffe said, "he had the longest arms in the NBA." Goodrich was left-handed and fearless going to the basket. He would disappear into a crowd of big men; then suddenly the ball would kiss off the glass and fall in.

At center was Darrell Imhoff, short on talent but long on willingness to sacrifice. He set scores of picks for Baylor, West, and Clark.

From the bench, van Breda Kolff urged this group along with an animation never seen in Los Angeles. "Butch was just all over the place," John Radcliffe recalled. "It was amazing how he would just throw himself down on the seats. The body language alone was enough to get him technicals."

The "Dutchman" drove his Lakers through the play-offs. They nailed the new Chicago Bulls, 4–1, then swept the Warriors in the Western finals, which left them eight days of watching the Celtics and 76ers battle in the

Eastern finals. They worked to stay fresh, but practices couldn't approximate the intensity of games. As van Breda Koff feared, they grew stale with the wait.

The Celtics had finished second in the divisional standings at 54–28, eight games behind the 76ers, who won 62 games, again the best in the league. Then Philly took a 3-1 lead in their playoff series, only to watch the Celtics come back. The Lakers followed the games on television and pulled for Boston, figuring player/coach Russell would be easier to beat than Chamberlain.

Boston did come back to whip Philadelphia, advancing to the championship round for the eleventh time in 12 years. Jack Kent Cooke was immensely pleased to have the Finals in his new Forum. The Lakers liked their chances going in. "If we can rebound, we can win," West told the writers. "We're little, but we match up well with Boston. We're quick, and we shoot well, and that can be enough in a seven-game series."

They alternated Mel Counts and Darrell Imhoff in the post, and Mueller's quickness helped out on the boards. Archie Clark joined West in the backcourt, with Goodrich and Crawford coming off the bench. Baylor was still the man in the corner, but Tommy Hawkins had returned to the team to provide depth at forward.

The Lakers opened the series with a not-too-surprising split in Boston Garden. They lost the first when West shot 7 for 24 and Baylor 11 for 31. But they pulled their usual surprise and won the second. The Celtics returned the favor when the series switched to LA, winning Game 3, 127–119. Then West scored 38 points, and Baylor added another 30 as Los Angeles evened the series with a 118–105 win in Game 4, after van Breda Kolff had been ejected.

West, however, sprained his ankle in the closing minutes, dampening the victory. It appeared serious enough to keep him out of Game 5 back in Boston. He played anyway and scored 35, but it wasn't enough to counter the Celtics, who jumped to a 19-point first quarter lead. By the third quarter, the lead was still 18, but LA came back after that, tying the score at 108 in the fourth. The Lakers were down four with less than a minute to play when West stole the ball and found Baylor downcourt for a lay-up. The Lakers then tied it when Clark got another steal and West scored. In overtime, Russell blocked a Baylor shot and Nelson hit a late free throw to give Boston a 3-2 series lead, 120–117.

Then, just as the series returned to Los Angeles for Game 6, and the tension turned high, things went terribly awry for the Lakers. It began with the national anthem. Johny Mathis, the featured vocalist, launched into "God Bless America," then switched to "The Star-spangled Banner." The best switch of the day, though, was made by Coach Russell, who moved Sam Jones to forward, where he scored over Goodrich and forced van

Breda Kolff to go with a taller, slower lineup. That didn't work either. The Celtics ended it in a blowout and took their tenth title.

That May, Philadelphia 76ers owner Irving Kosloff phoned Cooke at his Forum office and asked, "Would the Lakers be interested in Wilt Chamberlain?"

"Struggling to speak in measured tones," Cooke recalled, "I said that we certainly would be."

BIG NORMAN

His close friends called him "Big Norman." But to the basketball public, he was "Wilt the Stilt." He disliked that name, of course. He was a person, not a stilt. The name, as much as anything, defined his tenuous relationship with the fans and the writers. After all, he was a giant, and they expected giant things of him. That certainly was no more than he expected of himself. Unfortunately, the task was never up to him alone. Basketball is a five-man game. And that seemed to be the crux of the problem for Wilton Norman Chamberlain.

As big and talented as he was, Chamberlain's career progress had often been frustrated by the presence of Boston's Bill Russell. Where Chamberlain struggled most of his career out of context, Russell always seemed to have the right coach, the right teammates, and they got the right results. On the other hand, Chamberlain's career was a profound contradiction. For him, things were wonderfully easy and terribly difficult, all at the same time.

"The world is made up of Davids," he once explained, "and I am Goliath."

Since his freshman year in high school in the early 1950s Chamberlain had been the darling of eastern basketball. Scouts from college and pro teams followed his every move because, unlike most of the giants who came before him, Chamberlain showed the coordination and athletic skills of men much shorter. As a 6-foot-11 ninth-grader in Philadelphia, he led his undefeated Overbrook High team against West Catholic High in the finals of the city championship, where a scenario developed that would become miserably familiar to Chamberlain over the years. West Catholic packed four players around him inside, but his teammates couldn't make the open shots. Overbrook lost its only game of the season.

Over the next three years, his teams won 58 games and lost just three, while Chamberlain averaged 36.9 points (he scored 90 in one game). His junior and senior years provided a study in dominance, with Overbrook claiming consecutive city titles.

A friend in the NBA public relations offices got Chamberlain a summer job as a bellhop at Kutsher's Country Club in the Catskills. There, while still in high school, he played against the best talent pro and college basketball had to offer, humbling Philadelphia Warriors center Neil Johnston in one game. The pro scouts knew Chamberlain was ready then, but NBA rules forbade the drafting of a high-schooler. So he chose the University of Kansas, where the Jayhawks' offense focused on his towering presence.

Which meant that opposing defenses did the same. "That was always the problem when Wilt was playing with us," said former Kansas coach Dick Harp. "The defense was always going to concentrate on him. Teams would rig zone defenses around him with three and four men, making it impossible for him to move, particularly around the basket."

And defenders became quite physical with him. "It was difficult for the officials to be objective about Wilt," Harp said. "There were numerous opportunities for officials to call defensive fouls. But most of the time they didn't."

Regardless of the circumstances, Chamberlain kept his composure, Harp said. And even with the defenses he faced, he powered through opponents.

But, as Chamberlain himself noted, his frustrations led to errors in his method. When he rebounded, he liked to take the ball in one hand and slam it against the other, making a gunshot of a sound that startled the smaller players around him. What he should have been doing was whipping a quick outlet pass downcourt. When he blocked shots, he liked to smack the ball loudly and violently and usually out of play. As a result, opponents retained the ball and another chance to score. This habit would later hurt him when he faced Russell, who always brush-blocked the ball, often creating a Celtics fast break.

"Wilt understood the game of basketball," Dick Harp said. "He had an opinion about the game and was bright about it. He wanted to use his size in close proximity to the basket. But he didn't develop his skills beyond that. If he wanted to, he could have been a significant playmaker. Wilt had demonstrated he could have shot the ball and been an effective passer."

Over his sophomore season he averaged 30 points, 19 rebounds, and nine blocked shots. And Kansas was clearly the best team in college basketball. But in the finals of the NCAA tournament they lost in triple-overtime to North Carolina, an outcome that set the cornerstone of Chamberlain's frustrations. He returned to Kansas the next season, but the Jayhawks lost to cross-state rival, Kansas State, in postseason play.

Disgusted, Chamberlain decided to leave the University of Kansas. Because his class had not graduated, he was still ineligible for the NBA draft. So he played a barnstorming season with the Harlem Globetrotters, made a good sum of money, and waited his turn. That arrived the following season, 1959–60, when he made a heralded return to Philadelphia to play for the Warriors. His presence had an immediate impact on the league's statistical races. He led the NBA in scoring (37.6 points per game) and rebounding (27 per game). The next season, he became the first player in league history to shoot better than 50 percent from the floor. For the 1961–62 season, Chamberlain maximized man's potential for 48 minutes of basketball by averaging 50.4 points per game. The next season, he scored a mere 44.8 points per game and won the league rebounding title for the fourth straight season.

He made each season his statistical fiefdom, and yet they all ended in bitter disappointment. The reason, of course, was the Boston Celtics. Quite often Chamberlain would dominate Russell statistically, but he could never vanquish the Boston center and his teammates in the big games. Chamberlain was actually taller than his listed height of 7-foot-1 and towered over the 6-foot-9 Russell, which caused the public to marvel at the smaller man's success. To the basketball public's way of thinking, Russell had a winner's heart, while Chamberlain certainly had to be lacking in something.

In truth, the "something" was much more tangible than heart or desire. Russell was simply quicker than Chamberlain, said Bob Cousy, repeating a view that was held by insiders from the very first time the two met on a court.

"This is a tremendous advantage Russell had on Wilt," Cousy said. "He didn't give him the offensive position he wanted. Russell kept him from overpowering him and going to the basket. Russell had better speed and quickness, so he could always beat Wilt to the spot. He pushed Chamberlain out a little further from the basket, forcing him to put the ball on the floor once or twice. We always felt Russell could handle him one-on-one."

As a result, Chamberlain was forced to develop and shoot a fall-away jumper that was far less effective than his dunks and short bank shots. His critics, meanwhile, saw Chamberlain as a giant fascinated by his own statistics.

"It's interesting those things about him people would misinterpret," Jerry West said of Chamberlain. "They would say he was a selfish guy, that he didn't care, that he wasn't a team player. And that simply was not the truth. He's like all of us. No athlete wants to fail. Wilt Chamberlain certainly didn't want to."

The Warriors moved to San Francisco for 1963–64, and Chamberlain again led the league in scoring. He also broadened the scope of his game by finishing fifth in assists. It didn't matter. The Warriors lost in the NBA Finals that year to Russell and the Celtics.

San Francisco traded Chamberlain to the Philadelphia 76ers in the middle of the next season. "Chamberlain is not an easy man to love," Warriors owner Franklin Mieuli later said of the trade. "I don't mean that I personally dislike him. He's a good friend of mine. But the fans in San Francisco never learned to love him. I guess most fans are for the little man and the underdog, and Wilt is neither. He's easy to hate, and we were the best draw in the NBA on the road, when people came to see him lose."

Chamberlain quickly made the 76ers into a title contender, but that spring they lost a seven-game series to the Celtics again. The following year, Philadelphia actually beat out Boston for the Eastern Division's regular-season crown but got caught flat-footed in the Eastern play-offs and lost to the Celtics 4–1.

Chamberlain's frustrations were no deeper than those felt by West, Baylor, and the Lakers. Bill Russell had simply built a wall around the NBA title. He had made it his personal property, or so it seemed until 1967, when Chamberlain finally led the '76ers to a 68–13 record and the league title, leading many observers to call them the greatest team of all time. But Boston's comeback victory over the Warriors in the 1968 Eastern finals soon quieted that talk, and Wilt decided he wanted out of Philadelphia. Jack Kent Cooke was only happy to help him find a ticket.

They began their talks in June in the library of Cooke's Bel-Air mansion. Things got off to a good start when both noted that they each owned a 1962 Bentley Continental. "We talked about antique furniture, art, even the English language," Cooke said.

Finally they talked about money, a five-year deal at $250,000 per season, making Chamberlain what was believed to be the highest paid athlete in any pro sport. The Lakers shipped Archie Clark, Darrell Imhoff, and Jerry Chambers to Philadelphia for Chamberlain. The deal was announced in early July, setting off immediate speculation about Chamberlain, West, and Baylor on the same team. Could they share one ball?

"We'll simply have the best team in basketball history," Chamberlain replied.

Seeing an opportunity to tweak the Lakers, Red Auerbach told reporters, "I wonder if Jerry West and Elgin Baylor are going to be willing to be underlings to Wilt Chamberlain?"

Cooke and Chamberlain were infuriated. "A statement like that is typical of Mr. Genius," Cooke shot back. "It's preposterous."

Van Breda Kolff was at a party at Bill Bertka's house in Santa Barbara that July of 1968 when he learned that Chamberlain had been traded to the Lakers. "He was upset by the trade," Bertka recalled. "Butch didn't have anything against Chamberlain or his effectiveness. But you had to have Chamberlain in the post, and that dictated a style of offense that Butch didn't particularly like. He'd rather have all five men moving, all five men interchangeable and sharing the ball."

Within hours, the trouble started. First Chamberlain read in news accounts that van Breda Kolff said he "could handle" his new center, who'd make a great rebounder for the Lakers. Who needs "handling?" Chamberlain wondered. Then at the Maurice Stokes Game that summer at Kutsher's Country Club, van Breda Kolff asked Chamberlain to don a Lakers T-shirt and pose with him for a photo. When Chamberlain refused, the coach fumed.

In training camp, the tension increased a notch. Van Breda Kolff thought the center gave him one good day's practice, then began slacking off. Chamberlain thought the coach was trying to run a pro team with college rules.

Then came a season-opening loss to the 76ers where Chamberlain concentrated on defense and rebounding. The next game, Chamberlain scored big points and they beat New York. "Tell the coach," Wilt told the writers afterward when they asked about the difference in the two games.

A few games later, van Breda Kolff angrily benched Chamberlain when rookie Wes Unseld of the Washington Bullets outrebounded him, 27 to 21. The newspapers enjoyed the proceedings immensely, questioning Chamberlain's $250,000 salary and his sinking scoring average (20.5 points per game). "There are certain deficiencies with every club," Chamberlain replied. "Here with the Lakers I've tried to blend in, lend myself to the deficiencies, try to help overcome them. Here with the likes of Jerry and Elgin we have people who can score. So I've simply tried to get the rebounds, get the ball to one of them so we can score."

The questions about Chamberlain's salary were pointless, Hawks general manager Marty Blake told reporters. "There's no athlete in the world worth $250,000, or even $200,000, unless you can take it in at the gate. In LA, they take it in at the gate."

Indeed, for the first time in his career Chamberlain encountered a warm crowd. "Wilt was always the villain," Bertka said. "Wherever Wilt went in those days he was always booed and unappreciated. But, in tribute to the Laker fans, from the day he stepped on the Forum floor he was never booed, never shown disrespect. He was only appreciated. But it took him about a year here to realize that."

Some observers, however, questioned whether Chamberlain's presence hadn't weakened the team. He often set up on the left low post, dead smack in the way of Baylor's drives. Van Breda Kolff sought to move the center to a high post, but Chamberlain figured that only took him away from rebounding.

Privately, Chamberlain told friends that the coach favored West and Baylor and blamed him for the losses.

"What a lot of people forget is that they gave up some pretty good ball players to get Chamberlain," Atlanta's Paul Silas observed. "For example, Archie Clark. Guard is where they are hurting this year with Archie gone. You can concentrate a little more on West now, and that is something you couldn't do last season. Also, their style of play is slower."

Meanwhile the conflict raged on. Player and coach began shouting at each other during games. Finally, Schaus called the two in for a peacemaking session, where the general manager laid out new rules. No more bashing each other in the press. Van Breda Kolff is the boss. "I like both of them, but those two guys just couldn't agree on anything," Schaus recalled.

Six weeks later, he was forced to fly to Atlanta for yet another peace meeting. Then Schaus ordered the players to have their own meeting, which Baylor, as captain, conducted. Chamberlain was told to stop frowning at his teammates on the court when things went wrong. The other Lakers also asked him to ditch his aloofness, to socialize more.

That helped, but after a February 3 loss to Seattle, van Breda Kolff and Chamberlain screamed at each other for 20 minutes and would have come to blows in the locker room if Baylor hadn't stepped in. "It was embarrassing for everyone to hear them screaming like animals," one Laker confided to a writer. "It was ridiculous. The guys wanted to hide."

"Wilt being the dominant personality that he was and Bill being the dominant personality that he was, there were sparks," Bertka said. "Wilt had definite opinions about how the game should be played and how he should be used. So did Butch. Yet they both wanted to win in the worst possible way."

The Seattle blowup led to yet another meeting with Schaus, which brought a truce.

What do you want me to do? Chamberlain asked.

"Play defense and rebound," van Breda Kolff replied.

Chamberlain complied, and the Lakers won the conference title. By the 1969 play-offs, they were a picture of team defense, giving up just 94.7 points a game. Baylor, Chamberlain, and West were the heart of the lineup. But there was more. There was Keith Erickson out of UCLA, recently acquired from Chicago, as sixth man. There were John Egan, the veteran guard, to boost the backcourt, and Mel Counts, the 7-footer and former Celtic, to do the same up front. With Counts playing alongside Chamberlain, Los Angeles could close the lane and make opponents live off of jump shots.

On the strength of this defense, they advanced to the most disappointing of their Finals meetings with the Celtics. As hurt as the previous losses had left him, Jerry West justified them each year by remembering that Boston had the better team. But that was no longer the case in 1969. Los Angeles had taken the top seed in the Western with a 55–27 record and thus had home-court advantage for the Finals with the Celtics, who had finished fourth in the Eastern. "Most of the years we played they were better than we were," West said of the Celtics. "But in '69 they were not better. Period. I don't care how many times we played it; they weren't better. We were better. Period. And we didn't win. And that was the toughest one."

A week before the season ended, Los Angeles beat Boston, 108–73, on national television, emphasizing that the Lakers now had a center and a real shot at winning. With both Bill Russell and Sam Jones limping through their final season, the Celtics had slipped by, hoping to stay healthy for the play-offs and a shot at one final title. The Lakers were favored, but they didn't have many young legs either. Baylor, in particular, had begun to show his age. "I don't have to take his fakes as I always did before," Boston's Bailey Howell told the writers. "And he is not as quick on the drive or following the shot."

West, though, was determined not to face another championship loss. He scored 53 with 10 assists in the first game, which Russell called "the greatest clutch performance ever against the Celtics." It was just enough for a 120–118 Laker win. Afterward, West was so tired he iced down his arms. Boston had opened with Em Bryant covering West, but Bryant was too short to stop West's outside shot. When the Celtics tried to play West close on the perimeter, he drove right past them for a variety of lay-ups. In years past, Russell had always dropped off his man to stop those drives, but Wilt's presence meant the Celtics center couldn't get away with it anymore, West said. "I know he scares a lot of people, but if you're looking for Russell, you're not playing your game."

West cooled down to 41 points in Game 2, while Havlicek upped his total to 43. Very quickly the series became a shoot-out between these two. Chamberlain scored only 4, but he countered Russell on the boards. Even better, Baylor, who had been sluggish, came alive to score the Lakers' last 12 points for another Los Angeles win, 118–112.

Up 2–0, the Lakers had private thoughts of a sweep as the series headed to Boston. In Game 3, the Celtics took a big early lead but lost it after Keith Erickson poked a finger in Havlicek's left eye. The Lakers tied the game heading into the fourth and seemed poised to break the Boston curse and go up 3–0. But Havlicek, with his left eye shut, hit several late free throws to keep Boston alive, 111–105.

Game 4 provided yet another opportunity for the Lakers to strike the deathblow. The two teams combined for 50 turnovers and enough bad shots and passes to last them a month. The Celtics slowed the Lakers' scoring by double-teaming West, forcing him to make the pass rather than take the shot. Over the final four minutes, the two teams had one basket between them. But with 15 seconds left, the Lakers had an 88–87 lead and the ball. All they had to do was get the pass in safely and run out the clock. Instead Bryant stripped the ball from Egan and the Celtics raced the other way. Sam Jones missed the jumper, but Boston controlled the rebound and called time at 0:07. On the inbounds, Bryant threw the ball to Havlicek, then set a pick to his left. Boston's Don Nelson and Bailey Howell followed in line to make it a triple screen. At the last instant, Havlicek passed to

Jones, cutting to his right. Jones stumbled to a halt behind Howell, who cut off West. There, at the 0:03 mark, Jones lofted an 18-footer. He slipped as he took the off-balance shot, and it just cleared Chamberlain's outstretched hand. Jones knew it was going to miss and even tried to pull it back, he explained afterward. The ball went up anyway, hit on the rim, rose up, hit the back of the rim, and fell in. Chamberlain leaped up and lorded over the basket, his face a picture of anguish as the ball came through the net.

Boston had tied the series, 89–88, and a dagger in West's heart wouldn't have felt any worse. "The Lord's will," he said later.

"I thought to shoot it with a high arc and plenty of backspin," Jones told the writers. "So if it didn't go in, Russell would have a chance for the rebound."

Russell wasn't even in the game, a writer pointed out.

"What the hell," Boston's Larry Siegfried said. "You hit a shot like that, you're entitled to blow a little smoke about arc and backspin and things like that."

The Lakers regrouped and headed home for Game 5. In Los Angeles the Celtics just didn't have it. Russell scored two points with 13 rebounds. Chamberlain owned the inside, with 31 rebounds and 13 points, while West and Egan struck from the perimeter with 39 and 23 points respectively. Boston fell, 117–104, and trailed 3–2.

West, though, had injured his hamstring and was hobbled. He played in Game 6 and scored 26. But the Lakers needed more from him. And certainly more from Chamberlain, who made a measly two points. Boston won 99–90 and tied the series.

Once again a Celtics/Lakers championship had come down to a seventh game. Only this time Game 7 was in Los Angeles; this time there wouldn't be a Garden jinx. Or would there? West's hamstring had worsened. It was wrapped, and he declared himself ready to go. But everyone wondered. Everyone except Jack Kent Cooke, who began planning his victory celebration. He visualized the perfect finale for a championship season. He ordered thousands of balloons suspended in the Forum rafters. (Team employees spent hours blowing them up.) According to Cooke's plan, they would be released as the Lakers claimed the title. With the balloons raining down on the jubilant Lakers and their fans, the band would strike up "Happy Days Are Here Again." Cooke could see it clearly.

And so could Bill Russell. Laker legend has it that Red Auerbach walked into the Forum that May 5 and gazed up into the cloud of balloons in the rafters. "Those things are going to stay up there a hell of a long time," he supposedly said. But Hot Rod Hundley recalled that Russell, not Auerbach, made the comment. Auerbach later agreed, saying the balloons angered him, but he said nothing.

Regardless, no one was more infuriated by the balloons than Jerry

West. The thought of them made him sick with anger. The Celtics, always looking for that extra little boost of emotion, found it in the Forum rafters and in a Laker memo outlining plans for the celebration, which was passed around the Celtics' locker room before the game. They hit eight of their first 10 shots on the way to a quick 24–12 lead. The Lakers charged back to pull within 28–25 at the end of the first. At the half, it was 59–56. Celtics.

The Lakers tied the score in the third before going strangely cold for five minutes. West, playing brilliantly despite his heavily bandaged leg, finally hit a shot to slow down the Celtics, who led 71–62 with about five minutes to go in the third. Then, with 3:39 left, Russell took the ball inside against Wilt, scored, and drew Chamberlain's fifth foul to round out a three-point play. 79–66, Boston. Chamberlain had played his entire NBA career, 885 games, and never fouled out. Van Breda Kolff decided to leave him in. With Chamberlain playing tentatively, Boston moved inside and took a 91–76 lead into the fourth, and the balloons upstairs weighed heavily on Cooke's team.

The lead went to 17 early in the fourth, but both Russell and Jones picked up their fifth fouls. In the void, West went to work. A bucket. A free throw. Another bucket. The lead dropped to 12. They traded free throws. Then Havlicek got his fifth, and moments later, Sam Jones closed his career with a sixth foul. He had scored 24 on the day. After a Baylor bucket, and three more points by West, the Celtics answered only with a Havlicek jumper and the lead dropped to nine, 103–94.

At the 5:45 mark, Chamberlain went up for a defensive rebound and came down wincing. His knee. He asked to be taken out. Van Breda Kolff sent in Counts. West hit two free throws, and the lead was seven. Russell and his boys were out of gas, hoping to coast. Another West jumper. And moments later, two more free throws from West. The lead was three, 103–100.

Three minutes to go, and Counts, who shot 4 for 13 on the afternoon, surprised everyone by popping a jumper, 103–102. Chamberlain was ready to come back in.

"We're doing well enough without you," the coach told his center. West at the time was unaware of this exchange, and when he later learned of it he was incredulous.

Boston and Los Angeles traded missed free throws. With a little more than a minute left, West knocked the ball loose on defense. Nelson picked it up at the free throw line and threw it up. It hit the rim, rose a few feet, and dropped back through. The balloons were all but popped. The Lakers missed twice and the Celtics committed an offensive foul, all of which an angry Chamberlain watched from the bench. After a few meaningless buckets it ended. The Celtics had hung on to win their eleventh title 108–106.

The debate began immediately afterward. Chamberlain versus van

Breda Kolff. Although they had been friendly through their careers, Russell criticized Chamberlain for leaving the game. Perhaps a broken leg should have taken Chamberlain out, Russell said, but nothing else.

The comments caused a rift between the superstars and ruined their friendship. Some observers later commented that perhaps Russell had only feigned friendship during their playing days to prevent Chamberlain from becoming angry and playing well against the Celtics.

All of this mattered little to Jerry West. He was merely disgusted with another loss. He had finished with 42 points, 13 rebounds, and 12 assists. The Celtics went to the Los Angeles locker room immediately after the game. Russell took West's hand and held it silently.

"Jerry," Havlicek professed, "I love you."

"He is the master," Boston's Larry Siegfried said of West. "They can talk about the others, build them up, but he is the one. He is the only guard."

West was named the MVP, the first and only time in NBA Finals history that the award went to a member of a losing team. The gestures were nice, West said, but they didn't address his agony.

Yet there was a final insult. The car awarded with the MVP trophy was green.

Cooke, meanwhile, was left with the task of figuring out what to do with all the balloons. He finally decided to send them to a children's hospital. For years they would hang metaphorically over the Lakers' heads, the victory balloons that never rained down. The championships, it seemed, only belonged to Boston.

"It was a challenge to play against Russell and the Celtics," Baylor said. "It was fun. It was disappointing to lose. But it was the ultimate challenge. They were a proud team, and they had reason to be. Some people thought they were proud and arrogant. But I enjoyed playing against them. They were the best."

Two weeks after the 1969 season closed, Butch van Breda Kolff resigned to become the head coach of the Detroit Pistons and was replaced by Joe Mullaney, the veteran coach from Providence College. Mullaney was another practitioner of eastern basketball, but where van Breda Kolff was brash, he was mild. "Wilt is special and must be treated special," the new coach said with a smile.

"Mullaney is alright," Wilt observed. "He don't act like he wants to be *boss*."

Mullaney asked Chamberlain to help trap the ball in the corners. The big center was willing to cooperate, and this defense quickly showed that it would be effective. Alas, the 33-year-old Chamberlain suffered a knee injury nine games into the season. He had missed just 12 games in 11 seasons. Although the doctors said he would be out for the season, Chamberlain promised, "I will be be back." In his absence, Baylor found a spark. With Wilt in the post, Baylor had given up his drives and taken up jump shots the previous season, which sent his scoring average and effectiveness plummeting. And they had taken his influence over the team with them. Both he and Chamberlain were loud, forceful types, but as Baylor's physical skills declined so did his role as team leader. "It was painful to watch," said writer Merv Harris.

Chamberlain, meanwhile, worked diligently at rehabilitation and, as the 1970 play-offs neared, announced his intention to return, surprising even his doctors. "There's been so much unhappiness connected to my basketball—disappointing defeats, unfair criticism, and such—that I really hadn't realized how much the game meant to me," he said. "I've been surprised at the nice fan mail I've gotten since I've been hurt. I guess getting hurt has made me seem human and has made people sympathize with me for the first time. Usually, I've been regarded as some kind of animal."

He played the final three games of the regular season and was force enough to help the Lakers thrive in the Western play-offs. They had finished second in the regular season behind the Atlanta Hawks and Lou Hudson, but with Chamberlain the Lakers swept Atlanta in the divisional finals.

With Russell retired from Boston, the Celtics had collapsed in the East, only to be replaced by the Knicks, coached by Red Holzman and led by Willis Reed, Dave DeBusschere, Bill Bradley, and Walt Frazier. Which left only one question for the 1970 championship series: Who was the hungriest?

The Lakers ventured into Madison Square Garden for Game 1 and promptly lost 124–112, as Reed finished with 37 points, 16 rebounds, and five assists.

Asked why he had left Reed open outside, Chamberlain replied, "I just didn't come out after him. Next time I will."

As promised, Chamberlain was much more active on defense in Game 2. He hounded Reed into missing 17 shots and blocked the New York center's shot at the buzzer to preserve a 105–103 Laker win.

Back home for Game 3 on April 29, the Lakers rolled out to a 56–42 halftime lead while Chamberlain and Baylor ruled the inside. But the Knicks abruptly reversed that momentum in the third period. New York forward Dave DeBusschere and former Laker Dick Barnett started dropping shots in from the perimeter, setting off a run that allowed the Knicks to tie it at 100 with 13 seconds to go. The Laker defense forced New York out of a set play, but Dave DeBusschere took a pass from Frazier, gave a head fake, and dropped in a neat little jumper for a 102–100 Knicks lead with three seconds left. The Lakers were out of time-outs.

Chamberlain halfheartedly tossed the ball to West, who dribbled three times as Reed dogged him. Two feet beyond the key, just to the left of the lane, West let fly from 63 feet. Good. DeBusschere, underneath the basket, threw out his arms in disgust and collapsed.

Dr. Robert Kerlan, the Lakers' team physician, was excited enough to momentarily forget his arthritis. He jumped up from his courtside seat and began to celebrate. "I had my cane and I jumped out to the middle of the floor and started to dance," he told writer Scott Ostler. "I looked around and saw I was alone and I wondered where everyone was. Mendy Rudolph was the ref, and he signaled me to get back to my seat. I felt like a perfect ass."

Wilt was fooled, too. He laughed and ran off to the locker room, thinking the shot had won it. But only the ABA had a three-point rule back then. The officials brought Wilt back out for overtime, 102–102.

In overtime, Barnett, the former Laker, clinched it for the Knicks with a bucket at the 0:04 mark. West had no more miracles. It ended 111–108.

Game 4 was another nail-biter. It would come to overtime and the hands of Laker reserve forward John Tresvant, who would lead Los Angeles to a 121–115 win and a 2–2 tie in the series. Baylor did his part, too, with 30 points.

Wilt came out strong for the fifth game in New York and was determined to cover Reed all over the floor. With a little more than eight minutes gone in the first quarter, Los Angeles had raced to a 25–15 lead. Then Reed caught a pass at the foul line, and Chamberlain was there to meet him. Reed went to his left but tripped over Wilt's foot and fell forward, tearing a muscle in his thigh.

With Reed out, the Garden crowd grew quiet. Holzman tried to prop up his players' spirits during the time-out. He inserted Nate Bowman to play Chamberlain, and that worked for a time. Then Holzman went with reserve forward Bill Hoskett, all of 6-foot-7, who hadn't seen a minute of playing time in the entire play-offs. Hoskett hounded Chamberlain effectively enough, but it really wasn't getting the Knicks anywhere. By the half the Lakers led by 13.

In the locker room, Bradley suggested they go to a 3–2 zone offense, which would either force Chamberlain to come out from the basket or give them open shots. "Outside we had two wings with a point man," Bradley later explained. "Inside we had one guy on the baseline and a roamer. When we saw Wilt not playing a man, it was like attacking a zone. Just hit the open spaces in a zone."

It began working in the third. The Lakers seemed almost possessed by the notion of taking advantage of the mismatch in the post. Time after time, they attempted to force the ball into Chamberlain, and the Knicks got bunches of steals and turnovers. The fourth period opened with the Lakers holding an 82–75 lead and a troubled hand. They were in obvious disarray.

And the Knickerbockers were surging, cheered on by the awakened Garden crowd. "Let's go, Knicks. Let's go, Knicks," all 19,500 spectators chanted over and over. At just under eight minutes, Bradley hit a jumper to tie it at 87. The Knicks ran away from there, taking a 3–2 edge, 107–100. Los Angeles had been forced into 30 turnovers for the game. In the second half, West didn't have a field goal, and Chamberlain scored only four points.

"The fifth game," DeBusschere said proudly 20 years later, "was one of the greatest basketball games ever played."

The Lakers returned home and corrected their mistakes in Game 6. With Reed out, Wilt scored 45 with 27 rebounds. The Lakers rolled, 135–113, to tie the series at three each. But even with the victory, Chamberlain sensed doom. "American sports fans are spoiled," he declared afterward. "They only want to win. They can't just give credit to a team for getting this far. They can't just enjoy great games between great teams. They don't realize one team has to lose."

The stage was set in New York for the seventh-game drama. Would Reed play? The Knicks left the locker room for warm-ups not knowing. Before he had left, Bradley and DeBusschere had asked Reed to give the team just one half. About 20 minutes would do it, they figured. In the training room, Reed was set to receive injections of carbocaine and cortisone through a large needle. There were problems, though, because the skin on his thighs was so thick the doctor had trouble getting the needle in.

"It was a big needle, a big needle," Reed recalled. "I saw that needle and I said, 'Holy shit.' And I just held on. I think I suffered more from the needle than the injury."

In the Laker locker room West faced a similar situation—injections in both injured hands. "I don't even like to think about it," Mullaney told the writers. "A shooter getting needles in his shooting hand."

Reed appeared on the Garden floor just before game time that Friday, May 8, bringing an overwhelming roar from the crowd. "The scene is indelibly etched in my mind," Frazier said, "because if that did not happen, I know we would not have won the game." The Knicks watched Reed hobble out, and each of them soaked in the emotion from the noise.

The Lakers watched, too, and made no attempt at furtive glances. Reed took a few awkward warm-up shots. "I can't go to my right all that well," he jokingly told Chamberlain before the start. Reed couldn't go right when he was healthy.

He stepped into the circle against Wilt for the tip-off but remained immobile. That changed once play began. Reed scored New York's first points, a semijumper from the key, and he played incredibly active defense. Seventeen times the Lakers jammed the ball into Chamberlain in the post. Reed harassed him into shooting two for nine. And Reed hit another shot. (He would finish two for five with four fouls and three rebounds.) But it was enough. The emotional charge sent the rest of the Knicks zipping through their paces. They simply ran away from the Lakers. New York led 9–2, then 15–6, then 30–17. When Reed left the game in the third quarter, New York led 61–37. From there they rolled on to the title, 113–99.

"The Laker dressing room later was a morgue, in which living humans were interred," wrote Bill Libby for the *LA Times*.

Drenched in sweat, Chamberlain sat and pondered his painful comeback from injury, now rewarded with yet another championship loss. "My knee didn't hurt much," he said, turning down an excuse. "We just lost, that's all. I didn't lose. We lost."

Indeed. A hopelessness settled over the franchise.

West and Baylor missed much of the next season with injuries, leaving Chamberlain as the focal point of the offense. That wasn't enough as Kareem, Oscar Robertson, and the Milwaukee Bucks swept the Lakers aside in the play-offs 4–1.

In the aftermath, Cooke wanted Joe Mullaney's job. "I hated to see it happen to someone as nice as Joe," Fred Schaus said. "But when you're dealing with a guy like Jack Kent Cooke, when they've made up their mind, there's nothing you're going to say to change it."

9

First the Streak, Then Kareem

With their failure in the 1971 play-offs, it became clear that time was running out for Jack Kent Cooke's collection of talented Lakers. Bill Russell had been out of basketball for two years, and they still hadn't won a championship. Heading into the 1971–72 season, Elgin Baylor was struggling to come back from yet another injury. Chamberlain had turned 35, and West was 33. If this wasn't their last shot, it was close.

The answer, in Cooke's mind, was to try yet another coach. Having worked his way through Fred Schaus, Butch van Breda Kolff, and Joe Mullaney, the owner made overtures to UCLA coach John Wooden, who discussed the job over a cup of tea in the library of Cooke's Bel-Air mansion. "John turned it down," Cooke recalled. "He had had his time. He said he was too old to start into professional basketball."

Fred Schaus then asked Cooke to consider 45-year-old Bill Sharman, the former Celtic guard who had just coached the Utah Stars to the 1971 ABA title. Sharman's 1967 San Francisco Warriors had lost the NBA championship series to Wilt's 76ers. Before that, Sharman had made a winner of the miserable program at Cal State Los Angeles. He'd even coached the Cleveland Pipers to the old American Basketball League title in 1962. (The Pipers were owned by a young shipping magnate named George Steinbrenner, so it was established that he could get along in difficult circumstances.)

Cooke was intrigued by Sharman. "He had that inner intensity," the owner recalled, adding that he later saw the same quality in Joe Gibbs, who coached Cooke's Washington Redskins to three Super Bowl championships. "They were both seemingly quiet, almost shy. But I saw this quality after I talked to them five or 10 minutes."

Sharman's friends said he was crazy to consider the offer. They pointed out that the ideal situation would be a young team on the way up. Never get involved with an old team on the way down, they told him. After all, who needed the pressure of dealing with old superstars and a demanding owner? "Everybody told me, 'You don't want that job,' " he recalled.

He took it anyway, which left his Celtics buddies shaking their heads. The Lakers announced his hiring that July of 1971, after working out the legal details with the Stars, who claimed they still had Sharman under contract. Asked his goal, Sharman declared, "The world championship." That plot line, of course, was all too familiar to the reporters covering the team. They wondered what made Sharman think he could write a different ending this time.

The 1971–72 Laker roster presented a mishmash of gnarly egos. "Egads, they were prima donnas," Cooke recalled. The owner, of course, was the granddaddy of them all. His demanding style set the tone for what was a substantial cult of personality. Chamberlain had his giant pride. West was sullen with frustration, and "Motormouth" Baylor struggled with his declining skills and influence. To go with them were forward Happy Hairston, an irascible locker-room lawyer who chattered incessantly; Gail Goodrich, a determined scorer who liked to control the ball; and Jim McMillian, a chunky Ivy Leaguer pushing for a starting role.

Among the bit players were Pat Riley, Keith Erickson, and Flynn Robinson, all of whom sported healthy self-concepts. "On that one team you probably had more diverse, strong personalities than you had on any championship team in the history of the game," Bill Bertka observed.

The egos had tugged the Lakers in different directions for a few seasons now, and at times they had seemed on the verge of pulling the team apart. "We had a lot of players who'd had personal success but hadn't enjoyed team success," West said, "a lot of very frustrated people. It had been frustrating to lose each year. It was terrible."

"But," Bertka said, "you had the strongest personality in Bill Sharman. He was on fire right at that time. He was at the peak of his career with his personal intensity as a coach. He was a great communicator. No frills. No bullshit. With Bill, it was all down to productivity."

Intensity had always been Sharman's trademark as a player. Bob Cousy, his longtime Celtic roommate, said he thought he had the strongest killer instinct in basketball—until he met Sharman. "Bill matched mine," Cousy said.

Off the court, Sharman was a sweetheart. On it, he was a demon, a transformation that amazed and amused his teammates. He wasn't known for excessive fighting. But when he did square off, whether the opponent was a seven-footer or just another guard, the bouts were usually one-punch affairs. "Willie didn't talk," former Celtic teammate Ed Macauley recalled. "When he'd had enough, you knew it."

His one-punch victims included 6-foot-9, 230-pound Nobel Jorgensen of the Syracuse Nationals and Hall of Famer Andy Phillip. "I was always kind of aggressive," Sharman admitted. "When we played in the 'fifties, pro

Earvin "Magic" Johnson. *(Steve Lipofsky)*

Below: James Worthy in the
lane. *(Scott Cunningham)*

Right: Pat Riley. *(Steve
Lipofsky)*

Opposite page: Byron Scott.
(Steve Lipofsky)

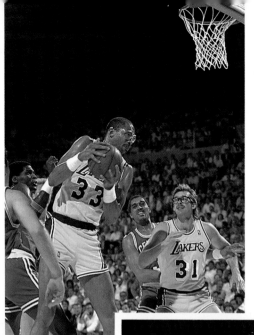

Opposite page, above: Kareem Abdul-Jabbar and Kurt Rambis out-muscle the Celtics. *(Steve Lipofsky)*

Above: Kareem launches his signature sky hook over Kevin McHale. *(Steve Lipofsky)*

Opposite page, below: A. C. Green. *(Steve Lipofsky)*

Opposite page: The Fabulous Forum. *(Scott Cunningham)*

Two familiar home-game sights: Jack Nicholson (left) at courtside *(Scott Cunningham)*, and (below) the Laker Girls. *(Steve Lipofsky)*

Magic and Bird: rivals of the 80s, with Pat O'Brien. *(Steve Lipofsky)*

basketball was still growing. It was kind of like hockey. The owners didn't say go out and fight. But they didn't discourage it. Back then they didn't throw you out of games for fighting. They kind of let it go. If you backed off and didn't hold your own, other players kind of took advantage of you. I always feel I never started a fight, but I never backed away from one. If you did, they just kept pushing and grabbing at you. I saw a lot of good basketball players in those days get pushed right out of the league because they wouldn't push back."

Beneath this tough exterior was a neat freak who always folded and put away his clothes on road trips, even for a 12-hour stay in a hotel room. On a Celtics roster bristling with partiers, he was the guy who filled 3x5 note cards with reminders on shooting technique and opponents' defensive tendencies and studied them in the locker room before games. He was the diet and exercise nerd, eating and working out at exact times during the day. Forget the usual beer and steak; Sharman wanted honey, toast, and tea as his pregame meal. Then, in the locker room, he would stretch and do warm-ups. Nobody did that stuff in the fifties. And they didn't jog either. But Sharman did. Strangest of all, he insisted on going to the gym each morning before a game for shooting exercise, running through exactly the shots he planned to take that night.

As a coach, he would insist that his players go through these same routines. They often grumbled, but Sharman's game-day shootaround soon became a staple of NBA preparation. So would his notions on diet and exercise. Beyond that, he required his players to become students of the game. His Lakers were the first NBA team to break down game film and study it as football coaches did. In that age before videotape, scout Bill Bertka would spend hours cutting and splicing film. When the players seemed a little bored with the idea, Bertka spliced in occasional shots of Playboy Bunnies.

"It kinda got their attention," Sharman recalled with a chuckle.

The son of a newspaper circulation supervisor, Sharman lettered in five sports (football, basketball, baseball, tennis, and track) in high school in Porterville, California. After a stint in the navy during World War II, he played basketball and baseball at Southern Cal. From there he joined the NBA's old Washington Caps, then moved to baseball with the Brooklyn Dodgers organization and even earned a brief spot on their roster in 1951. But that fall Red Auerbach coaxed him back to basketball. Sharman had been a 6-foot-2 forward in a control offense at Southern Cal. He couldn't handle the ball too well, but he could shoot, and Auerbach's freelance system required scorers. "Sharman was just perfect for it because he moved constantly," Cousy said.

Defenders hated Sharman's Energizer style and the cunning way he would run his man into the Celtics' bruising picks. "He would move in a circle, and eventually he would come free," Cousy said. "I almost knew where he was going before he got there." Most often he would circle and emerge on the weak side just as the defense was collapsing, which left him with an open shot. He was a quick shooter, hoisting the ball from his shoulders up. "He was a complete technician in terms of the mechanics of the shot," Cousy said. "He never took a low percentage shot." For four seasons, 1956–59, he led the Celtics in scoring and had the league's top free-throw percentage for eight.

An eight-time All-Star, Sharman would later author an instructional book on shooting. As a coach, he used his understanding of the mechanics to improve his players' touch. In Los Angeles, however, he soon met his match. Chamberlain's foul shooting presented an unconquerable mountain. After years of trying everything, Wilt admitted he was befuddled at the line. Crowds at the Forum took to cheering wildly when he made one. Dolph Schayes and previous coaches had become obsessed with improving Chamberlain's free throws, thinking that practice would make perfect. Chamberlain did, in fact, become a good practice shooter, only to resume his impotence during games.

"I never could figure out how to help him with free throws," Sharman said.

At first, the Lakers weren't quite sure what to make of Sharman. They found him to be a strange mix of fight and quiet innovation. He was a Southern California boy, but he was also a Celtic. "It was difficult for us to relate to him in the beginning, because he was covered with Boston green," recalled Pat Riley, a Laker sub at the time. "But in time we came around. He was a low-key guy, but very competitive, very feisty."

It didn't help that Sharman gave them another dose of green when he added K. C. Jones, his Boston teammate, as the first assistant coach in Laker history. "We've never had an assistant coach before," Cooke grumbled, "except, of course, Chick Hearn." The two former Celtic guards had seen Red Auerbach's running game work wonders with Bill Russell snatching rebounds and firing outlet passes on the fast break. They understandably wanted to perpetuate Red's revolution in Los Angeles.

Sharman's announcement that he planned to make the Lakers a running team brought a lot of laughs around the league. Use Chamberlain, the NBA's resident dinosaur, in a running game? Absolutely loony. Chamberlain was the premier post-up weapon.

Sharman knew he would have to sell the key players on the idea.

First he invited Chamberlain to a pricey LA restaurant for lunch. Once there, they discussed the need for Wilt, the greatest scorer in the history of the game, to focus on defense and rebounding. The big center had heard this line from other coaches. But Sharman was different. He listened to Chamberlain's opinions on the issue. Sharman had played the running game, and he knew exactly what it took. Chamberlain had his doubts but said he would cooperate fully.

"When they got up to go, Sharman had forgotten his billfold," Schaus recalled. "Wilt had to pay for the meal."

Chamberlain grinned and reached for his cash. Wherever he played, the tabs were left to him. He was used to it by now. Some observers believed he wouldn't have it any other way.

Next, Sharman asked Happy Hairston to shelve his funky offensive game to concentrate on rebounding. Dominating the defensive boards was a two-man job. Every great center needs a tough power forward to help out. Hairston's sacrifice would be a key to winning the title, Sharman said. A muscular 6-foot-7, 225-pounder, Hairston agreed. (It helped that Cooke had just awarded him with a new contract. "Management has been very generous to me," Hairston explained.) The new emphasis would cause his scoring to dip from 18.6 in 1971 to 13.1 in '72. But he would average 15 boards over the last half of the season and become the first forward to pull down 1,000 rebounds while playing alongside Chamberlain.

With Hairston and Wilt controlling the defensive boards, the Lakers had West and Gail Goodrich to run the fast break. But Goodrich, who had started his career in LA, then gone to Phoenix, liked to control the ball. Now that he had returned to the Lakers, Sharman wanted him to give up the ball and use his great ability to move without it, working to get open for a pass from West. "Gail always had the ball in Phoenix," Bertka recalled. "People said we were going to need two balls with West and Goodrich in the backcourt, but Gail began taking great pride in playing without it."

He and West would both average 25 points per game over the season as they hauled in pass after pass from Chamberlain. West, who was working his way back from knee surgery, would run the break from the center, with Goodrich finishing from the wing. "Jerry was a great player, and I think we complemented each other," Goodrich said. "We blended and didn't hurt each other's games."

The last remaining problem was the other forward, where Baylor was a painful question mark. The team's captain, he had been the Lakers' dominant figure for most of his 13-year career. But he had missed all but two games of the previous season with injury. In the off-season, he had worked hard to come back and was now able to play again, only Sharman's new running system required a very active small forward. Baylor just didn't have the mobility. At first, Sharman wasn't sure exactly how to handle it. So he waited. The answer would come soon enough.

BUTTER

Bill Bertka was ill the first time he scouted Jim McMillian at a college holiday tournament. Maybe it was because Bertka had the flu or because he had ridden cross-country with Red Auerbach and they ate candy bars the whole way. Whatever, Bertka was so sick he couldn't sit up. So he climbed to the nosebleed section, lay on his side, and watched McMillian, a senior at Columbia. Ill as Bertka was, he still liked what he saw. Columbia was playing Villanova with Howard Porter. "I was surprised by McMillian's ability to play Porter in the post," Bertka said. "The thing I saw about him was how smart he was."

With Bertka's recommendation, the Lakers made McMillian the thirteenth pick of the first round of the 1970 draft. Soon afterward, Fred Schaus endured a tongue lashing from Cooke. Knicks owner Ned Irish had phoned Cooke and told him, "I can't believe you guys drafted Jim McMillian. Why, he's an overweight small forward."

Schaus, one of Cooke's favorite shouting targets, was worried. "I can't believe we drafted this guy," he told Bertka.

"Look; you have to wait and find out," the scout said. "He's got character. He's gonna play in this league."

McMillian did have a tendency to gain weight. Baylor thought he looked like a chubby Floyd Patterson and dubbed him "Floyd Butterball," or "Butter" for short. But he slimmed down on a grapefruit diet and steadily improved over his rookie season. "He came to epitomize what you wanted in a small forward," Bertka said. "He could run the floor. He could post-up. He could pass the ball. He had a nice medium-range jumper. He had a quick release on his shot. And he was smart."

By the opening of the 1971–72 season McMillian was pushing Baylor for the starting role at small forward. The Lakers broke out to a 6–3 record that first month. "But Bill wasn't happy with the results," Bertka said.

"Elgin started every game," Sharman said. "But Jim McMillian was coming on strong."

He hustled and ran the floor just like Sharman wanted, which put him in position to run the break with West and Goodrich. After those first nine games, Sharman decided McMillian should start. The coach knew he had to approach Baylor carefully about a reserve role. Before practice one morning at Loyola University, Sharman informed his captain that McMillian would start. "He just wasn't the Elgin Baylor of old," Sharman said. "I knew he felt bad, and I wanted him to keep playing. But he said if he couldn't play up to his standards he would retire."

Baylor announced his retirement the next day, and their 33-game win streak began that night. The 1971–72 Lakers would win more games than any other team in NBA history with a 69–13 record. "One of the happiest times of my life was when the Lakers were on that 33-game winning streak," Cooke said, "a record I dare say will never be broken in the history of professional sports. It's as good as my Washington Redskins winning three Super Bowls. Each time they'd play, we'd wait for the win with bated breath."

"All the pieces just fit," Sharman said.

Especially the big one, the Big Dipper.

With Baylor's retirement, Sharman had asked West and Chamberlain to become team captains. West declined, but Wilt relished the leadership role. In the past, he had infuriated Laker coaches, sometimes snacking on hot dogs or fried chicken on the bench before a game. But now he was all business. He had 25 rebounds, six assists, and a dozen points in the first victory of the streak, at home over Baltimore. Next came Oakland and a 19-rebound effort, followed by 22 rebounds and seven assists against New York in the Forum. In Chicago two nights later it was 20 rebounds and eight assists. Most of the assists came from his pulling defensive rebounds and hitting the streaking Goodrich, West, and McMillian for fast-break buckets. Yet even those statistics said little about the blocks and changed shots he forced on defense. Instead of smacking the ball out of bounds as he had in years past, he began brush-blocking shots and starting a fast break the other way.

Their twenty-fifth straight came in Wilt's hometown of Philadelphia, where he celebrated with 32 points, 34 rebounds, and 12 blocks.

"Sharman has Wilt playing like Russell," Joe Mullaney said after watching the Lakers on television.

"Wilt should be the MVP in the league this season," Baylor told one writer, a sentiment echoed by Philadelphia's Billy Cunningham.

Many observers rushed to credit Sharman for the "new" Wilt. "I don't think I should get the credit," the coach quickly pointed out. "He's always had a bad rap. Whatever they ask of him he's done. He's just doing more things better now that he is not mainly a scorer. He must block a zillion shots a game. And he scares guys out of other shots or makes them take bad shots."

The secret to the entire running game, Sharman added, "has been Wilt's rebounding and fast passes."

"I really like the man," Wilt said. "I've never had a coach as conscientious as Bill."

Still, Chamberlain, always a stat freak, admitted feeling a twinge every time he looked at his drooping scoring average, down to 14.8 for the season. "I'm happy about it," he said of the streak, "but here I am the greatest scorer in the game of basketball and I've been asked by many coaches not to score. Now where else in a sport can you ask a guy to stop something he's the best in the world doing? It's like telling Babe Ruth not to hit home runs, just bunt."

*　　*　　*

Each win brought more notoriety for Sharman's shootaround. Soon just about every coach in the league had instituted a game-day practice. Which was bad news for Wilt. A night person and late sleeper, he had reluctantly agreed in his preseason meeting with Sharman to give the shootaround a try. "I'm still not for those 11 o'clock practices," he said as the streak rolled on. "I don't think they've done anything personally for Wilt Chamberlain except to make him lose some sleep. But we're winning and I'm not going to do anything to knock the winning way."

"After we started out 6 and 3, Wilt started to vacillate on the shootaround," Sharman said. "But after we won 33 straight, it was hard for him to say anything. Wilt only missed two morning practices all season, and he called ahead both times."

The streak ran through January 9, 1972, when they lost a road game to rival Milwaukee and Kareem, 120–114. Bucks coach Larry Costello had scouted the Lakers' thirty-third consecutive win, a road victory over Atlanta, and quickly devised a defense to cut off their fast break.

"We knew it had to end sometime," Sharman said.

Through each game, he'd been a fiend on the bench, shouting incessantly. "I was always a yeller," he said. "When I got back from Milwaukee my throat was sore that whole week. It got to where I couldn't even be heard. I went to the doctor and he told me I really had a bad case, not to even talk for a week or 10 days. I couldn't do that. We were in the middle of a season, a championship season.

"So I tried using one of those battery-operated megaphones. But in a game I couldn't use it. So I just kept hollering. The doctors said I shouldn't do it. But I thought after the season it would come back. But the damage had been done. My voice never came back."

The voice damage suffered during the streak was permanent and would eventually force Sharman from coaching.

They went 30–10 over the last half of the season. Each win brought them a little closer to that unreachable goal. But as the play-offs neared, the team sensed that old Laker jinx hovering somewhere nearby. "We were waiting for something to happen, something bad to happen again," Riley said. "But it didn't."

By the end of the season McMillian was averaging 18.8 points and 6.5 rebounds and had become a Forum favorite, with the crowd erupting over his long jumpers from the corner. "I really can't tell you how I fit into this team," he told reporters. "I'm just the fat little dude wearing Number 5."

Chicago, their first-round opponent, had won 57 games, but the Bulls had no center and were forced to play a control game. They fell in four. The Lakers' big challenge came in the Western finals, against the Bucks and

Kareem. In Game 1 at the Forum, the Milwaukee defense overplayed and double-teamed the Lakers, forcing them out of their favorite shooting spots and into a 27 percent performance from the floor. Los Angeles scored a mere eight points in the pivotal third period, and the Bucks took away the home-court advantage, 92–73.

In practice before the start of the series, Goodrich had complained about the ABC television lights that had been added for broadcasts. Cooke asked the network to remove some of the lights, which it did. Cooke wanted even more removed, and ABC again complied. After Game 1, the Los Angeles owner wanted still more adjustments.

It wasn't the lights, Sharman finally said. "It was that our good shooters were all way off."

The Lakers did manage a win in the second game, 135–134, but they were obviously shaky. West had shot 10 for 30 from the field. "I know what I'm doing wrong," he said afterward. "I'm turning my hand too much. But I can't get it stopped. It's got to go away by itself."

Somehow they overcame 61 percent shooting from the Bucks in Game 3 in Milwaukee. The Lakers drove frequently, drawing fouls and shooting free throws. On defense, Wilt overplayed Kareem to stop his skyhook, forcing him instead into short jumpers and lay-ups. At one point, Chamberlain blocked five shots. In the critical fourth period, Wilt held Kareem scoreless for the last 11 minutes. Abdul-Jabbar still finished with 33, but Chamberlain had done the job. The Lakers won, 108–105, and regained the home-court advantage. Goodrich had scored 30 and McMillian 27 to lead Los Angeles.

The Bucks lashed back in the fourth game, taking a 75–43 rebounding advantage and tying the series at two-all with a 114–88 blowout. Abdul-Jabbar celebrated his 25th birthday with 31 points. West, on the other hand, was only 9 of 23 from the field, and afterward he complained that Cooke was requiring him to play too many minutes.

The Lakers headed back to the Forum, where they ran away with the fifth game, 115–90, despite West's continued slump. They returned to Milwaukee for the sixth game, and in practice West kicked at a press table after missing an open jumper. In the past, he told the writers, nobody seemed to notice when he had great-scoring games because the Lakers always lost in the Finals. Now that they were winning, he said, all that people seemed to be interested in was his slump. As usual, Sharman said, people had failed to notice that West could virtually rule the floor with his defense alone.

The cure for these frustrations was another win; they vanquished the Bucks in Milwaukee, 104–100, to take the series, 4–2. Their opponent in the 1972 Finals would be the New York Knicks, who had beaten a resurgent Boston club in the Eastern finals, 4–1. The Knicks, however, were not the team of old. Cazzie Russell had been traded away after the '71 season to get

Jerry Lucas from the Warriors. And Mike Riordan and Dave Stallworth had been shipped to Baltimore in exchange for Earl Monroe. Willis Reed was out of action with his nagging knee injuries; his absence changed the entire nature of the team. "We operate on such a small margin of error," Bill Bradley told the writers. "We don't have Willis there to take care of our mistakes."

But the Knicks made no mistakes in Game 1 in the Forum. Lucas scored 26 points, and Bradley hit 11 of 12 shots from the field as New York shot 53 percent from the floor. They used a nearly perfect first half to jump to a good lead and won much too easily, 114–92. Early in the second half, the Forum crowd began filing out dejectedly. It looked like another Los Angeles fold in the Finals. The Lakers had lost their home-court advantage again.

But in Game 2, Dave DeBusschere hurt his side and didn't play after intermission. With no one to hold him down, Happy Hairston scored 12 points in the second half, and Los Angeles evened the series, 106–92. Luck had always been such a big factor for the Lakers, West said. Each of the previous Finals, they were overcome with a sense that fortune had turned against them. But that all changed after Game 2 in 1972. That night West lay awake wondering how he would act if they actually had a championship to celebrate. What would he do?

At Madison Square Garden for Game 3, DeBusschere tried to play but missed all six of his field-goal attempts. The Lakers dominated the frontcourt and danced out to a 107–96 win. Their momentum was holding, although they felt a tremor in the first quarter of Game 4, when Chamberlain fell and sprained his wrist. Obviously in pain, he decided to stay in. It was a crucial decision. The game went to overtime, but at the end of regulation the Los Angeles center picked up his fifth foul. In 13 NBA seasons he had never fouled out of a game, a statistic of which he was immensely proud. Immediately speculation started along press row that he would play soft in the overtime. Instead, he came out in a shot-blocking fury that propelled the Lakers to a 116–111 victory. At 3–1, their lead now seemed insurmountable.

"The patient is critical and about to die," Walt Frazier observed.

The early word on Chamberlain was that he would be unable to play Game 5 at the Forum. But as game time neared, he received a shot of an antiinflammatory drug and took the floor. To assure the title, he scored 24 points and pulled down 29 rebounds as Los Angeles finally broke the jinx, 114–100. The effort earned Chamberlain his second Finals MVP award. Afterward, the Lakers sipped champagne from wineglasses and toasted each other quietly. There was no shaking and spewing. No riotous behavior. And certainly no rain of balloons from the Forum rafters. "Wilt," West said, raising his glass, "was simply the one who got us here."

There was, however, Jack Kent Cooke's championship smile. "Mr. Cooke walked in with the biggest smile I'd ever seen on his face," Sharman recalled.

"I was very, very, very happy," Cooke said. "In sports, it's the winning that counts."

Yet those moments of joy, which had taken so many years to wrench from the circumstances, evaporated within hours. As a postseason bonus, Cooke gave each of his players $1,500, the only problem being that the previous season, when they hadn't even reached the Finals, the bonus had been $5,000. The players were miffed and suggested that rather than take the money, everybody should just turn their share over to Sharman. That, West said, would have meant a $15,000 gift for the coach. That would be greater than the $12,500 share of play-off money, the players reasoned. That would be a good way to get Cooke to pay the coach's play-off share.

Cooke, however, disagreed, saying that Sharman's money should come from the players' allotment. The morning of the team championship dinner, the *LA Herald Examiner* published a story saying that the players were trying to cut Sharman out of his play-off share. "Cooke got [columnist] Melvin Durslag to write that story," West said. "Whenever he wanted something derogatory written about me or Wilt, he got Durslag to do it."

The story broke the morning of their team banquet, which left the players furious that Cooke had used their disagreement to cast them as selfish. "That night of the team party was a tremendous brouhaha," recalled Pete Newell, who was replacing Fred Schaus as general manager. "It was worse than an Irish wake."

Actually, an Irish wake would have been better, because at least it carries a spirit of celebration, Cooke said.

The players refused to speak to the owner at the banquet. Chamberlain walked in and Cooke rose to greet him, but the center walked past as if the owner weren't there, Newell said.

"I was just appalled by their behavior and very hurt," Cooke said. "It was just an air of sullenness. It was Jerry West again. He went up and down the hall sulking."

That was not true, West said. "It's too bad that it got blown out of proportion. Everyone there that night felt bad for Bill Sharman. All the players loved him. One of the good things that happened to me in my career was having him as a coach."

The blowup helped prompt Schaus to take the head coaching job at Purdue, said Newell, who had just begun work as general manager. "I know when I got in there nobody was speaking to anybody. That was one reason Freddie Schaus wanted to get out. All the players were mad at him, too."

* * *

There was one final, unsatisfying peak before the Lakers descended into the great valley of the 1970s. They put their differences with Cooke aside long enough to make a run at one more championship. Considering the age of the 1972–73 roster, just reaching the Finals was an achievement. Chamberlain was 36. West was 34 and philosophical about it. "There's no question that there are a lot of things I can't do that I once could, particularly on offense," he said. He was no longer among the scoring and assist leaders in the league. Neither was Wilt. Although he led the league in rebounding and shot an incredible .727 from the floor, critics complained that Chamberlain seemed increasingly lethargic.

Goodrich still led the team from the backcourt, and Keith Erickson and Jim McMillian worked from the corners. But Happy Hairston spent much of the season injured, and to bolster the frontcourt the team picked up veteran forward Bill Bridges.

This group won the Pacific Division with a 60–22 record and prospered in the play-offs, defeating Chicago in a seven-game series, then brushing aside the surprising Golden State Warriors, who had upset Kareem and Milwaukee. For the fourth time in five seasons, the West- and Chamberlain-led Lakers advanced to the championship round. And for the third time, they faced the Knicks, who had won 57 games. New York had finished 11 back of Boston, who had topped the league at 68–14, but the Knicks had upset the Celtics in Boston the seventh game of the Eastern finals on Sunday, April 29. Then they had to scramble to Los Angeles for a Tuesday-night Game 1 with the Lakers. New York phoned to ask if the Lakers would consider delaying the series until Wednesday.

No way, the Lakers said.

Regardless, the players looked forward to this rubber match. New York and Los Angeles had won a championship apiece in their series. Now they had an opportunity to settle the issue. "It will be nice to see Jerry," Walt Frazier said of West and his Lakers. "Between us it will be a battle of pride."

Not to mention age. The Knicks were just as long in the tooth as the Lakers. Exhausted, they arrived that first Tuesday of May and promptly met a rested monster. Chamberlain blocked seven shots and intimidated five others. Mel Counts, the Lakers' other seven-footer, had nine rebounds. Los Angeles owned the interior, while the Knicks shot from the perimeter and rebounded poorly. The Lakers jumped out to a 20-point lead with 26 fast-break points. The Knicks did make a good run in the second half, cutting it to 115–112 in the closing seconds. (West, who had 24 points, had fouled out with three minutes to go.) But Erickson got a defensive rebound at the end and whipped the ball out to Bridges to preserve the win.

That, unfortunately, would conclude the highlights for the Lakers. The momentum abruptly shifted to the Knicks once they had rested. "After that, we took names on them and won the next four games in a row," Willis Reed recalled with a chuckle.

The Knicks' defense threw a cowl over West, Chamberlain, and McMillian. Chamberlain, in fact, would make only 22 field goals in the series and miss 24 of 38 foul shots. New York claimed Game 2, 99–95, when McMillian botched a pair of free throws with 24 seconds to go. Chamberlain himself missed eight of nine and drew quick fouls just about every time he looked to score, which wasn't often.

Chamberlain took only three shots in Game 3 in New York, and West was slowed by strained hamstrings. Still, the Lakers had an opportunity to win it until Willis Reed's jumpers and nine fourth-quarter points from Earl Monroe did them in, 87–83. They got close again in Game 4. With the Knicks up by two, Bradley missed a jumper. Chamberlain and Reed went for the rebound and deflected it to DeBusschere, who laid it in as Wilt fouled him. The free throw gave New York a 3–1 lead in games, 103–98. From there, the Knicks closed it out in the Forum, 102–93, with Earl Monroe sealing the championship by scoring eight points over the last two minutes.

Afterward, Chamberlain peeled off his soaked Laker jersey for the last time. Never close, this cluster of personalities had run out of things to say to one another, and Sharman didn't have the voice to keep them together another year.

What followed is a time Jerry West describes as "the worst period in my life." It is no coincidence that the same could be said about the entire organization.

In early March 1973, Jack Kent Cooke was having dinner while watching a Kings hockey game when he got a call from his doctor, who, reporting on the results of a life insurance physical, told Cooke he had "the constitution of a 25-year-old man and the heart of an ox." Elated, Cooke hung up the phone and immediately suffered a massive heart attack. "My lower jaw went numb, and my chest tightened," Cooke recalled. "Fortunately, I was having dinner with Dr. Bob Kerlan. He took one look at me and said, 'Get out of here.'" Kerlan helped Cooke to an office couch, where the doctor administered mouth-to-mouth resuscitation until Cooke could be rushed to a nearby hospital.

Cooke's first visitor during recuperation was his mother. "She was just a beautiful lady," Pete Newell said. "She would go to all the Forum games. Jack just loved her and was so proud of her. He was also very proud of his vocabulary. He was a walking dictionary, and when she came to visit he described in great detail what he'd been through, the catheterization and everything. He used the exact medical terminology. 'Mother,' he said, 'believe it or not, for 30 seconds I was dead. But Dr. Kerlan revived me.' His mother smiled and said, 'Tell me, Jack, which way were you going? Heaven or hell?' "

As it turned out, neither would have him. Just one month after his heart attack, Cooke suffered a second blow. The stock of Teleprompter, his cable television company in New York, plunged because of huge losses. Against doctor's orders, Cooke went to New York, fired most of the management, and ran the company himself. "I spent exactly a year in New York," he said. "I was not about to preside over a bankrupt company."

"That's the way he did things," Newell said of Cooke. "In six months, he had the stock going in the right direction again, all the fat cut out."

"I later sold that company for a major profit," Cooke boasted. "An ungodly amount."

Other endings weren't so happy. That same year, Sharman's wife, Dorothy, was diagnosed with cancer. She spent much of the 1973–74 season hospitalized in New York. "It was a tough period," Pete Newell said. "Jack Kent Cooke lost his health; Sharman lost his voice; then his wife, Dorothy, died of cancer."

"It was very difficult," Sharman recalled. "After the doctor told me she only had a few months to live, I wanted to be with her all the time. I'd go with the team for a few days, then fly to New York, then go back with the team again."

In his absence, John Barnhill, now his assistant, ran the Lakers. "Bill spent more time back in New York than he did with the team," Newell said. "Mr. Cooke loved Bill. He took care of all those expenses with his wife's illness."

"When she was in the hospital in New York, Mr. Cooke called her every day," Sharman said.

The season became a study in chaos as Newell hastily put together a lineup. Chamberlain departed in September of 1973, leaving the Lakers without a center. The Buffalo Braves had 23-year-old Elmore Smith, a 7-foot 250-pounder known for blocking shots. "To get him, we had to give up Jim McMillian," Newell said.

McMillian was popular with his teammates. Word of the trade stunned the team. "I cried like a baby when we traded Jimmy McMillian," Bill Bertka recalled. The Lakers also shipped Keith Erickson to Phoenix for the legendary Connie Hawkins and drafted a bruising but unpolished rookie, Kermit Washington. Sharman and Barnhill worked at getting the new faces introduced, but their efforts were further complicated by injuries that caused West to miss 51 games. Despite all the setbacks, the Lakers trailed Golden State by just three games with seven left on the regular schedule. From there they found a last burst of emotion and fought their way to the Pacific Division championship with a 47–35 record. But the effort left them spent, and they fell to Kareem and the Bucks in the first round of the play-offs, 4–1.

West played just 14 minutes in the series and scored four points, renewing rumors that he would retire, but he came to training camp in the fall of 1974 in good shape. His mental state, however, had deteriorated with constant bickering with Cooke over money. West believed Cooke had promised him that he and Chamberlain made the same salary, but after Chamberlain departed in 1973, West learned otherwise, which left him stewing.

"Jerry West was a brilliant young man in many areas," Cooke said. "But he was very naive back then in the ways of the world. Jerry was obsessed with money. He's a very rich man now. He's been very careful in the handling of his money. From the moment I purchased the Lakers in 1965, it was a continuing battle every year between Jerry West and me as to whether Elgin Baylor got a penny more than Jerry. Jerry felt the amount of money he got should be greater than Elgin because he did so much more.

"As far as Wilt Chamberlain was concerned, I never made such a commitment to Jerry. I did, however, make a commitment to him concerning Elgin Baylor. But Wilt Chamberlain was an entirely different story.

"I should point out," Cooke continued, "that I did not dislike this constant clamoring for equal financial treatment with Elgin Baylor. That revealed Jerry's spirit. It was part of the man."

West said his rounds with Cooke had very little to do with other players' salaries and a lot to do with the owner's manipulation. Cooke used salaries to play mind games, West said. "No one ever had to pay me to play basketball. But Mr. Cooke's manipulation made me not want to play for him. My relationship with Mr. Cooke was acrimonious because the negotiations were a game to him. I knew that. It was very frustrating."

West abruptly retired in October 1974. Then he filed suit against the Lakers, claiming Cooke owed him back wages, which set in motion an estrangement between West and the team that would last over the next two seasons.

West's departure was a setback, further complicated by the knee injury of newly acquired free agent Cazzie Russell. The Lakers finished 30–52 and for the first time in 14 seasons did not make the play-offs. "I kept thinking, 'It's got to get better,'" Sharman recalled. "But it never did."

Having gone through one season without a superstar, Cooke knew he didn't want to go through another. The Laker roster had always featured an exceptional talent. So Newell and Cooke set out to find another one. Fortunately, they didn't have to look too far.

In Milwaukee, Kareem Abdul-Jabbar had grown weary of life with the Bucks in a small, cold city and no longer wanted to play for coach Larry Costello. With a year to go on his contract, he informed the team that he wanted to move to New York or Los Angeles. "Milwaukee had to make a tough decision," Newell said. "Kareem was going to leave the Bucks anyway. They could trade him or end up in a year with nothing."

The choice then fell to the Knicks and Lakers. The Bucks decided they wanted a center and draft choices to replace Kareem, Newell recalled. "The Knicks were trying hard to get Kareem, too. They had a lot of money and no center and no draft choices. We had a center, Elmore Smith, and draft choices."

The Lakers held the second and seventh first-round picks in the 1975 draft, which they used to select David Meyers of UCLA and Junior Bridgeman of Louisville. They packaged those two rookies with Smith and second-year guard Brian Winters for Abdul-Jabbar, a deal that left Knicks executive Alan Cohen fuming. He later complained that the Bucks had never given New York a real chance.

Jack Kent Cooke merely smiled. The crafty old dealmaker had just landed another big one.

FOREVER

Kareem had wanted to go home again, to New York's own special noise. To Amsterdam Avenue and the playgrounds. To jazz and Harlem and the Lower East Side. To Madison Square Garden and lost love.

Ah, the Garden. He was 14 and already seven feet tall the first time he played there. Promoters had decided that one of his high school games at Power Memorial Academy should be moved to the Garden to accommodate the crowd. "It was like stars in my eyes," he said of that night in 1961. He couldn't understand, when he returned there eight years later as an NBA rookie, why those once-friendly fans booed him so vociferously. He didn't see that it was he who had jilted them first, when he decided to attend college in Los Angeles.

It didn't matter. He was bigger than New York anyway. He was Egypt and Africa and Islam and Westwood and Malibu and Manhattan and the West Indies, all rolled into one.

So the trade took him back to Los Angeles. They knew him there. Still, it wasn't home, not then. He knew that the love, like the hate, would have come much easier in New York. California was a place where the emotions seemed to run more tepid, which wasn't exactly conducive to finding the one thing he really wanted. Eventually he would come to understand that they loved him in Los Angeles. Yet even then, after all those years, he could really never be sure.

Born Ferdinand Lewis Alcindor on April 16, 1947, he grew up in Manhattan, the only child of Al and Cora Alcindor. His mother was a singer, and his father studied the trombone at the Juilliard School of Music while working at a variety of jobs to support the family.

Young Lewis was 13, already 6-foot-8 and the darling of New York's considerable hoops cult, when he conducted his first newspaper interview.

Quiet and bookwormish, he had decided he wanted to be an engineer. "I know I can't play basketball forever," he explained to a reporter.

He was wrong, of course. But how could he know then that he was built for the long run? The evidence only grew with each succeeding season. His years at Power Memorial produced two national high school titles and a 71-game winning streak. By the spring of his senior year college coaches all over the country wanted him, and they weren't alone. "I'll trade two first round draft picks for him right now," quipped Gene Shue, coach of the Baltimore Bullets.

But it was UCLA's John Wooden who got him, and together they formed the linchpin of the Bruins' college basketball dynasty. "I always related to him," Kareem said of Wooden. "He was about what you had to do to win games."

They did plenty of that, claiming three straight NCAA championships and forcing the college rules committee to adopt the "Alcindor Rule," outlawing dunking his final two seasons. As Wooden often pointed out, Alcindor was the most valuable player ever. The coach emphasized that most valuable didn't necessarily mean most talented. It simply meant that Alcindor was the kind of gifted, versatile center who could take a team beyond the sum of its players.

From UCLA he catapulted to the year-old Milwaukee Bucks. Even to the wise old tough guys of the league he presented a mystery. "How tall is he really?" they asked. The answer in college had been 7-foot-1. The official word from the Bucks was 7-2, but nobody believed it. "You could start the guessing at 7-4," said Nate Bowman of the New York Knicks, "but his arms seem to be eight feet long."

Whatever his size, it was big enough to take the Bucks to the Eastern Conference finals his rookie season. They lost to New York, but for 1970–71 Milwaukee added Oscar Robertson, and the two of them led their teammates on a businesslike march to the title in just the team's third season of NBA operations.

That championship season also marked the completion of Alcindor's conversion to Islam, which he had pursued since 1968. Just before the 1971 All-Star Game, he quietly changed names and married a woman named Habiba. "The game means so much to him that he postponed his honeymoon to play," Robertson told reporters.

The new name, Kareem Abdul-Jabbar, meant "noble, generous, powerful servant of God," yet the task of living up to it seemed quite a test. In October 1972 he was jailed briefly in Denver for suspicion of marijuana possession, only to be released after teammate Lucius Allen was charged. Three months later, in January 1973, seven people, including five children, were murdered in Abdul-Jabbar's Washington, D.C., town house. The victims, who belonged to the orthodox Hanafi Muslim sect, were the family

of his close friend and adviser Hamaas. The repercussions from that incident left Kareem stunned and doubtful about his own marriage. Before the
year was out, he had separated from his wife and retreated within the
cocoon of his Milwaukee apartment.

The Bucks, meanwhile, had traded or released key members from the
1971 championship team, moves that led to play-off losses in 1972 and '73.
They had mustered the effort to challenge the Celtics for the 1974 championship but lost in an intense seven-game series. The next season, his last
in Milwaukee, he broke his hand, smashing it against a basket in anger.
With him on the injured list for long stretches, the Bucks sank to 38–44 in
1974–75, and afterward they consummated the deal he had requested.

His years in Milwaukee had produced three league MVP awards and
yet another name, when Bucks play-by-play man Eddie Doucette tagged his
bread-and-butter shot the "skyhook," certainly a worthy weapon for a
noble, generous, powerful servant of God.

The California drug culture was in full bloom when Kareem arrived there
in 1975. Since Lou Mohs first ran the team in the sixties, Laker management
had employed off-duty LA police detectives to identify hookers hanging
around the team's locker room. As drugs became more prevalent later in the
decade, team officials had asked their security consultants to keep track of
that, too. At first the concern was only marijuana. Then, as the seventies
progressed, freebasing cocaine, or playing "baseball," became the Hollywood party rage.

"You worried like hell," Laker general manager Pete Newell recalled.
"Marijuana and drugs always seemed to break out at parties. The players
were celebrities, so they were always invited. And they were anxious to
meet the people they saw in the movies. A lot of Hollywood power people
liked to showcase the athletes."

When David Stern stepped in as commissioner in 1982, he quickly
instituted a drug policy. But the seventies offered no such protection. "We
really didn't test the players for drugs because cocaine was not something
that was feared that much back then," Newell said.

Having experimented with cocaine and heroin in college, Kareem
recalled that he had little interest in the coke crowd that sought him out,
although there were Lakers who did. After all, powder could be had at
every stop on the road. Hotels around the league were transformed into
party palaces that drew regular crowds eager to greet the players as the
teams came and went. "The marijuana smell, if you stayed one place in
Oakland, it would keep you awake it was so pungent," Newell said. "The
place was wall-to-wall hookers. And the lounge was a nonstop party."

"I think we were in an awkward era for the league itself," West said
of the seventies. "It was floundering, and we didn't have any direction."

With the league front office unprepared or unwilling to take on the drug issue, the Lakers protected their interests the best they could. "We had two detectives that worked the Hollywood beat in terms of drugs and gambling," Newell recalled. If a player kept the wrong company, the team hoped to intervene, he explained.

But sexual frivolity presented a more difficult issue. The team was reluctant to get involved, although Newell admitted, "We were all appalled by the women who just flaunted themselves. The players just kind of passed these gals around. There was no deterrence about AIDS and sex in those days. The players just didn't have as much to lose."

The league, however, was on the verge of losing quite a bit. Pro basketball survived in an atmosphere of decline in 1975. The ABA was on its last legs, and the NBA lagged behind the NFL and pro baseball as a second-rate sport. It was often portrayed as a black game struggling to find support in white America. To make matters worse, the league's television contract was measly, which suggested limited potential. These conditions weren't as bad as they appeared, but that hardly mattered. Basketball's future lay in its development as an entertainment medium, and in the entertainment business appearances were everything.

Critics charged that the sport was boring, that an overly long season resulted in games that seemed meaningless. Kareem was the NBA's top star, and his brooding image did little to help the situation. His last season in Milwaukee had been his first ever as a loser, and many sportswriters read his unemotional response as a lack of interest. Laker fans, however, mostly remembered Big Lew of UCLA fame, the Dominator. They welcomed him and expected great things.

The troubles, of course, began almost immediately, and the vast majority were not of his making. As Pete Newell explained, the Lakers had given up most of their young talent and their draft picks to get Abdul-Jabaar, leaving a mishmash of a roster to greet him. The real complications, however, began on the bench, where the personal tragedies had finally caught up with Sharman. "I was not a good coach my last two years," he admitted.

Kareem won the rebounding title with a 16.9 average and scored 27.7 points per game, good enough to bring his fourth league MVP award. But the 1975–76 Lakers could not win on the road and finished 40–42, out of the play-offs for the second consecutive season. "My coaching contract ran out after the season," Sharman recalled, "and Mr. Cooke said, 'Bill, I want you to be the general manager.' "

With Newell retiring, Sharman moved up, and Cooke set out in hot pursuit of UNLV's Jerry Tarkanian as the Lakers' next coach. Cooke recalled that he ultimately decided to pass on Tarkanian. But Tarkanian remembered it very differently. He said he was offered the job and accepted it, only to change his mind. At the time, his lengthy court battle with the NCAA was just getting started, Tarkanian said. "I was afraid that if I took the Laker job the case would be dropped and my name would never be cleared. I backed out at the last minute. The press conference had already been scheduled. So they went ahead and called Jerry West."

Sharman had pushed West as the best choice, and finally Cooke agreed, only to find that West wouldn't return his calls. Actually, West dreamed of coaching the Lakers but still couldn't bring himself to talk to Cooke. Adjusting to retirement had been a dream-turned-nightmare for West. He indulged himself in golf, travel, and what the writers called his "penchant for stewardesses."

"I found out it wasn't a very good way to live," he once said. "I won't go into detail, but that period played hell with my marriage."

Finally, desperate to get ahold of West one morning in July 1976, Cooke ordered Chick Hearn to find him. The broadcaster tracked him down at a local golf course and instructed the pro to have West phone between rounds. Still, West refused to budge. When Cooke ordered Hearn to try yet again, he angrily resigned as the voice of the Lakers, only to take the job back moments later when Cooke phoned to patch things up.

West eventually relented after Cooke agreed to bring in more talent. Sportswriter Mitch Chortkoff said West's hiring was part of a settlement of his suit against the team. Cooke, however, denied it, saying it was merely a "coincidence" that the suit was settled at the same time West was hired. West refused to discuss the suit in his interviews for this book.

"I needed something to do with my life besides play golf," he recalled.

West promptly hired two assistants, Stan Albeck for offense and Jack McCloskey for defense, when most NBA teams only had one. "I wanted to coach the Lakers one day," West explained a few months later. "I mean, I love the Lakers. I always felt that loyalty was a tremendously important part in the life of an athlete. But I had this lawsuit going against Cooke, and I figured that would do it for me as coach of the Lakers. Then Cooke asked me if I wanted to coach the team. It was a tremendous adjustment. I guess I'd seen one Laker game in two years. I called all of the players and told them I would be honest with them and that we were going to have fun. I went out and hired Stan and Jack, because I hated organizational work and I needed a crutch to help me through that part. I'm still nervous. Sometimes I don't know what to say to players after a game. I'm still learning."

Before long, it would become apparent that the coach was the best guard on the roster. Every time the team would go into overtime, Albeck would turn to West and say, "Suit up, Jerry. Just five minutes. Then you can retire again."

DOC HOLLYWOOD?

"Frankly, I've tried to block those years out of my life because they weren't real pleasant for me," West says now.

His frustration began almost immediately after agreeing to coach. The ABA folded operations after the 1976 play-offs, with the NBA greedily gobbling up the rosters of its dying teams. The New York Nets would survive to join the NBA, but they were willing to peddle their star player, Julius Erving, to any team with the cash. The Philadelphia 76ers stepped up and offered a $6 million package, three to the team, three to Erving, for Dr. J.'s rights.

West said he asked Cooke to go after Erving. "Obviously, we weren't going to do anything to spend a little bit of money to make us better," West recalled. "We could have gotten Julius Erving. That's the only time I ever got involved. I told Mr. Cooke, 'You should take this guy. He's very exciting. Plus he's a terrific player.'

"He told me it wasn't my money; it was his money. So be it. I never talked to him about those things anymore. The only time I knew about personnel changes, I'd show up at practice; we'd have a different face there. Cooke would tell me how great the guy was, and we'd have picked him up off of waivers. We picked up a lot of people that were retreads. It was like an open-door policy. We had a lot of guys running in and out of there. It wasn't a very comforting thing. When you're letting people who don't know a damn thing about basketball make your decisions, you're going to have a problem eventually."

It was Abdul-Jabbar who bore much of the hardship from the failures of Laker teams in the late 1970s. Fifteen years later, he was stunned to learn that he could have played with Erving. "That blows my mind, knowing that they turned down Dr. J.," Abdul-Jabbar said. "Mr. Cooke screwed up royally on that one. You do what you can to improve your team."

Cooke denied that he passed on the opportunity to acquire Erving. "Jerry is excusing himself for the dreadful job he did as coach," he said. "That is sheer balderdash. My record speaks for itself. My God, we acquired the giants of basketball, Wilt Chamberlain, Kareem Abdul-Jabbar. There is no truth whatsoever to it."

Sharman, then the general manager, said Cooke told him, "Bill, I don't want you to talk to the coaches about personnel. Get a general idea of what they like. But every time you talk to coaches they always want the best players in the league and it gets out of hand."

"Mr. Cooke loved to win," Sharman said. "But he was also a financial genius."

Three months after taking over as coach, West figured the Lakers were spending $1.4 million on their payroll, while the Philadelphia 76ers were spending twice that. "Shit," he said. "We've got the bodies of a YMCA pickup team. . . . The only thing going for us is that we have fun, and we have Kareem. Cooke promised me some help. He promised. Then these players come up, and he doesn't move."

The first thing West did after agreeing to coach the Lakers was phone Kareem and set up a meeting. You don't know me, and I don't know you, the coach said. But you need to know what I believe in. I don't know much about offense, because I never had to have plays run for me.

Where West thought he could help the team was in building a defensive mentality. Always one to believe in chain of command, Kareem readily agreed. "Who's going to doubt one of the best players of all time?" he would explain later.

Soon opponents noticed a new life in Kareem and the team. "With Jerry, there was something in the atmosphere that became infectious," Abdul-Jabbar explained. "Everybody wanted to feel about the team the way Jerry did. He was never arrogant. He had great intuition. He wanted to see what each of us could do. When you get that kind of atmosphere going, it does something to bring you near the top of your skills. Maybe something like that happened with me."

Those 1976–77 Lakers started slowly, winning four and losing six, but they found some chemistry on an early eastern trip and ran off a 28–10 streak from there. By March they were challenging for the best record in the league, which they achieved in a win over Denver. But that same night, power forward Kermit Washington was lost for the season to a knee injury. Then Lucius Allen went next. The Lakers still finished with the best record, but they had lost what help Kareem had. "In 1977, we could have won the world championship had we not had Kermit Washington and Lucius Allen get hurt in the last month of the season," Abdul-Jabbar said. "Prior to their getting hurt, we had beaten Portland every time. After they got hurt, we never beat Portland again. We had a chance to win the world championship, and it got away."

Lost with the opportunity was the special atmosphere West had created. Four times in 11 play-off games Kareem scored better than 40 points. But Bill Walton and the Blazers swept Los Angeles in the second round, leading to media criticism that Kareem had been outplayed. "I'm a target," he responded. "Always have been. Too big to miss."

Over the next two seasons, this criticism would gain momentum, leaving West furious at two reporters, Ted Green of the *LA Times* and Rich Levin of the *Herald Examiner*. "We had two writers that were killing him in the newspaper that should have been fired," West said. "It was unfounded bias. People expected more than what he was doing. It was never good enough."

Yet West himself contributed to this atmosphere, at one point calling

Kareem a dog after a bad game, then losing his temper when the quote made the morning papers. "I should never have coached," West says now. "My personal life was in turmoil. It just wasn't a good time for me. That spilled over into it and made me do and say things I should never have said."

Among their many differences, this was one subject upon which Cooke and West agreed. "It was a terrible mistake on my part to make him coach," Cooke said, adding that like other great athletes, West couldn't understand why the players he coached couldn't duplicate his feats.

As a coach, West seemed to eat himself alive in silence, said Stu Lantz, a former Laker who spent the '76–77 season on injured reserve. "He didn't try to put the handcuffs on players," Lantz said. "But a lot of the players then did not have the mental capacity to make quick decisions, or to be intuitively decisive in their decision making, and that would drive Jerry crazy. Especially a flashy player like a John Neumann. There were nights at halftime where Jerry would be totally upset because Johnny had tried a wraparound pass that went up in the stands."

"Our guards never could seem to get the job done to his satisfaction," Kareem recalled. "But you wouldn't hear a lot about it. Jerry usually was not vocal at all, especially if you were doing a good job. He would just say supportive things. He wouldn't get into any critiques."

For all its trauma, the 1976–77 season closed with Kareem being named the league MVP for a fifth time. "Those teams in the late 1970s would have been lucky to win 20 games without him," West said of Abdul-Jabbar. "Yet we were always in the play-offs. We just didn't have enough pieces."

The heartbreak that followed came in a blur. Lost in a strange turn of violent events were the hopes of a promising 1977–78 season. The trouble started just hours into the campaign when Kareem exploded in anger at Milwaukee rookie Kent Benson for shooting a forearm into his solar plexus. Abdul-Jabbar knocked him unconscious with a punch. Even worse, the blow broke Kareem's hand, forcing him to miss 20 games.

The incident derailed plans for an imposing Laker frontcourt. Power forward Kermit Washington had returned from his knee injury but was suddenly left to man the boards alone. Like Sharman before him, Washington was a sweet, gentle family man off the floor. On it, he was a tense, muscular intimidator, the kind of competitor who had worked hard for everything he had achieved. He wasn't about to allow it to be taken from him easily.

He had come to the Lakers as a rookie in 1973 after leading the nation in rebounding at American University. Pete Newell had hoped he would make the conversion from college center to pro power forward. Washington was only 6-foot-7, but he had catlike quickness and an overpowering strength. However, he had played little organized ball until he reached American, where he played center in a zone defensive alignment. Thus his man-to-man defensive understanding was weak, and on offense he had never played facing the basket. The Lakers soon realized he lacked many of the skills necessary to make it in the NBA.

What he did have was incredible desire and strong work habits. That was enough to impress Newell, who decided to tutor Washington in all the nuances of post play over the summer of 1975. Their sessions working together formed the basis of an NBA institution, Pete Newell's "Big Man Camp." Over the ensuing summers, undeveloped players from across the league would come to California to work with Newell, a Hall of Fame coach, on developing frontcourt skills. Each year these informal sessions would grow in scope, and nearly a decade later, when the retired Newell decided he could no longer run the camps, he would turn their operation over to Washington and former Laker Stu Lantz.

"Kermit is a special person to me," Newell said.

The work Washington did with Newell in 1975 expanded his game, and he willed himself to become the power foward the Lakers needed. He played the position with the toughness of a stevedore. In the terms of the trade, Washington became an enforcer.

"When Kermit was there nobody messed with Kareem," Newell explained.

Washington's reputation soon spread around the league. One night Boston center Dave Cowens punched him in the jaw. "That didn't faze Kermit," Newell said. "He backhanded Cowens, and Kevin Stacom came running out from the Celtics bench. Kermit just smacked him in the nose."

Boston's Don Nelson rushed to help his teammates but saw how Washington had handled them and thought better of it. "Nelly said, 'I made the greatest hook slide in the history of the game,' " Newell recalled with a laugh.

Such brouhahas were standard fare in the NBA of the 1970s, and Washington was one of the regular participants. The league issued fines on occasion but generally responded as if it considered these flare-ups part of the business. (Kareem had been fined $5,000 by new commissioner Larry O'Brien but received no suspension.) A few games after Kareem punched out Benson, Washington took on the Buffalo Braves in a wild melee.

"Kermit was hit from behind and beside in Buffalo, which left him gun-shy," Stu Lantz said.

Afterward Washington told Newell he had a great fear of people attacking him from behind, stemming from his days growing up in the inner city. "He told me that in the ghetto you always made sure there was a wall at your back when you got into hassles," Newell recalled.

The tragedy that these circumstances set up came in December in the Forum. Kevin Kunnert of the Houston Rockets was headed upcourt when Washington grabbed his shorts to hold him back. Kunnert turned and threw a couple of punches. When both players squared off, their teammates rushed in to help. Kareem, who had returned to action, grabbed Kunnert and swung him around away from Washington to break up the fight.

At the same time, Houston's Rudy Tomjanovich ran up to help his teammate. Washington abruptly whirled and struck Tomjanovich. Laker statistician John Radcliffe, sitting a few feet away, said the blow sounded like a melon striking concrete.

Tomjanovich's face collapsed in a shower of blood.

"It was the most physical blow I've ever seen anybody throw or receive," Newell said. "When he saw this uniform coming at him, from then on it was a blur. He responded almost instinctively."

"Kermit was into karate and happened to throw the right punch at the right time," said former Laker Lou Hudson.

"All Kermit did was turn and throw, just as Rudy was coming in," Stu Lantz said. "With those forces colliding, that's what made the damage as severe as it was. It wasn't like Kermit was this big man-eater waiting to destroy someone's career and face."

Videotape of the gruesome incident was replayed regularly on television, creating further furor. "I know it had a tremendous effect on his life, his family life," Lantz said of Washington. "He got hate mail for a long time, a long time."

His face shattered, Tomjanovich missed the rest of the season while undergoing a series of reconstructive operations. A former All-Star, he resumed his career the next season, yet he never achieved his previous level of play.

Washington was fined and suspended without pay for 60 days, bringing an additional $50,000 in salary losses. Shortly after the incident, the Lakers traded Washington and Don Chaney to the Boston Celtics for Charlie Scott. Tomjanovich later filed a civil suit against the Lakers and won.

The league's handling of the incident and its aftermath cast a pall over the Lakers. "All of a sudden we were the negative people," Hudson said. "We knew that if Kermit had hit another black player, nothing would have happened. But since he hit a white player and broke his face, he was thrown out of the league."

"Kermit didn't fight it the right way," Kareem said. "I don't know about his legal representation, but he should have fought it. He could have made it difficult for them to do that to him. But the Lakers weren't supportive either. They knuckled under. I don't know if Mr. Cooke made a deal or whatever. We had to trade Kermit because they didn't want me and Kermit on the same team."

Newell, who testified at the civil trial in Texas, said, "The club never stood behind him, and that's the thing that bothered me."

With Washington gone, the Lakers had only small forwards Don Ford and Jamaal Wilkes to play the power position and subsequently lost to Seattle in the '78 and '79 play-offs. "You know how far we went with them," Kareem said. "It was unbelievable how all of that turned around. We couldn't rebuild it."

When he met Jerry West to offer him the Laker coaching job in July 1976, Jack Kent Cooke sported a broken arm, which he had sustained just days earlier trying to stop Jeannie, his wife of 42 years, from leaving their vacation home in the Sierra Nevadas. Jeannie, though, made a clean getaway from the marriage she had tried to escape for the previous decade. Weary of life with Cooke and his endless schedule of sporting events, she'd tried suicide four times.

"I can't measure up to your competitive nature," she explained in one note.

Bereft of companionship, Cooke packed up his life and moved to Las Vegas, becoming in the process an absentee owner, ruling the Lakers with daily phone calls. For urgent matters, general manager Bill Sharman would jump a flight to Vegas to confer with Cooke in person.

The Lakers owner became even more of a tyrant after the separation. For years the rule around Forum offices had been that if the phone on your desk rang three times, you were fired. And when you answered, you had better know the starting times for all major Forum events. If you didn't, that would get you a pink slip, too. The tales of his insensitivities grew with each passing season. Supposedly there was an occasion when he stood on the Kings' hockey ice, holding his dog Coco and talking to a Forum employee.

I need your coat, Cooke told the employee, who quickly surrendered it only to watch him wrap the dog. Cooke has denied these and many other stories of his brash style, but along with the Fabulous Forum, the Kings, and the Lakers, they remain part of his legacy in Los Angeles.

Forum employees saw the first indication that this reign was coming to an end in 1979, when Jeannie Cooke finally collected the payback for her decades of misery. Judge Joseph Wapner, who would go on to television fame on the syndicated "People's Court," hit Cooke with a $41 million divorce settlement. At the time, the *Guinness Book of World Records* decreed it the largest in history.

To pay up, Cooke would have to sell his Forum sports empire, and when it happened, that, too, would go down as another record deal.

No one could have been more pleased by this news than Jerry West. It wasn't exactly clear who would be running the team, but things had to get better. "It was time for a change," West said. "It was a positive divorce, that's what it was."

10

Vanity Fair

The lines in his face suggest the price of being forceful. They run deep, particularly the furrows cutting perpendicular to his mouth, framing the jutting chin and leaving him gaunt, almost haggard. It's a hard look, but then again, Pat Riley is a hard guy.

His arms folded, he stands at courtside, waiting intently for his New York Knicks to muscle their way through yet another game. The tension tightens his face until he looks like he might gnaw the leg of the scorer's table. "I'm still the kind of coach to get jacked up for a regular-season game," he explained not so long ago. "I'm not searching for the meaning of life in the NBA, okay? But it gives me a feeling of being totally alive every time I'm out on the floor."

Tonight he's jacked. His old love, the Lakers, have come to town to confront this specter from their past.

Vanity Fair magazine is here, too, sniffing out a piece on how the Garden of the 1990s is like the Forum of the 1980s. Just the other night, the Orlando Magic and Shaquille O'Neal were here, and the Garden's court-side seats were thick with celebrity. "It was almost like what the Forum must have been like," says Kirk Ruddell, the 22-year-old writer for *Vanity Fair*. Dustin Hoffman, Spike Lee, and Arnold Schwarzenegger were there, he says, and Branford Marsalis blew the national anthem. Woody Allen showed up, too, only since his very nasty custody battle with Mia Farrow he has deserted the spotlight of courtside to sit up by the railing at the exit tunnel.

"The level of peroxide isn't quite as high in the Garden as it is in the Forum," Ruddell observes. "But it's the whole Riley aura. It's been a while since we've had a glamour team here."

To mirror the Laker Girls, New York even has its Knicks City Danc-ers, who tonight are wearing black tights while lying facedown on the floor and squeezing their buttocks. "Supposedly the Knicks girls do more club, hip-hop, athletic dancing as opposed to posing," Ruddell says. "I don't know how valid that is."

Later the Knicks City Dancers will bring folding chairs onto the floor, straddle them provocatively, then move to a spread-eagle pose. "It's a popular move, and the chairs are a nice touch," Ruddell says.

In Washington, Jack Kent Cooke has read a newspaper account of celebrity row in the Garden and crows that he started it all. In 1968 when the Forum opened, he declared that all those unwashed reporters sitting along press row should be moved up to the nosebleed section and those prime seats should be sold at top prices to celebrities and high rollers. "I take great pride in that," Cooke says with his usual zest.

He takes great pride in Riley, too. Cooke recalls that Riley's playing career died in the late 1970s. "He was the twelfth man on a twelve-man squad," Cooke says. "We didn't know what to do with him, so finally we made him a broadcasting assistant to Chick Hearn. Look at him now."

Yes, look at him. He's the toast of New York. The man who once drove those Showtime Lakers till their minds went numb has a new basketball show, led by Patrick Ewing, John Starks, and Anthony Mason, all ugly and mean. They don't shoot straight, but Riley has them playing defense like repo men. "Pat should be coach of the year for winning with that goddamn bunch," Bill Bertka will say later.

And this, Ruddell later concedes, is why the Garden/Forum comparison doesn't hold. Showtime was the sleekest, greatest team in the history of basketball. These Knicks wouldn't rate an inch of consideration in that category.

Pat Riley does have them playing with fire. But, Ruddell admits, the only real connection between the Forum of yesterday and the Garden of today is that Riley image. The intense, chiseled face. The folded arms. The $1,500 Armani suits. The slick hair.

Ah, that hair. Riles, as the Lakers call him, guards it jealously. When Kareem signed on with Lays potato chips to do a commercial in 1991, the idea was for Riley to lose a betcha-can't-eat-one, shaved-head wager with Abdul-Jabbar. "But Pat didn't want to be bald," says Lorin Pullman, Kareem's publicist, "so he turned it down."

Riley, who seemingly has a line on every dollar, who loves to knock down those $20,000 speeches on the motivational circuit, who went so far as to patent the phrase "Three-peat" to scoop up all the T-shirt revenue when the Lakers were on the verge of winning three straight titles in 1989, turns down easy advertising money? Everything is for sale but the hair?

It's true, Pullman says.

Instead, Kareem shot the spot with Larry Bird, who at first thought he had to shave his head until it was explained that he'd only have to wear a skin cap.

It had been a battle to find the right endorsement contracts for Kareem, Pullman said, and the marketing types had wanted a white player or coach to appear with him. Riley's slick look would have been the perfect lampoon, and Bird's golden locks weren't a bad second. But it wasn't the first time Riley had passed on a good opportunity. Hollywood producers had wanted him to play the role of an obsessed narcotics cop in *Tequila Sunrise* in the 1980s. When Riley declined, the producers filled in with a greased-back Kurt Russell.

There've been other attempts to appropriate the look, most notably by Laker coaches, who've made it a team tradition. Upon arriving in LA, Mike Dunleavy, a guy not known for pretensions, immediately slicked down his thinning rug. And Randy Pfund later did the same, only the ribbing made Pfund a little self-conscious, so he made a point of dropping to one knee on the sideline rather than squatting in the old catcher's stance that Riley liked. After all, it was one thing to be an imitator and quite another to be a clone.

Not that Riley could be cloned.

It seems all of these people, the celebrities, the producers, the coaches, were learning one great lesson together: that while image may make the man, it doesn't have shit to do with burnishing the soul of a great basketball team.

As Randy Pfund points out, most people focus on Riley's image and fail to comprehend his intensity. It has been three seasons since he left the Lakers, and they still feel it. New Yorkers are beginning to understand this. "I think he's a condescending asshole," says one radio reporter, "but he's a hell of a coach. Ewing respects him tremendously. It's been a while since Patrick called anybody 'coach.' He calls Riley 'coach.' "

Riley himself played for the greatest asshole in the history of basketball, Adolph Rupp at the University of Kentucky, where Riley was an All-American forward in 1966. "He was the ultimate when it came to discipline," Riley says of Rupp. "He taught me how to be disciplined. He had a system, he had a great philosophy, and he made you believe in that philosophy. He had a great plan that got him great results. He taught us to take great pride in it, which I do.

"You do it the same way every day of your life. He was the most repetitious man I've ever been around. Every day we did the same drills. He never ever scouted opponents. He would give our offense to the opposition, saying, 'If you want to stop us, we've got a counter for everything.'

"He was unique, and I only appreciate him now because I've gotten into coaching and I understand what he was trying to do."

Riley pauses for the mea culpa. "When I was a player, I probably hated him." Then he pauses again. "There's a lot of his philosophy in mine."

There are other influences. Riley's wife, Chris, a psychologist, has had a profound impact, says Lon Rosen. "Like Hillary Clinton."

The Riley reading list includes a major influence, *The Art of War,* a collection of aphorisms on aggression from the fourth century B.C. by Sun Tzu.

When his troops are disorderly, the general has no prestige, says Sun Tzu in his section on forced marches.

Riley also studied John Wooden's writings, his "pyramid of success," and the UCLA coach's near-mystical approach to the game. From there Riley fashioned his own paradigm, the "three commitments." The first, he said, was "commitment to your life plan, to family, retirement, things like that." Second came the "Laker plan," a total commitment to winning and all the little extra efforts it required. The third, the one he constantly hammered into his players' minds, was unity. "You gotta totally get out of yourself and into the unity of the team," Riley explained. "The spirit of unity does not guarantee you anything, but without it you can't be successful."

Riley's own personal transformation was one of the fascinating developments of Showtime. Like Lee Pfund, Riley's father, Leon, was a big leaguer, and later Leon became a minor-league coach. But he then went into business and failed, requiring that he work late in life as a school custodian, a station that Riley recalls his father carrying with dignity. The youngest son, Riley was a strong-armed high school quarterback in Schenectady, New York, and Bear Bryant wanted him to play football at Alabama. (Even after college he would be drafted by the Dallas Cowboys.) But Rupp talked him into basketball in the bluegrass. From Kentucky, Riley went on to a nine-year pro career over which he averaged 7.7 points. Lacking in speed, he relied on hustle and drive, says former Laker general manager Pete Newell. But he injured a knee in 1975, and the Lakers dealt him to Phoenix. "I felt betrayed," Riley said. "My only pro blood is Laker blood. They were the only team I cared about or had a passion for."

A year later he ended his career and found himself an ex-jock caught in the throes of postpartum funk. He spent a lot of time staring at beach sunsets or sitting in his Santa Monica home without a clue, at one point attacking his cabana with a chainsaw in a misguided remodeling attempt. Finally Chick Hearn saved him from this purgatory with an offer to be his broadcast assistant. Riley tackled the job with relish, until 1979, when Paul Westhead asked him to serve as assistant coach. Two years later, he was thrust into the head job and had to learn, at Jerry Buss's urging, to exert his will over the team. Once he learned, he came to relish the struggle for "unity."

"He does know how to put a team together," says A. C. Green. "That's always been his biggest asset. He makes the nucleus jell. He takes the players' strengths and potential and tries to bring it all together and make it work for everybody."

Sort of like hard-boiling an egg.

This "unity" extended from the players right down to the coaches and staffers. Riley kept the group small, the dozen players and four or five staffers. "He called it the family," said Rosen, who was once part of the inner circle. Riley, of course, was the patriarch.

"It meant that you fit into a slot and everything was done for the good of the team," recalled Gary Vitti. "Pat drove that home. That was the philosophy. He didn't care if you had to stay up all night to do your part."

As trainer, Vitti worked closely with Riley for five seasons and learned to live with his drive. "He thrives on intensity," the trainer said. "He thrives on it. There was always pressure, always pressure."

It stemmed from a desire to win matched only by Earvin Johnson's. "They will sell their souls, sell your soul, whatever it takes," Vitti said. "I don't care what it is. Pat will claw and scratch. He will rip your eyes out.

"It was kind of like, if you were going good, Pat would say, 'You gotta keep the edge, man. You gotta practice hard.' And if you're not going good, it was, 'We gotta get back, man. The only way to get back is to go hard.' So there was never any letdown."

Riley became fanatical about every little detail with the team. The staffers had to report everything to him, because it was the little things that led to winning. "Behind his back, Kareem began calling him Norman Bates," Lon Rosen recalled with a laugh.

"If somebody makes you be your best all of the time, puts that pressure on you all of the time, there's going to be resentment," Vitti says. "I respect Pat because most of us aren't tough enough to do that. We're not tough enough to piss people off to get 'em to be their best. As soon as they start retracting from you because you're harassing them, then you soften up. He wasn't like that. He made you give more and more, and when you didn't have any more to give, he made you give more."

When the troops continually gather in small groups and whisper together, the general has lost the confidence of the army, says Sun Tzu.

Frank Brickowski came to the Lakers in the fall of 1986 and was quickly awed by the team dynamic. "I've never encountered anything like it before or after," he said. "Riley was intense, but Magic and Kareem only let him get away with so much stuff. When it came to a point of drawing a line, they would not have a part of something. The first day I was there, they had just gotten done playing back-to-back preseason games. We were sitting in a circle at the start of practice, and Riley said we'd go for two and a half hours and get out of there. Magic stood up as we were ready to break and said, 'All right, an hour and a half and we're outta here.' Riley said, 'No, I said two and a half hours.' Magic said, 'Oh, I thought you said an hour and a half because we're tired because we played the last two nights.' There was a dead silence. Then Riley said, 'All right, if we do this and that, we'll be out of here in an hour and a half.' "

In nine seasons Riley shoved and pressured the Lakers into four championship performances and got them close to three others. But by 1990, the human possibilities had been exhausted. Publicly, Riley sought to make it appear that he made the choice to leave, but veteran Laker beat writer Mitch Chortkoff believes that Riley was forced out. Regardless, the circumstances of his leaving remain somewhat mysterious.

Riley confided to Ted Green, a former *LA Times* writer who then produced the Lakers' pregame television show, that he was a victim of Jerry West's "toxic envy."

"Jerry West was 100 times the player Pat Riley was," Green said. "When Jerry West became coach, he didn't have the horses to win. Then Riley comes along and gets the coaching job by serendipity and gets to coach Magic. West saw Riley as a lucky sonofabitch. West thought, 'I got stuck with the crap that I had to coach, and then Riley wins all these championships, and I get shunted into the background.' There was a tremendous amount of jealousy."

It was Riley who claimed all the endorsements and the big profile in the 1980s, and West, still struggling to regain the public accolades he had enjoyed as a player, couldn't deal with that, Green said. "Jerry's a brilliant basketball mind and a very unhappy individual."

Many Laker staffers considered Ted Green's opinion outrageous hogwash. The general manager was obsessed with the team's success, they said. But he wasn't petty. In fact, Jerry West served as something of a father figure for many Laker employees, said a staff member. "Riley didn't care about people, unless he could use them. Jerry's a great guy. He's made all of us feel like we're an important part of the organization. He has a great sense of humor. He remembers all the funny stories from his playing days, stories about Ray Felix and all those characters from the sixties. But he seldom tells those stories to reporters and writers, and he never lets them see his sense of humor. He never puts it on display. He's not trying to win some public relations game. Whatever he does, he does quietly. Jerry jealous of Pat? That's a joke."

If West was envious then he wasn't alone. In his first few seasons with the team, Riley kept a low profile. But as the Lakers won championship after championship, he harvested a bundle in endorsements and motivational speech royalties. "The players started thinking that he was profiting from their work and success," explained a Laker staffer.

During the celebration of their back-to-back championships in 1988, Byron Scott led the fans in a chant. Gary Vitti recalls the words as "Three-Repeat." But other Lakers staffers says Scott used the phrase "Three-peat." Riley soon filed a trademark on the term, a move that infuriated some players, who believed he had appropriated Scott's creation.

"Pat made you be the best you could be, so you looked for things to be mad about," Vitti said. "You think anybody was gonna look themselves in the mirror and say, 'I'm mad at Pat because he made me be the best that I could be?' No. But you could look in the mirror and say, 'I'm mad at Pat because he copyrighted Three-peat.' Nobody cared about that. It was an excuse to be angry."

Still, there is ample evidence that Riley's leaving followed a shipwide mutiny and that West was faced with keeping order. West believed pro basketball to be a players' game. The coach had to give the players freedom to be creative. Yet West fielded many complaints over the 1989–90 season that Riley's iron will was choking the life out of the roster. Scott and Worthy, in particular, had come to loathe Riley's high-pressure tactics. "It got to the point where we'd heard this speech before and to the point where he got tired of saying it," Scott said.

With Riley flashing his anger and stamping his feet on the sideline, the Lakers powered their way to a league-best 63–19 record that spring of 1990. It was their first season without Kareem, and Riley was determined to make the transition. But the acrimony thickened with each passing day, until the Phoenix Suns closed down the Lakers 4–1 in the second round of the play-offs.

"By the end of the season, the fire was not there," Worthy said. "As far as the team was concerned, the locker room was dead. For the first time since I had been with the Lakers, it was a job."

When orders are consistently trustworthy and observed, the relationship of a commander with his troops is satisfactory, says Sun Tzu.

"That year was ugly," one Laker staffer said of 1990. "By the end of the year, Byron and James wouldn't even talk to the guy. Pat would come in the locker room and ask a question, and they wouldn't respond. It was his personality. Riley treats big people, the people who can do him favors, one way, and the rest of the world another way. He's really that mercenary. The people that can't help him he doesn't care about. He upset just about everybody on the staff. Lots of people wanted to quit because he would swear and scream at them. I almost quit myself. Then he finally left, and it was like everyone in the whole organization rejoiced."

When the season ended, Riley told reporters that he was considering leaving his post. Laker staffers figured the coach was fishing for entreaties to stay from West and Jerry Buss. Neither, however, was about to suggest that, because both had had enough. Seeing he had no support, Riley knew it was over, explained one Laker staff member.

Yet any rejoicing over Riley's leaving was mixed with mourning. An era had ended. And after they had time to reflect on it, his players would realize something special had passed through their lives.

"We didn't see eye-to-eye on a lot of issues," Byron Scott said, "but I respected him because of what he had done. And he gave all of the players respect.

"Now that I look back on it, I even respect him more because of what he helped us achieve. Looking back on all that, I say he's probably the best coach in the game."

To his credit, Randy Pfund hadn't tried to mimic Riley's intensity. First of all, he didn't have Kareem and Magic, the two great pieces of the basketball puzzle that Riley had. Second, Pfund knew a hard-driving approach wouldn't work with the current Laker veterans. Worthy readily agreed, saying he much preferred Pfund's cooperative style to Riley's pressure treatment.

Yet the results were mixed, and it was becoming increasingly clear as the 1992–93 season progressed that, fair or not, Pfund's future was hanging in the balance. After beating Orlando, the Lakers opened 1993 with more of their strange cadence, losing to teams they should have beaten, then producing inspiring upsets of the Bulls in Chicago and winning their third against Portland. Late in January, *USA Today* columnist Peter Vecsey came to Los Angeles for a day, talked to Pfund, West and other assorted sources, then produced a column suggesting that Pfund's job was in peril and that Michael Cooper, now a special assistant to West, was waiting in the wings to take over the team.

Pfund laughed and shrugged it off, joking that being tweaked by Vecsey was a sign he belonged in the league. Still, he couldn't help being concerned and wondering what West was saying about him "off the record."

They closed January with a solid 3–3 record on yet another eastern road trip, defeating Charlotte, Boston, and Washington while falling to Utah, New Jersey, and Indiana. However, a sense of foreboding settled on the coaching staff. Pfund gave up his plans for a major move toward the motion offense. After the Indiana loss, the usually quiet Sedale Threatt had groused to reporters that the Lakers needed to run. Pfund agreed, and they made the effort to break more often. But to run, a team needs great defensive rebounding, and the Lakers seemed to shy away from that commitment.

So they persisted in their weird ways, out of synch some nights, just getting by on others, with their moments of inspiration coming at odd intervals. "This is a tough team to figure out," West conceded.

"When you don't have a leader on the floor, you get lost," assistant coach Larry Drew observed in late January. "I think that's happened to us. Right now we're soul-searching, and other teams are taking it to us. They're not doing anything fancy. We can sit up all night drawing X's and O's on the board, but we're getting beat on just sheer effort now, and we're not taking the challenge. Veteran players know that you have to come out night after night and play hard. We're just not playing with a lot of effort, a lot of intensity, a lot of fire, a lot of energy.

"Somewhere along the line we're gonna have to put our foot down and find five guys who will come out and play with the energy that people are used to seeing Laker teams play with."

The situation left them all pining for Magic. "Earvin was one of those guys to challenge people individually," said Drew, who played with Johnson for two seasons. "He would set the tone in practice, and once he set the tone, it was up to everybody else to follow the lead. If you didn't, he let you know. That's why he was so successful. Teams would die to have people like that on their roster. It was just unbelievable. I've been with teams where we thought we had leaders. But when I came with the Lakers, Earvin started in training camp. He just demanded perfection.

"Earvin would look at a challenge and meet it head-on. He came out every day with a lot of energy and that filtrated down to everybody else, because he'd get really hyped up, really psyched up. You'd see him going out and playing as hard as he could, and it really just rubbed off on you."

"There's nine or 10 points gone from my game just from his passing ability," Worthy said of Johnson, "just from his getting the ball to you in unique situations. His leadership qualities were unique. Here's a guy who didn't mind getting on you. Some guys can do that; most can't. Plus Earvin had energy all the time. Energy at shootaround, energy on the bus, energy in the locker room, energy while he slept. He was just that type of guy. He would not let you get down. He would not let this team lose."

With every game the Lakers had grown more desperate for a player to step forward, Drew said. "Everybody talks about it, but it's one thing to talk about it and another to do it."

Worthy said, "We have energy, but we don't have Earvin Johnson. We don't have that same level. We're trying the best we can, but we don't have that special talent that he had."

Jerry West's solution, just before the trading deadline at the All-Star break in February, was to ship Perkins to Seattle for the rights to unsigned rookie guard Doug Christie and center Benoit Benjamin.

Perkins, of course, had seen it coming. He had told Vitti after a February 18 loss in Portland, "Well, it's been nice working with you."

"What are you talking about?" the trainer said.

"I'll never make it through the All-Star break," Perkins replied.

Sure enough, he hadn't, and the trade left him very depressed. After hearing the news, Vitti phoned Perkins and told him that no matter where he played, "you'll always be one of my guys."

Later, as the season and its opportunity slipped away, Pfund and the rest of the team often wished the same thing, that Perkins was still one of theirs.

Later it would turn out to be false hope. But on this night in New York in early March, there was reason for optimism among the Lakers. Despite their obvious problems, they had gone 8–3 over the past four weeks, including a road win last night in Detroit in which Worthy scored 28.

Seeking to build on that and to pin one on their old coach, Scott and Worthy came out strong in the first period against the Knicks, and Los Angeles took a 25–18 lead. But Pfund soon noticed that Riley was countering his every move, not dramatically, just subtly. After all, Riley had Ewing. Riley once explained that the center position is the most important in basketball, but it's only important if you have a great one. If Ewing wasn't great, he was near it. And Pfund had no answer, not with Perkins in Seattle.

Therefore when those experienced in war move they make no mistakes; when they act, their resources are limitless, says Sun Tzu.

The two coaches, with their slick hair and histrionics, mirrored each other on the sideline. At one point, the action boiled over and Riley rushed out on the floor. Later Pfund came out of his coaching box and was cautioned not to do it again by official Steve Javie.

"What about my buddy down there?" Pfund asked, nodding toward the New York bench.

Javie agreed and went to the other end to caution Riley about getting on the floor. Pfund heard Riley yell in anger at the warning. The Laker coach tried to catch the eye of his former boss and share a laugh over the incident. But Riley wouldn't look at him. This was a game, and it had to be won.

Former Laker Tony Campbell scored 10 quick points in the second period, and Ewing had his way with Elden Campbell and Benoit Benjamin, the Laker reserves, which pushed New York back in front, 54–47, at the half.

Without Perkins, the Lakers' interior defense was particulary awful, and when Charles Oakley scored easily inside to open the third period, Pfund yelled for a 20-second timeout. "Let's go!" he shouted, charging out to meet his players as they came off the floor. The plea went unheeded, however, as Charles Smith got position and dunked seconds later. The Knicks muscled the lead to a dozen, and the Lakers trimmed it back to four with seven minutes left. But they couldn't find any defensive inspiration and lost again. In the closing seconds, Pfund walked to the end of the bench and kicked at the air.

"What happened to Showtime, Randy?" a fan bellowed from the end zone. "Where's Showtime now?"

11

The Once and Future Kings

Randy Pfund isn't the only one haunted by the past. They all are. The players. The coaches. The extras. To borrow Pat Riley's phrase, Showtime was the game's "defining moment," and they were happily caught up in it. Yet even as they lived it, the period was addressed in the past tense, leaving the marketing minds behind the scenes to wonder if they would survive it. Showtime was a hoops fairy tale, pro basketball's Age of Camelot, when Magic Johnson and Larry Bird were the boy wonders who pulled the proverbial sword from the stone. Until they came along, the game had struggled to find an identity among American professional sports. It had a reputation for selfish athletes and boring, meaningless games. But Bird and Johnson changed all that. They first took their college teams to the 1979 NCAA finals, where Johnson and Michigan State ended the hopes of Bird and his little team that could, the Indiana State Sycamores.

Born overnight, their rivalry drew a massive television audience for that NCAA title game, and just six months later many of those fans followed them into the NBA. For decades pro basketball had attempted to appropriate the excitement of college hoops. At last Larry and Magic delivered the goods, transforming the NBA into a new kingdom, ruled by the wondrous pass and the unforeseen assist. They took a royal pride in their competition.

Ah, Camelot.

Who can blame the NBA of the 1990s for trying to reinvent itself? Or the Knicks and Riley and *Vanity Fair* for trying to recreate its glory? It was pure storybook, or so it seemed.

The Showtime cast was filled with a complement of honorable knights, all of whom were armed with an array of low-post moves and jump shots. Kareem. Coop. Riles. Silk. Worthy. Rambis. Byron. Norman. To the fans, their very names suggested a depth of character.

And the script? Nearly perfect.

Leave it to Hollywood to screw up the opening with a giant business deal and a murder mystery, neither of which has ever been completely resolved.

First the deal, actually a classic American rags-to-riches story, of which the protagonist is Jerry Buss, who grows up disadvantaged, first in Southern California, then in Wyoming. The plot includes a harsh stepfather, poverty, icy walks to school, rebellion, and a record of remarkable and persistent academic achievement. Buss becomes frustrated, drops out of high school, works at manual labor, returns to school, and graduates. From this background, he goes to college, earns a degree, gathers momentum, and picks up a Ph.D. in chemistry. Thus credentialed, he goes to work in the aerospace industry, with occasional stints teaching chemistry at Southern Cal. The money is decent, but the job is boring. Besides, his real genius is numbers, and his real love is sports. Buss and college buddy Hampton Mears will go anywhere to see a Southern Cal football game. On the side, Buss and a friend from his work in the aerospace industry, Frank Mariani, buy an old apartment building and become landlords. Here the plot drags, as it often does in critical financial junctures. Scenes of late nights with Buss and Mariani painting and doing maintenance on their building. Then the purchase of another building, followed by shots of Buss hovering over a calculator for long hours, figuring out how to finance even more properties, interspersed by frames of Buss gleefully rolling the dice playing Monopoly, with a French subtitle suggesting that life imitates leisure. From there yet another plot twist, as Buss, the father of four, gets a divorce and emerges as a budding real estate tycoon and blue-jeans-wearing playboy who dates attractive young women as often as they will say yes and dances till his knees ache. Then still shots of business-page headlines about the Southern California real estate boom, followed by more scenes of Buss rapidly working his calculator to acquire more property. Other leisure moments include Buss playing high-stakes poker with stacks of chips in front of him, or spending time with his growing stamp and coin collections. Ultimately, however, stamps and coins prove too tame. With success comes angst that the protagonist is merely a landlord. He wants to play in the great sandbox of American professional sports, so in 1972 he and partners buy the LA Strings of World Team Tennis, and promptly lose a bundle trying to promote tennis at the Sports Arena, sending Buss looking for a better deal at the Forum. There in 1975 he gets to know Jack Kent Cooke, setting in motion the chemistry that makes it all happen. Tennis losses run heavy, but Buss is determined to move beyond real estate into pro sports ownership. He searches for baseball, football, and basketball options, all the time not daring to hope that the answer to his desires is very close.

Cooke and Buss made for a fascinating pair of business adversaries. One, soft-spoken and intense, given to wearing dirty blue jeans and open-collar shirts. The other a loud, overbearing sort, always eager to get the best of every situation. Together they would hatch what was billed at the time as the "largest sports deal in history."

Since 1975, Cooke had watched Buss battle to build the Strings' woeful tennis attendance from 2,000 to 7,000 and complimented him on the effort. Buss, in turn, overlooked Cooke's personal shortcomings to view him as a mentor, a rare resource who could teach him much about sports ownership. They even became friends. Sort of.

One day, in the midst of one of their many talks, Cooke mentioned that he might like to sell the Forum. Buss jumped. It was just the opportunity he wanted, but Cooke was coy. "I'd fly up to Vegas every six weeks or so, and we'd talk about it," Buss recalled.

Mostly, he listened as Cooke told tales of running his two teams. Little actual business was discussed, but the inside details of the two franchises fascinated Buss. He would hop a plane every time Cooke called just so he could get the current scoop. But, outside of that, his hopes of getting the Forum seemed mired in Cooke's parlor games. "It was a very frustrating time," Buss said. "I guess I always believed that it would happen, although it seemed like forever. I would alternate being down and depressed. Then I'd think it was going to work and I'd be elated."

Slowly, as Cooke's divorce proceeded, the sale talks warmed up. They met often at the Regency in the Sands Hotel, and afterward Buss sifted through what had been said, trying to figure Cooke out. "There were times when I felt I'd gotten in a little over my head," he said. "Jack Kent Cooke is remarkably charming when he wants to be, and he's a very, very tough-willed man. He may have the toughest will I've ever seen. It's like iron. And he was very quick to take advantage of turns in the negotiations."

To make things happen, Buss had to arrange a trade on seven of his properties for the Forum, which allowed Cooke to avoid the taxes of a cash transaction. Then in late 1978, Cooke mentioned that he might like to include the Lakers and Kings in the package. "How would you like to buy the whole thing?" he asked.

Buss's heart jumped again. "The size of the deal doubled," he recalled.

Buss told Cooke he'd love to purchase the teams, but he'd need time to see if it was possible. "I started thinking," he said, "and I went to LA and started rummaging through my holdings. I had no idea what I could get on the open market for them."

"That deal was going to work regardless," Cooke says now. "He was so eager to get it. It was just a matter of the price."

Fortunately, the real estate market was strong in 1979, and Buss soon realized he was in a position to move. But then Cooke decided that he wanted the Chrysler Building in New York instead of Buss's properties. Buss laughed, shook his head, then hustled to find buyers for his buildings.

That done, he worked out a trade: his high rises, complete with buyers to soften the tax blow, for the Chrysler Building.

Then Cooke wanted to include his 13,000-acre Raljon Ranch in the Sierras. "I drove up to the ranch, saw it, came back, and made an offer," Buss said. "I don't think he knew for sure he wanted to sell, but once he made up his mind, things went smoothly."

Well, almost.

With everything in place in early May 1979, Cooke phoned and said, "Jerry, we're going to make the deal." Buss would pay what amounted to $67.5 million for the Forum, Lakers, Kings, and Cooke's ranch. Cooke would get the Chrysler Building and properties in three states. The high rises would go to the owners of the Chrysler Building.

But on midnight May 17, Buss learned that one of the high-rise buyers in the Chrysler deal had backed out, creating a $2.7 million shortage. Buss scrambled to get the cash together, calling in favors from Mariani and other associates, and just made it by the 12:30 closing time the next day. Afterward, he was too exhausted to celebrate, other than a few private moments in the Forum, sitting at courtside in the empty building, then walking upstairs to gaze at photographs of Lakers and Kings. "My players," he thought proudly. No longer was he just another landlord.

"It announced the ending of my real estate career and the beginning of my sports career," he says now.

In the aftermath, *Sports Illustrated* turned loose one of its investigators trying to isolate all the elements of the deal. After a good effort, the investigator phoned his editors and said it would take six weeks or more just to track the deeds involved. So *SI* hired an accounting firm to cut the time to a week. Three weeks later, the accountants were still trying to figure it all out.

Apparently, Buss had sold 15 to 20 limited partnerships in the acreage on which the Forum sat, with plans to buy out those partnerships over the next 15 to 20 years. It was estimated that Buss actually had only $125,000 cash invested in the entire transaction, not including the costs of the deal itself.

"We had a lot of people working on it," Buss said. "A conservative estimate of the lawyer and accountant hours would be $500,000."

"The deal," Cooke says, "was not complicated at all to me."

Now the murder mystery.

Buss knew he had learned much from Cooke about managing an arena, but he figured the former Lakers owner really didn't know how to market the team. Buss, on the other hand, had exact ideas about what he wanted. His notions about entertainment dated to a seminal experience in the early sixties when he was a regular at The Horn, a small nightclub on

Wilshire Boulevard in Santa Monica. The club's nightly opener captured his fascination, no matter how often he saw it. The lights would dim, the spotlights would come up, and from one of the tables a singer would rise to croon, "It's showtime." Then a second and a third would stand to join the harmony. Buss would sip his rum and Coke, draw on his lighted cigarette, and let himself drift away in the moment.

He wanted that same atmosphere for his new arena. It would be a place where fans could settle into their courtside seats with a mixed drink and a cigarette and enjoy the show. There would be dancers and celebrities and a hot band to replace the Forum's dead-zone organ music. And there would be no more waitresses running around in cheesy togas. But the real change would have to come with the team itself. Buss thought pro basketball was more than a little boring in 1979. He needed an exciting running team to take center stage for this new "Showtime" atmosphere. Otherwise it wouldn't work. To run, the Lakers had to have the right players and the right coach.

In early May of 1979, after Buss and Cooke agreed to the deal but before they closed it, they sat down to discuss coaches. Cooke recalls that Buss asked him what he thought of Jerry Tarkanian, coach of UNLV's Runnin' Rebels.

"He's a first-class coach," Cooke replied.

"Could you arrange a meeting with him?" Buss asked.

In a flash, Cooke phoned for Tarkanian, who was in New York recruiting Sidney Green. Tarkanian agreed to meet, and they exchanged a vow of silence on the matter. In 1976, the deal to make Tarkanian the Laker coach had been queered when UNLV boosters found out about it and pressured him into staying in Vegas. "This time we kept it a total secret," Tarkanian said. "This time I wanted the job."

Their first meeting in California went well, so Tarkanian called in his agent and friend of many years, Vic Weiss, to work out the details the next day with Buss and Cooke. (Buss doesn't recall his involvement in hiring Tarkanian, although Cooke and Tarkanian do.) Weiss, a 51-year-old San Fernando Valley auto dealer, boxing manager, and sports aficionado, drove a white Rolls-Royce to the meeting that morning. He hadn't talked to Cooke and Buss long when he pulled out what Cooke called "a roll of bills that would have choked an ox." Weiss casually informed Cooke that he always carried $5,000 to $10,000.

"I was distracted by this, and he calmly put it back in his pocket," Cooke recalls. "I am sure he did it to show us how well off he was."

The distraction aside, the parties agreed to a five-year, $1 million contract for Tarkanian to coach the Lakers, but there remained small issues—season tickets and autos for Tarkanian's family—to be settled. So Weiss agreed to return the next day with Tarkanian for a final meeting to close the deal.

Weiss, however, failed to show the next morning, prompting Cooke to phone Tarkanian at his Newport Beach hotel room. He didn't show here either, Tark replied. Then Weiss's wife phoned Tarkanian because her husband hadn't been home the night before.

Almost a week later, a parking garage attendant at the Universal Sheraton noticed a terrible odor. Weiss was there, stuffed in the trunk of his Rolls. He reportedly was still carrying the rough draft of Tarkanian's agreement with the Lakers.

Tarkanian said he didn't know it at the time, but Weiss was apparently involved "in shady deals with Rams owner Carroll Rosenbloom [who had long generated suspicion of high-stakes gambling and underworld connections]. I heard he was transporting money for Rosenbloom."

Rosenbloom himself had drowned in Florida under mysterious circumstances just a few weeks earlier. Federal authorities had for some time been investigating Weiss's role in transporting cash to Las Vegas, ostensibly to place bets for Rosenbloom. Reportedly, investigators had even surveilled Weiss during a briefcase exchange in a Las Vegas airport rest room, but no connection could be proved.

And although the Los Angeles Police Department spent years working on the Weiss murder, the case was never solved, although authorities indicated that it appeared to be an organized crime hit.

News reports of the murder tipped UNLV backers that their coach was planning to leave. "A bunch of Vegas boosters got to me and put the guilt trip on me," Tarkanian explained. "It got to me, really got to me, so I turned it down. I told Jerry Buss it was gonna be a big mistake for me to turn it down. Going in with Magic would have been something."

Simultaneously, the incident cooled the Lakers on Tarkanian. His "Tark the Shark" motif (which would later add the "Jaws" theme music to be played at UNLV home games) would have been an added touch to Buss's Showtime plans at the Forum. But the Lakers decided their brief encounter with Vic Weiss was as close to "sleeping with the fishes" as they wanted to get. Instead, Buss first attempted to get West to stay on as coach. When he declined, the Lakers turned to Jack McKinney, a protégé of Portland coach Jack Ramsay. Although he had never been a pro head coach, McKinney loved an up-tempo offense. Buss wasn't sure about McKinney's credentials, but he came highly recommended. And he knew the running game, which was all the new owner needed to hear.

In the final days, as he waited to close the sale, Cooke turned his interest to the team's number-one pick in the 1979 draft. His Forum empire was the jewel of his collection, and while his divorce may have forced its sale, the owner wanted to add one last bauble before he turned it loose.

In 1976, 33-year-old Gail Goodrich had played out his option with the Lakers and signed a contract with the New Orleans Jazz. Under the league rules in force at the time, the Jazz owed the Lakers compensation for luring Goodrich away, so Cooke ordered his lawyer to strike a tough bargain with New Orleans general manager Barry Mendelsohn. The Lakers demanded New Orleans' number-one picks in 1977 and 1979 and a second-round pick in 1980. It was a blatantly unreasonable asking price for the graybeard Goodrich, who would only play part of three injury-plagued seasons for the Jazz. But Cooke knew he had an edge. If the two teams failed to agree on compensation, Commissioner Larry O'Brien would settle it for them. The Jazz feared that O'Brien, who didn't like one team signing away another's players, would come down hard on them. So they agreed, only to have the Lakers then offer the three picks back to them for veteran power forward Sidney Wicks.

As fortune would have it, the Jazz refused that Wicks deal, and then helped the Laker cause tremendously by finishing last in the league in 1979, thus ensuring Los Angeles a coin flip with Chicago, the worst team in the East, for the top pick in that spring's draft. Commissioner O'Brien made the flip at the NBA's New York offices while the Lakers and Bulls listened over the phone in a conference call. Cooke was so nervous, he couldn't go in Hearn's office, where Chick was taking O'Brien's call. The Bulls asked to call the flip; Hearn agreed. Heads, said Chicago general manager Rod Thorn.

Tails it was.

"Chick let up a yell that could have been heard in downtown Los Angeles," recalled Cooke, who had waited anxiously down the hall in his executive suite.

Exciting as it was, the victory set up an immediate dilemma. Should they draft Magic Johnson or Sidney Moncrief out of the University of Arkansas? "There was no question in my mind that we should draft Magic Johnson," Cooke recalled. Maybe so, but the rest of the Laker staff seemed to have questions. Johnson had decent athletic skills, but what would you do with a six-foot-nine point guard? Moncrief, on the other hand, was a big, strong off guard with court sense, leadership skills, and smarts.

The team had faced a similar choice in 1975, when the Lakers had the option of acquiring Kareem or Bill Walton. All of the inner sanctum except Chick Hearn favored Kareem, and the trade for him was made with little anguish.

But Magic was a tough call. The Bulls offered to trade their top pick, plus Reggie Theus, for the rights to Johnson. When Tarkanian came to interview, the Laker brass asked what he thought of the trade. Gosh, he said, I love Reggie because he played for me, but I can't really help you on that one.

Buss, though, wanted Magic, and with owners future and present weighing in, the choice was obvious. Little did they realize then that Show-time had just found its master of ceremonies.

* * *

His religious mother disliked it, because it suggested the occult, but sportswriter Fred Stabley, who followed Johnson's high school team, first gave him the nickname Magic.

Magic because of his beamer of a smile. Magic because of uncanny ability with a basketball. But mostly he was Magic because he somehow transformed good teams into great ones. He did that everywhere he played. At Everett High School in East Lansing. At Michigan State. And finally in Los Angeles.

"I'm asked a lot what was the greatest thing Earvin did," Michigan State coach Jud Heathcote said. "Many say passing the ball, his great court sense, the fact that he could rebound. I say the greatest things Earvin did were intangible. He always made the guys he played with better. In summer pick-up games, Earvin would take three or four nonplayers, and he'd make those guys look so much better and they would win, not because he was making the baskets all by himself, but because he just made other players play better."

Johnson entered State in the fall of 1977 and 19 months later delivered the Spartans an NCAA championship victory. "I'd heard about him at Everett High School," Terry Donnelly, his college teammate, recalled, "and I'd even seen him play. But it didn't really hit me until I got in the backcourt with him, on the first day of practice. You're running down the floor and you're open and most people can't get the ball to you through two or three people, but all of a sudden the ball's in your hands and you've got a lay-up."

To his credit, Heathcote immediately recognized Magic's unique talent. Although the Michigan State program was short on big men, the coach didn't hesitate to run Johnson at the point. "I still remember the first game that Earvin played," Heathcote said. "We were playing Central Michigan. I think he had seven points and about eight turnovers, and everyone said, 'Heathcoate's crazy. He's got Earvin handling the ball in the break; he's got him playing guard out there on offense; he's got him running the break; he's got him doing so many different things. Nobody can do all those things.' It's just that Earvin was nervous playing that first game and he didn't play like he played in practice. Actually, he was very comfortable in all those areas. When he went to the pros and right away they had him playing forward, I said sooner or later they'll realize that Earvin can play anywhere on defense and he has to have the ball on offense."

The Lakers needed many things in the fall of 1979. They needed rebounding help for Kareem in the frontcourt, and as Heathcote projected, Johnson filled in nicely as a power forward on the defensive end. The Lakers also needed help for Norm Nixon in the backcourt. And although Nixon was already a young, promising point guard, the Lakers eventually moved him to shooting guard, and as Heathcote also projected, they gave Magic the ball at the point.

Yet perhaps the team's biggest need was enthusiasm. No one player needed this more than Kareem, who had carried the Lakers through five frustrating years. Each passing season had brought more noise about his failure to take the team to a title. The criticism had been particularly stinging when the Lakers were thumped by Seattle in the second round of the 1979 play-offs. "They fixed on me as the reason for everything bad," Kareem says now. "It was like 'our star can't do it all for us here in Los Angeles.' "

"At that time, Kareem seemed to be going through a peculiar questioning in his life," said former *LA Times* writer Ted Green. "He seemed to be wondering if he wanted to continue playing basketball. He was often lethargic and apathetic on the floor. Many nights he operated on cruise control. One night in Madison Square Garden he scored 24 points and had only one rebound. I wrote a story and called him Kareem Abdul-Sleepwalker. He got very upset and didn't speak to me for several months."

"I always felt that Kareem was misunderstood," said Stu Lantz, his former teammate.

"Understanding me meant that I was supposed to come around to the writers' point of view," Kareem said.

His response to the circumstances was to pull even deeper within his shell. His already-cool approach to the game turned chilly.

According to the story line, Magic then arrived and recharged the great center's competitive battery, an interpretation that irritates Abdul-Jabbar. Yes, Magic was influential, he would say time and again. But he contended that what really juiced him up was his new contract and the Lakers' decision to acquire two power forwards, Spencer Haywood and Jim Chones, to help him in the frontcourt.

Still it was hard to deny that Earvin Johnson had all of Los Angeles jumping with excitement in 1979. The once sparsely attended summer league games in the balmy gym at Cal State Los Angeles suddenly opened to overflow crowds. The feeling grew from there and coursed through the whole season, pushed along by the verve of a 20-year-old. For Johnson, life was one big, joyful disco, a trip from one jam to another. All he had to do was pop on his Walkman headset, snap his fingers, and let the good times roll. Sometimes his youthful charm might be as ostentatious as wearing a full-length fur coat and chartering a helicopter as his personal limousine. Usually, though, it was as simple as his smile.

"His enthusiasm was something out of this world," said Laker small forward Jamaal Wilkes, "something I had never seen prior to him and something I haven't seen since. It just kind of gave everyone a shot in the arm."

In training camp, Norm Nixon took to calling Johnson "Young Buck," later shortened to "Buck," because of his zeal. Johnson's soulmate in this energy zone was a little-known second-year player out of the University of New Mexico named Michael Cooper who was fighting for his basketball life. He could execute spectacular dunks and had lots of raw athletic talent, but he was 6-foot-7 and weighed only 185. Johnson would have breakfast with Cooper and tell him not to worry, that he had the team made. But the coaches had to choose between Cooper and another second-year player, Ron Carter out of Virginia Military Institute. The team needed some defensive toughness, and the coaches pondered which of the two would be more likely to provide it.

Assistant Paul Westhead recommended they keep Carter, but Jack McKinney chose Coop. Carter went off to earn a bundle in the real estate business with Buss, and Cooper stayed around to play the vulture in Showtime's feared defense.

With a rookie leading the way, the Lakers charged out of training camp in 1979 and into a bright future. When Kareem won their opening game at San Diego at the buzzer with one of his skyhooks, Magic smothered him in a youthful celebration. The big center was obviously startled. Take it easy, kid, he said. We've got 81 more of these to play.

"Everybody was shocked," Johnson recalled, "but I was used to showing my emotions."

The first setback came just 13 games into that inaugural season. The Lakers opened with nine wins and four losses and were primed to scoot. McKinney's offense offered something for everyone. It would obviously require adjustments, but the atmosphere was open and getting better with every game.

Then McKinney suffered a serious head injury in a bicycle accident while headed to a tennis match with Westhead. For a time it appeared McKinney might not make it. At the very least, he faced months of convalescence. So Westhead, another Ramsay protégé, served as interim coach, and selected Pat Riley, then serving as Chick Hearn's color man, to become his assistant.

The Lakers resumed their pace in the aftermath of the accident. Westhead was just as big a proponent of the running game as McKinney. Still, there were problems. Johnson wasn't exempt from rookie growing pains, which are especially tough for point guards. The veterans complained that he was controlling the ball too much, keeping it to himself. And his no-look passes kept catching teammates unaware.

Norm Nixon, who had run the point since being drafted by the Lakers in 1978, had rather selflessly given up that role and moved to shooting guard. His presence took some pressure off the rookie and made his adjustment easier.

"You talk about people that weren't given their due," Kareem said.

"Norm could handle the ball as well as Earvin. Norm was faster up the court, and he had just as good a vision. But Norm couldn't get to the basket like Earvin because he didn't have the size.

"But when other teams tried to pressure Earvin and he gave the ball to Norm and let him run the break, then Norm and Jamaal [Wilkes], that was an incredible break right there. If the other teams tried to stop Earvin, that gave Norm and Jamaal the open court. They got us a lot of points. We went to two world championships that way."

"Magic had to learn to keep everybody in the game," Nixon told the *New York Times* later that season. "He was losing 'em. He had to make an effort, and he did. I like playing with him much more now. We complement one another."

Very quickly opponents realized that the Lakers had the best backcourt in the league. Combined with a dominant offensive center, they presented a formidable challenge. Kareem won the league's MVP for an unprecedented sixth time (Boston's Bill Russell had won five), and the Lakers topped the Western Conference with a 60–22 record.

Bird, meanwhile, had led the Celtics to a 61–21 finish. The Boston forward had averaged 21.5 points in helping his team to what was then the best turnaround in league history. The year before Bird arrived, Boston had finished 29–53. That upswing of 32 games resulted in Bird being named rookie of the year.

It was an insult that left Johnson with plenty of incentive. During the regular season he had averaged 17.6 points, 7.7 rebounds, and 7.3 assists while shooting 52 percent from the floor. He upped those numbers during his 16 play-off games that spring of 1980 to 18.3 points, 10.5 rebounds, and 9.4 assists. With the team in synch and Kareem playing his best ball in years, the Lakers ditched Phoenix and defending champion Seattle on their way to the Western Conference championship and the Finals.

Bird's Celtics, meanwhile, had run aground against Julius Erving and the Philadelphia 76ers in the Eastern Conference finals and lost 4–1. Coached by Billy Cunningham, Philadelphia had finished 59–23, just two games behind Boston during the regular season. They brought a strong, veteran lineup to face the Lakers for the 1980 title. Julius Erving was still at the top of his high-flying game. "I don't think about my dunk shots," he had said during the Boston series. "I just make sure I have a place to land."

But Kareem quickly overmatched Philadelphia's centers, Caldwell Jones and Darryl Dawkins, and put Los Angeles in position to win the championship. In Game 1 in the Forum he scored 33 points, with 14 rebounds, six blocks, and five assists, to push the Lakers to a 109–102 win. Nixon had 23 points and Wilkes finished with 20 while doing an excellent double-team job on Erving. "Every time I caught the ball I had two people on me," the Philly star said afterward. Magic, too, was a factor with 16 points, nine assists, and 10 rebounds.

In the earlier rounds of the play-offs, Westhead had begun playing Johnson at power forward on offense, while Nixon and sixth man Michael Cooper ran the backcourt. "That's our best lineup," the coach told reporters.

Philadelphia coach Billy Cunningham made his adjustments for Game 2, of which the most prominent was relieving Dawkins of the task of defending Kareem, which had brought "Chocolate Thunder" quick foul trouble in Game 1. "I ain't afraid to go to the hoop on Kareem," Dawkins had said afterward. "But when the refs are callin' 'em that way, it's a waste of time. I lost my funk."

Kareem scored 38 in Game 2, but Philly's team effort was impressive. They virtually shut down the vaunted Laker fast break and did it without fouling. The 'Sixers led by as much as 20 in the fourth period, but the Lakers raced back, trimming the lead to 105–104 late in the game. Then Bobby Jones popped in a jumper with seven seconds left, and that was enough for a 107–104 Philly win that tied the series at one-all.

The Lakers blamed the loss on the "distractions" of Spencer Haywood, who had fallen asleep during pregame stretching exercises. Once an ABA star and now a Laker reserve, Haywood had been disgruntled most of the season, at one point saying that Westhead's reasons for not playing him more were "lies." The Forum fans loved Haywood, and he often encouraged their affection by waving a towel to urge their chanting his name. Game 2 brought the final straw, however, when he picked a fight with teammate Brad Holland. Afterward Westhead suspended Haywood for the remainder of the season, which left the Lakers thin in frontcourt just when they needed the help.

Westhead made two key defensive switches for Game 3. First, he moved Jim Chones to cover Dawkins. With only the nonshooting Caldwell Jones to worry about, Kareem parked his big frame in the lane and dared the 'Sixers to drive in. Then he switched Magic to covering Lionel Hollins on the perimeter, which stifled Philly's outside game. The result was a 111–101 Laker win. Kareem had again given the 'Sixers a headache—33 points, 14 rebounds, four blocks, and three assists. And once again he got plenty of help from Nixon, Johnson, and Wilkes.

As expected, Philly lashed back for Game 4. The lead switched back and forth through the first three periods, then the 'Sixers took control in the fourth. Doctor J. unleashed one of his more memorable moves, scooting around Laker reserve Mark Landsberger on the right to launch himself. In midair, headed toward the hoop, Erving encountered Kareem. Somehow the Doctor moved behind the backboard and freed his right arm behind Kareem to put it in. It was pure magic, the Philly variety, and the 'Sixers went on to even the series at two-all with a 105–102 win.

All of which served to set up a marvelous Game 5 back at the Forum.

Los Angeles clutched to a two-point lead late in the third quarter when Kareem twisted his left ankle and went to the locker room. At that juncture, he had 26 points and was carrying the Lakers despite an uneven performance from Magic. But the rookie took over with the captain out. He scored six points and added an assist as Los Angeles moved up by eight.

That was enough to buy time for Adbul-Jabbar, who limped back into the game early in the fourth period. His appearance aroused the Forum regulars, and despite the bad ankle, he acknowledged their support by scoring 14 points down the stretch. With the game tied at 103 and 33 seconds left, Kareem scored, drew the foul and finished Philly by completing the three-point play. Los Angeles won 108–103 and took the series lead, 3–2.

That next morning, Thursday, May 15, the Lakers arrived at Los Angeles International Airport for their flight to Philly and learned that Kareem wouldn't be making the trip. His ankle was so bad, doctors told him to stay home and try to get ready for Game 7.

Westhead was worried about the effect the news would have on the team. In a private meeting, the coach told Magic he would have to move to center. No problem, the young guard replied. He had played center in high school and loved challenges such as the one he was about to face.

"Paul's fear was that we couldn't match up with Dawkins and Caldwell Jones," Johnson recalls now. "I told him I could play Caldwell Jones, and he looked at me like, 'Jesus, he's seven feet tall!' He couldn't believe that I could match up. I told him, 'Coach, on the other end, what are they gonna do with us? Who's gonna guard the guys we're gonna have?'

"And that's what he couldn't understand. Because once we got the ball, we were gone. We beat Philadelphia in the transition game because they couldn't keep up."

When the team boarded its United Airlines flight to Philadelphia, Johnson plopped himself down in the first-class seat always set aside for Abdul-Jabbar. "It was like a sacrilege to sit in Kareem's seat," Ted Green recalled. Then Johnson went through Kareem's normal routine, stretching out in the seat and pulling a flight blanket over his head. This done, he looked back at his coach and winked.

"Never fear," he told his teammates. "E.J. is here."

Somehow the folks in Philly never really believed the Lakers would head into the game without their captain. Radio stations reported regular sightings of Kareem at the airport. One taxi driver even claimed to have taken the center to his hotel.

Billy Cunningham was just as distrusting as the man on the street. "I'll believe he's not coming when the game ends and I haven't seen him," the 'Sixers' coach told the writers.

The Lakers, meanwhile, were almost too loose, Westhead feared. Magic was his normal jammin', dancin' self. About the only thing that punctured his mood was reporters' questions about his thoughts for Game 7. It was perfect, he told his teammates. Nobody expects us to win here.

In reality, most of the Lakers figured they didn't have a chance.

But when they arrived at the Spectrum that Friday evening they were greeted by the sounds of carpenters hammering out an awards presentation platform. The NBA rules required that Philadelphia provide some facility to present the trophy, just in case Los Angeles happened to win.

"It should be interesting," Westhead told his players before the game. "Pure democracy. We'll go with the slim line."

Which meant Magic, Chones, and Wilkes in the frontcourt while Nixon and Cooper took care of things up top. Kareem, who was sprawled on his bed back at his Bel-Air home, sent a last-minute message.

Go for it.

With that last blast pushing them sky-high, the Lakers took the floor. Magic grinned broadly as he stepped up to jump center against Dawkins. He lost the tip, but the 'Sixers seemed puzzled. Los Angeles went up 7–0, then 11–4. Finally Philly broke back in the second quarter and took a 52–44 lead. Westhead stopped play and told them to collapse in the middle. Steve Mix had come off Philly's bench to knife inside for 16 points. The Lakers squeezed in and closed to 60-all at the half. Then they opened the third period with a 14–0 run, keyed by Wilkes's 16 points in the period. But the 'Sixers drew it close again in the fourth.

Back home in Bel-Air, Kareem was twisting and turning and going crazy watching the television from his bed. Finally, late in the last period, he got up and hobbled out to his backyard to let out a scream.

With a little over five minutes left, it was 103–101, Lakers. Westhead called time again and made one last attempt to charge up his tired players. They responded with a run over the next 76 seconds to go up by seven. Then Magic scored nine points down the stretch to end it, 123–107.

Alas, the Lakers were too exhausted to celebrate. Wilkes had a career-best outing, scoring 37 points with 10 rebounds. And Chones lived up to his vow to shut down the middle. He finished with 11 points and 10 rebounds. He held Dawkins to a Chocolate Blunder type of game, 14 points and four rebounds.

For the Lakers, even Landsberger had 10 boards. And Cooper put in 16 points.

But the big news, of course, was Magic, who simply was. He scored 42, including all 14 of his free-throw attempts. He had 15 rebounds, seven assists, three steals, and a block.

"It was amazing, just amazing," said Erving, who led Philly with 27.

"Magic was outstanding. Unreal," agreed Philly guard Doug Collins, who was injured and watched from the sideline. "I knew he was good, but I never realized he was great."

Despite Abdul-Jabbar's fine performance in the first five games, Johnson was named the series MVP. "What position did I play?" he replied for the reporters afterward. "Well, I played center, a little forward, some guard. I tried to think up a name for it, but the best I could come up with was CFG-Rover."

How had they done it without their center? Johnson was asked. "Without Kareem," he said, "we couldn't play the halfcourt and think defensively. We had to play the full court and take our chances."

Then in the postgame interview on national television, Johnson turned to the camera and addressed Kareem back home. "We know you're hurtin', big fella," he said. "But we want you to get up and do a little dancin' tonight."

Buss, in fact, was already jumping. He hadn't been a pro basketball owner a full year and already he was on national television, soaked in champagne and accepting a championship trophy. It was something he'd worked for a long time, he told CBS.

The Lakers partied all the way back to Los Angeles, where Kareem and a cast of thousands greeted them at the airport. There were hugs and cheers and high fives all around.

Yet inside Kareem had been seething since he sat at home and watched stupefied as Johnson was named the MVP. Kareem suspected that CBS had tampered with the voting process so that there could be a presentation after the game. Johnson would later admit as much. "He was robbed of it," Lon Rosen agreed. "Kareem should have been the MVP."

"I had to give away the MVP," Kareem said. "I had won it. The writers voted me for the MVP, and then somebody from CBS went and asked them to change their vote so they could give it to Earvin. Earvin talked to me right afterwards. The next day after he got the award he said, 'Hey, I should give this to you. I didn't deserve this.'

"But I wasn't going to get into a thing with Earvin about that. I was thrilled with everybody else that he did what he did and we ended up with a World Championship. I was able to put it behind me, but it was one of the things that happened to me in my career that makes me bitter. It all came from me not being popular."

So many writers and media people failed to understand his contribution, Kareem said. "I kind of see it like the Chrysler Building. You can't build a building like that without an incredible foundation. My game was the foundation which enabled James and Earvin and Byron and Norman and all these guys to do their thing on the perimeter while I created what I created inside. We played off that, which is what teamwork is all about.

"Because of Earvin's special charisma," Kareem continued, "the story was written a different way. It was always what he did. It got to the point that I had no real belief in the objectivity of the press. I guess I was a victim of my success, the team was a victim of its success, and Earvin was the victim of his success. We compounded each other's successes and difficulties. I should emphasize that I would rather be dealing with these problems than dealing with the problems of not ever winning a World Championship."

Unable to enjoy the celebration was Jack McKinney, whose recovery from head injury had moved slowly. Against doctors' advice, he decided to attempt a comeback during the spring of 1980. When the Lakers questioned the wisdom of his move he became frustrated and criticized Buss in a newspaper story. After the championship series, the Lakers informed McKinney that Westhead would remain head coach. The decision left McKinney embittered at the team and Westhead, his longtime friend. McKinney later coached the Indiana Pacers and eventually acknowledged that the Lakers made the right decision, that he was still debilitated when he attempted to return.

"He had some memory loss for a while," Bill Sharman said. "It was just kind of a no-win situation for the team."

Sad as it all seemed, nothing could deter Johnson from savoring the special season. Over the years to come, he would treasure the videotape of his sixth game performance, playing it over and over again, almost weekly, even watching the old commercials, squeezing every moment.

From the staid confines of Bobby Knight's program at the University of Indiana, Butch Carter came to the Laker wonderland in the fall of 1981. He had just departed the from NCAA championship team to join the NBA champions. The difference was profound, as he learned in training camp.

"We had to run a mile after our first practice in Palm Spring," Carter recalled. "I'm a rookie trying to make the team. I mean I'm hauling ass; I'm trying to be first, trying to impress the coaches. And I couldn't catch Magic Johnson. This was a guy who had just earned the MVP of the championship series, and he's like 40 yards ahead of everybody else, and I'm asking myself, 'How do you ever make it up?' I always figured if you worked hard, things would work out. That's what I'll always remember about him. Not only was he the most talented, he was the hardest-working and the nicest guy I've ever been around."

Carter and another rookie stayed in the same apartment building as Johnson. Because Magic had a big contract he could afford to have meals prepared for him, so he invited the rookies over to eat every day.

Once he made the team, Carter was in for more wide-eyed amazement with his first game in the Forum. "I went from sitting beside my teammates at Indiana to sitting beside Freda Payne and Pam Grier," he recalled. "It was a little difficult trying to pay attention in the huddle."

And road trips simply meant more ambience. "Every city we went to, there was a party for us, the defending world champs," Carter said. "They would provide transportation, everything. That was the tone in every city. I guess that's the way it's gonna be if you're defending world champs."

The parties also gave Carter an understanding of true athletic stamina. "People don't understand the godly gift some of these people have," he said. "They could stay out all night and be no slower the next day out on the floor."

Despite their "godly gifts," the Lakers' good fortunes declined during their season of celebration. Johnson suffered a cartilage tear in his knee, then struggled back from surgery to rejoin his team late in the schedule, only to see the atmosphere disrupted by bickering. Nixon and Johnson sniped at each other in the press as the play-offs opened. The acrimony was relatively mild but clearly disruptive. More serious was the conflict between Abdul-Jabbar and Jim Chones, because it factionalized the team when Westhead decided to bench Chones. Nixon, Johnson, and others felt the coach made the move to keep Kareem happy. "We just lost our best inside player," Nixon told reporters.

The Lakers lost to Moses Malone, Mike Dunleavy, and a plodding Houston Rockets team, 2–1, in the opening round of the 1981 play-offs when Johnson, faced with a last-second shot to tie it, threw up an air ball. Then Bird's Celtics claimed the league title, which only increased the Lakers' suffering.

In the off-season, management shipped Chones, Brad Holland, and draft picks to Washington for power forward Mitch Kupchak, whose megasalary served to keep the locker room stewing. By no means had the atmosphere cleared by the time training camp for the 1981–82 season opened. Instead, the Lakers' long list of troubles was growing:

- News was leaked that in the off-season Buss had renegotiated Johnson's contract to a $25 million, 25-year deal, prompting an angry Kareem to call a press conference to question if Magic had become part of team management. "I'll tear up the contract if it's gonna cause problems," Magic said. But Buss gave Abdul-Jabbar a new contract at $1.5 million per season to quiet the complaints. Yet observers wondered just how the guard and center would get along in the aftermath.

- Just weeks before training camp opened, forward Jamaal Wilkes lost his second infant daughter to crib death. (His first daughter had died of heart disease.)

- Through training camp, the players bitched about Westhead's apparent attempts to slow the offense down. The coach explained to the Laker front office that he was merely trying to install a halfcourt offense so the team would have an option if the break wasn't available. But Westhead failed to make this clear to his players, who had been grousing about coaching since the '81 play-offs. Privately Buss began planning to change coaches, but general manager Bill Sharman pleaded patience.

- Johnson was among a group of players frustrated with Westhead's new offense. In mid-November, during a road win over Utah, Johnson and Westhead argued on the bench. "Things came to a head in Utah," Sharman recalled. "There was a miscommunication between Paul and Magic. The band was playing; Magic was toweling off and seemed not to listen. Paul kind of hollered at him and upset him." That night Johnson told reporters he wanted to be traded, saying he felt the new offense was stifling the team's creativity.

- The next day Buss fired Westhead, who had just directed the team through a five-game winning streak. "I defended him for a while," Sharman said of Westhead. "But it got to the point where, 'What'll you do?' Jerry West, Jerry Buss, and I all thought it was better to make a change."

- The team was then caught in confusion over the identity of the head coach. Buss had wanted West, then a personnel consultant to the team, to return to the bench. West vehemently declined and instead offered to help the 36-year-old Riley adjust to being the team's boss. At the press conference announcing the coaching change, Buss told the media that West was the coach, only to have West deny it. Instead, West served as an assistant to Pat Riley for two weeks, until Bill Bertka was hired.

- In the Lakers' next home game, Magic was stung by a chorus of boos from the Forum crowd. For months afterward he would hear extensive booing on road trips. "What you must do," Riley told him, "is ride it out and not break concentration. Just play your head off and you'll turn the crowd around."

- The ensuing weeks brought round after round of condemnation from editorialists across the country who labeled Buss a meddlesome owner and Johnson a spoiled, overpaid crybaby. His new contract was cited as part of the problem. The *LA Times* called him a "glory hog," while the New York *Daily News* said he was a "spoiled punk."

• In December, power forward Mitch Kupchak, for whom the Lakers had spent a bundle of cash, blew his knee out in a game at San Diego and was lost for the season.

• Just days after Kupchak went down, Kareem suffered a severe ankle sprain.

The injuries left the Lakers decimated in the frontcourt, and the controversy left them numb. Faced with this adversity, they responded with a short winning streak, much of it coming from Johnson's emotion. But it was clear that enthusiasm could only carry them so far. Even when Kareem returned they would face the same dearth of rebounding.

But then help arrived in two very unexpected forms. First came the acquisition of 30-year-old free agent Robert McAdoo, who while playing in Boston, Buffalo, and Detroit had been branded as selfish. Still, the Lakers were intrigued. McAdoo had a league MVP award and two scoring titles under his belt. Few people figured he would fit in, but he showed a remarkable willingness to play off the bench. Even better, he was good at it, giving the team just the scoring punch it needed at key times.

The other unexpected aid came with the emergence of power forward Kurt Rambis, the Clark Kent lookalike and free agent who reluctantly signed with the Lakers only after management assured him he had a solid shot at making the team. Not long after Kupchak went down, Rambis got an unexpected start and responded with 14 rebounds. He couldn't shoot and had a noticeable lack of athleticism. But the Lakers had enough of those properties. They needed his hustle, his defense, his rebounding, and his physical play. Combined with the other Showtime elements and Kareem's return, McAdoo and Rambis were immense help.

It seemed that the Lakers only needed direction to find their way out of the morass.

At first Pat Riley wasn't sure if he should take Westhead's place. After all, Westhead had given him the chance to be an assistant. Riley did not want to show disloyalty. He sought the advice of West, his old teammate.

"Yes," West said. "Take the job."

"I was numb," Riley said later. "I thought the firing was horrible."

Not to mention unfair. "Contrary to what people think, Paul was flexible," Riley said. "He was beginning to make changes in the offense. He was aware there were problems, but he was judged too quickly. It seemed to be the feeling of the media, the fans, the players, and the front office that it wasn't happening fast enough. I think it was more of an emotional decision than anything else."

Although confused, Riley agreed to take over the team and, more important, to make the fast break the team's top option. Still, there were problems aplenty. After Westhead's firing, the Lakers surged on emotion but fell back between January and March, barely playing .500 ball.

"Don't be afraid to coach the team," Jerry Buss finally told Riley in one meeting.

"I was giving the players too much responsiblity," Riley explained later.

He began to assert himself. When the team lost at home to Chicago on March 12, he flashed his anger. "I got fed up," he said. "I didn't know what I wanted to do when I took the job. I looked at the players and I respected their games so much and I respected them as people. I gave them too much trust. I said, 'This is their team.' It was their team, but they needed direction. That's my job. It took me three months to realize it, but I have certain responsibilities to push and demand. They have to play. I have to coach. They were waiting for me to put my foot down. That's my nature anyhow."

Weigh the situation, then move, says Sun Tzu.

Riley put his foot down, and no one shouted. In fact, the players seemed relieved. Despite their struggles, they finished the regular season with a best-in-the-West 57–25 record. But more important, they were peaking as the play-offs opened. They won 21 of their final 24 games. From there, they would break loose, sweeping nine straight play-off games before finally closing out the championship with a record-tying 12 wins against only two losses.

Suddenly Buss raised his eyebrows. The coach he hadn't particularly wanted was getting the job done.

Much of the success, of course, was due to Johnson, who was getting reacquainted with his fans. "The crowds still get me going," he said toward the end of the regular schedule. "They still jack me up. And I still love the game. I don't think I'll ever lose that."

"Magic has become a great player," Jerry West told the writers. "I've watched him go from one level to another, higher level this year. He's become solid; that's the big thing. He's in control out there. He knows what he's doing every minute he's on the floor. He's had a great, great season, especially under the circumstances."

Despite a 63–19 record, the Celtics fell to Philadelphia in a seven-game Eastern Conference Finals. The Lakers watched this drama on the tube, having dispatched Phoenix and San Antonio, 4–0 each. Their last game against the Spurs ended a full 12 days before Philly finished off Boston. Rather than get rusty, they had worked two-a-days in practice and battled each other to pass the time.

"That's the best thing about this team," Riley said, "the work ethic."

As the 1982 Finals opened, he acknowledged that Philadelphia and Los Angeles faced the challenge of not wasting their superstars' best years. "Maturity," Riley said, "makes the veterans ask, 'How many more times are we going to have the chance to win it with Kareem or with Doc?' I see that with this team, and it could be a tremendous motivating force. They talk about it constantly."

Erving, a poetic player if there ever was one, with his acrobatic moves to the basket, his twirling dunks, his well-spoken, diplomatic manner, was 32 as the 1982 play-offs opened, and he was making his third trip to the Finals since coming to the NBA in 1976. Each time the 'Sixers failed, they had to fight the public perception that they were wasting Erving's bountiful talent.

Kareem, too, was thinking about age. He had turned 35 during the season, and with each year speculation had increased about his impending retirement. In 1982, it would have seemed unimaginable that Johnson's presence could keep the great Laker center playing another seven years. By no means would those seasons be easy or uncomplicated. Still, they would be fruitful, bringing the Lakers three more titles. And if that didn't keep Abdul-Jabbar young, it at least made him ageless.

Philadelphia had the home-court advantage in the 1982 Finals, but the Lakers had their nifty zone trap, devised by assistant Bill Bertka, which they produced at just the right time in the opener at the Spectrum on Thursday, May 27. Fresh from the battle of Boston, the 'Sixers worked their offense to precision until midway through the third period. At the time, Philadelphia led by 15. Then, over the next 11 minutes or so, the Lakers ripped through a 40–9 blitz. The bewildered 'Sixers fell, 124–117. In the postgame autopsies, Billy Cunningham called it both ways. He said the zone trap wasn't hurting his team all that much. Then he called it an obviously illegal zone.

Riley then decided to back off the trap a bit for Game 2. "The officials read the papers, too," he explained. Instead, he switched Magic to cover Erving on defense. "Magic on Doc seemed like an ideal matchup to me," Riley said. "Doctor J. is a great offensive rebounder. He'd hurt us real bad. Defensive rebounding, that's Magic's greatest strength. So we put him in the position we wanted him to be in. It was great to watch. No pushing, no shoving, no hammering. They played with their talents. Magic played him as honestly as he could play him. Two great players going against each other."

"I've always been his fan," Johnson said of Erving. "I respect him. I'm in awe of him. But when you've got a job to do, you do it the best you can."

Perhaps there was too much respect. Erving brought the 'Sixers back with 24 points and 16 rebounds for a 110–94 Philadelphia win that evened the series at one-all. The Lakers, however, dominated the next two games in the Forum. Norm Nixon led a parade in Game 3 with 29. Again the zone trap was Philly's undoing, 129–108. In fact, it worked so well, they employed it again in Game 4 to take a 111–101 win.

Down 3–1, the 'Sixers seemed finished. But they lashed back in Game 5 to pin an embarrassment on Kareem, holding him to just six points, his lowest total since 1977–78 when he was tossed out of a game for punching Kent Benson. Afterward the Lakers center hurried from the locker room before speaking with the media.

"They pushed and shoved a lot," he explained in a terse memo handed out to the writers.

Dawkins said, "I tried stopping him from getting position. It's hard. He's strong, and if you let him get position he gets the skyhook. You can't block that. Wilt Chamberlain couldn't block it, so how do you expect me to block it?"

Philadelphia had closed it to 3–2, but had to return to the Forum for Game 6, where the Lakers got the lead early. The 'Sixers held Los Angeles to 20 points for the third quarter and several times cut the lead to one. "I had a few butterflies about then," said Wilkes, who led six Lakers in double figures with 27.

The Lakers then surged to boost their lead to 11 early in the fourth period. Philly again responded and with a little under four minutes to go trimmed the edge to 103–100. But Kareem completed a three-point play to put Los Angeles up by six. At the end, Wilkes got a breakaway layup to close it out, 114–104.

Riley and Buss smiled broadly as the Lakers owner accepted the trophy. "It seems like a millennium since I took over," Riley said of seven months as a head coach. "Yeah, a millennium. I've got brain drain right now, mush brain. I dug down for everything I could find. I need four months to rest up."

Johnson with 13 points, 13 rebounds, and 13 assists in Game 6 was named the series MVP, an award that raised more than a few eyebrows. The Lakers, though, had had about all the controversy they could stand for one season. "There were times earlier in the year when I didn't think this would be possible," Wilkes said as champagne cascaded over his face. "We had so many unhappy people around here you wouldn't believe it."

Winning had made them all happy, at least for the time being. And they were soon set to get richer. Trading Don Ford to Cleveland during the 1979–80 season had brought them the Cavaliers' first-round pick for 1982.

Cleveland had finished last in the league, and the Lakers again won the coin toss with the worst team in the West, the San Diego Clippers. The prize was James Worthy, who had just come from leading North Carolina to the 1982 NCAA championship.

Worthy made a nifty fit into the Showtime review. His quickness to the basket was almost startling. "I knew it was going to be special as soon as I was drafted," Worthy recalled. "For two years I had watched Earvin just kill teams with his passing. I used to watch Jamaal Wilkes and Coop get out on the wing, and I knew I was gonna benefit from Earvin. I didn't realize then how much. But I knew it was going to be good running the break with somebody who could deliver it to you at the right time."

The '82–83 Lakers boasted a deep roster. Johnson, Nixon, and Cooper in the backcourt. Rambis, Wilkes, Worthy, and McAdoo at the forwards. Kareem was in the last year of his contract and playing like a man who wanted to reap millions, the only problem being that his agent, Tom Collins, and Buss had fallen into nasty bickering over a new deal. Each day brought increasing speculation that Kareem's days as a Laker were growing short.

Yet no one could argue with the results. They ran off to a 34–9 record and had just finished a loss to the Celtics in Boston when the bad news came. Kareem's Bel-Air mansion had burned to the ground, taking with it his personal sports memorabilia and vast collections of Oriental rugs, jazz albums, and books. His longtime girlfriend, Cheryl Pistano, and son, Amir, had escaped unhurt. But the loss was in excess of $3 million. Abdul-Jabbar took the next flight to Los Angeles while the team went on to Dallas. The media immediately speculated that the loss of his home would make it easier for Abdul-Jabbar to leave Los Angeles.

Riley and West figured that Kareem would miss at least a week while trying to get his personal life in order. But he flew to Dallas before that Wednesday's game and played, scoring a season-high 34 points. "It's absolutely incredible to me that he'd come here under these conditions," remarked West, who was traveling with the team. "You know why greatness endures when you look inside a person."

Even more amazing was the fan response to the disaster. Beginning in Dallas that night and lasting months afterward, people would come forward in NBA cities to present Abdul-Jabbar with records and books to replace those lost in the fire. Josh Rosenfeld, then the Lakers' P.R. director, recalled Kareem being amazed that first night in Dallas when a young fan gave him an Ella Fitzgerald record. For years Pistano had been urging Kareem to seek a warmer relationship with his public. The fire had at last brought that about. "Kareem was showered with a lot of love and a lot of heartfelt concern for the first time in his entire career," Riley said. "I don't think he had ever seen that before."

Even with the support, the Lakers' momentum slipped after the fire. They finished 58–24, good enough for best in the West. But their hopes for a repeat championship dimmed a week before the play-offs when Worthy jumped for a tip-in against the Suns and landed unevenly on his left foot, causing a fracture of his leg just below the knee that finished him for the season. "I went airborne and got slightly pushed by someone, just hard enough in my back to throw me off," Worthy recalled. "I hyperextended and snapped the leg."

Rambis, too, was hobbled by foot injuries and missed stretches of action. The Lakers were still deep enough to stifle Portland and then San Antonio in the Western play-offs. They were up 3–1 against the Spurs and should have ended it in Game 5 in the Forum, but they lost and had to return to San Antonio for a sixth game, where McAdoo got hurt. The cumulative damage doomed their hopes in the 1983 championship round against Philadelphia. Determined to win a title, 'Sixers owner Harold Katz had shipped Darryl Dawkins to New Jersey and acquired Moses Malone, the scoring/rebounding machine, from the Houston Rockets for Caldwell Jones. Thus armed, the 'Sixers ripped through the regular-season schedule with a 65–17 record. When writers asked Malone how the 'Sixers would fare in the play-offs, he uttered his famous "fo, fo, and fo" prediction. They had come close, sweeping the Knicks in the Eastern semifinals and losing a single game to the Milwaukee Bucks in the conference finals before moving on to the NBA Finals for the third time in four years.

The Lakers quickly found more trouble in the championship round; Nixon went down with injuries. Without help, Kareem found himself in a situation similar to the one that had frustrated him so during the late seventies. Malone dominated the boards, outrebounding Adbul-Jabbar 72–30 over the course of the series, and the Lakers fell in line with Philadelphia's other victims. Each game they would lead at the half, yet each time the 'Sixers would power ahead. Philadelphia took Game 1 at home, 113–107, after Nixon suffered a partially separated shoulder. He continued to play, but the injuries mounted. The 'Sixers also took Game 2, 103–93. In the Forum, the 'Sixers sensed their opportunity. Game 3 was a blowout, 111–94, that left Nixon with a wrenched left knee and four stitches in his chin. He sat out Game 4, yet without him the Lakers still took a late lead, 106–104. Then Philly called time-out. "I'm taking over," the Doctor said in the huddle.

He immediately stole the ball and dunked it to tie the game. Next he produced a three-point play, then followed it moments later with another score, a one-hander in Johnson's face from the perimeter. The momentum from those seven late points pushed the 'Sixers over the edge, 115–108.

The aftermath of the sweep was not pleasant. That summer Norm Nixon, long a thorn in the side for Laker management, said he suspected that the team was having him investigated for drug use. Specifically, Nixon believed that West, who had replaced Sharman as general manager, was out to get him. The two had not been close since 1978, when West was coach and Nixon his rookie point guard. "Norm Nixon was Jerry West's personal whipping boy," said Ted Green, who covered the team for the *LA Times*. "Norm hated it. The day after the 1978 season ended Norm and I were standing curbside at LAX, and Norm said, 'I put up with his shit a whole year because I was a rookie, but I'm not taking it anymore.' "

For his part, West saw a talented young player in need of heavy tutoring, as young point guards often are. The position was about decisions, and if you wanted to play it, you had to live with a coach's second-guessing.

Nixon went on to build a reputation as an excellent guard and a team leader over the ensuing seasons. His teammates thought highly of him, but from time to time his fiery personality had clashed with players, coaches, and management alike. "Norm was a very cocky little guy and not afraid to voice his opinion," Kareem said. "He was a team player, but he could also disagree with you. That summer he just got into it with them [management]. When you're winning, nobody cares. When you lose like that . . ."

"He was conscious," said Worthy, who considered Nixon something of a mentor. "He was aware; he was tapped into all categories and aspects. Not your average jock."

But the situation worsened as camp opened that fall. There were trade rumors that Nixon was gone, and there was talk around other teams that he had a drug problem. Nixon saw the drug talk as West's attempt to manufacture an excuse to get rid of him. As camp opened, West told him to relax and play. But the issue ate at the guard, and Lon Rosen, then a Laker staffer, recalls Nixon finally declaring in camp that he'd had enough. He wanted to go.

During the exhibition season, West triggered a deal sending Nixon and Eddie Jordan to the Clippers for the center Swen Nater and the rights to unsigned draft pick Byron Scott.

"I think Jerry West made it easier on himself and the team," Kareem said. "That's what general managers are supposed to do. Norm went over to the Clippers and was an All-Star and had a good career. It would have been a lot better for him to finish with the Lakers. But he did okay."

The deal meant that rookie Byron Scott faced difficult circumstances when he joined the Lakers with two exhibition games left. "I caught a lot of trouble," he recalled. "Norm had been traded, and the people in Los Angeles weren't happy about it. And the team didn't seem real happy. They thought they'd been betrayed and were losing a friend. It all came down to me, a rookie who had nothing to do with it. Earvin and Cooper were the two that gave me the most trouble, because Norm was very close to both of them. Mostly it was just pushing and shoving, things like that. Taunting and talking, trying to make me upset. As a rookie you have to do what they say. Go get water. Get this and that. I think they took it a little bit overboard, but I never complained and kept doing what I could until one day Coop threw an elbow and I told him, 'You throw another one, I'm gonna throw one back.'

"After that, they started to respect me a little bit. Earvin told me they had done it number one, to see if I could play; number two, to see what kind of heart I had; and number three, to see if I could fit in. He told me I passed all three with A's."

Scott was not as good a ball handler as Nixon, but his presence didn't complicate the offense with two guards wanting the ball. An excellent shooter, he knew the role of off guard well. He spotted up, waited for Johnson to drive, then caught the kick pass when Johnson drew the double-team. From there, it was merely a matter of hitting the open shot, which Scott was born to do.

By January the Lakers had assimilated him into the lineup and were on their way tó compiling a 54–28 record, once again the best in the West. Along the way, Kareem passed Wilt as the game's all-time leading scorer in an April game against Utah in Las Vegas. With a smiling Johnson making the assist, Abdul-Jabbar racked up a total of 31,421 with a skyhook over Utah's Mark Eaton. "I'd like to give thanks to the great Allah for gifting me," he told the audience afterward. "I'd like to give thanks to my parents, who are both here tonight for inspiration and a lot of courage and support. I want to give my best to my family, and lastly, I want to thank all of you fans for your tremendous support."

12

Showtime Versus Shamrocks

LOS ANGELES 1984

For four seasons they had danced around each other in the NBA, meeting only twice each year in regular-season games. Still, Larry Bird and Magic Johnson were always aware of each other. They searched the headlines and kept their eyes on the standings and the box scores. They were trying to find some way of measuring who was best, and both would later admit that they wanted to meet for a championship. In 1984 it finally happened. Bird's Celtics versus Magic's Lakers.

"It's like the opening of a great play," Jerry West told the writers just before the 1984 Finals. "Everyone's waiting to see it."

Pro hoops had never enjoyed such media hype. As Scott Ostler and Steve Springer pointed out in their very fine book, *Winnin' Time,* it was a clash of symbols. Bird versus Magic. West versus East. Showtime versus Shamrocks. LA Cool versus Celtic Pride. But beneath all the symbols and media hooks, at the heart of everything, were two guys with immense confidence, supreme talent, and a mutual desire to dominate.

"With Magic, it's a macho thing," West explained. "He wants to be better than everybody else."

The same was true with Bird. "The number-one thing is desire," he said, "the ability to do the things you have to do to become a basketball player. I don't think you can teach anyone desire. I think it's a gift. I don't know why I have it, but I do."

Bird talked as tough as he played, Worthy recalled. "He'd always say, 'Get down!' or 'In your face!' or 'You can't guard me!' Whatever he could use to throw you off balance. That was his biggest weapon over the years. Back then, when I was young and didn't know any better, I thought he was a jerk. But after reflecting back, I realized that was just part of his game. He was measuring and analyzing his opponents, and he would do it from the moment he stepped on the floor. In the lay-up line, he'd be looking down there at you, just checking out your tendencies and your mannerisms and your posture. He could tell if your confidence wasn't right. He could tell. He could sense the vibe. If you came out on him and really didn't bump him or weren't aggressive with him, he knew. He knew he had you. If you showed any signs of doubt, you were through with Larry."

These forces of pride and ego collided in the 1984 championship series, and the league was ever so thankful for it. The Boston/Los Angeles fling in the Finals was the juice that grew the NBA. Over Bird and Johnson's first dozen years in the league, television rights money alone zoomed from roughly $14 million per year to more than $100 million. "There's no question that Bird and Magic together, with the rivalry they brought us, was an important factor," said Russ Granik, the NBA's executive vice president.

In sports bars, living rooms, and cocktail lounges across America, the competition spawned a running debate as to who was the greatest. Bird would be named the league MVP for three consecutive seasons, 1984–86. On the heels of that, Red Auerbach went so far as to declare him the greatest basketball player ever, greater even than Bill Russell, a five-time MVP.

Yet even as Bird claimed his awards, plenty of observers, including Chamberlain, thought Johnson was being shortchanged. "I don't know if there's ever been a better player than Magic," Wilt said.

Bird himself readily agreed. "He's the perfect player," he said of Johnson.

It was a nice public statement, but in 1984, as both teams were fighting their way to the championship round, the two superstars held an abiding dislike for each other, which meant that they were more than eager to prove something on the court.

The Lakers finished off the Phoenix Suns and took the Western Conference title. Once again, they were lucky to be there, having overcome injuries and other problems. Johnson had missed 13 games early in the schedule with an injured finger. Then in February, Jamaal Wilkes had contracted an intestinal infection that would hamper him the remainder of the season. Still, they possessed a solid confidence as they prepared for the Celtics. Kareem was no longer dominant, but he still gave the Lakers a formidable half-court game when they needed it. Beyond that, Worthy had quietly come into his own as a forward. He had brilliant quickness, and once Johnson got him the ball in the low post, the result was usually a score. He took delight in faking one way, then exploding another. And he continued to add range to his shot, building consistency from 15 feet out.

And the Lakers again got good frontcourt minutes and scoring from McAdoo. In the backcourt, Michael Cooper had found his identity as a defensive and three-point specialist, while third-year guard Mike McGee contributed 9.8 points per game.

Once Johnson put his finger injury behind him, they won 56 of their last 61 games, including a nice little roll through the early rounds of the play-offs. As the Finals opened, there was a sense that Los Angeles was the better team. But the Celtics had ended their conference finals series on May 23, while the Lakers didn't wrap things up until Friday night, May 25. With the first game of the Finals set for Sunday, May 27, in Boston Garden, the Celtics' four days' rest seemed to be a major factor. It had been 15 years since Los Angeles had last faced Boston in the Finals, yet old-timers needed no reminder of the numbers. Seven times the Lakers had met the Celtics for the championship, and seven times they had lost. "We had heard a lot about the Boston jinx," Worthy said, "but it wasn't something we worried about. We knew we could win."

Yet the Lakers soon realized that Boston took on a "weird atmosphere" at championship time. "There were fire alarms at two or three o'clock in the morning every night in the hotel, so you didn't sleep well," Worthy said. "and the humidity in Boston Garden was terrible. They made you deal with all the external things."

It was a long-held Laker suspicion that Red Auerbach was responsible for these things. In the locker room before Game 1, Byron Scott reached over to pick up some tape on the floor and felt warm air coming out of a vent. The Celtics were heating the locker room, he concluded.

"The Celtics did all kinds of dastardly things," said Lon Rosen, echoing the Laker company line. "It was all Red Auerbach. The guy is classless. That's old-time bullshit."

The schedule required the Lakers to make three cross-country trips. With each visit they changed hotels, hoping to avoid the harassment. To no avail. "The Boston papers and TV stations were publicizing our hotel locations," said former PR director Josh Rosenfeld.

Hours before Game 1, Kareem was wracked by one of the migraine headaches that had troubled him throughout his career. Team trainer Jack Curran worked the center's neck and back an hour before game time, at one point popping a vertebra into place. That seemed to do the trick on the 37-year-old captain. He walked out and treated the Garden crowd to 32 points, eight rebounds, five assists, two blocks, and a steal. He made 12 of his 17 shots from the floor and eight of nine free throws. He did all of that only when the Lakers slowed down. They spent the rest of the time running their break in one door and out another for a 115–109 win.

Kaput went Boston's home-court edge.

Game 2 then became a Worthy showcase for the first 47 minutes or so. He hit 11 of 12 from the floor and scored 29 points. Even better, the Lakers had come from behind to take a 115–113 lead with 18 seconds left. McHale went to the free-throw line for two shots but missed both. Thoughts of a sweep crossed 14,890 Boston minds. But the Lakers picked that particular moment for a snooze. Pat Riley had told Johnson to call time-out if McHale made the shots. But Johnson misunderstood and called time-out after the misses, which gave Boston time to set up the defense. Inbounding at mid-court, Johnson then tossed the ball to Worthy, who spied Byron Scott across the court and attempted to get the ball to him. Lurking in the background praying for just such an opportunity was Boston's Gerald Henderson. He stepped in, snatched the fat pass, and loped down the court for the lay in. The game was tied, but again Magic made a mistake. He allowed the clock to run down without attempting a final shot.

"The other players never did anything to help him," Riley would say later in defense of Johnson. "They stood out on the perimeter and didn't get open. Kareem moved with 12 seconds left, which meant he was open too early. Magic got blamed."

Late in overtime, Celtic reserve forward Scott Wedman hit a jumper from the baseline to give Boston a 124–121 win and a 1–1 tie in the series.

Afterward Riley was haunted by the steal. "What will I remember most from this series?" he asked rhetorically. "Simple. Game 2. Worthy's pass to Scott. I could see the seams of the ball, like it was spinning in slow motion, but I couldn't do anything about it."

"I had the first big blooper of my career," Worthy recalled. "I threw the ball to Gerald Henderson. We could have gone up 2–0. That set the tone for them."

The Lakers quickly recovered back home in the Forum. Johnson had a Finals record 21 assists, and Showtime rolled to a 137–104 win. Bird was outraged at Boston's flat performance. "We played like a bunch of sissies," he said afterward.

The next day the Los Angeles papers began touting Worthy as the series MVP, a development that infuriated the Celtics. None was angrier than Dennis Johnson, who had scored only four points in Game 3. "I thought I was into the game," he said, "but Game 3 convinced me I wasn't. It was a case of getting mentally and physically aggressive."

Coach K. C. Jones adjusted the Boston defense, switching Dennis Johnson to cover Magic. Regardless, the Lakers took an early lead and seemed poised to again run off with the game. From the bench, Boston's M. L. Carr vociferously lobbied for the Celtics to become more physical. Kevin McHale complied in the second quarter when he clotheslined Kurt Rambis on a breakaway, causing a ruckus under the basket. The incident awakened the Celtics and gave the Lakers reason to pause.

Later Riley would call the Celtics "a bunch of thugs."

Maxwell, on the other hand, was overjoyed with the development. "Before Kevin McHale hit Kurt Rambis, the Lakers were just running across the street whenever they wanted," he said. "Now they stop at the corner, push the button, wait for the light, and look both ways."

Still, Los Angeles held a five-point lead with less than a minute to play in regulation. But Boston's Robert Parish stole a bad pass from Johnson, and the Laker point guard later missed two key free throws, allowing the Celtics to force an overtime. Late in the extra period, Worthy faced a key free throw. But Carr hooted loudly from the bench that he would miss. Worthy did, and Maxwell stepped up and greeted him with the choke sign. The Celtics vaulted to a 129–125 win to tie the series again and regain the home-court edge.

The free-throw misses and the turnover would trouble Magic for a long time. "I thought the free throws more than the pass were mistakes," he would say later. "Those were things I—not the team—I should have taken care of. When you miss the shots you go home and sit in the dark."

The Celtics realized they were on to something. The Lakers could be intimidated. "We had to go out and make some things happen," Boston's Gerald Henderson recalled. "If being physical was gonna do it, then we had to do it. I remember in the fourth game that was the turnaround. We had to have that game or we were gonna be down 3–1. We had to have it."

The Celtics found their mental and physical tactics worked. "Cedric Maxwell and M. L. Carr would try to talk you out of your game," Worthy said. "They'd do a good job of it. They made me mad with the choke signs. I really didn't say anything, except, 'Forget you,' or something like that. But they were good at taunting you and keeping you disoriented."

The series hinged on Game 5 in Boston, where the Lakers sought an edge with oxygen tanks on the bench. "The so-called 'heat game' in 1984," *Boston Globe* writer Bob Ryan remembers. "The fifth game with Los Angeles. It was 97 degrees in the Boston Garden, and the one player that you could have predicted turned this game into a positive was Larry Bird. That sums up Larry Bird. The Lakers were sitting there sucking on oxygen, and Bird is saying, 'Hey, we've all played outdoors in the summer. We've all played on asphalt. We've all done this. Why should this be different? It's just because we have uniforms on and it's a national television audience.' That game and that performance summed up Bird to me as much as anything else he's ever done."

In that crucial match, Bird was 15 for 20 from the floor for 34 points as Boston won, 121–103. Kareem, meanwhile, appeared to be just what he was—a 37-year-old man running in sweltering heat. How hot was it? a reporter asked. "I suggest," Kareem replied, "that you go to a local steam bath, do 100 pushups with all your clothes on, and then try to run back and forth for 48 minutes. The game was in slow motion. It was like we were running in mud."

"I love to play in the heat," Bird said, smiling. "I just run faster, create my own wind."

"He was just awesome," Riley said of Bird. "He made everything work."

The Lakers then answered the Celtics' aggressiveness in Game 6 back in the air-conditioned Forum. In the first period, Worthy shoved Maxwell into a basket support. From there, the Lakers rode their newfound toughness and an old standby. Kareem scored 30, and Los Angeles pulled away down the stretch for a 119–108 win to tie the series at three apiece. As Carr left the Forum floor, a fan pitched a cup of liquid in his face, enraging the Celtics. Carr said afterward that the Lakers had declared "all-out war." Bird suggested that the Lakers had better wear hard hats on the bench for Game 7 in the Garden because the fans might get wild.

The entire city of Boston was juiced up for the event that Tuesday night, June 12. The Lakers needed a police escort just to get from their hotel to the Garden. Carr came out wearing goggles to mock Kareem and told the Lakers they weren't going to win. Not in the Garden.

Cedric Maxwell further ensured that, presenting a high-action low-post puzzle that the Lakers never solved. He demoralized them on the offensive boards. He drew fouls. By halftime, he had made 11 of 13 free throws. When they tried to double-team him, he passed them silly. He finished with 24 points, eight assists and eight rebounds. Bird had 20 points and 12 rebounds, Parish 14 points and 16 rebounds. And Dennis Johnson scored 22 while covering Magic.

Even against that barrage, the Lakers fought back from a 14-point deficit to trail by just three with more than a minute left. Magic had the ball, but Dennis Johnson knocked it loose. Cooper recovered it, and Magic again went to work and spied Worthy open under the basket. But before he could make the pass, Maxwell knocked the ball away yet again. Later the vision of Worthy open under the basket would return to Johnson again and again.

At the other end, Dennis Johnson drew a foul and made the shots, spurring the Celtics to their fifteenth championship, 111–102. Bird was named the MVP after averaging 27.4 points, 14 rebounds, 3.2 assists, and two steals over the series. But Maxwell's seventh-game performance had been incredible. All of which was celebrated deliriously by the Garden crowd. Kareem had made the mistake of retrieving a rebound as the final horn sounded and was caught up in the rush. "People tried to snatch my glasses," he said. One fan jumped on Rambis's back and would later file suit when the Laker forward slung him off. "There was no crowd control, and they just went nuts," Josh Rosenfeld said.

In the Celtics' locker room, Auerbach enjoyed yet another of his very fat, very special cigars as Commissioner David Stern presented the league trophy. The Celtics president clutched it with satisfaction and asked, "Whatever happened to that Laker dynasty I've been hearing so much about?"

Reporters packed the tiny visitors' dressing room waiting for Johnson and Cooper, who sat on the floor of the shower too disconsolate to come out. Mark Aguirre and Isiah Thomas waited, too, Rosenfeld said. "Finally they went back to Earvin and told him, 'Why don't you get this over so we can get out of here?' "

Then the Lakers tried to escape the bedlam in the streets outside the arena, but the crowd spotted their bus headed down the exit ramp. "It was a slow exit from the arena down that ramp," Worthy recalled. "The crowd was shaking and hitting our bus."

"People were throwing stuff at the bus and banging on the windows," said trainer Rudy Garciduenas. "There was this one guy in a wheelchair shooting us the bird. I remember people laughing at him. He was smiling and flipping everybody off. He was just sitting there so out of it about the Celtics."

BREAKTHROUGH

Unfortunately, the Lakers couldn't get out of town after the 1984 Finals. They had to spend one more night in their hotel, trapped inside of Boston with the Celtic blues again. Needless to say, it was a sleepless night. Owner Jerry Buss chain-smoked. Michael Cooper spent the time in deep and miserable mourning sequestered in his room with his wife, Wanda. Riley quickly put away the white tuxedo he had planned to wear for the championship celebration and began thinking about next year.

Joined by Isiah Thomas and Mark Aguirre, Johnson talked the night away. About music. Cars. Old times. Anything but the series. Occasionally the conversation would drift that way, but they'd steer it away. It was too tender a subject.

"We talked until the morning came," Thomas said later, "but we never talked about the game much. For that one night I think I was his escape from reality."

Early the next day Kareem had agreed to appear on the CBS morning news. "When we showed up at the studio, Cedric Maxwell was there," Laker PR director Josh Rosenfeld recalled. "The producer's idea was to have Cedric and Kareem on together. We were there about 10 minutes, and Cedric was sitting across from Kareem. Cedric had said a lot of things during the series. Kareem asked the producer, 'Is he on first, or am I on first?' She said, 'Oh, no, we want the two of you on together.' Kareem got up and very politely said, 'Thank you for inviting me. I can't do that.' This poor girl, the producer, she was frantic. She was in tears. She followed us out to the limo and said, 'We can reformat the show. You can go on after Maxwell.' Kareem said, 'No, I'm not in the mood anymore, but thank you.' Then he explained to me, 'Maxwell accused Worthy of choking. I can't be seen on national TV with him. It would be offensive to my teammates.' "

The Lakers' humiliation would remain for months. Johnson returned to California, where he was set to move into his new Bel-Air mansion, only the furniture hadn't arrived. His palace sat as empty as his heart, so he hid out for three days in his Culver City apartment. His mother, Christine, phoned to see how he was doing. He told her he just couldn't talk about it.

Yet everywhere he turned there seemed to be something to read about it. The Celtics were having fun with their victory. McHale even dubbed him "Tragic Johnson." Asked about the 1984–85 season, Bird said of the Lakers, "I'd like to give them the opportunity to redeem themselves. I'm sure they have guys who feel they didn't play up to their capabilities." Asked if he meant Magic, Bird replied, "You think we don't love it? Magic having nightmares [about his poor play]."

Johnson retorted that he had no need for redemption.

Even worse than the Celtic cockiness was the trashing he took from the LA newspapers. "I sat back when it was over," he said later, "and I thought, *Man, did we just lose one of the great play-off series of all time, or didn't we?* This was one of the greatest in history. Yet all you read was how bad I was."

The Lakers returned to Palm Springs for training camp that fall. "When we walked on the floor that first day of camp, we saw it in everybody's eyes," Byron Scott recalled. "This was going to be a serious year."

Especially for Riley. "Pat was screwed down pretty tight, like a spring," Gary Vitti said of the '85 season. "And it escalated from there."

"Riles made us aware of exactly what he wanted," Scott said. "He let us know from day one, 'I'm gonna work you from the first day of camp to the last day of the play-offs.' He didn't let up. That's the main reason we kept going all year, because we had a coach who wouldn't let us stop."

Riley later explained that his team's psyche was fragile. They had won two championships on their talent, but the Celtics had challenged them with psychological warfare and won. The Lakers would have to either form as a team and fight back or fall apart.

"That first series that we gave them in '84 really seasoned us," Kareem said. "It gave us the mental tenacity that we didn't always exhibit. We couldn't outrun everybody. We had to understand that sometimes there were other ways to skin the cat."

By the 1985 play-offs the Lakers had regained their composure and their strength. The frontcourt was bolstered by the return of Mitch Kupchak and Jamaal Wilkes to go with Kareem, Worthy, Rambis, McAdoo, and Larry Spriggs. The backcourt showed Magic, Scott, Cooper, and McGee. As a group, they were driven by their '84 humiliation.

"Those wounds from last June stayed open all summer," Riley said as the play-offs neared. "Now the misery has subsided, but it never leaves your mind completely. Magic is very sensitive to what people think about him, and in his own mind I think he heard those questions over and over again to the point where he began to rationalize and say, 'Maybe I do have to concentrate more.' I think the whole experience has made him grow up in a lot of ways."

After all, Johnson was a mere 25, and at a time when most pro players were just beginning to feel comfortable in the game, he already owned two championship rings. Across pro basketball, observers sensed that he was about to add to his jewelry collection. The Celtics, however, were conceding nothing. With a 63–19 regular-season finish, they had again claimed the home-court advantage. The Lakers had finished 62–20. And neither team dallied in the play-offs. Boston dismissed Cleveland, Detroit, and Philadelphia in quick succession. The Lakers rolled past Phoenix, Portland, and Denver.

For the first time in years, the Finals returned to a 2-3-2 format, with the first two games in Boston, the middle three in Los Angeles, and the last two, if necessary, back in Boston. The situation set up an immense opportunity for the Lakers to steal one in the Garden, then pressure the Celtics back in Los Angeles.

Yet on the eve of the Finals they were struck by old doubts. "We really weren't sure of ourselves," Worthy recalled. "We got back to the Finals and said, 'Golly, we got the Celtics again. How're we gonna do it?' We just came out and played like a bunch of women, really. Didn't have any aggressiveness. No killer instinct. We paid the price for it."

Which was one final, profound embarrassment. Game 1 opened on Memorial Day, Monday, May 27, with both teams cruising on five days' rest. The Lakers, however, quickly took on the appearance of guys who had just come off two weeks on the graveyard shift. The 38-year-old Kareem, in particular, slogged up and down the court, while Robert Parish seemed to glide. Often Kareem would just be reaching the top of the key to catch up when all of a sudden the action raced the other way. He finished the day with 12 points and three rebounds. And Johnson had only one rebound. Meanwhile the famed Showtime running game had been slowed to a belly crawl.

And the Celtics?

They placed a huge red welt on the Lakers' scar from the previous year, 148–114. Scott Wedman hit 11 for 11 from the floor, including four three-pointers. Danny Ainge fired in six straight buckets at the end of the first quarter to finish the period with 15 points. "It was one of those days," K. C. Jones said, "where if you turn around and close your eyes, the ball's gonna go in."

Abruptly, the Celtics quieted their trash talking, as if they sensed that they had gone too far. They hadn't expected it to be this easy. And the last thing they wanted to do was rile the Lakers. "It's definitely time to back off," Maxwell said. "It's not like backgammon or cribbage, where if you beat someone bad enough you get two wins."

But it was too late. The teams didn't play again until Thursday, and there was an uneasy air in Boston despite the big win.

The next morning in the Lakers' film sessions, Kareem moved to the front row, rather than recline in the farther reaches as he usually did. And he didn't blink when Riley ran and reran the gruesome evidence of his terrible performance. In fact, the captain went to each of his teammates later and personally apologized for his effort.

"A lot of the discussion was pointed at Kareem," Worthy said. "But it was all of us, because none of us played well. But he was our leader."

"He made a contract with us that it would never happen again. Ever," Riley said later. "That game was a blessing in disguise. It strengthened the fiber of this team. Ever since then, Kareem had this look, this air, about him."

"That set the tone," Worthy said. "That game was the turning point in Laker history, I think. We came back strong and Kareem led the way. Riley, too. He stepped forward. It was the turning point in his career, too. He took his coaching to another level. It brought the last development of his coaching technique. It was to utilize all aspects. After that particular game it wasn't pretty. It was factual. It was the truth, and it was presented to us in a way we couldn't deny. We had to go out and do something about it."

As the second game approached, the Lakers knew exactly what they had to do. "Our break starts with good, tough defense," Rambis said. "That forces teams out of their offense. Then we must control the boards. That's where the work comes in. If we do those two things, the fast break is the easiest part."

Before Game 2 on Thursday, Kareem went to Riley and asked if his father, Al Alcindor, could ride on the team bus to the Garden. Riley consented and thought of his own father. "Pat talked about when he was a little boy," Gary Vitti recalled. "His big brothers would take him down to the playground. He was the smallest guy out there, and he'd get beat up every day and go home crying. They'd take him home, and his father would say, 'Take Pat back down there tomorrow.' And the big brothers would say, 'Dad, the guy's getting beat up.' His father said, 'Take him back. At some point, you gotta plant your feet, kick some ass, and make a stand.' "

Just before he died, the elder Riley had reminded his son that to survive you had to make that stand. Riley recalled those words to his players in his pregame talk. It was time, he said, to make a stand.

"That's why Pat is what he is today, those types of influences," Vitti said of Riley's father. "Riles is an inspiring guy. I mean after hearing him, I wanted to go out there and kick some ass, too."

And the Lakers did. Kareem, in particular, reasserted himself with 30 points, 17 rebounds, eight assists and three blocks. Cooper hit eight of nine from the floor to finish with 22 points. And just like that, the Lakers evened the series, 109–102. Best of all, they had stolen a game in the Garden and now returned to the Forum for three straight.

"They expected us to crawl into a hole," Lakers assistant Dave Wohl said of the Celtics. "It's like the bully on the block who keeps taking your lunch money every day. Finally you get tired of it and you whack him."

They hosted the Celtics on Sunday afternoon and really whacked 'em again, returning the favor of Game 1, 136–111. This time Worthy was the man, with 29 points. But Kareem's presence was felt again, too. He had 26 points and 14 rebounds.

At one point, Boston had led, 48–38, but Worthy dominated the second quarter and Los Angeles charged to a 65–59 edge at intermission. The Lakers ran away in the second half, during which Kareem became the league's all-time leading play-off scorer with 4,458 points.

Bird, meanwhile, had fallen into a two-game shooting slump, going 17 for 42. He had been troubled by a chronically sore right elbow and bad back, although some speculated his real trouble was Cooper's defense.

As with '84, the series was marked by physical play, although this time it was the Lakers who gained an edge. "We're not out to physically harm them," Kareem offered. "But I wouldn't mind hurting their feelings." Before Game 4, the NBA's vice president of operations, Scotty Stirling, warned each coach that fighting and extra rough play would be met with fines and suspensions. Riley told his players of Stirling's warning, but K. C. Jones chose not to. With their uninhibited play, the Celtics stayed in it, and the game came down to one final possession. Bird had the ball but faced a double-team, so he dumped it off to D. J. above the foul line. From there, Johnson drilled the winner with two seconds left. Boston had evened the series and regained its home-court advantage, 107–105.

Game 5 two nights later in the Forum was another showdown. The Lakers went on a 14–3 run at the close of the half to take a 64–51 lead. They stretched it to 89–72 after intermission, until the Celtics closed to within four at 101–97 with six minutes left. But Magic hit three shots and Kareem added four more, giving him 36 on the day, as the Lakers walked away with a 3–2 lead, 120–111.

"People didn't think we could win close games," Johnson said afterward.

From there it went back to Boston. Jerry West didn't dare make the trip for fear of spooking the proceedings. Across the country old Lakers held their breath and watched the tube. After eight painful losses, this seemed to be the best chance yet to end Boston's domination. The Celtics would have to win the final two games. With a mere 38 hours' rest between games, that just didn't seem possible.

Kareem was there again, this time with 29 points, 18 of them in the second half when it mattered. The score was tied at 55 at intermission.

Kareem sat much of the second period in foul trouble while Kupchak did admirable work at backup. The Celtics had played only seven people in the first half, and Magic could see that they were tired. It was written on their faces. Riley told him to keep pushing it at them, not to worry about turnovers. Just keep up the pressure.

He did.

And the Celtics did something they had never ever done before. They gave up a championship on their home floor, on the hallowed parquet, 111–100. McHale had kept them alive with 36 points, but he got his sixth foul with more than five minutes left. And, thanks in part to Cooper's defense, Bird was closing out a 12-for-29 afternoon. "I thought I'd have a great game today," he said afterward.

In the end, the Lakers' victory was signaled by the squeaking of sneakers in the deathly quiet Garden as the crowd slipped away. It was the same crowd that had so riotously jostled the Lakers the year before. "They fought as dirty as they could until they realized they were gonna lose," Kareem recalled. "Then they came back with Celtic pride and all this crap."

"We made 'em lose it," Johnson said with satisfaction.

Kareem was named the MVP. "He defies logic," Riley said of the 38-year-old Laker center. "He's the most unique and durable athlete of our time, the best you'll ever see. You better enjoy him while he's here."

Johnson's trophy was the sweet redemption he had said he didn't need. "You wait so long to get back," he admitted afterward. "A whole year. That's the hard part. But that's what makes this game interesting. It's made me stronger. You have to deal with the different situations and see if you can come back."

With the building empty and the last reporters taking notes in the locker rooms, Jerry Buss and Hampton Mears, his old sports friend, quietly slipped out to the center of the Garden parquet to giggle and exchange high fives. What Buss called the "most odious sentence in all of sport"—"the Lakers have never beaten the Celtics"—was no longer true. From the Garden, the Lakers retreated to their hotel, where at last Riley got to celebrate in his white tuxedo from the year before.

The team's next business was to vote on Pres. Ronald Reagan's invitation to visit the White House. If the coaches hadn't cast ballots, too, the team might have passed. It was a close vote, but the '85 champions became the only Lakers to visit the presidential quarters. They were tossed about on a bumpy flight into Washington, but once there Kareem and Riley had a nice chat with Mr. Reagan. Then it was on to LA. "We wanted to get back home to party with our families and friends," Byron Scott recalls.

Across the country, old Lakers felt a weight lifted. "All those Celtic skeletons came out of the closet," Riley said.

*   *   *

In the wake of the '85 title, the Lakers decided to ditch two old favorites. They waived Jamaal Wilkes and declined to pick up the option on Robert McAdoo's contract. Both were popular with their teammates. "Without a doubt," Johnson says now, "that was the Lakers' greatest moment. Those years with McAdoo, that team was awful close. We were all so tough-minded. We would go on the road and just say, 'OK, how many games we got?' We'd see there was six. 'We're gonna win all six.' And then we'd go and win all six. We would push each other to make sure. Coop would be on me. I would be on Coop. If the game got tight, Coop would say, 'Buck, take over.' And I'd take over. Or I'd say, 'Kareem, it's time for you to dominate. Take over the game.' And it was just that way.

"Or we could get on one another. 'Man, your man's beatin' you! What's up?' You would get so mad, you'd just shut 'em down. That was the respect we had for one another. That was the sign of a true championship team, that we could get on one another."

To bolster the frontcourt after McAdoo's departure, the team signed veteran bruiser Maurice Lucas. It was figured that he would give the roster a little toughness, but it didn't work out. A veteran, Lucas expected the perks of one. He expected a first-class seat on planes but was told they belonged to the Lakers' inner core of veterans, most of whom had far less time in the league than Lucas. He fumed at the snub, and Riley tried to explain. "These guys have been together a long time," he told Lucas. "Are you gonna be the guy to break that up? You gotta look beyond yourself to the team."

The friction, however, persisted and became one of several factors in the Lakers' ultimate failure. "Winning the '85 title took tremendous energy from our guys," Gary Vitti said. "It was really mentally fatiguing to break that Celtic barrier. That next year, we needed an injection of something and it just wasn't there."

The end came abruptly against Houston in the first round of the 1986 play-offs. They fell 4–1, finished off by Ralph Sampson's last-second shot in the Forum that bounced up and in. "We beat them the first game and thought it was going to be a cakewalk," Byron Scott recalled. "Then they caught up and got us in Houston and we never recovered."

"Houston was playing great," Gary Vitti said, "and we were going through the motions."

Once again the Lakers sat back and watched Boston defeat Houston for the title. Jerry Buss didn't like it. He was convinced they should trade Worthy to Dallas for Mark Aguirre. But Jerry West talked him out of that deal, saying no team wanted to make a trade based on emotions. Bird and his Celtics had held their breath, hoping that Buss would break up the team. The owner's anger at their lackluster play eventually cooled.

Riley, though, had other changes in mind. Kareem was 40 years old heading into the 1986–87 season. As long as anyone could remember, he had been the focus of the Lakers' offense. But the center's retirement was inevitable, and Riley wanted to begin shifting the burden to other players. He wanted Magic, and to a lesser degree James Worthy, to become the focus of the offense. So the coaches began roughing out their ideas of how this transition should work. They took their notions into training camp that fall and were promptly confronted with confusion and frustration. Abdul-Jabbar didn't like the change. "By then he kind of felt he was the team," Kareem says now of Johnson. "When we lost in the play-offs to Houston. I was the failure and Earvin was the answer. I was being written out of the mix."

With Westhead's demise in the back of his mind, Riley had second thoughts and told longtime Laker assistant Bill Bertka that maybe they should junk the idea.

No, Bertka replied, now is the time to make the change.

"This was Kareem's team," Johnson says now. "He was the dominating type. I played my role, and it was great. I didn't mind it, but it was other people saying things. They figured I couldn't dominate like Kareem."

Despite the clash of egos, the players found their comfort zone in the new system. Kareem personally reassured Riley that everything was working fine. Johnson's play over the season would confirm it. He became the first guard since Oscar Robertson to win the league MVP award. His scoring zoomed to a career-high 23.9 points per game, and he was tops in the league in assists, at 12.2 per game.

He didn't do it alone, of course. Kareem. Worthy. Byron Scott. Cooper. And rookie A. C. Green. All of them wanted to establish their superiority. They had the opportunity to prove themselves one of the greatest teams in basketball history. And they were about to get better.

The big boost arrived February 13, when the front office acquired Mychal Thompson from San Antonio. Larry Bird was heartsick at the news. How could the Spurs give Thompson to the Lakers? he asked. The 6-foot-10 Thompson gave the Lakers just what they needed up front. He could play backup to Kareem at center, and he was a solid power forward. Better yet, he was an excellent low-post defender, and having played with McHale at the University of Minnesota, Thompson knew better than anyone how to defend against Boston's long-armed forward. It was, Kareem says now, West's most brilliant move as general manager, because it made them championship contenders again. With Thompson, the Lakers surged to a 65-win regular season, the best in the NBA.

"We rolled in 1987," Gary Vitti recalled. "It was almost a piece of cake. It was like, 'Who's next?' Every night we knew we were gonna win. All we had to do was keep it close. Then they could just turn it on and finish."

* * *

It had been 18 seasons since a team had won back-to-back championships in the NBA. The 1986–87 Celtics had hopes of being the first modern team to stretch to that achievement. Standing in their way was a tall, skinny guy with an inferiority complex. For several seasons Michael Cooper had shown the league that he was Showtime's defensive backbone. The '87 season finally brought his recognition as the NBA defensive player of the year. He had made Larry Bird his personal challenge, spending hours studying the Boston forward on videotape, even going so far as to take the tapes on vacation. "Coop just drove himself," said Rudy Garciduenas. "He wanted to be the best. His wife, Wanda, used to give him hell all the time because that's all he did was watch tape. He didn't pay attention to her or the kids when he was home. Coop was that way. He wanted to know what was coming at him, what to expect."

"Larry didn't talk as much with Coop," Worthy recalled. "Coop would be right back in his face. Most of the time, Coop would get the first lick in. He would come out on the floor and say, 'Nothing tonight, Larry. Nothing for you. I'm sorry.' Then that would get it started right there.

"I learned a lot from Coop in that aspect, because there wasn't any backing down. If you got 55 points against him, it was gonna be the toughest 55 you had ever gotten. Coop and Larry had that same talent, because if Coop saw you weren't ready or you weren't gonna work hard, it was history. He'd shut you down in a minute."

"It wasn't just Bird," Gary Vitti said. "Coop talked to everybody out there. The guy was 175 pounds. He was nothing. He was like a feather. He was afraid of no one. We weren't a bunch of bruisers. We were a finesse team. But when there was a fight on the court, Michael was always a part of it."

Cooper was the best athlete in the Showtime retinue, in Vitti's opinion. His quick first step. His speed. His timing. The hand-eye coordination. And what the trainer called "the kinesthetic sense, knowing where his body is in space.

"One of the greatest things to watch in those days," Vitti said, "was Coop baiting somebody on the breakaway. Coop would give 'em a step and they would go to the hole, and Coop would be a step behind and time it perfectly to leave his feet and block the shot. It was a vintage thing. He knew what they were gonna do before they even did. And his mental toughness. It was like Coop was so insecure about his body and size that everybody had told him he couldn't make it. He was too thin, too small. He wasn't strong enough. That's why he was so great, because he had to prove to himself that he was.

"Magic's motivation in many, many ways came from Michael Cooper. He motivated Magic. We play too many games. We have too many practices. You cannot be 100 percent mentally and physically ready every single day in this league. When Magic wasn't there, it was Coop that was grabbing him by the jersey saying, 'C'mon, Earvin! C'mon, Earvin!' They really thrived off each other in a verbal sense. Kareem and Magic maybe thrived in a mental sense. They were on the same wavelength, but they didn't have to talk to each other. Coop and Magic talked to each other a lot on the court, getting in each other's face."

"Coop was probably the most superstitious player in the league," said Rudy Garciduenas. "You had to come to understand Coop and accept him for his oddities. He had to have his socks pulled all the way up to his knees. If he was going through a slump, he would walk in one day and everything had to be new. His socks, his jocks, his wristbands. He shaved his face. It was like he would cleanse himself of everything and that would break his slump."

As a young player, Cooper was an acrobatic leaper and quickly became a Forum favorite executing his "Coop-a-loop," the alley-oop slam dunk that fired up the fans. But as he aged, he legs diminished, and he made himself into a great defensive player and a solid three-point threat. Best of all, he had an iron will, reflected in his streak of 556 straight games played, which ended fittingly enough in January 1988 when he was suspended one game for fighting.

The Lakers scorched the earth as they moved through the 1987 play-off field. Detroit assistant Dick Versace scouted them and came away shaking his head. "They're cosmic," he said. "They're playing better than any team I've ever seen."

Denver fell 3–0 in the first round. Then Golden State dropped out of sight, 4–1. Seattle, the opponent in the Western finals, went down, 4–0, meaning the Lakers concluded their conference work on May 25, while the Celtics and Pistons fought through a seven-game series. Faced with a week off, Riley set up a minicamp in Santa Barbara to keep them focused. They had a pancakes-and-strawberries breakfast buffet on Saturday, May 30, and watched the Celtics advance with a 117–114 win over Detroit.

Three days later, on Tuesday, June 2, the Finals opened in the Forum before a crowd peppered with celebrities. The regulars, Jack Nicholson and Dyan Cannon, were there, but the series attracted many more. Bruce Willis, Don Johnson, Whoopi Goldberg, John McEnroe, Johnny Carson, Henry Winkler, and many others. Their presence only seemed to inflame Pat Riley more. He had begun stewing with the end of the Eastern finals, when the press described the injured Celtics as a blood-and-guts brigade. Riley threw this up to his troops as an affront. The Celtics get all the respect for being hardworking, while the Lakers are packaged as a bunch of glitzy, supertalented guys who glide through their Showtime without much character or thought, Riley alleged.

And he considered the presence of all the celebs just another reason for the press to underestimate his team. "A bunch of glitter-group, superficial laid-backs," Riley spat. "This is the hardest-working team I've ever had, but regardless of what we do, we're minimized . . . we're empty people . . . and most of us aren't even from California."

The tirade brought puzzled looks from reporters, but most of them figured he was looking for something to whip his team to the next level. The eight-day layoff had left some questions in his mind about intensity.

Riley was faced with two probable scenarios. Either the Celtics would come in game-sharp and take it to the Lakers, or they would come in weary from two straight seven-game battles. The latter very quickly established itself as the operating format for the day. Their tongues wagging, the Celtics could do little more than watch the Lakers run weave drills up and down the floor. "The Celtics looked like to me like they were keeping up pretty good," Mychal Thompson quipped, "just at a different pace."

Johnson led the rout with 29 points, 13 assists, 8 rebounds, and no turnovers. On the receiving end of many of Johnson's passes, Worthy had 33 points and nine rebounds. The Lakers ran 35 fast breaks in the first two quarters and led by 21 at intermission. They settled into a canter thereafter, finally ending it 126–113.

The Celtics knew they were reeling and to catch themselves they had to stop Johnson. Which they did in Game 2, but in the process they allowed Michael Cooper to switch specialities, from defense to offense. Boston trailed by seven in the second quarter, when Cooper pushed the Lakers through a 20–10 outburst, accounting for all 20 points himself by either scoring them or assisting. "He was so invaluable," Kareem said. "Coop could come in for a few minutes and really change everything in a game."

When it was over, he had laced in six of seven trey attempts. And the Celtics had spent another day gasping in pursuit of the Laker break. "One of the Laker girls could've scored a lay-up on us," backup center Greg Kite said later. Kareem flicked in 10 of 14 shots for 23 points, while Magic put up nice boxy numbers, 20 assists and 22 points. In Coop's big second quarter, he racked up eight assists, tying a finals-series record. His six treys broke a play-off record as well.

It all added up to a 141–122 rout, Boston's sixth straight road loss in the play-offs. The LA papers enjoyed these developments thoroughly and took to calling the Celtics "Gang Green." Before doubt crept too far into Celtic minds, they righted themselves in Game 3 with a 109–103 win.

"We're just too good a team to be swept," Bird said.

The pressure of Game 4 shifted to the Lakers, which made Riley's mood even blacker. During a closed Los Angeles practice in the Garden, Riley requested that the cleaning staff leave the building. "Maybe he thought they had VCRs in their brooms," the Garden security director quipped. When they weren't playing cloak-and-dagger games in the Garden, the Lakers were sequestered in their hotel rooms, waiting on nightmarishly slow room service and jumping at the fire alarms that always greeted their stays in Boston. Any sane observer could have determined that the Lakers were too tight. But there weren't many sane observers around. This was the Lakers and the Celtics. And this was the Finals. Riley expected the worst.

He sure got it. Boston went up by 16 just after the half. Jack Nicholson, who had wormed a seat in the upper press area, spent most of the evening getting choke signs from Boston fans. "There was one guy," Nicholson said. "He was giving me the choke sign so hard, I almost sent for the paramedics. He was wearing a gray sweatshirt, and his face turned almost as gray as his shirt. I couldn't believe it."

At one point, Jack allegedly mooned his tormentors. "I was surprised he didn't get arrested," Rudy Garciduenas said. "But the Boston fans loved him being there. He gave them somebody to jeer at."

Shortly thereafter, relief came to Nicholson and the Lakers. LA cut the lead to eight with three and a half minutes to go in the game. From there, the conclusion, the series actually, came down to one Magic sequence.

With half a minute left, the Lakers called time to set up a pick for Kareem. But Johnson told Kareem to fake it as his defender, Parish, attempted to fight through the pick. When Parish tried to fight through, Kareem should roll to the basket, Magic said.

He did. The pass was there, and the Lakers took a 104–103 lead. But Bird grabbed it back at the 0:12 mark with a three-pointer, putting Boston up 106–104.

On the next possession, Kareem was fouled and went to the line, where he made the first and missed the second. McHale grabbed the rebound, but Mychal Thompson gave him a gentle push and the ball went out-of-bounds. McHale signaled Boston ball and had the boys in green headed back to the other end until the officials got their attention and notified them that it was Laker ball.

What followed of course was another of those plays for the ages. For years afterward Magic Johnson would sit in the private screening room at his mansion, playing and replaying the scene thousands of times, each time tingling with a glee that would refuel his competitive fires. The play replenished his spirit every time he watched it.

Perhaps the definition of a Celtic hell is being assigned to Magic's screening room for eternity, watching the sequence and listening to his delighted laughter over and over and over.

Magic took the ball on the inbounds pass at the left of the key and at first contemplated a 20-footer, but McHale came out to change his mind. So Magic motored into the key, where Bird and Parish joined McHale in a trio of extended arms as Magic lofted a hook. Parish almost brushed it.

But the ball rose up and then descended to a swish. K. C. Jones, watching in a standing twist from the Celtic bench just feet away, felt his heart sink into an abyss.

"See everybody thought I couldn't score," Johnson says now. "I had said, 'You know, I'm just gonna go along, and one of these days it's gonna be my show.' That shot proved it to everybody, and that was the year I won the MVP. That's the year Pat said, 'OK, Earvin, I want you to take over.' And that's what happened. After that, people said, 'It *is* Larry and Magic,' instead of 'Larry can do this, and Magic can't do that.' You always had to fight that."

The Celtics got a time-out with two seconds left, and the Lakers even left Bird open for a shot, which went partially in. But it didn't stay down, and Magic ran off happily, having stolen Game 4, 107–106.

Red Auerbach, however, was anything but happy. He chased veteran official Earl Strom off the floor, and in front of the press contingency and the television cameras he made pointed, disparaging remarks, suggesting that Strom was a gelding, that Strom had given the game to the Lakers.

Strom ducked into the officials' dressing room, then stuck his head back out to tell Auerbach, "Arnold, you're showing the class that you always have."

Auerbach later explained that he chased Strom in an attempt to fire up his team. "People say, 'Relax, the game is over. The game is over.' Well, the game is never over," he said.

Alas, Red was wrong. The game was most definitely over, and Magic had retired to the locker room to be lost in his eternal joy. He dubbed the shot "my junior, junior, junior skyhook."

"You expect to lose on a skyhook," Bird said with a sickly smile. "You don't expect it to be Magic."

The Celtics made the mistakes down the stretch, Bird continued. "We turned the ball over twice. We missed a rebound after a free throw. We really can't blame anybody but ourselves."

Would the game be remembered just for its last minutes? Bird was asked. "It should," he replied. "A lot happened in the last minute and a half. Robert gets the ball taken away from him. I throw the ball at Kevin's feet. They miss a free throw, and we don't get the rebound. How many chances do you need to win a game?"

Then someone asked how he liked the Celtics' chances for the rest of the series. "How do I like my chances?" he asked and grinned. "How would you like it? I know, when we're up 3–1, I always say it's over. It's not a good position. There's no question we're in trouble. We're not a good road team. I don't know if we can beat them twice out there. But we'll give it a try."

Bird had told his teammates, "If they want to celebrate, let's not let them do it on the parquet." At one point during Game 5, the Laker staff even iced down several cases of champagne. But the Celtics had incentive enough. They got their second win, 123–108, and the series jetted back across the continent.

Kareem arrived for Game 6 with a shave job on his balding head. And for a time it seemed Los Angeles was intent on cutting it close. Magic had only four points by the half, and the Celtics led 56–51. But like Kareem's pate, the Lakers glistened after intermission. Worthy finished with 22, and Kareem had 32 points, six rebounds, and four blocks. Mychal Thompson had 15 points and nine rebounds. And Johnson led them with all-around brilliance. His 16-point, 19-assist, eight-rebound showing brought him the MVP. And the Lakers claimed their fourth title of the decade, 106–93.

"Magic is a great, great basketball player," Bird conceded. "The best I've ever seen."

"He's the best in the game," Riley agreed. "He proved it in the regular season and the play-offs. We wouldn't be anywhere without him. We wouldn't be a championship contender without him."

Johnson saw the reflection of his special talents in the team. "This is a super team, the best team I've played on," he said. "It's fast; they can shoot, rebound, we've got inside people, everything. I've never played on a team that had everything before. We've always had to play around something, but this team has it all."

Bird had to agree. "I guess this is the best team I've ever played against," he said. "In '85, they were good. In '84, I really thought they should have beaten us. . . . I don't know if this team's better than they were, but I guess they are. Their fast break is better. They're deeper."

Bird's assessment was nice, but the major questions about the Lakers remained unanswered. How deep? How good? How tough? Would they live up to their promise?

13

Repeat

Even before the Lakers had put the wraps on their 1987 title, Pat Riley had begun plotting the course for next year. While the champagne sprayed across the locker room in celebration, he set the board for his first move. It would begin with a reporter's question. Riley waited until someone got around to asking if this Laker team could repeat as champions.

"I guarantee it," he said flatly.

The reporters, the players, the staffers all stopped in their tracks. Say what?

He guaranteed it.

His players were instantly infuriated. The game was tough enough without asking for trouble. Championship pro basketball is essentially a matter of taking on the pressure that builds over the course of a long season, the goal being to conquer that pressure and ultimately eliminate it. The greater the player, the greater the ego; the greater the ego, the greater the pressure. The reward, for truly great players, is a summer away from the pressure, a time in which they can say that they've lived up to their potential.

"In '87, we win the thing," Gary Vitti recalled, "and then Pat turns right around and lays all that pressure right back on them."

"Just when we thought we'd done everything we could do, Riles makes this guarantee," Byron Scott says now. "I thought he was crazy."

Nineteen seasons had passed since the Celtics had won consecutive championships in 1968 and '69. Many observers had come to the conclusion that the feat couldn't be accomplished in the modern NBA. Riley rejected that notion. He believed that winning again was a test of will, that greatness was available to the team with the mental toughness to fight for it. He knew the Lakers were a team of mentally strong individuals. They just needed someone to drive them to greatness. He was that person.

Ultimately, Riley got away with it because the Lakers remained haunted by their missed opportunities. 1981. 1983. 1984. 1986. "The fact is," Gary Vitti says, "we had teams that could've and maybe should've won all those years."

Beginning with training camp the next fall and throughout the following season, Riley pushed them like a man obsessed. He was Captain Ahab, and the back-to-back championship was the elusive great whale. On occasion the crew came close to mutiny, but then he would read their mood and lighten up just enough to keep them going.

The biggest factor, of course, was the team itself. They had the image of Showtime, of Magic's smile and the electraglide fast break, of run and gun and fun. But all in all they were a serious lot. Kareem and Worthy and A. C. Green were as businesslike as they come. Johnson, too, had his fun face, but he had hardly been frivolous in his pursuit of basketball excellence over his career. As a team, they practiced like accountants. Detail mattered. Distraction wasn't tolerated. They had to be tough. They had to work. And they didn't slip often, but when they did, Riley was there to remind them, to irritate them with his professorial tone and his mind games.

In the end, the Lakers' intensity became a way of life. And quite simply, the Boston Celtics couldn't match it.

The Lakers' 1987 championship season had only confirmed that the Lakers would need Worthy's low-post game if Riley's obsession was to be realized. With the 1987–88 season, Kareem would be 41, and while he was still the presence that the Lakers needed in their halfcourt game, he simply couldn't carry the load that he once had. Much of that burden would fall on Worthy's shoulders.

Heading into his sixth NBA season, the former North Carolina forward had come to enjoy a reputation for consistent excellence. In every facet of his life and his game he seemed to opt for quiet dignity and grace rather than for flash and fame. It wasn't that he disliked the Hollywood aspect of playing for the Los Angeles Lakers. He just didn't immerse himself in it. Rather than own a mansion, he lived quietly with his wife, Angela, in a middle-class neighborhood in Westchester, not too far from the Forum. If he wanted, he could ride his bike to work. Other folks could take the limos.

Even so, he was the Lamborghini in the Laker fleet. At 6-foot-9, Worthy was incredibly quick and swift. No man his size in the league could stay with him. Without a doubt, Johnson was the guard who drove the Showtime machine, but Worthy was the forward who made it go. "Earvin can push the ball upcourt at an incredible tempo," Riley once explained. "But he needs someone even faster than himself to break for the wing and fly upcourt. James is the fastest man of his size in the NBA. In terms of finishing the fast break creatively and swiftly and deceptively, no one else compares."

And when the game slowed down a bit, Johnson liked to send the ball to Worthy in the low post. Then, the guard said with a smile, it would be over in a matter of seconds.

"His first step is awesome," Maurice Lucas said.

As a veteran pro, Worthy showed an array of moves, a repertoire of head fakes and twitches and shifts that he used to reduce his defenders to nervous wrecks. "He'll give a guy two or three fakes, step through, then throw up the turnaround," Riley said. "It's not planned. It's all just happening."

That season would mark the crescendo of Worthy's career, sealing his reputation as "Big Game" James. He would lead the Lakers through the postseason, earning himself the play-off MVP distinction in the process.

Other Lakers stepped forward as well. Byron Scott had labored to find his shot during the 1987 Finals, but the 1987–88 season brought new confidence. He led Los Angeles in scoring, averaging 21.7 points over the regular season while shooting .527 from the field. Also vital was the development of A. C. Green at power forward. He didn't shoot much, but when he did the selection was good. He rebounded well and continued to learn the intricacies of low-post defense.

Johnson once again showed consistently brilliant play, although he missed 10 games at midseason due to a groin injury. If there was a problem for the Lakers, it was Kareem's age. His decline was marked throughout the season, yet Mychal Thompson's presence off the bench provided just enough patchwork to make the Lakers effective in the post.

They started the schedule with an 8–0 run, the finest opening in their history, but from there it became a test of survival. "The season was a trainer's nightmare," Vitti recalled. "We didn't know who was gonna play from one game to the next."

Worthy's knees ached. Byron Scott was plagued by patella tendinitis. Johnson had his groin injury. And Cooper got hammered. "Coop sprained his ankle badly in March in Houston," Vitti said. "He was never the same after that. That was really the injury that slowed him down. When he came back from that injury, Karl Malone threw him into a press table and bruised his foot. He still played every single game after that, but he was hurting."

Somehow they overcame these ups and downs to claim the league's best regular-season record at 62–20. "Guaranteeing a championship was the best thing Pat ever did," Byron Scott said as the schedule drew to a close. "It set the stage in our mind. Work harder; be better. That's the only way we could repeat. We came into camp with the idea we were going to win it again, and that's the idea we have now."

To do so, they had to face the ultimate test. They dumped San Antonio 3–0 in the first play-off round but then had to fight their way through three consecutive seven-game series to win the title, something that no team had done before. Next came Utah and a full series battling Karl Malone, followed by seven games with Dallas.

They arrived at the Finals to meet the Detroit Pistons, who had put down the Celtics in six. Isiah Thomas's team had acquired the sobriquet "the Bad Boys," because of their penchant for hard fouls and rough play. Despite this newfound toughness, the Pistons weren't projected as much of a problem for the Lakers. Maybe the series would go six games, the observers figured. Maybe it wouldn't.

It opened at the Forum on June 7 with both sides professing determination to win a championship. Yet it was all tempered a bit by the sight of Magic and Isiah holding hands and kissing before the tipoff of Game 1. It was a display of brotherly love, they explained. That didn't stop it from wearing a bit thin as the matchup intensified. Detroit wasted little time casting doubt on LA's repeat plans. The Pistons' Adrian Dantley stepped forward, making 14 of 16 shots from the floor, enough to lead the Pistons to a shocking 105–93 win. Suddenly, the Los Angeles press noticed that the Lakers bore a remarkably striking resemblance to the Celtics: i.e. they looked old and tired. As the shock of the loss wore off, the Lakers felt nothing but humiliation. "It was an embarrassing loss for us," Riley told reporters the next day. "The players came in this morning a little angry, a little upset, and I hope they get worse. We're going to have to bring an attitude different than the one they took into Game 1."

Playing with the flu, Johnson scored 23 points in Game 2. Worthy scored 26 while Scott had 24, and the Lakers evened the series with a 108–96 win. "I don't think there's any doubt Earvin Johnson showed the heart of a champion," Riley said afterward. "He was weak. Very weak. But this is what I call a hope game—you hope you get through it—and we got through it."

The site then switched to the Pontiac Silverdome, the football arena, where crowds of 40,000 or more were expected. Ignoring the crush of fans, the Lakers shoved past the Pistons to take the third game and a 2–1 lead, 99–86.

Which put the pressure on the Pistons for Game 4. Johnson repeatedly used his size and strength to get to the basket, and Detroit's answer was to try to knock him down, which left him fuming and complaining. "Magic is tough because he likes to penetrate," Detroit's Dennis Rodman said afterward. "But I try to distract him, and hopefully he won't be able to look up the court and make one of those great passes."

The tactic worked, and Johnson was obviously frustrated. At one point, he knocked Thomas to the floor with an elbow. By then it was too late. Detroit blew past the Lakers and won by 25 points, tying it at two-all.

Determined to counter, Los Angeles opened Game 5 with a fury of physical intimidation, scoring the game's first 12 points. But that approach soon stalled, then backfired into foul trouble. The Lakers got away from what they do best—rebounding and running. "We couldn't contain anyone on the boards," Riley said. "We had [two] defensive boards in the fourth quarter, and they had 10 offensive boards. You're not going to beat anyone with that."

The Pistons won, 104–94, and took a 3–2 lead. Riley's dream seemed to have gone gray. But Detroit would have to claim the championship in the Forum, and that wouldn't be a cakewalk.

The Pistons fell behind, 56–48, early in the third quarter of Game 6. Then Isiah Thomas scored the next 14 points in trancelike fashion—two free throws after a drive in the lane, then a five-footer off an offensive rebound, followed by four jumpers, a bank shot, and a lay-up. But, with three minutes to go in the period, Thomas landed on Cooper's foot and had to be helped from the floor. Despite a severely sprained ankle, he returned 35 seconds later and continued the assault. By the end of the quarter he had hit 11 of 13 shots from the floor for 25 points, setting an NBA Finals record for points in a quarter and driving Detroit to an 81–79 lead.

That momentum boosted the Pistons down to the wire, and with a minute left in the game, they held a 102–99 edge. They were a mere 60 seconds from an NBA title, the franchise's first ever. The league trophy was wheeled into the Pistons' locker room. Iced champagne was brought in. CBS requested the presence of Detroit owner Bill Davidson to receive the trophy. Minutes later, those plans were rapidly disassembled, the trophy taken away before Davidson could feel it.

"A minute is a long time," Johnson would say later. "A long time. It's just two scores and two stops and you're ahead."

The first Laker score came on Byron Scott's 14-foot jumper, to bring LA within one, 102–101, at 52 seconds. Detroit struggled for the right shot on its possession and failed when Thomas missed an 18-footer. At 14 seconds, Abdul-Jabbar positioned for his skyhook from the baseline, but Detroit's Bill Laimbeer was whistled for a foul. Kareem made both free throws, giving LA a 103–102 lead.

The Pistons had the ball and a chance to win it. At eight seconds, Joe Dumars took the shot for Detroit, a six-foot double-pumper. It missed, the rebound slipped through Dennis Rodman's frantic hands, and Byron Scott controlled the loose ball. The Lakers were smug again.

"I thought I could get it to the hole," Dumars said afterward. "I thought there was an opening, but then they converged on me. They just cut me right off."

Rodman sat at his locker thinking only of the missed opportunity. "You look up," he said, "and that clock runs r-e-a-l s-l-o-w. I was tasting it. I was going to come in here to the locker room, have my championship hat on, everything. I guess I've got to wait until Tuesday."

There was only one major question for Game 7. Would Thomas play with the bad ankle? He answered with relative ease: "I'm playing—period," he declared.

The ankle took Thomas to the third quarter and no further. Despite limping badly in warm-ups, he scored 10 points in the first half, leading the Pistons to a 52–47 lead. But the down time between halves brought on stiffness, and he could no longer be effective.

The Lakers, meanwhile, got going behind Worthy's low-post scoring and raced to a seemingly insurmountable lead, 90–75, in the fourth quarter. Yet just when Riley could taste the reality of his repeat fantasy, the Lakers got fat. Seemingly headed down in a blowout, the Pistons fought back with a pressure lineup that consumed the Lakers' lead in gulps. At 3:52 Detroit's John Salley knocked in two free throws to close to 98–92, and the Lakers were in obvious panic. At 1:17, Dumars hit a jumper to make it 102–100. Then Magic scored a free throw off a Rodman foul, stretching it to 103–100. Detroit had an opportunity, but Rodman took an ill-advised jumper at 39 seconds. Scott rebounded and was fouled. His two free throws pushed the lead to 105–100. Then Dumars made a lay-up, Worthy hit a free throw, and Laimbeer canned a trey, running the score to 106–105 with six seconds showing. Green finished a lay-up, making it 108–105, and although the Pistons got the ball to Thomas at midcourt with a second remaining, he fell without getting off a shot.

Riley could only give thanks. "It was a nightmare to the very end," he said. "I kept saying, 'Please don't let this end in a nightmare.' We were a great team trying to hold on. Hey, they just put on one of the greatest comebacks in the history of this game and they have nothing to be ashamed of. We're a great team and they had us hanging on at the end. We were able to do it because of who we are, but they gave us all we could handle."

Worthy had racked up 36 points, 16 rebounds, and 10 assists, the first triple double of his career. For that and his earlier efforts in the series, he was named the MVP. Self-effacing as usual, Worthy said he would have voted for Magic. The big news, though, was the team. At last, the league had a repeat champion. The Lakers had grasped the greatness about which Riley had rhapsodized so often. "He pretty much got it all out of us that year," Byron Scott says now. "We went seven games every series and ended up winners."

They were all relieved. And to make sure Riley had no more wise ideas about the future, Kareem kept his eye on the coach during the postgame interviews. It did little good, though.

The Three-peat pressure began immediately and swirled throughout the 1988–89 season, mixed with night after night of Abdul-Jabbar's retirement tour. He was 42 and announced that this campaign was his last. It was a painful year. His skills obviously diminished by age, Kareem labored through many nights, which led to a flurry of media questions as to whether he was just playing for the money. In retrospect, it seems a little odd that a team going for a third title would have to weather such scrutiny. But some of Kareem's nights were difficult. There were even discussions with Jerry West about an abrupt departure. However, wisdom prevailed. Kareem stayed, and the Lakers prospered. With each day that spring, hope grew that they could send Abdul-Jabbar out with another ring. They finished with a 57–25 record, once again the best in the West, yet short of the Pistons' 63–19 march. The Lakers, though, had confidence that they could win in Detroit and leave no doubts as to their supremacy.

In the NBA, 1989 was the Year of the Broom. The Knicks swept the Philadelphia 76ers in three close first-round games, and in a fit of youthful excess the New York players grabbed brooms from the custodial staff in Philadelphia and began doing the floor. It was a hoot. At least it seemed that way until Chicago upset New York in the next round, leading the Knicks to realize they had been grossly cocky.

For better or worse, the tone had been set for the play-offs. The Lakers furthered the notion, sweeping their way along an 11–0 run to the Finals. Portland, Seattle, and Phoenix—each had gone out with the dustpan. The wins meant that Pat Riley needed only one more victory to become the winningest coach in play-off history. As it turned out, that achievement was far more remote than it seemed.

Detroit, too, had made a sweep of the first two rounds. In Boston, Larry Bird had spent the season on the sidelines after undergoing heel surgery in November. As a result, the Pistons easily pushed aside the Celtics in the first round, 3–0. The same fate befell the Milwaukee Bucks in the second round, 4–0. Only Michael Jordan and the Chicago Bulls interrupted this trend. They won a pair of games from Detroit before falling, 4–2.

Left to wait while Detroit beat Chicago, Riley took the Lakers to Santa Barbara and worked them hard. They cursed him for it. "The thing that upset us more than anything," Byron Scott said, "was how hard we worked. It was like training camp all over again. We didn't feel that we really needed that."

The Detroit papers had fun with the Pistons/Lakers rematch in the Finals, calling it "The Sequel." As things turned out, it had the properties of a sequel. Big on staging, hype, and promotion. Plenty of talent. A bit short on dramatic sequences.

The Pistons' worries—not to mention the dramatic possibilities— began to soften before Game 1 in Detroit, when Scott suffered a severe hamstring injury. He would miss at least the first two games, the injury report said at first. But the muscle was torn. He wouldn't return. Suddenly the hard workouts became an issue in the Lakers' minds. "I felt my hamstring first twinge in Santa Barbara and I had to stop practicing," Scott said. "Then, the first practice in Detroit, I completely tore it."

Without Scott to help contain the Detroit guards, the Lakers faced an onslaught. With six minutes to go in Game 1, Detroit led, 97–79, and they glided from there to a 109–97 win. The Lakers then targeted Game 2 as their opportunity. Sure enough, they snapped right back to pound the boards and take a 62–56 lead at intermission. Cooper was hitting, and Johnson had that look in his eye. But events turned upside down in the third period. With about four minutes left, Detroit's John Salley blocked a Mychal Thompson shot, starting the fast break. Johnson dropped back to play defense and, in so doing, pulled his hamstring. Sensing immediately that the injury was serious, he flailed at the air in frustration. "I felt a twinge early in the third quarter but thought everything was okay," Johnson said later.

Even without him, Mychal Thompson led a Los Angeles comeback. Down 106–104, the Lakers had the ball with eight seconds left when Worthy was fouled and went to the line. He missed the first and made the second, leaving the Lakers short at 106–105. Thomas hit two free throws with a second remaining for the final, 108–105. Down 2–0, Los Angeles was short on options. The immediate speculation centered on Magic. Could he play in Game 3 in the Forum? He tried but left the game in the first quarter with the Lakers leading 11–8. "I wanted to play so bad, but I just could not," Johnson said later. "I could not make the cuts, defensively, that I had to make."

"He made a heck of an effort," Joe Dumars said, "but it just wasn't there. You could tell by his motion. One time, the ball was right there a couple feet away, and he just couldn't get it."

Without Johnson, the Lakers still did a fair imitation of a championship contender. Worthy scored 26, and Kareem played out of his 42-year-old body, scoring 24 points with 13 rebounds. The only veteran in the backcourt, Cooper had 13 assists and 15 points. Grand as it was, that didn't do it. The Pistons won a third time, making the ending a foregone conclusion.

Down 3–0, the Lakers still talked of making history. Specifically, they would have to be the first team to ever overcome a three-game deficit. Tony Campbell, a former Continental Basketball Association player the Lakers had picked up at the end of the season, asserted that such a comeback was in the works. Wiser voices weren't quite so optimistic.

"It's like you have a real nice sports car and a great driver," Kareem said of the circumstances, "and then all of a sudden you have to find somebody who has been driving a bus to be a driver. That's a learning experience."

The crowd came to Game 4 expecting an event, Kareem's final game. The big center conducted his final warm-up, his bald pate glistening a regal green and red from the Forum lights. He was composed, spending much of the session standing silently in a half-slouch, his hand on his hip. He did one final finger roll in the lay-up line and headed down to the bench. With that signal, the team followed, igniting a growing applause that spread across the arena. Riley told Worthy that he would have to up his game a few notches and get them a win. Worthy responded with a championship effort—40 points on 17 of 26 from the floor. But the Pistons weren't about to let up.

When Worthy blasted the Lakers into the lead late in the third quarter, the crowd began chanting, "Three-peat." It was nice Hollywood stuff, but it would never see the light of reality. They nipped and tucked from there. The Lakers held a 78–76 lead at the end of the third, but the Bad Boys turned the chores over to James Edwards, who slammed and picked his way along, giving Detroit the lead in the process. The Lakers appeared drained.

When Detroit got the ball back with 3:23 left and leading 100–94, the crowd rose to a standing ovation, not to try and pull a miracle out of exhaustion, just a note of thanks. At 1:37, Kareem executed a neat spin move and bank shot, his last NBA points, bringing the Lakers to 100–96. In the closing seconds, with the game clearly over, Riley sent Laker sub Orlando Woolridge in for the Cap, a bittersweet hug time for the Lakers. Johnson came out to meet Kareem. The crowd's applause was large and warm, and the Pistons all stepped onto the floor, faced the Laker bench, and helped out.

Then Isiah Thomas went to the line to shoot two final free throws. Nobody even noticed if he made them. "Kareem. Kareem. Kareem," the crowd intoned over and over.

Some would argue that the curtain closed on Showtime with his departure. Others would say that Magic's style and personality defined the era. Riley ushered them through the next season and resigned to become an NBC broadcaster for a season, to be replaced by Mike Dunleavy. Coop left, too, asking to be waived so that he could play in Europe.

Dunleavy had Johnson, Worthy, and Scott to go with the crop of young players West had brought together. They began with a losing streak to open the 1990–91 season, but Dunleavy frantically righted the team and coached them to the Finals yet again. The Trail Blazers had ruled the regular season in the Western with a 63–19 finish, but the Lakers survived in the play-offs, ousting Portland in the conference finals, 4–2.

For most observers, the Finals seemed a dream matchup: Michael Jordan and the Bulls against Magic and the Lakers. In 1990 promoters had come up with an idea for a one-on-one game between Magic and Michael to be staged for pay-per-view television. But the NBA vetoed the idea— which would have paid big money to the participants—after Isiah Thomas, the president of the NBA Players' Association, objected.

Jordan lashed out at Thomas's intervention, charging that the Detroit guard was jealous because no one would pay to see him play.

Thomas offered no response to Jordan's comment. Privately peeved at Isiah, Johnson said he would love to play the game. But he declined to get involved in the scrap. "That's their thing," he said of Thomas and Jordan.

Johnson, however, did have some fun speculating over the outcome. Jack Nicholson had said that if he were a betting man, he'd put his money on Jordan, the premier individual star in the game, as opposed to Johnson, the ultimate team player.

Johnson, though, wouldn't concede a thing. "I've been playing one-on-one all my life," he said. "That's how I made my lunch money."

Asked his best one-on-one move, Johnson said, "I didn't have a best move. My best move was just to win, and that's it. I did what I had to do to win."

Although the 1991 Finals wouldn't be a one-on-one matchup of the superstars, it seemed like a great opportunity to see them battle. Many observers, including Riley, then at NBC, figured the Lakers' experience made them a sure bet. Los Angeles was making its ninth Finals appearance since 1980 and had five titles to show for it.

"The Lakers have experience on us," Chicago's Scottie Pippen conceded as the series opened in Chicago Stadium, "but we have enough to win."

The big negative for the Lakers was Worthy's ankle, sprained in the Western finals against Portland, which took away much of his mobility. Some insiders figured Worthy's injury would cost the Lakers the series. Game 1, however, seemed to confirm Riley's prediction. The Lakers won, 93–91, on a late three-pointer by Sam Perkins. The Bulls got the ball to Jordan, but his 18-foot jumper with four seconds left went in the basket and spun out.

"We won the first game, we said, 'Hey, we can beat these guys,' " Byron Scott recalled.

The only problem, says Gary Vitti, is that they forgot to win the rest of the games. The trainer remembered telling the young Lakers on the roster that year, "You guys just don't understand. You join the Lakers, you see the history, you think that this is part of the deal, that every year we'll play for a championship. This may be the only time you will ever be in this position in your life, and you must win. You have to win because you may not ever get another chance."

The Bulls, however, found success by pressuring Johnson's ball handling over the next four games. And the Lakers could find no means of helping him out. The tumble started with a Chicago blowout in Game 2, 107–86. The Bulls starters shot better than 73 percent from the floor, with guard John Paxson going eight for eight to score 16 points. "Does Paxson ever miss?" Sam Perkins asked.

In Game 3, Jordan hit a jumper with 3.4 seconds left to send the game into overtime. There, the Bulls ran off eight straight points for a 104–96 win and a 2–1 lead. Jordan was elated, but he refused to dwell on the victory. The Lakers had plenty of experience in coming back, he said.

But experience proved no match for the Bulls' young legs and determination. For Game 4, the Bulls harried the Lakers into shooting 37 percent from the floor, good enough for a 97–82 win. The Lakers' point total was their lowest since before the shot clock was adopted in 1954. They managed a total of 30 points over the second and third quarters. Perkins made just one of his 15 shots.

"I didn't even dream this would happen," Magic said.

The Bulls then took their third straight in the Forum to close the series on a Wednesday night, 4–1. It was a finish without glory for LA, but the Lakers weren't cut too deeply. They had had plenty of glory over the past dozen years. Besides, they expected to get another shot at the title next year. Wasn't that the way it always happened?

No one—least of all Earvin Johnson—would have believed it at the time, but the 1991 championship series was the swan song for Showtime.

Their pride intact, the Lakers and Jerry West would likely resume their championship tradition. But this golden era had ended. Excalibur soon settled into the lake, and Arthur rested on the barge, leaving Randy Pfund alone to answer the rude, mean questions.

"Where is Showtime now?" the Knicks fan bellowed from the end zone on that night in New York in 1993.

The answer, of course, was left hanging in the air with the question.

Like the great Laker teams of Pollard and Mikan and Baylor and West and Wilt, Showtime is just a memory. Just a sweet, sad, wonderful memory.

Epilogue

Exel-ent, Dudes

CHARLOTTE COLISEUM, JANUARY 11, 1995

The fan in the front row at the Charlotte Coliseum doesn't know it yet, but he's about to make Nick Van Exel's night. It's another tough road game, and Van Exel, the Lakers' precocious second-year point guard, has started slowly. Early in the first quarter, with his energy level seemingly stuck in low gear, he begins searching the sidelines for a lift.

And there, on the front row, he finds just the guy to do the trick. Best of all, the fan is a Brother, one who knows how to talk a little trash. "You're selling out, Nick!" the Brother yells. "It's gonna be a long ride home, baby!"

That's my man, Van Exel thinks.

And with that, the plucky young guard begins a "conversation," a verbal battle with his heckler. To counter the fan's barrage of insults, Van Exel uses chest-thumping, self-congratulatory displays and a full array of grins, quick comments and sideways looks.

All of which are met by the Brother's relentless reminder: "You're selling out, Nick."

Finally, just before he's about to shoot a free throw, Van Exel turns, grabs his crotch, tugs at it and nods defiantly at the heckler. The message is clear: "Bite me."

It sends a ripple of laughter through the courtside seats. Even the Brother can't suppress a grin. "You're selling out, Nick," he answers lamely.

To the contrary, Van Exel seems to have shaken off his road weariness and is now fully energized. The mind game firmly in control, the young guard drives the Lakers to a steady comeback. In the fourth quarter with Charlotte holding a narrow lead, he faces full-court pressure from Muggsy Bogues, the Hornets' muscular little point guard whose quickness is a nightmare for most guards in the league but not for Van Exel. Left to bring the ball up alone against Bogues' pressure, Van Exel looks smugly at his defender, does two quick jab steps, then pirouettes and zips away, leaving the NBA's supposedly quickest man sitting dumbfounded.

At midcourt, Charlotte's Dell Curry attempts to step in and pick Van Exel up, but the Laker guard merely does a spin dribble — a majestically graceful 360-degree move around him — and keeps motoring straight to the basket, where Hornets center Alonzo Mourning awaits. Mourning seems surprised that the 6-1, 170-pound Van Exel keeps coming. The surprise then spills into full disbelief when the guard rises up right in the center's face and flips in a layup. Van Exel has gone end to end, first blowing off the quickest, then challenging the most ferocious. The result, as you might expect, is devastating for the Hornets. Once seemingly in control of the game, they stumble.

With 20 seconds to go, Bogues fouls Van Exel, who makes a free throw to push the Laker lead to 106-102.

"Damn you, Nick," the Brother in the front row yells hoarsely.

Moments later, the game ends, and, as Van Exel heads off, the fan yells, "Nick." Van Exel turns around, and the Brother points at him and smiles. Van Exel points back and grins.

"On the court, when he gets into a conversation with the fans, that motivates him," Lakers rookie guard Eddie Jones says of Van Exel. "That motivates him every night. I'm like, 'Nick, shut up!' Off the court, he's calm and quiet, but on the court he's like a different person."

"On the road, it seems I play a lot better when I have somebody harassing me," Van Exel says, smiling. "I like that. It gets me fired up. It's fun. We were getting on each other during the game. He was saying things. I was saying things. But when it was all said and done, we pointed at each other and said good-bye. It's all in fun."

Tremendous fun, unless you happen to be the home team faced with the challenge of the Lakers' brilliant young guards. Van Exel possesses a nearly indefensible quickness, and Jones has the long arms to snatch the ball right out the passing lanes, which gives opponents stress attacks as they try to work their offenses against the Lakers' pressure.

"These guys are truly amazing," says Laker assistant Larry Drew.

Perhaps the most amazing thing about this new edition of the Lakers is how quickly and brilliantly Jerry West has rebuilt them. As it turned out, Randy Pfund had every reason to be concerned about his coaching job in March 1993. West was displeased with how unorganized the team seemed. Pfund, of course, countered that the club was clearly one in transition, that it was impossible to get much more out of the roster than he did. James Worthy, in particular, struggled with his declining skills and with his waning passion for the game. Trading him, however, had become an impossibility because of the balloon contract with which Jerry Buss had rewarded him, a deal that paid him a reported $7 million per season over the final two years of the agreement.

This problem, and the team's lack of leadership and a point guard, seemed to have Pfund locked into a course for failure over the spring of 1993. The Lakers suffered through a record six straight home losses at the Forum in

March (they would finish 20-21 at home, their first losing home record since moving to LA in 1960).

They finished the year at 39-43, fifth in the division, yet somehow managed to make the playoffs, where their first-round opponent was the top seed, the Suns with Charles Barkley, the team with a league-best 62 wins and the momentum for a championship. The Lakers were figured to be a mere speed bump on the Suns' roll to the 1993 NBA Finals. Yet, the circumstances somehow stirred something in Pfund's players, particularly Worthy. Playing with a fire not seen all season, the Lakers came out and promptly claimed the first two games in Phoenix. Never in NBA history had an eighth-seeded team taken the first two games on the road against a top seed. Better yet, never in league history had a team fallen behind 2-0 in a five-game series and survived it.

Unfortunately, the Lakers hosted the next two games, and the Forum had been quite friendly to the Suns in recent seasons. Barkley bore down, and like that, Phoenix evened the series with two wins in Los Angeles. With Game 5 in the Suns' brand new America West Arena on May 9, the Lakers seemed finished. But once again, they came out strong, hitting a team playoff record seven of 15 three-point attempts and seemed on the verge of a stupendous upset until they lost their lead in the last minutes of regulation and went to overtime, where Barkley and the Suns finally found an edge for a 112-104 win.

The series performance was just enough to save Pfund's job. But the 1993-94 season was doomed to be yet another phase of transition. In the '93 draft, West went for North Carolina forward George Lynch with the 12th pick of the first round, but the real prize was Van Exel out of the University of Cincinnati with the 37th selection in the second round.

Most pro scouts had seen talent in Van Exel but worried about his shot selection and questioned his attitude and character. Part of the problem stemmed from Van Exel's seeming reluctance to visit certain teams that were interested in him, including Charlotte.

West has often said that if you don't have a top pick you have to wait around and hope that other people make mistakes. With Van Exel, the entire NBA made a mistake in 1993. It could be argued that even West wasn't aware that he had gotten a star. But soon after Van Exel came to work, the Lakers realized they had a rare, rare find, a rookie who could start and excel at point guard.

He was, however, just that — a rookie — and that contributed to an immense problem for Pfund. The Lakers began the season with a starting lineup that averaged just 23.4 years in age, the youngest in the league. Plus, the team still lacked strong rebounding and a leader. West had hoped that Lynch, whose defense and rebounding had helped Carolina to the '93 NCAA title, would contribute in those areas. But Pfund seemed unimpressed with the rookie, who had a power forward's game in a small forward's body. The

Lakers needed scoring and rebounding from the small forward slot, and Lynch's jump shot was suspect. But where Lynch struggled, Van Exel immediately found a comfort zone and a job as the team's starting point guard.

Unfortunately, the roster was strangely unmotivated, which frustrated both rookies, not to mention Pfund. The Lakers opened the season with a losing month, then proceeded to stack up the kind of forlorn defeats not seen since their dark days in Minneapolis. "It's tough," Van Exel had confided during his first season. "There are a lot of games where we go out and see guys who really don't want to play and are not giving their all. That really hurts the most because we know they can do better."

Sitting and watching this lack of effort was particularly tough on the immensely proud and workmanlike Lynch. "George didn't lose many games in his college career, and he's won a national championship," Van Exel said. "It was hard for him losing so many games. He felt there were a lot of games where we should have won, where people should have tried harder."

Ultimately, the thing that worked in Lynch's favor was a run of injuries that forced Pfund to play him. Given time, he showed a knack for offensive rebounds and putbacks and defensive energy. Some still doubted that he would ever possess the skills of an NBA starter, but it became clear that he was a strong bench player, the kind of frontcourt depth the laconic Lakers badly needed. Most important, he had intensity.

Yet when a team has to draw on rookies for its strength, there's trouble. And there was plenty of that for Pfund. Strangely, the Lakers picked March, the team's only month with a winning record, to release the second-year coach. In a move typically classy of Buss and West, they first extended his contract an additional year in early March, although their decision was already made. From there, the Lakers went on a rare winning streak, claiming a 6-1 record from March 7 up to their March 23 game against the Mavericks, before which management relieved Pfund and assistant Chet Kammerer of their duties.

For two games, Bill Bertka ran the team until new coach Magic Johnson and assistant Michael Cooper could get situated. The emotion and excitement of Johnson's return generated renewed interest in the Forum, where ticket sales had sagged through the miserable season. Those feelings grew when Magic won five of his first six games. Yet it soon became clear that his presence on the bench was a halfhearted experiment, and the problems that had plagued the Lakers remained very malignant.

The end of the season was quite ugly, a 10-game losing streak, the longest in franchise history. The losing gained momentum after Johnson announced that he wouldn't take the job on a long-term basis. Frustrated by the lack of concern among key players, Johnson reportedly smashed a player's beeper against a wall when it went off during practice. He wanted full commitment to winning, and they weren't willing to make it. Johnson himself wasn't ready to take on the challenge and stress of coaching. Instead, he acquired a minority ownership of the team and settled in as a vice president not long after the Lakers finished 33-49 and out of the playoffs for the first time in almost two decades.

Someone else would have to do the coaching.

For that, West turned to Del Harris, a well-traveled veteran known for his slowdown offenses. Actually Harris had been a proponent of the push game during his days in Houston. But he slowed down the Rockets' offense to match the skills of then-center Moses Malone, and that resulted in a trip to the 1981 NBA Finals against the Boston Celtics. The Rockets lost, but Harris' record for flexibility was established among keen observers. Which is why West could hire him with a clear conscience before the 1994-95 season. West knew that Harris wasn't wed to any one system and would find the style of play suited to the young roster.

The other big holes for the Lakers included a small forward who could score and rebound consistently and a superstar. For years that had been James Worthy's domain, but his declining game and the sudden death of his mother led to retirement in the fall of 1994. To fill the small forward spot, West struck a deal with Phoenix that brought in Cedric Ceballos, a fifth-year forward with a rapidly developing game.

Added to that was the selection of Eddie Jones out of Temple with the tenth overall pick in the '94 draft. Chicago Bulls general manager Jerry Krause had badly wanted Jones. In fact, Krause's real effort in attempting to trade forward Scottie Pippen for Seattle power forward Shawn Kemp in 1994 was to get into position to draft Eddie Jones. The Pippen/Kemp deal fell through, however, and Jones went to the Lakers. Teamed with Van Exel at the point, Ceballos at small forward, Elden Campbell at power forward and Vlade Divac at center, Jones proved he could contribute immediately as the Lakers' off guard. As a result, they were one of the NBA's big surprises in 1994-95.

That was especially true of the development of the young guard tandem. "We're one of the best teams in the league," the 57-year-old Harris said unabashedly eight weeks into the season. "I think Nick and Eddie Jones have got to be the most exciting backcourt in the league," he added. "I mean these kids are 23 years old and they play like salty veterans. We are really blessed."

Jones says that away from the game Van Exel is a quiet sort who likes listening to music, playing video games and going to movies. Off the court, about the only time Van Exel gets riled is if he sees a teammate staying out too late or engaging in behavior detrimental to the team.

Then Van Exel doesn't hesitate to confront that player, even if it involves an older veteran. This policing is an extension of Van Exel's natural leadership abilities. But it also comes at the urging of Magic Johnson, who used to run the team with the same intensity.

Since Johnson's abrupt retirement in 1991, the Lakers had drifted along without a leader. That helps explain why Van Exel's intense competitiveness and leadership abilities were so welcomed in Los Angeles. "He's very competitive," said assistant coach Larry Drew. "If you find a guy with a passion to win, you got yourself something special. Hopefully he can pass that will to win on to some of these other guys. Nick's very passionate. He wants to win badly and gets frustrated when he doesn't."

"I got a lot of competitive relatives," Van Exel said of his hunger. "All of my aunts, when they were growing up, played softball and were great competitors. My Dad, my uncles, everybody in my family always wanted to win."

The leadership abilities weren't exactly an acquired facet of his personality but something Van Exel wanted to develop. "He came in this season really focused on trying to lead," Drew said. "And he did a good job. Our players look at him as a leader. He has commanded that kind of respect. He's demanded it, too."

"I think he's a great floor leader," said teammate Anthony Peeler. "The Lakers gave him the ball as a rookie and told him to run the team. This year he's had a lot of things on his shoulders, a lot of pressure from everybody, to see if he can do well. He's proven that he can. He's focused as a leader. In the hotel on the road, if you're hanging out too late, he'll go to the player and pinpoint 'em. That's what we need in a captain. He's letting everybody know he's a leader.

"Last year as a rookie, Nick was just witnessing a lot of stuff that he couldn't really do anything about. This year he's taken it upon himself to really get eye contact and really get inside each player on the team."

At least part of the motivation for this leadership effort stemmed from Van Exel's frequent talks with Johnson. "Magic's very inspirational," Van Exel said. "The rule we have about night life is that you can go out as long as you're ready on the court to handle your business and be professional. The Lakers gave me a lot of confidence last year to be the leader, and it's a role I want."

As Drew pointed out when other players struggled with the leadership mantle following Johnson's retirement, the efforts to lead the team only work if you have the talent and competitiveness to make it stick. In that regard, Van Exel's quickness is a key factor because it makes him a unique player. "I call him 'Quick.' That's his nickname," Peeler said, "because nobody in the NBA can keep up with him right now. They had a year during his rookie season to see him. But now they're trying to use the excuse that they didn't know he had all of these moves. But this year they know. They've scouted him, and they still can't stop him. I'm waiting to see if there is somebody in the league who can keep up with him. Nick's been going up against the best guards in the league all season, and I haven't seen one of them take the ball away from him yet, or stop him. He's just doing what he wants to right now. He knows he's good."

"The thing that first opened my eyes about Nick Van Exel," Larry Drew said, "is how easily he broke the defender down. That's something that few point guards can do. You find a lot who have the speed to blow by defenders. But actually breaking them down off the dribble with your moves is another matter. Nick's doing it time and time again. And once he breaks them down he knows what to do once he gets around them. He came to me at the start of this season and said, 'Did I shoot the ball too much last year?' (Van Exel led the team in field-goal attempts but only shot 39 percent from the floor as a rookie.) Personally, I didn't think he did, because it's so easy for him to get around a defender and make things happen in a transition game. He finds himself open for a lot of shots. You gotta take those shots.

"You look at the point guards today, most are scoring guards. If you find one who can score and distribute the ball, you got yourself something special. In Nick, we have something special."

Sometimes, Van Exel admitted, he surprises even himself with his moves and quickness. "I play a lot on instinct," he said. "Sometimes when I do a move, I think, 'I never did that before.'"

The summer after his rookie season, Van Exel spent his time in the LA summer leagues focusing on becoming a better distributor. "I wanted to get the ball to guys in scoring position," he explained. "I wanted to learn to set guys up and work on staying focused and running a team, being in control of a game."

Peeler swears that Van Exel, who has been rewarded with a handsome contract, is using his draft-day slight as motivation to drive the Lakers to road win after road win, and the other teams around the league are discovering paybacks are heck. "He's coming out wanting to destroy every team that overlooked him," Peeler said. "He doesn't talk about it. He just goes out there and does it."

"I guess they'll hold it against me forever," Van Exel says, implying that other teams harbor a grudge against him because of the draft. This, of course, is obviously disingenuous. It is Van Exel himself who seems intent on showing the rest of the league that he has a long, long memory.

Regardless of its origin, Van Exel's motivation keeps Del Harris immensely pleased, although player and coach had to overcome an early season misunderstanding. Harris quickly downplayed a playing time disagreement they had during a game in Portland. The incident, Harris said, "was a nothing kind of situation. I love working with him. He's a special player. It's amazing to watch him get better all the time. Tougher. More heads-up. The guy can beat you every way. He can score outside, inside, make the play off the dribble. He works on the defender and is good off the ball, too. He's terrific."

Both Harris and West offered similar endorsements of Jones, who at 6-6, 190, has the body and temperament to play both big guard and small forward. Guard, however, is his first position, because he has the size to post up opponents. The Lakers spent much of his rookie season building his confidence and skills, with Drew schooling him on his midrange jumper and

Cooper teaching the nuances of tough defense and stopping the pick-and-roll.

The confidence building began the moment Jones was drafted. "Jerry West came to me several times and said, 'Man you can be great,'" Jones recalled. "He's like THE basketball guru, the best of scouts. So that just made me want to work harder over the summer so I could come here and perform to his level of expectation. I just tried to do my best to play my heart out."

There was little question that Jones did that, although his coaches thought he was too reckless in taking the ball to the basket and challenging the league's bigger, stronger inside players. Sure enough, Jones' fine rookie season was interrupted when he injured a shoulder dunking. Losing his scoring and defense could have been disastrous, except that Peeler, long in management's doghouse and slowed by a series of injuries, came through with a tremendous spring.

After leaving Charlotte, the young Lakers closed out the schedule with a show of strength, winning 48 games and finishing in fifth place in their conference. Better yet, Van Exel proved to be an immense factor in the playoffs, guiding the Lakers to a first-round upset over fourth-seeded Seattle.

In the second round, they were derailed 4-2 by David Robinson and the San Antonio Spurs, winners of a league-best 62 games. But there was little doubt that the young Lakers had put the league on notice. With Divac having developed into a solid center and Ceballos offering all-star caliber play at small forward, Harris' club had a bright, bright future.

At the height of the excitement, Van Exel was asked if it was the most fun he'd ever had in basketball. "It's not the most fun in my life," he said. "Not yet. I think that's still to come."

Heading into their fiftieth anniversary, that seemed a promising enough forecast for the Lakers. More good times ahead. Brought on by a tough little guy who likes to search the sidelines for a motivational ploy. Will it be enough to bring more championships? If Van Exel's heart has anything to do with it, the answer will be affirmative.

"He's got that burning desire to win," Drew said of Van Exel. "You just don't teach that. It has to come from within."

Sources

A number of excellent books and periodicals provided me with background for this project:

Magazines and Newspapers
Extensive use was made of a variety of publications, including AirCal, *Basketball Times, Boston Globe, Boston Herald, Business Week, Chicago Tribune, Chicago Sun Times, The Detroit News, The Detroit Free Press, Esquire, Flint Journal, Forbes, GQ, Hartford Courant, Hoop Magazine, Houston Post, Let's Talk!, Los Angeles Business Journal, Los Angeles Daily News, Los Angeles Lakers Illustrated, Los Angeles Times, L.A. Herald Examiner, Los Angeles Sentinel, The National, New York Daily News, The New York Times, New York Post, New West, The Oakland Press, The Roanoke Times & World-News, The Charlotte Observer, USA Today, Vanity Fair, The Orange County Register, Philadelphia Inquirer, San Diego Tribune, Sport, Sports Illustrated, The Sporting News, Street & Smith's Pro Basketball Yearbook,* and *The Washington Post.*

The Writers
Without the front-line work of a variety of reporters and writers over the years, the compilation of this book would not have been possible. That group includes the following:

Mitch Albom, David Aldridge, Jim Alexander, Elliott Almond, Neil Amdur, Dave Anderson, Ira Berkow, Greg Boeck, Cliff Brown, Bryan Burwell, Kelly Carter, E. Jean Carroll, Mitch Chortkoff, Marlene Cimons, Doug Cress, Tim Deady, Frank DeFord, David Dupree, Larry Donald, Mike Downey, Ron Dungee, Melvin Durslag, Joe Fitzgerald, Mal Florence, John Freeman, Bud Furillo, Sam Goldaper, Alan Goldstein, Ted Green, Allen Greenberg, Don Greenberg, Milton Gross, Donald Hall, Merv Harris, Mark Heisler, Bruce Horovitz, Scott Howard-Cooper, Mary Ann Hudson, Bob Hunter, Michael Hurd, Doug Ives, Bruce Jenkins, Roy S. Johnson, William Oscar Johnson, Dave Kindred, Leonard Koppett, Tony Kornheiser, Doug Krikorian, Rich Levin, Bill Libby, Mike Littwin, Leonard Lewin, Jack Madden, Allan Malamud, Jack McCallum, Sam McManis, Jackie MacMullen, John L. Mitchell, David Leon Moore, Morton Moss, Bruce Newman, Scott Ostler, Sandy

Padwe, John Papanek, Charles Pierce, Pat Putnam, Brad Pye, Jr., Ron Rapoport, Bob Ryan, Steve Springer, Bill Steigerwald, Marc Stein, Larry Stewart, Eric Tracy, Michael Ventre, George Vecsey, Peter Vecsey, Lesley Visser, Mike Waldner, Peter Warner, Mark Whicker, and Alex Wolff.

Books
24 Seconds to Shoot by Leonard Koppett, Macmillan, New York, 1980.
50 Years of the Final Four by Billy Packer and Roland Lazenby, Taylor Publishing, Dallas, 1987.
100 Greatest Basketball Players by Wayne Patterson and Lisa Fisher, Bison Books, Greenwich, Conn., 1988.
100 Years of Hoops by Alexander Wolff, Oxmoor House, Birmingham, 1992.
Bad Boys by Isiah Thomas and Matt Dobek, Masters Press, Grand Rapids, 1989.
Basketball's Greatest Games, edited by Zander Hollander, Prentice Hall, Englewood Cliffs, 1971.
Basketball's Hall of Fame by Sandy Padwe, Grossett and Dunlap, New York, 1973.
Bird, The Making of an American Sports Legend by Lee Daniel Levine, McGraw, New York, 1989.
Cages to Jump Shots by Robert Peterson, Oxford, 1990.
Championship NBA by Leonard Koppett, Dial Press, New York, 1970.
Coach by Ray Meyer and Ray Sons, Contemporary, Chicago, 1987.
College Basketball's 25 Greatest Teams by Billy Packer and Roland Lazenby, The Sporting News, St. Louis, 1989.
From Set Shot to Slam Dunk by Charles Salzberg, Dutton, New York, 1987.
Giant Steps by Kareem Abdul-Jabbar and Peter Knobler, Bantam, New York, 1983.
Holtzman on Hoops by Red Holtzman and Harvey Frommer, Taylor, Dallas, 1991.
Kareem by Kareem Abdul-Jabbar and Mignon McCarthy, Random House, New York, 1990.
Magic's Touch by Magic Johnson and Roy S. Johnson, Addison Wesley, Boston, 1989.
March to the Top by Art Chansky and Eddie Fogler, Four Corners Press, Chapel Hill, 1982.
Miracle on 34th Street by Phil Berger, Simon and Schuster, New York, 1970.
My Life by Earvin Johnson and William Novak, Random House, New York, 1992.
Magic by Earvin Johnson and Rich Levine, Viking, New York, 1983.
Pro Basketball Champions by George Vecsey, Scholastic, New York, 1970.
Rick Barry's Pro Basketball Scouting Report by Rick Barry and Jordan E. Cohn, Bonus Books, Chicago, 1989.
Second Wind, The Memoirs of an Opinionated Man by Bill Russell and Taylor Branch, Random House, New York, 1979.
Showtime by Pat Riley and Byron Laursen, Warner Books, New York, 1987.
Sportswit by Lee Green, Fawcett, New York, 1986.
Tall Tales by Terry Pluto, Simon and Schuster, New York, 1992.
The Bird Era by Bob Schron and Kevin Stevens, Quinland Press, Boston, 1988.
The Breaks of the Game by David Halberstam, Knopf, New York, 1981.
The Glory and the Dream by William Manchester, Little Brown, Boston, 1974.
The Golden Boys by Cameron Stauth, Pocket Books, New York, 1992.
The History of Professional Basketball Since 1896 by Glenn Dickey, Stein and Day, New York, 1982.

The Jim Murray Collection by Jim Murray, Taylor Publishing, Dallas, 1989.

The Legend of Dr. J by Marty Bell, New American Library, New York, 1981.

The Modern Basketball Encyclopedia by Zander Hollander, Dolphin, Garden City, N.Y., 1979.

The NBA Finals by Roland Lazenby, Taylor Publishing, Dallas, 1990.

The Night Wilt Scored 100 by Eric Nadel, Taylor Publishing, Dallas, 1990.

The Official NBA Basketball Encyclopedia, edited by Zander Hollander and Alex Sachare, Villard, New York, 1989.

The Sports Encyclopedia, Pro Basketball by David S. Neft and Richard M. Cohen, St. Martin's Press, New York, 1992.

The Story of Basketball by Dave Anderson, New York, 1989.

They Call Me Coach by John Wooden and Jack Tobin, Word, Waco, Texas, 1972.

Walt Frazier by Walt Frazier and Neil Offen, Times Books, New York, 1988.

Winnin' Times by Scott Ostler and Steve Springer, Macmillan, New York, 1986.

Gail Goodrich's Winning Basketball by Gail Goodrich and Rich Levin, Contemporary, Chicago, 1976.

Wilt by Wilt Chamberlain and David Shaw, Macmillan, New York, 1986.

About the Author

Roland Lazenby has addressed a wide array of subjects — ranging from sports to government and prisons — over his 20-year writing career. His most recent project is *And Now, Your Chicago Bulls!*, an illustrated history scheduled for fall 1995 release from Taylor Publishing. Lazenby is the editor of *Lindy's Pro Basketball Annual* and over the years has written for a variety of publications, including *The Sporting News*, *Basketball Times* and the Basketball Hall of Fame yearbook. In 1993 he served as the senior writer for the *Chicago Tribune's* commemorative book *Three-Peat!* about Michael Jordan and the Bulls.

Besides *The Lakers*, Lazenby has written or coauthored 28 other books, including four titles with CBS college basketball analyst Billy Packer. Lazenby's books have been excerpted by the Associated Press, *The Sporting News*, *Basketball Times* and several other publications. His work has also been highlighted in CBS Sports public service announcements aimed at encouraging reading and aired annually during the NCAA basketball tournament.

A 1975 graduate of Virginia Military Institute (where he played one year of football and two of rugby), Lazenby holds a master's degree in creative writing from Hollins College. Before becoming a freelancer in 1984, he worked seven years as a newspaper reporter. In 1980 he won an Easter Seals Society National Communications Award for writing about a handicapped woman. His years as a reporter afforded him a broad range of experiences, covering prisons, crime, government and circuit court beats for the *Roanoke* (Va.) *Times*. In that capacity, Lazenby was among a team of reporters that produced an award-winning series on the status of African-Americans in Virginia in 1983. He has also won Virginia Press Association first-place awards for feature writing and sports writing.

Prior to becoming a writer and reporter, Lazenby was an English teacher and head varsity wrestling coach at Blacksburg (Va.) High School. Lazenby is a native of Wytheville, Virginia. For the past 15 years he has lived in Roanoke with his wife of 20 years, Karen. They have three children, Jenna, Henry and Morgan. Since 1992, he has taught journalism and speech communication at nearby Radford University.

Success is a Slam Dunk
with Masters Press!

Masters Press has a complete line of books on basketball, and other sports to help coaches and participants alike "master their game."

All of our books are available at better bookstores or by calling Masters Press at 1-800-9-SPORTS. Catalogs available by request.

Coaching Basketball

Jerry Krause

Sponsored by the National Association of Basketball Coaches, this book is a collection of more than 130 articles and essays by the game's leading coaches, covering every aspect of the game.
$22.95
ISBN 0-940279-86-X

Winning Defense

Del Harris

Considered by many to be the bible of halfcourt, man-to-man defense for serious coaches everywhere, this book is an advanced guide for coaches and players written by the head coach of the Los Angeles Lakers.
$14.95
ISBN 0-940279-76-2

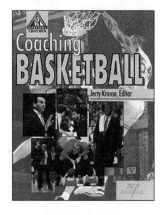

Basketball's Balanced Offense

Jim Harrick

The 1995 NCAA National Championship coach of the UCLA Bruins explains the offense perfected by legendary coach John Wooden, explaining numerous options, step-by-step and illustrated.
$12.95
ISBN 1-57028-023-1

Big Ten Basketball

Peter C. Bjarkman

Similar to the book *ACC Basketball*, this is an enjoyable and informative look at the history, coaches and players of one of the nation's top collegiate basketball conferences.
$14.95
ISBN 1-57028-038-X

Boom Baby! The Sudden, Surprising Rise of the Indiana Pacers

Conrad Brunner

The most extensive account of the history of the NBA's Indiana Pacers ever written. Charts the 1993-94 season, when the team climbed to within a few seconds of its first-ever berth in the NBA finals.
$14.95
ISBN 1-57028-036-3

Call Toll Free 1-800-9-SPORTS To Order

Success is a Slam Dunk with Masters Press!

Masters Press has a complete line of books on basketball, and other sports to help coaches and participants alike "master their game."

All of our books are available at better bookstores or by calling Masters Press at 1-800-9-SPORTS. Catalogs available by request.

Basketball's Offensive Sets
Tom Reiter

A must of any coach or player who wants to thoroughly understand the halfcourt offense, its potential, which defensive weaknesses it exploits, and the type of personnel at each position which make it most effective.
$12.95
ISBN 1-57028-040-1

Basketball Abstract
Dave Heeren

Using the internationally acclaimed TENDEX system, the most accurate system to date for rating players, this book is a must for fantasy league participants and rabid hoops fans.
$14.95
ISBN 1-57028-005-3

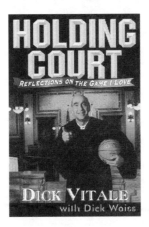

Holding Court: Reflections on the Game I Love
Dick Vitale with Dick Weiss

Former NBA and college head coach, and legendary ESPN and ABC Sports college basketball analyst Dick Vitale candidly shares his insights and opinions on significant issues facing basketball as well as other sports-related topics.
$22.95 (hardcover)
ISBN 1-57028-037-1

Tourney Time: It's Awesome Baby!
Dick Vitale with Mike Douchant

Stuffed full of trivia, features, statistics, and rare photographs of the players, teams, and coaches who have made the NCAA basketball tournament so unique.
$7.95
ISBN 0-940279-84-3

ACC Basketball
Peter C. Bjarkman

Similar to the book *Big Ten Basketball*, this book contains school-by-school team histories and stats, all-time great coaches and players, a look back at some of the conference's most memorable moments and games, all-time team selection and a trivia section.
$14.95
ISBN 1-57028-038-X

Call Toll Free 1-800-9-SPORTS To Order